HOTEL CATERING

HOTEL CATERING

A HANDBOOK FOR SALES AND OPERATIONS

Patti J. Shock

John M. Stefanelli

William F. Harrah College of Hotel Administration
University of Nevada, Las Vegas

John Wiley & Sons, Inc.
New York • Chichester • Brisbane • Toronto • Singapore

Library of Congress Cataloging-in-Publication Data

Shock, Patti.
    Hotel catering : a handbook for sales and operations / Patti Shock,
John Stefanelli.
        p.   cm.
    Includes bibliographical references and index.
    ISBN 0-471-54418-3 (alk. paper)
    1. Caterers and catering.   2. Hotels, taverns, etc.—Food service.
I. Stefanelli, John M.   II. Title.
TX943.S546   1992
642'.4—dc20   91-30707

Printed in the United States of America

10 9 8 7 6 5 4

To our students —
past, present, and future;
and to the members of the
National Association of Catering Executives (NACE)

Foreword

The excitement of the hospitality industry is never more evident than when the doors to the grand ballroom are swung open to reveal a magnificent event. The ambience of the room, its lighting, theme props, music, sound, temperature, table decor, and place settings combine to create memories for the guest that will leave positive impressions of your hotel for years to come.

The menu, wine, and spirit selections, and the level of service provided work together to create harmony. The same feeling is evident regardless of whether you are experiencing a standard meeting room setup, elaborate audiovisual presentations, a simple sandwich luncheon, or a routine coffee break.

The catering executive interfaces with the client to plan, coordinate, and orchestrate all details of the catered event. The end result is a smooth, professional experience for the event planner and his or her constituents, your guests.

These important scenarios have existed for many years, yet education directly related to the influential role of the catering executive has, for the most part, been informal or addressed as an addendum usually entitled: "the restaurant that books private parties."

Recently, as the need for qualified catering executives has become more critical, our industry has become more focused on this very profitable segment of the hospitality spectrum. Owners now address the need for quality banquet and meeting space in their hotels, suppliers direct new products toward the banquet/catering segment, professional associations like the National Association of Catering Executives (NACE) grow in membership and scope, and books are written by industry leaders to address the "how to" of catering.

This book is unique. Unlike others dealing with catering operations, it offers a complete, logical outline of catering-management principles and procedures. It is designed to enlighten the reader to the detail, planning, dedication, precision, versatility, and fun involved in being a successful catering executive in today's hospitality industry. Its authors are talented educators who have recognized the need for such a book in our dynamic and ever-changing field, and it has been reviewed by industry professionals to ensure the proper dose of reality.

Remember, excellence is in the details.

GARY BUDGE
Corporate Director, Food and Beverage
Princess Hotels International, Inc.
Past President, National Association of
   Catering Executives (NACE)

Preface

Over the past few years, the catering segment of the United States food-service industry has grown significantly. Convention catering, mobile catering, and social catering enjoy above-average growth. National Restaurant Association (NRA) statistics indicate that catering sales increased nearly 7 percent per year between 1987 and 1990. It is one of the fastest growing segments of the food and beverage industry.

Convention and social catering are especially popular. Patrons are rediscovering the advantages and pleasures of catered events and are engaging professional caterers at an ever-increasing rate. There is such a shortage of professional caterers today that the NRA and the National Association of Catering Executives (NACE) have tried to fill this void by providing catering seminars to restaurateurs who want to expand into this exciting and lucrative field. The NRA offers two types of catering courses: on-premises and off-premises. The on-premises course is aimed at restaurateurs who want to get involved with banquets and catering.

The primary objective of this book is to provide hotel catering professionals, as well as aspiring professionals, with an in-depth, one-stop source of generally accepted hotel catering principles and practices. Readers will find that this book contains a discussion of the: (1) organization and administration of hotel catering, (2) major hotel catering activities, (3) hotel catering production and service techniques, and (4) hotel catering department's working relationships with internal departments and external organizations.

The book includes several major topics. Readers wishing to gain a general perspective of the hotel catering business will be

interested in Chapters 1 and 2. Those who want specific information that can be used to plan, develop, implement, supervise, and
follow-up on a catering function should read and study the remaining chapters.

Chapters 3 through 12 contain an in depth discussion of hotel
catering procedures. They also serve as the hotel catering professional's desk reference. This book will help the reader who needs to
know approximately how many servers to schedule for a particular
type of function, how to price meal functions, and how to develop
banquet proposals.

During the writing of this book, the authors have benefited
from the thoughtful and constructive feedback of colleagues who
continually reviewed our efforts. We would especially like to ac-
knowledge our expert reviewers who diligently corrected our errors
and oversights. Thank you Gary Budge, Peter Gunther, Jane Jaeger,
Andy Nazarechuk, Robert Neville, Laura Silverman, and John
Steinmetz.

Patti Shock would also like to thank Angela Barbara, Judy
Cantu, Ron Charest, Joe Jeff Goldblatt, Klaus Inkamp, Helen
Roberts, Michael Roman, and Harold Weese for sparking and sus-
taining her interest in catering and the NACE organization, and for
their continuing inspiration and support.

The appropriate methods used to organize a memorable catering function are subject to a certain amount of discussion, opinion,
and interpretation. Since a textbook is a living document, subject to
revision as our industry changes, we welcome your ideas and suggestions for the next edition.

While no book can claim to be the last word on any subject, we
feel that the material presented in this volume provides a thorough
view of hotel catering. We hope that our discussion of this exciting
and rewarding field will be a worthy contribution to each reader's
professional career development.

PATTI J. SHOCK
JOHN M. STEFANELLI

Las Vegas, Nevada
December 1991

Contents

HOTEL
CATERING

1

Overview of Hotel Catering

I approach catering as an art which mixes both creativity and management. It is essential in any catering operation to express an image which is consistent with your company. Further, in the case of The Mirage, it must represent the collected creativity of a staff from around the world. Finally, it must be a managed process which serves the needs of both the client and the company.

Angela Barbara
Director of Catering
The Mirage Hotel
Las Vegas, Nevada

In our fast-paced society, people are less and less inclined to prepare meals or entertain at home. Between personal and professional activities, the typical individual does not have the time, nor the desire, to work in the home kitchen.

The U.S. food-service industry has benefited greatly from this trend. According to the National Restaurant Association (NRA), U.S. food-service sales equal about 5 percent of the U.S. Gross National Product (GNP). This is expected to increase throughout the 1990s.

Today, over 40 percent of all money spent for food in the United States is spent in a food-service operation. In 1950, less than 25 percent of the food dollar was spent away from home.

On the average day, almost 50 percent of the U.S. population will spend money at a food-service establishment. About $3/5$ of them will eat in a food-service operation, while the remainder will purchase food for off-premises consumption.

The on-premises and off-premises catering segments of the U.S. food-service industry have enjoyed similar success and growth over the years. Every day thousands of business and social groups get together to enjoy each other's company and the refreshments that are usually found at these gatherings.

1

Some of these events are catered by the group members themselves. But since time is a precious commodity, more and more groups are demanding professionally prepared and served food and beverages. This allows people to concentrate solely on their personal, social, and business activities while simultaneously enjoying the events. And, as a bonus, they can leave the clean up to someone else.

The NRA estimates that catering sales have increased about 7 percent per year between 1987 and 1990. The catering segment is one of the fastest growing segments of the U.S. food-service industry. It is thought that catering and take-out sales will generate considerable growth in U.S. food-service sales throughout the 1990s.

TYPES OF CATERING

Catering can be classified several ways. The most common method is to categorize catering into social catering and business catering.

Social catering includes such events as high school proms, high school reunions, society balls, weddings, birthday parties, charity benefits, and costume balls. It is estimated that social catering accounts for about 25 percent of all catering sales.

Business catering includes such events as association conventions, civic meetings, corporate sales meetings, seller-buyer entertaining, service awards banquets, recognition banquets, product showings, and educational training sessions. It is estimated that business catering accounts for about 75 percent of all catering sales.

Catering can also be categorized into off-premises catering and on-premises catering. Off-premises catering usually involves production at a central kitchen with delivery to and service provided at a client's location, though at times the caterer may do on-site production as well as service.

Off-premises catering also includes less complex functions, such as carry-out party trays and other similar refreshments.

Hotel catering is a form of on-premises catering. Almost all production and service is handled at the hotel property. The hotel controls all aspects of the catered event. Patrons usually receive a one-stop shopping opportunity from the typical hotel caterer.

In the food-service industry, on-premises catering sales exceed off-premises catering sales. While exact statistics are not kept for these two catering segments, it is estimated that on-premises catering accounts for about two-thirds of all catering sales, with off-premises catering accounting for the remaining one-third.

The NRA classifies catering into two categories: mobile catering and social catering. The vast majority of these sales are off-premises catering sales. Hotel food and beverage sales, which include hotel catering sales, are noted separately.

The U.S. food-service industry's annual amount of all types of food and beverage sales exceeds $250 billion. Total hotel food and beverage sales are approximately 7 percent of all types of food and beverage sales in the United States, while social-catering and mobile-catering sales are about $1^1/_2$ percent of U.S. food-service industry sales.

Mobile catering involves primarily the companies that provide prepared foods and beverages from the back of a truck or portable stand to cash-paying customers. This type of food service is very common at construction sites, busy street corners, and special outdoor events. Firms engaged in this type of activity must prepare finished products at a central location (or purchase prepared merchandise from a third party), and then package and transport those products to customer locations. Many mobile caterers also provide vending machine service to places such as office buildings, school grounds, and shopping centers.

Some types of mobile catering are very similar to typical restaurant meal service, in that they usually involve cash sales to individuals. For instance, a mobile caterer may stock a complete set of vending machines in an office park and employ a cashier and servers on-site to handle cash sales, clean-up, limited table service, and so forth.

Some mobile caterers provide complete meal production and service on location. For instance, a few companies specialize in feeding forest-fire fighters, movie and television productions in the field, in-home parties, in-office parties, and people taking extended camping trips. Caterers working in this field furnish both mobile-catering and social-catering services. There is no sharp line that distinguishes social catering from mobile catering in these cases.

According to the NRA's classification scheme, social caterers outsell mobile caterers by about three to one. Generally speaking, for every dollar spent by guests for mobile catering services, they will spend three dollars for social catering services.

Social catering includes primarily on-premises catering, where guests are served in a banquet room or other similar facility owned and operated by the caterer. As the term implies, social catering generally involves a planned, hosted event. Generally speaking, each event has one host and one bill. Events range from small business meetings to large awards banquets.

The typical hotel catering department specializes in this type of catering. You do not usually find a hotel property heavily involved in mobile catering. A few of them though, have entered the off-premises catering industry and are capable of providing on-site production and service.

There is a growing trend in the hotel industry of more and more hotels moving into off-premises catering in order to maintain profitability during the off season. Some hotels are responding to the challenge of off-premises caterers by going outside the hotel to obtain additional sales revenue. Going after the large corporations or charity functions held in civic locations can help the hotel catering department survive during slow periods.

Off-premises functions can be a significant source of additional sales revenue and profits for those hotel properties that have the necessary equipment and personnel to handle large off-site catered affairs. However, unless the property is set up to do this correctly, the work can be too distracting and the added expense could wipe out any incremental profits.

TYPES OF CATERERS

The hotel caterer is only one of many types of caterers that seek to satisfy customer catering needs. The hotel usually has the advantage in this competitive atmosphere because normally it can offer many services under one roof as well as sufficient space to house the entire event, thereby enticing the customer with a one-stop shopping opportunity. The hotel also tends to be a more glamorous and exciting location. The hotel must realize though, that other caterers abound in the industry and, even though they may be much smaller and unable to offer a smorgasbord of choices, they eagerly court many of the same customers.

In some parts of the country, there are independent banquet halls, convention facilities, and conference centers. Many of these properties are able to compete with hotels for the same customers because they have more flexible price structures due to their lower overhead expenses. In some instances, they may also have the advantage in some instances because they can offer a client a generous price reduction if the client can buy out the entire facility.

Some restaurant operations have attached banquet rooms that can be used for several types of catered events. The typical restaurant though, cannot afford this luxury; it is too expensive to maintain a room that might be empty three or four days per week. As a result, restaurateurs who want to book banquet business usually will go after the smaller functions that can be housed in one section of the restaurant's regular dining room.

The hotel may lose these small functions to the local restaurant unless it takes the time to court this business. However, before going after this business, the catering executive must be careful to avoid those catered events that cannot be charged enough money to cover all variable and fixed-overhead costs associated with opening a function room. For instance, the restaurant that uses a section of its regular dining room to house a catered event will not incur significantly greater heating and cooling expenses; the dining room must be heated or cooled regardless of the number of guests expected. The hotel though, must consider the feasibility of opening a function room; if the room is opened, incremental heating and cooling expenses will be incurred, whereas if the room remains closed, these expenses are avoidable. In some cases, while a particular group might turn a profit for the average restaurant, the hotel property may be less fortunate.

Some mobile caterers are able to service major functions. For example, many vending machine companies use their central kitchens and transport equipment to cater events at independent halls (such as a church multipurpose room) or at a client's facilities. Again, some hotels will solicit this type of business during the slow season if it can secure the proper equipment and personnel to do it adequately and profitably.

Private clubs do a great deal of catering for their members. Country clubs concentrate on social events, such as weddings and dances. City clubs specialize in business catering, such as corporate meetings, board luncheons, and civic events.

Resorts often have outdoor functions at remote locations on the property. For example, The Pointe at Tapatio Cliffs in Phoenix, AZ, has a special "hayride" party where guests are transported in a horse-drawn wagon to a hilltop where they enjoy a mountain-side, steak-fry barbecue with all the trimmings.

Profit-oriented hospitals do catering for medical meetings and staff functions. In most cases, they compete directly with hotels for these functions.

There are several types of tax-exempt organizations that offer catering services to anyone willing to pay for them. For instance, universities, colleges, hospitals, museums, and fraternal organizations vigorously compete for these events because they help subsidize their major, nonprofit activities. Small, tax-paying businesses are especially unhappy with these so-called "nonprofit" competitors; however, nonprofit groups consistently fight any types of government restraints on these activities.

Contract food-service companies operate many facilities that are capable of supporting catering events. For instance, many of these firms operate food services in large office buildings, where executive dining rooms can be used to house special parties and meetings. Some contract food-service companies are also capable of handling off-premises catering functions.

Lately a new competitor has edged its way into the catering arena: the retail food-service operation that concentrates on take-out service. For instance, there are now many "super-store" supermarkets that house complete kitchen and deli facilities. Several department stores and discount stores also contain these facilities. Given enough lead time, these competitors can prepare buffet platters that would be the envy of many hotel catering executives.

Many restaurant operations are also heavily engaged in take-out service. For instance, it is not unusual for new restaurants to have a separate entrance devoted strictly to take-out business. Customers do not have to enter the regular restaurant. In fact, some of these restaurants, borrowing a page from their fast-food neighbors, have drive-through windows.

Restaurants that have a thriving take-out business often seem to flirt with delivery business. Take-out and delivery business could be considered forms of off-premises catering. They share many of the same traits that characterize more traditional forms of off-premises catering.

Take-out and delivery business accounts for an ever-increasing proportion of total U.S. food-service sales. It is unlikely that the hotel caterer would want to compete in these business segments. However, hotel properties have done some of this quite successfully. For example, at the Camelback Inn in Scottsdale, AZ, people living next to its golf courses can dial the hotel's room-service department. A room-service server hops on a catering "golf" cart and delivers the finished products. The hotel also takes orders for box lunches.

HOTEL CATERING DEPARTMENT FUNCTIONS

The person in charge of the hotel catering department must perform the normal management functions. As the head of a major hotel department, he or she must engage in the following:

1. *Planning.* The department must accomplish its financial and nonfinancial objectives. To do so, it must develop appropriate marketing, production, and service procedures. It also must ensure

that the department's operating budgets and other action plans are consistent with the hotel's overall objectives.

2. *Organizing.*   The department must organize the resources needed to follow the plan. Staff members must be recruited and trained. Work schedules must be prepared. And performance evaluations must be administered.

3. *Directing.*   Employee supervision is an integral part of every supervisor's job. Supervisory style will emanate from top management. The catering department's supervisory procedures must be consistent with company policies.

4. *Controlling.*   The catering department manager must ensure that actual performance corresponds with planned performance. Effective financial controls ensure that actual profit-and-loss statements are consistent with pro forma budgets, while effective quality controls ensure that production and service meet company standards.

HOTEL CATERING DEPARTMENT OBJECTIVES

Hotel catering departments have a variety of objectives. The weight and priority given to each will depend on corporate policy. Some of the most common objectives are:

- Earn a fair profit on assets employed in the catering business.
- Generate sufficient catering sales volume to defray all expenses and leave a fair profit. Hotel caterers must be careful not to generate a lot of business that will not pay for itself. They must practice selective sales strategies in order to maximize profits. Usually the only time a hotel catering executive will consider booking a marginally profitable event is if it is a party designed to show off the catering facilities. It may also be contemplated if the hotel wants to host those who may directly or indirectly generate future catering revenues.
- Deliver customer satisfaction. This will lead to repeat patronage as well as positive referrals. A food-service operation thrives on repeat patronage; the same holds true for the hotel catering department.
- Provide consistent quality and service. The best surprise is no surprise. Customers are happy when the actual quality and service received parallels those that were promised. Punctuality and consistency are hallmarks of the well-run catering department.

- Convey a particular image. Hotel caterers want to be known as specializing in certain types of products and services. They strive to be unique because they want customers to think of them whenever a specific atmosphere or ambience is required. Catering is often the hotel's most visible characteristic on the local and national levels. It alone has the most potential to become a hotel's "signature," that is, its major claim to fame.

- Develop a reputation for dependability. Regardless of the pressure that any event places on the catering department, hotels want clients to have confidence that their needs will be met. The catering department must fill adequately the liaison role between clients and all hotel services.

- Develop a reputation for flexibility. To be dependable, the typical hotel caterer must be flexible. The department must be able to react on a moment's notice. Clients will remember fondly the service that bailed them out at the last minute.

HOTEL CATERING DEPARTMENT ORGANIZATION

Hotel catering departments are organized according to the needs of the particular hotel properties. Usually a hotel's primary profit center is its sleeping-rooms division, with the catering department being the second most profitable department. Consequently, all hotel departments generally are organized and administered to maximize the sales and profits of sleeping rooms and catered functions.

There are two general types of hotel catering department organizations. In one form, the department is organized in such a way that all catering personnel are under the supervision of the hotel's food and beverage director. (See Figures 1.1 and 1.2.) In this example, the food and beverage director is responsible for the hotel's kitchens, restaurant outlets, and banquet operations as well as for client solicitation and service.

Alternatively, the catering department may be organized so that some catering personnel are under the supervision of the sales and marketing director, with other employees, such as the banquet staff, reporting to the food and beverage director. (See Figure 1.3.) In this situation, the director of catering must work closely with the director of sales and marketing as well as with the food and beverage director. The catering department takes clients secured by sales and marketing, matches them with the necessary services provided by food and beverage and other hotel departments, and develops the appropriate service procedures needed to plan and implement successful and profitable catered events.

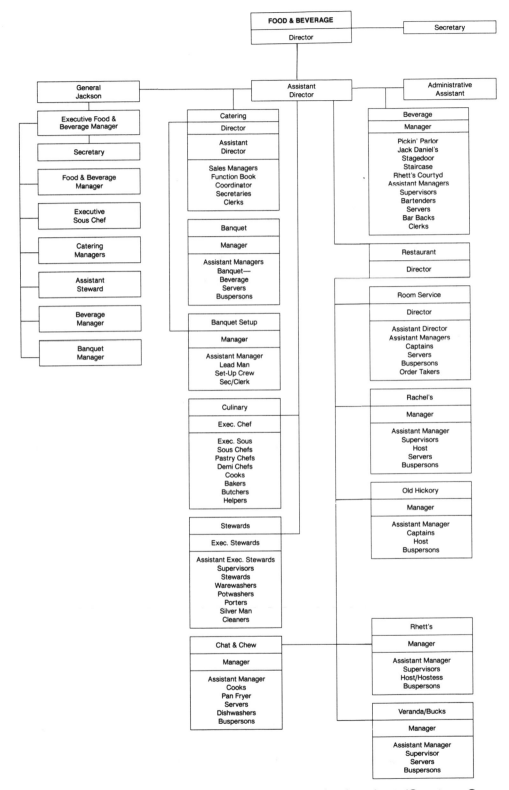

Figure 1.1. Food and beverage department organization chart. (Courtesy Opryland Hotel, Nashville, TN.)

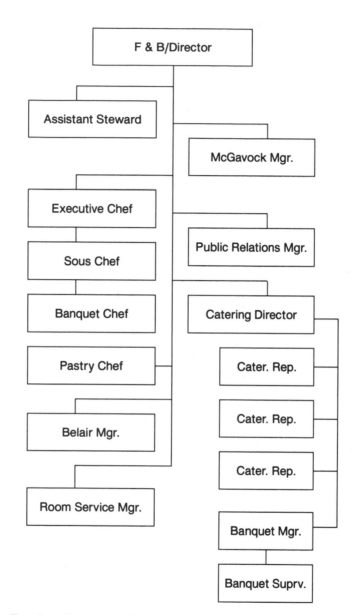

Figure 1.2.   Food and beverage department organization chart. (Courtesy Music City Sheraton Corporation.)

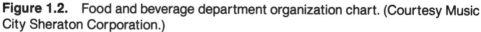

In this second type of organizational pattern, the sales and marketing and food and beverage directors "split" the workload and coordinate catering sales and service. For example, in some hotels, convention service personnel handle any food function that uses more than 20 sleeping rooms while the catering department handles the local functions. In other hotels, the catering department handles all food and beverage service, while convention service personnel take care of all nonfood logistics, such as function-room setups, tear downs, and so forth.

There are advantages and disadvantages with each organizational form. The major advantages associated with the organizational forms in Figures 1.1 and 1.2 are:

1. *Increased efficiency.*   Clients work with one designated person who has the authority to oversee the event from inception to completion. Last-minute requests and changes can be implemented quickly.

2. *Isolated responsibility.*   Responsibility is assigned to one person. Management and clients know exactly who to contact if questions arise. This contact person occupies a key role in that he or she is the sole liaison between clients and all hotel services. It is a very critical position in that the contact person is responsible for translating a client's needs and wishes into reality.

3. *Job enrichment.*   A person in charge of an event enjoys more variety than does the person involved with only one or two aspects. When the event is a success, the person in charge can rightfully take a bow.

4. *Repeat patronage.*   When clients deal with one person, there are additional opportunities to solicit repeat patronage and referrals.

5. *Improved communications.*   Since there are fewer persons on the communications chain, ambiguities and misinterpretations should be minimal.

The major disadvantages of the organizational forms in Figures 1.1 and 1.2 are:

1. *Excessive workload.*   One person may not have enough hours in the day to perform all the necessary tasks.

2. *Too many bosses.*   The food and beverage department cannot be totally isolated; it must interact to some degree with the sales and marketing department. Unfortunately, this overlap may violate established chain-of-command policies unless the relationships are spelled out clearly.

3. *Lack of specialization.*   Some industry experts feel that it is difficult to train one person to be expert in so many areas. However, if the hotel caterer is only the information point of exchange between clients and all other hotel services, this potential problem can be minimized.

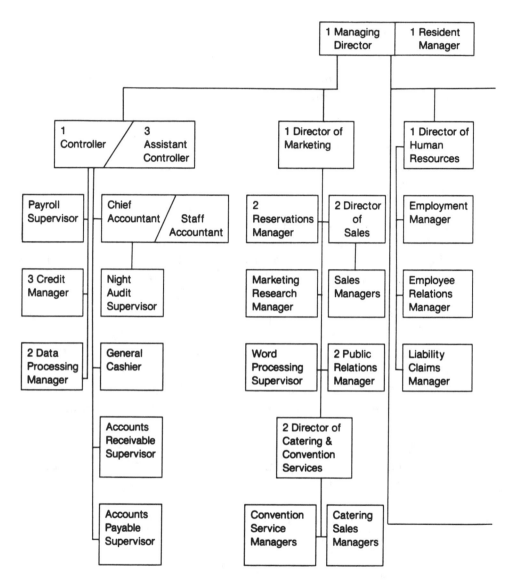

Key:
    1 - Executive Committee/Operations Committee and Department Head
    2 - Operations Committee and Department Head
    3 - Department Head

Figure 1.3. Hotel organization chart. (Courtesy Westin Peachtree Plaza Hotel, Atlanta, GA.)

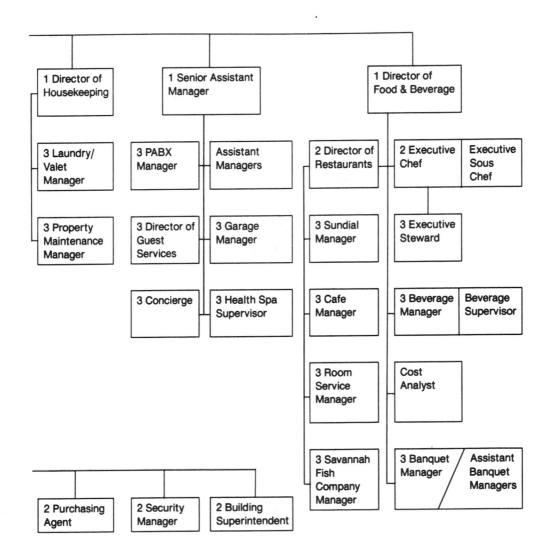

4. *Excessive delegation.*   If one person is not expert in all areas, the odds are he or she will delegate responsibility freely. This can defeat the positive aspects of including all tasks under one person's direction. It also can confuse catering staff members.

The advantages and disadvantages associated with the organizational form shown in Figure 1.3 are the opposites of those associated with the organizational form in Figures 1.1 and 1.2.

Which organizational form is appropriate? As a general rule, the hotel catering department organization will be influenced by: (1) the size of the hotel; (2) types of functions catered; (3) corporate policy; and (4) overall level of service offered by the hotel.

While there is no one single organizational form suitable for all hotels, it would appear that the most typical organizational pattern is the one in Figure 1.4. In this case, the catering and convention service staffs work together, each handling specific activities. Catering typically handles all food and beverage requirements while convention service handles all nonfood arrangements.

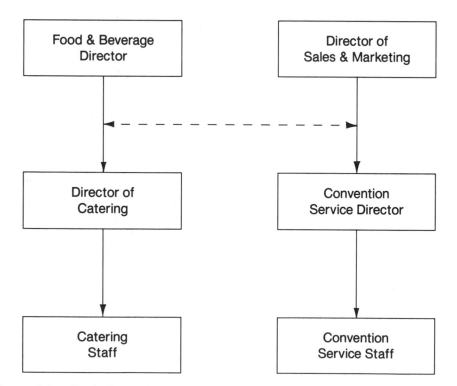

Figure 1.4.   Typical catering organizational pattern.

Catering Staff Positions

Hotel catering departments require a variety of staff positions in order to operate effectively and efficiently. Depending on the type of catered event, they also depend on other hotel departments' employees to handle meal and beverage functions. In a large hotel property, the typical positions needed to service clients are:

1. Director of catering (DOC)
2. Assistant catering director
3. Catering manager
4. Catering sales manager
5. Catering sales representative
6. Director of convention service/Convention service manager
7. Banquet manager
8. Banquet setup manager
9. Assistant banquet manager
10. Scheduler
11. Maitre d' hotel
12. Captain
13. Server
14. Food handler
15. Bartender
16. Sommelier
17. Houseman
18. Attendant
19. Clerk
20. Engineer
21. Cashier
22. Ticket taker
23. Steward.

Job Specifications

A job specification contains the qualities sought in a job candidate. Before hiring a catering department employee, a superior generally looks for at least five major qualities.

1. *Technical skills.*   Ideally, catering employees will have food and beverage preparation and service skills. At the very least, they must have the aptitude to learn these skills. All catering employees must be familiar with the products so that they can respond adequately to customer inquiries.

It is felt that most, if not all, catering employees must have sales skills. For some job positions, the primary job qualification is the ability to sell. For instance, a sales representative's major asset is his or her ability to sell. However, even those employees primarily involved with guest service should have the ability to upsell clients. They should be able to encourage clients to purchase additional, or higher quality, products and services, thereby increasing hotel profits.

Communications skills are absolutely essential for catering staff members. Each function is a unique undertaking. There is no standard pattern. Consequently, open and intelligible communications are critical to the success of a catered event.

2. *Conceptual skills.*   As much as possible, catering department employees must be able to view the entire catering function and not see things exclusively from their particular job perspectives. For instance, a banquet chef must appreciate the ceremonies involved with a wedding function and not ignore them when preparing and coordinating food courses.

Catering staff members must be able to take a client's "vision" of the function (including needs, wishes, purpose of the function, and budgetary constraints) and develop an event (through negotiations) consistent with this vision that can be delivered effectively and efficiently by the hotel. The planned catered event must meet the client's requirements.

3. *Human (interpersonal) skills.*   Customer-contact skills are extremely important in the hospitality industry. Getting along with people, and satisfying them while simultaneously making a profit, is a challenge that must be met and overcome by all catering staff members. Unlike technical and conceptual skills, basic human skills generally cannot be taught by the hotel training department. As Ellsworth Statler once said before the turn of the century, "Hire only good-natured people."

4. *Honesty and integrity.*   Most staff members will be handling a considerable amount of hotel property. They also will be making promises to clients, other customers, and several intermediaries (such as entertainers and florists). To say the least, they must be above-board in all their dealings. Kickbacks are not an acceptable practice.

5. *Other qualities.*   Other characteristics that superiors look for in job candidates depend on the type of position and company policies. For instance, if the hotel has a promotion-from-within policy, a superior would seek a job candidate who has the ability and desire to advance and grow with the company.

Job Descriptions

A job description contains a list of duties an employee must perform. It also includes the job candidate's superior, job performance evaluation criteria, the job objectives, and a career path. It is usually prepared before, or in conjunction with, the job specification.

Example abbreviated job descriptions for the staff positions involved directly or indirectly with catering are:

1. *Director of catering (DOC).*   Assigns and oversees all functions; oversees all marketing efforts; interacts with clients and catering managers; coordinates with hotel sales director; creates menus; usually reports to the director of food and beverage, but in some hotels reports to the director of sales and marketing.

2. *Assistant catering director.*   Services accounts; helps with marketing.

3. *Catering manager.*   Maintains client contacts; services accounts.

4. *Catering sales manager.*   Oversees sales efforts; administers the sales office.

5. *Catering sales representative.*   Involved only in selling; handles outside sales and/or inside sales.

In some hotels, jobs 3, 4, and 5 are one and the same. The rule in these properties seems to be: "If you book it, you work it!"

6. *Director of convention service/Convention service manager.* In some hotels, he or she handles catering for meetings and conventions, with the catering department handling the local/social market. In other hotels, this person handles all services except food and beverage. In some hotels, this person has the title director of catering and convention service and is responsible for both areas.

7. *Banquet manager.*   Implements the director of catering's requests; oversees captains; supervises all functions in progress; staffs and schedules servers and bartenders; coordinates all support departments. He or she is the operations director, as opposed to catering executives, who handle primarily the selling and planning chores.

8. *Banquet setup manager.*   Supervises the banquet setup crew; orders tables, chairs, and other room equipment from storage; supervises tear down of event.

9. *Assistant banquet manager.*   Reports to banquet manager; supervises table settings and decor. There may be two (or more) assistants; for example, a hotel may have one for the day shift and one for the evening shift.

10. *Scheduler.*   Sometimes referred to as a diary clerk. Enters bookings in master log; oversees the timing of all functions and provides adequate turnover time; responsible for scheduling meeting rooms, reception areas, pool-side areas, other areas, meal functions, beverage functions, other functions, and equipment requirements; keeps appropriate records to ensure against overbooking and double booking; responsible for communicating this information to all relevant hotel departments.

11. *Maitre d' hotel.*   Floor manager; in charge of all service personnel; oversees all aspects of guest service during meal and beverage functions.

12. *Captain.*   Room manager; in charge of service at meal functions; typically oversees all activity in the entire function room or a portion of it during a meal; supervises servers.

13. *Server.*   There are two types: food servers and cocktail servers. Food servers deliver foods, nonalcoholic beverages, and utensils to tables; clear tables; attend to guest needs. Cocktail servers perform similar duties, but concentrate on serving alcoholic beverages. Servers are sometimes backed up by buspersons, whose primary responsibilities are to clear tables, restock side stands, and serve ice water, rolls, butter, and condiments.

14. *Food handler.*   (Sometimes referred to as a food steward.) Prepares finished food products noted on banquet event orders (BEO). Responsible for having them ready according to schedule.

15. *Bartender.*   Concentrates on alcoholic-beverage production and service. Bartenders are sometimes assisted by bar backs, whose primary responsibilities are to stock initially and replenish the bars with liquor, ice, glassware, and direct operating supplies.

16. *Sommelier.*   Wine steward; usually used only at fancy, upscale events.

17. *Houseman.*   Sometimes referred to as a porter or convention porter. Physically sets up rooms with risers, hardware, tables, chairs, and other necessary equipment; reports to assistant banquet manager.

18. *Attendant.*   "Refreshes" meeting rooms, i.e., does spot cleaning and trash removal during break periods, and replenishes supplies—such as note pads, pencils, and ice water; responds to requests for service by meeting function hosts. Some catered functions may require restroom attendants. And some events may require cloakroom attendants.

19. *Clerk.*   Handles routine correspondence; types contracts; types banquet event orders (BEO); handles and routes telephone messages; distributes documents to relevant staff members and other hotel departments.

20. *Engineer.*   Provides necessary utilities service, such as setting up electrical panels for major exhibits; hangs banners; prepares special platforms and displays; sets up exhibits; maintains catering furniture, fixtures, and equipment (FFE). He or she may also handle all audiovisual (AV) and lighting installation, tear down, and service.

21. *Cashier.*   Collects cash at cash bars; sells drink tickets; may also sell meal tickets.

22. *Ticket taker.*   Responsible for collecting tickets from guests before they are allowed to enter a function.

23. *Steward.*   Delivers the proper amounts of china, glass, silver, and other similar items to function rooms, kitchens, and bars areas.

HOTEL CATERING DEPARTMENT POLICIES

The hotel property must establish policies to guide the catering department's relations with clients. The typical policies include:

1. *Food and beverage prices.*   These must be clearly listed. It is a good idea to note that any listed prices are subject to change; in other words, the hotel should not assume responsibility if potential clients are viewing outdated menus. Usually hotels note that published menu prices are subject to change unless firm price guarantees are negotiated and noted on a catering contract. If competitive bids are being prepared, all prices must be computed according to standard company pricing procedures.

2. *Taxes.*   Clients must be informed that all relevant state and local consumption taxes, such as sales tax and entertainment tax, will be added to the catering prices. Tax-exempt clients usually must furnish an exemption certificate to the hotel prior to the event.

3. *Gratuities.*   These are mandatory charges for service added to the catering prices. Most properties add a 15 to 19 percent gratuity to the bill. You cannot assume that clients are aware of these traditional charges: they must be informed about them up front.

4. *Tips.*   These are voluntary gifts. Some clients will want to tip some or all employees if they receive exceptional service. If you have a no-tipping policy, clients must know about it.

5. *Deposits.*   The deposit procedures must be spelled out clearly. Clients must be informed of the amount that must be paid, when it must be paid, and how it will be applied to the final billing.

6. *Refunds.*   While no one likes to broach a negative subject, it is important to detail your refund policies and procedures in advance.

7. *Guarantees.*   Usually a client must give a firm guarantee two or three days in advance of the event. The hotel will prepare for that number plus a stipulated percentage to handle any guests who decide to attend at the last minute. For instance, most hotels will agree to handle the guaranteed number of guests and to overset about 3 to 5 percent.

If the function is very large, the hotel usually will use a sliding-scale guarantee. For instance, while it may agree to a 5 percent overset for parties up to 500 persons, it may agree to accommodate only a 3 percent overage for parties in excess of 500.

Negotiating guarantees is a very tricky undertaking. The wise catering executive makes sure that clients understand clearly the hotel's position.

Guarantees, as well as deposits, refund policies, miscellaneous charges, menu prices, and so forth, should always be spelled out in the catering contract.

8. *Set-up charges.*   If these are not included in the food and beverage menu prices, clients must be told in advance about these extra charges. Usually a large function will not incur additional set-up charges; however, small groups may be subject to them.

9. *Room-rental rates.*   The typical hotel will usually charge clients rent for function rooms if they are used for meetings and other functions that do not include significant food and beverage sales. For instance, usually a hotel will charge for the room if the function does not generate at least a $15-per-person food and/or beverage tab. The rental rate is usually calculated to cover the fixed overhead and provide a fair profit for the hotel.

10. *Other extra charges.*   Depending on the size of the function, the hotel may add on extra charges for bartenders, cashiers, coat-checking facilities, and directional displays. If clients require additional labor because their functions are scheduled to last longer than normal, they usually will be assessed an additional charge to cover the extra payroll cost.

11. *Credit terms.*   Clients who have established credit ratings with the hotel will usually be allowed to put up a minimum deposit and pay the remaining balance within 30 days. Clients without credit approval usually must put up a large deposit and pay the remaining balance at least two days prior to the event or immediately after the function. Clients who are somewhere between an established credit rating and no credit rating normally must put up a deposit and pay the remaining balance at the end of the catered event.

12. *Outside food and beverage.*   Hotels generally will not allow clients to bring in their own food and beverage supplies. In most situations, the hotel's liquor license, health permit, and/or business license forbids the use of personal products. The same restrictions may apply to other materials, such as paper products, decorations, and equipment.

13. *Set-up service charges.*   If the law and the hotel allow clients to bring in their own products, there usually will be a charge for set-up service. For instance, if a client is allowed to bring in his or her own liquor, there may be a standard, one-time fee for the service, or the hotel might charge a standard fee for each drink prepared and served.

14. *Underage guests.*   The hotel must ensure clients realize that the pertinent liquor laws will not be suspended during their catered events. For instance, wedding hosts may not see anything wrong with serving wine to an underage guest at a private party. However, the law does not make this distinction. The same thing is true for service to visibly intoxicated guests; they cannot legally be served by the banquet staff.

If clients request self-service bars, some caterers will require them to sign a waiver of liquor liability so that they are not held responsible for guest actions. This type of waiver is necessary because in the case of self-service, the hotel does not have bartenders and cocktail servers on site to monitor underage drinking and service to visibly intoxicated guests.

15. *Display restrictions.*   Many clients need to use their own signs, displays, decorations, and/or demonstrations at booked events. Usually the hotel will reserve the right to approve these and to control their placement and location. If clients are allowed to have displays, the hotel usually expects the clients to be responsible for any damage done and any extraordinary clean up that may result.

16. *Responsibility for loss and/or damage.*   Personal property brought into the hotel by clients usually will not be covered by the hotel's insurance policies. Consequently, they need to be informed of this policy, and agree to it, before receiving permission to use their own property.

17. *Indemnification.*   The hotel usually expects clients to agree to indemnify the hotel against any claims, losses, and/or damages, except those due solely to the negligence and/or willful misconduct of the hotel staff. The hotel also wants protection from claims made by outside service contractors, such as florists, decorators, or audiovisual (AV) firms engaged by clients. Furthermore, clients are expected to stipulate that, by paying the final bill, they agree that there are no disputes with the products and services received.

18. *Uncontrollable acts.*   There are times when the hotel will be unable to perform through no fault of its own. For instance, strikes, labor disputes, travel agency mistakes, and so forth, could hamper the hotel's ability to service its clients. Consequently, clients must agree to hold harmless the hotel under these types of conditions.

19. *Substitutions.*   This is similar to the uncontrollable acts policy mentioned above. Occasionally supply problems may force the hotel to substitute menu products. Or it may be necessary to move a function from one meeting room to another. For instance, an outside event may have to be moved indoors at the last minute because of inclement weather. Or a contractor's strike could force the hotel to substitute other space of comparable size and quality. While few of us want to think about these potential problems, the clients must be advised in advance that they could happen.

20. *Security.*   A hotel may require a client to provide additional security for his or her event. For instance, a convention of diamond dealers may be expected to schedule a great deal of personal security that is provided by or approved by the hotel. Alternatively, the hotel may reserve the right to hire additional security guards and bill the convention host.

21. *Licenses and permits.*   Some functions may need to be approved and/or licensed by the local government licensing agency. For instance, a function that has a cover charge may need a temporary admission license. The hotel should reserve the right to refuse service to any client who does not hold the appropriate licenses and permits prior to the event.

MAJOR CHALLENGES

The catering department encounters several challenges while working to attain its objectives. Some of the major ones are:

1. *Marketing the department's services.*   A great deal of time must be spent in this effort to distinguish your property in the minds of potential clients. Too many caterers are exactly alike. Clients tend to perceive caterers as interchangeable as busses: there is always another one available who can handle their needs. You will need to battle constantly this perception.

2. *Excessive time spent with clients.*   Unfortunately, only a small number of persons and groups contacted will end up purchasing catered events. Moreover, once business is booked, a great deal of time must be spent planning and coordinating the events. While some clients need more hand holding than others, the wise catering executive expects to devote a lot of time to these tasks.

3. *Unique demands.*   For instance, refreshment breaks sometimes are permanently set; customers do not have a particular schedule in mind and merely visit the refreshment area when time permits. This is especially true in conference centers, where attendees can break at will. Consequently, setups need to be freshened periodically, which requires an employee to be constantly alert to fluctuating needs.

4. *Difficult costing and pricing.*   Special requests and last-minute needs will cost more because of the specialized circumstances. The refreshment breaks noted above fall into this category. Since the demands these events present cannot always be predicted in advance, function hosts usually must wait until a final accounting is made by the catering department. This can cause ill will among clients, especially those who are on a tight budget and would appreciate price guarantees.

5. *Ethical traps.*   Sometimes the catering department may encounter conflict-of-interest dilemmas. For example, clients who need outside contractors, such as tour buses, entertainers, and decorators, may ask the hotel for a recommendation. The hotel, always mindful of its image and reputation, will tend to recommend only a few outside contractors that can fill the bill adequately. However, such favoritism could be perceived by some as shady dealing.

6. *Responsibility greater than authority.*   It is very important to determine in advance who is responsible for each part of the event. For instance, a convention may want to hire its own band, but simultaneously expect the hotel to coordinate the details. This can easily lead to misunderstanding and unhappy clients unless everything is spelled out clearly.

7. *Time pressures.*   The catering department is a pressure cooker. It seems as if everything must be ready "yesterday." Catering personnel must learn to work well under time constraints.

8. *Working and coordinating with others.*   Proper advance planning is necessary to avoid service glitches that could cause guest dissatisfaction.

9. *Maintaining qualified staff members.*   Many hotel catering departments experience severe volume swings. For instance, convention centers pose a unique challenge in terms of volume and staffing. One day you might have a breakfast for 5,000, which requires a lot of labor. You may not have another similar function for two weeks; as a result, it is very difficult to keep qualified employees, many of whom prefer more predictable work schedules.

In addition to full-time management and hourly employees, many hotels maintain two lists of service-staff (i.e., banquet-staff) employees: an A-list and a B-list. The A-list personnel are the steady extras; they are the first ones called by the manager when help is needed. If enough people are not available on the A-list, the manager will call those on the B-list.

The B-list personnel are casual labor. They are used to fill in the gaps. They present more problems than do A-list people because the typical B-list worker is probably on the B-list of every hotel in town. As a result, major functions can go begging for adequate staff. The catering executive must be a creative personnel recruiter and a superb planner in order to overcome these obstacles.

A unionized hotel will be obligated to go through the local union hiring hall for its steady and casual servers. The union generally keeps lists of steadies and extras similar to the A-list and B-list kept by nonunionized properties. If the union has enough advance notice of all hotels' labor requirements, chances are it can plan for them and satisfy every catering department's needs.

10. *Lack of experience.*   Due to the rapid growth of the catering industry, there are fewer and fewer experienced catering executives to go around. This has allowed more women into the field, but often at lower salaries because many of them are willing to work for less. Also, since many women catering executives started out as catering secretaries, their food and beverage knowledge is often quite limited.

11. *Scarce technical skills.*   The lack of technical food-service skills is not restricted to women catering executives. Many caterers today, both men and women, have less food knowledge than ever before. They are more and more reliant on chefs and food and beverage directors for advice. This would not be a major problem if standardized menus were used consistently; however, things are more trendy these days, there is more competition, and many clients want something special. This can make it difficult to respond quickly to unusual customer requests.

A potential client may become restless with the catering executive who needs to confer constantly with other food and beverage people in the organization. However, an executive's confidence and poise can transcend the bonds of ignorance. Instead of dismay, a potential client may be quite pleased with the executive who may not have the answer at that very moment, but who promises to get it quickly.

No one is expected to know everything. They do, however, need to know where to get the expertise/information to handle client needs. In the well-run hotel, there is a tremendous network of specialized professionals available as well as a sophisticated communications system that can be used to tap into this bundle of resources. As catering clients become more sophisticated and/or jaded, the hotel cannot remain competitive without them.

2

Markets

We caterers sell only memories. It is our responsibility to make these memories happy ones!

Greg Mosser
Director of Catering/Conference Services
PGA National Resort
Palm Beach Gardens Florida

The number and types of potential clients are limited only by the imagination. Hotel catering departments, especially those housed in large hotel properties, can expect to service the smallest business meeting to the largest industry convention and exposition.

The hotel has the advantage over other types of caterers because, generally speaking, it can handle most types of meal and beverage functions and can provide under one roof, all the function-room space needed. Its ability to offer one-stop convenience to the function host suggests that it can cast its marketing net far and wide. Usually the typical hotel catering department is in the enviable position of deciding whether it wants to specialize and concentrate on certain markets; or it can strive to service any legitimate type of event.

Clients are everywhere. Our society has a never-ending love affair with meetings, conventions, celebrations, ceremonies, and various other special events. The purpose of this chapter is to outline these markets and provide a detailed discussion of each one.

BUSINESS MARKET

The business market represents approximately 75 percent of total catering sales in the United States. It is generally divided into three segments: shallow, mid-level, and deep.

The shallow segment is characterized by low-budget functions. These events usually involve a short lead time for the caterer. For instance, an office party that needs a few deli platters and salads delivered tomorrow afternoon would be a typical event.

Clients in this segment usually shop around for the best price. This does not mean that they ignore quality and service; however, they normally are on a limited budget and cannot afford the very best. The shallow customer of today though, can very easily be the corporate meeting planner of tomorrow. As a result, the caterer who does a good job with this group is apt to win repeat patronage as well as gain an inside track on securing potentially more profitable functions in the future.

The mid-level segment usually involves a sit-down meal function. For instance, an executive luncheon for a few persons, complete with all the trimmings, is a typical mid-level catering opportunity. These events usually are planned well in advance. While price is important, clients will not quibble for a few dollars; it is imperative that the event be memorable and consistent with the executives' status in the business community.

The mid-level function can quickly lead to repeat business. For instance, the executive business luncheon can easily become a monthly affair. The caterer who provides excellent value will more than likely become the favored provider for these clients.

Businesspersons are trained to shop around for the best value; however, when it comes to their personal pleasures, they are no different from the rest of us in that they will not switch loyalties on the spur of the moment. Furthermore, these small functions can lead to bigger and better things in the future.

The deep segment involves especially fancy business meal functions. These are expensive events where cost takes a back seat. Furthermore, these functions oftentimes represent repeat business. While most large conventions and other similar events tend to move around the country, many tend to patronize the same locations or geographical areas on a regularly scheduled basis. For example, COMDEX and the Consumer Electronics Show (CES) always meet in the same locations.

Even though most large business events are booked years in advance, the caterer who specializes in the deep segment must still be prepared to service a client at a moment's notice. The loyal client expects this and is willing to pay for it.

BUSINESS MARKET EVENTS

Companies have several catering needs. Since most hotels are capable of servicing many demands, they enjoy a competitive edge in the catering industry. The hotel that can handle a variety of business functions will earn considerable catering, food and beverage, and sleeping rooms profits.

Business functions range from small meetings to lavish conventions. Some of the typical events that hotel caterers service are:

1. *Meetings and conventions.*   These events represent the bulk of the business market. Some, such as sales meetings, can be rather routine affairs easily serviced by the typical hotel catering department. Others though, such as an annual stockholders meeting, can severely test the catering executive's skill and ingenuity.

Probably the biggest advantage of working with the corporate-meetings segment is that these types of clients can give you more accurate predictions. They usually can note a precise number of attendees. For instance, if a company plans a meeting for 100 persons, it usually will have 100. If a person cancels, normally he or she will be replaced by the company.

A corporate group also tends to allocate more money per attendee than do other types of markets served by hotel catering departments. As a general rule, off-site corporate events are usually attended by businesspersons accustomed to judging overall value without concentrating solely on price.

The corporate-meeting market is also considered to be a more stable market group than others. Oftentimes its off-site events are scheduled months or even years in advance. Furthermore, there are many events, such as sales meetings, that must be held periodically.

Another advantage of this market segment is the general level of professionalism that exists among those who plan and organize their events. These persons tend to know exactly what they want. They also are in business, and so they can understand and appreciate the hotel catering department's capabilities and problems much better than can, say, a family-reunion organizer.

Business-related associations generate a tremendous amount of meetings and conventions business. The hotel caterer will encounter two major types of business-related associations: the trade association and the professional association.

The trade association represents persons employed in a particular trade. Membership usually is sponsored and paid by the member's employer. For instance, the National Association of Catering Executives (NACE) is a trade association, with membership dues generally paid by the catering executive's employer.

The professional association represents persons who practice a particular professional activity. Membership usually is sponsored and paid by the individual member. For instance, the American Medical Association (AMA) is a professional association, with each doctor paying his or her own membership dues.

The combined association market is the largest segment of the meetings and conventions trade. Association members participate in local chapter meetings, educational events, charitable works, and regional, national, and international conventions. Most have conventions and/or meetings at least once each year.

There is an association for almost every vocation or avocation in existence. According to the American Society of Association Executives (ASAE), about 70 percent of Americans belong to one association, about 50 percent belong to two, and about 25 percent belong to four or more.

There are over 20,000 national associations based in the United States. In addition to their membership rosters, they employ approximately 500,000 people to manage their affairs.

2. *Incentive events.*   The purpose of these events is to encourage company employees to meet or exceed sales and/or production goals. When the goals are met, a celebration is planned to honor those who contributed to their successful achievement.

Usually a company's marketing department plans these types of events. They typically are used to motivate salespersons. In addition to a special celebration, high achievers can also be rewarded with a free trip (incentive travel) or some other prize.

Incentive events are very profitable for the hotel catering department. Companies usually reward their star performers with lavish functions. Economy is not in their vocabulary. Maximum reward leads to maximum effort and results.

3. *New product introductions.*   These types of events range from new film to new model car releases. These are usually very elaborate, expensive events. First-class food, beverage, entertainment, and decorations are standard fare—all designed to attract maximum media coverage.

Periodically companies present news conferences. These also represent potential catering business.

4. *Building openings.*   Most companies celebrate ground breakings, topping offs, and grand openings with gala parties. Many of these are off-premises functions; however, usually there are many preopening functions that could be held at a hotel. For example, a building developer's leasing department may host a party at a hotel to promote interest among potential tenants.

5. *Recognition events.*   These are similar to incentive events. Generally though, they are less elaborate. Typically they involve awards dinners and other types of ceremonies intended to recognize several employees at many levels of performance. For instance, many companies and associations will hold an annual recognition luncheon to recognize long-term employees and to honor the employee of the year.

Some recognition events are actually a form of public relations. A company or association may hold a function that, while it is designed to honor someone, is also used to generate publicity. For example, the National Academy of Motion Picture Arts and Sciences holds Oscar parties and other similar events that honor industry members as well as generate interest among the movie-buying public.

6. *Training sessions and seminars.*   If an educational event is expected to last one day or more, the company usually will want to hold it at a place where food and beverage are readily available. The typical hotel fulfills this requirement. Furthermore, the hotel may be able to provide the necessary equipment that most companies will not have in house; for example, a company usually does not own elaborate video and sound equipment.

7. *Anniversaries.*   Most companies will celebrate decade anniversaries. They will also celebrate silver, golden, diamond, centennial, sesquicentennial, bicentennial, and tricentennial anniversaries. Coca Cola's 100th birthday celebration held in Atlanta was an incredible event. Coca Cola executives and other guests from around the world were feted at parties over a period of several days. The celebration encompassed events at all the major hotels and culminated in a reception for 16,000 people at the city's convention center.

Sometimes several companies join to defray the cost of a community anniversary. For instance, many firms contributed to the Statue of Liberty Centennial restoration in New York. It was a spectacular event that was televised nationwide. One of the authors was attending a conference in Dallas that carried out the theme during an evening reception. There were televisions placed around the room so that guests could watch the fireworks displays and ceremonies in New York.

8. *Traveling exhibitions.*   There are many traveling "shows," such as entertainment extravaganzas, trade-show exhibitors, and sports teams. They have an obvious need for sleeping rooms and food and beverage. The hotel that is part of a chain organization will be preferred by this market segment because of the efficiency the chain can offer to the person who needs to book space and meal and beverage functions in several cities.

Sports teams are a particularly good market segment. Whether major league, college, high school, or intramural, when they are on the road they tend to play their sport and spend the rest of their time in the hotel. This increases indirect income, such as telephone revenue, valet revenue, and gift shop sales.

Sports teams usually have several support persons traveling with them who will also spend time and money at the hotel. If there are any "groupies" following the teams, they will probably generate additional revenues for the hotel.

Celebrity watchers are also attracted by sports teams. Some of these fans will stay at the hotel in order to be close to their favorite athletes. Those who cannot stay at the hotel will usually spend a few dollars on other hotel services, such as restaurants and gift shops, while awaiting a glimpse of their favorite star.

Sports teams also are usually very profitable ventures for the hotel because athletes are big eaters. While at times they may be difficult to service because of their time constraints, generally speaking, their catered functions involve very specific types and quantities of foods and beverages and relatively simple service procedures.

SMERF MARKET

SMERF is an acronym that refers to the social, military, education, religious, and fraternal market. Since these groups have limited resources and are very cost conscious, the SMERF market is sometimes referred to as the "Grunt" market.

One of the biggest segments of this market is the fraternal segment. Fraternal organizations abound. Most areas of the country have Rotary, Kiwanis, Lions, Seroptomist, and other similar organizations. They can represent a good source of steady business because of their desire to meet at the same location each month. They do not like to move around. They like it when their members know that, for example, the monthly meeting is held on the third Tuesday of the month at the Boulder Dam Hotel. This avoids confusion. It also makes it easier for members to plan their personal calendars—an important point, as most members tend to belong to more than one fraternal organization.

The military segment can represent a good source of catering business, particularly in those cities that house major military bases. There are many awards, armed-forces-day, and birthday events. For instance, every November 8th, or closest weekend, the Marine Corps holds its Marine Birthday Ball.

While it is true that most military bases have club facilities capable of providing catering services, local hotels can expect to attract their fair share of business, particularly since the typical hotel offers more space as well as a welcome change of pace.

The education segment can also generate a respectable amount of revenue and profit. There are many continuing-education seminars, symposiums, and fraternity and sorority events. There are also many high-school functions. For instance, proms can represent considerable revenue in April and May. Unfortunately, experience shows that proms require proportionately more work than just about any other type of catering function and can test the mettle of the most intrepid catering executive.

The SMERF market is not as profitable as the business market. However, the hotel can use these groups to fill in the slow-period gaps (i.e., the "shoulders") between more lucrative events. And, since many of the attendees are bona fide business and/or community leaders, their exposure to your property may convince them to use your property for catered functions instead of a competing hotel.

The SMERF market is similar to the business market though, at least in terms of the types of events desired. For instance, these groups have meetings, attend conventions, and sponsor training sessions and other types of educational functions. Consequently, the catering sales and service procedures are similar for the SMERF and business markets; however, the sales revenue and profits are not.

Since this market has less profit potential, new, inexperienced catering salespersons usually are assigned to it. These neophyte salespersons though, should not be turned loose on any market segment without proper training and guidance from top management. Absent the right preparation, the new salesperson tends to promise products and/or services to clients unwarranted by their budgets, or which cannot be handled adequately by the hotel. A poorly sold event can increase product and payroll costs.

As catering salespersons gain experience, they quickly learn what can be sold and how they can maximize revenue and profits. Experience with officials of civic, political, church, school, museum, senior-citizen, charity, condo-association, and other similar groups is invaluable and necessary for the catering professional who intends to advance to the business and/or special events markets.

SPECIAL EVENTS MARKET

According to Joe Jeff Goldblatt, "a special event recognizes a unique moment in time with ceremony and ritual to satisfy specific needs." In his book *Special Events: The Art & Science of Celebration,* he states that all human societies celebrate, privately and publicly, individually and as a group.

To some extent, every catered event could be considered a special event, at least for some clients and their guests. To that end, functions scheduled by the business and SMERF markets could involve some ceremonial and/or ritualistic elements. For instance, a convention could book several "refueling" functions, such as breakfasts and luncheons, but also schedule one special event, such as a surprise birthday party for the company president.

Special events differ from daily, ordinary events in at least three ways. A daily event generally occurs spontaneously, while a special event is always planned in advance. A daily event does not necessarily arouse expectations, but a special event always does. And while a daily event usually occurs for no particular reason, some type of celebration is the motivating force behind a special event.

TYPES OF SPECIAL EVENTS

Most special events are life-cycle events. Birthdays, anniversaries, reunions, and so forth mark time in our lives. They are usually celebrated with specific ceremonies and rituals.

Many of these events are celebrated privately; professional caterers are not used. Others are small celebrations that are catered by off-premises social caterers at clients' homes or other locations. And some are larger affairs that would be of interest to the typical hotel catering department.

Some of the special events that hotel caterers usually handle are:

1. *Weddings.* Today's wedding is longer and more expensive than ever before. Many women are marrying later in life and have more time and money to devote to this special day. Hotels that can

provide a one-stop service are apt to have a competitive edge among women who have many demands on their time.

Hotels that have unique surroundings, picturesque views, and/or romantic settings are especially preferred by wedding planners. For instance, the Del Coronado Hotel in Coronado, CA, is located in an absolutely beautiful area—a stone's throw from the ocean. It is such a favorite spot for weddings that it is not unusual for two of three parties to be held each day—one right after the other.

Many weddings have specific religious requirements. For instance, the Jewish wedding requires a canopy and the breaking of a glass. The hotel will need to be aware of these types of traditions or else it might disappoint and/or insult guests.

Ethnic weddings, such as Italian and Greek weddings, are quite often very extravagant affairs. Guests normally come from all over the country and sometimes from other countries. Sleeping rooms are almost always needed for these types of events. The large hotels can accommodate these needs, whereas the other types of caterers usually cannot.

2. *Wedding anniversaries.*   These are usually surprise celebrations hosted by adult children on milestone years. The silver wedding anniversary is especially popular.

The children party planners generally need a good deal of advice when putting together their celebrations. The hotel caterer should consider advising them to center a theme on what was going on in the world at the time the parents were married. This is usually a very popular theme, especially with guests who are contemporaries of the anniversary couple. The local library has plenty of information about what was happening during the wedding year, as well as on the specific wedding date.

3. *Reunions.*   The reunion market encompasses everything from high school classes to military units. High school reunions are especially popular these days because of the recent development of private reunion planners that specialize in locating alumni and planning memorable events, tasks that a few well-intentioned alumni are usually unable to perform.

Reunions require a lot of preplanning. A successful event usually needs a one-year lead time. Usually there are a few faithful alumni who shoulder the bulk of the planning burden, or they will engage a professional reunion planner. The hotel catering department though, oftentimes will be part of the overall planning process.

Many reunion organizers will benefit from any advice the hotel caterer can offer. The amateur clients usually have no experience in planning and organizing these types of events. Consequently, the sales representative must be able to recommend little things that will be a big hit with attendees. For instance, one very popular technique is to put each school reunion attendee's original graduating-class picture on a name badge. Another strategy sure to please the school reunion attendee is to recreate the yearbook, using the attendees' current pictures.

4. *Funerals and memorials.* These are the most delicate of all social events. Death is a shock, even when it is expected.

More and more funeral services will be held in hotels because they offer sleeping rooms for overnight guests, food and beverage, and function rooms for the service.

The hotel catering department must consult with the appropriate clergy to determine the correct rituals and customs to follow. Family members also must be consulted to ensure that other pertinent rituals and customs are honored. For instance, if the deceased was a military veteran, the hotel catering department must plan to accommodate the relevant military rituals. Or, if the traditional Irish Wake is planned, an abundance of food and beverage is required.

5. *Bar Mitzvahs.* A Bar Mitzvah is the traditional Jewish ceremony celebrated on a Jewish boy's 13th birthday. It marks the coming of age in the Jewish faith. During the ceremony, the young man publicly recites benedictions from the Torah, the Jewish scripture, and accepts personal responsibility for observing the commandments set down in the Torah.

The Bas Mitzvah, for young Jewish girls, is similar to the Bar Mitzvah.

The celebrations of these events traditionally are very serious and glamorous, similar in scale to large wedding receptions. Important elements include the blessing of the bread and wine, and the lighting of candles. Menus and food preparation and service usually follow the Kosher dietary restrictions.

6. *Baptisms.* A baptism is the Christian rite which results in the acceptance of the baptized person into the faith. The reception is most often held at the parents' home, though larger functions would need to be held at a hotel or other similar location.

7. *Confirmations.* A confirmation is the Christian rite confirming a child's infant baptism into the faith. The ceremony allows the young person to confirm that he or she knows right from wrong and that Christ is the chosen savior. Receptions usually are very popular, with the confirmed receiving several gifts and a considerable amount of attention.

8. *Graduations.*   This can be a very attractive market segment these days, especially given the fact that many older persons are graduating from college. They have fulfilled life-long dreams and usually are very anxious to celebrate. Hotel caterers are an obvious choice to service these clients and their guests.

Some hotels will shy away from the high-school graduation market. They may not want to deal with adolescent mind sets and all the potential trouble they represent. However, usually hotels are not as interested in them primarily because these guests are under-age and cannot purchase profitable beverage functions.

9. *Proms.*   These are high-school affairs that are not high on the priority list of the typical hotel catering department. Underage adolescents, coupled with tight budgets, do not normally result in profitable, successful affairs. As with high-school graduations though, if you impress these guests today, they may remember it and reward you with catering business when they grow up and are in a position to book functions.

10. *Birthdays.*   The large, expensive birthday celebrations tend to be surprise parties. The caterer must be involved in a considerable amount of preplanning and subterfuge. Since many of these affairs involve out-of-town guests, the hotel may be required to house them at least overnight.

11. *Gourmet clubs.*   Groups such as the Chaine des Rotisseurs and the American Institute of Wine & Food (AIWF) host extremely fancy, high-priced meals. When evaluating a caterer, the members will give priority to those establishments that are fellow members. Consequently, the hotel seeking this type of business must see to it that the chef, director of catering, and/or food and beverage director hold active memberships in these organizations.

12. *Customer-appreciation parties.*   These are another type of unique, special event. They are quite common in some industries. And they are normally based on some sort of theme. For instance, a company may throw an anniversary party for current long-time clients as a way of showing its appreciation for their patronage.

Oftentimes customer-appreciation parties can be used by a company to solicit future business. For example, an equipment manufacturer can host a party that might also include a brief display of its collection of equipment prototypes. This can encourage its current and potential customers to preorder this merchandise. It is also a good bet that these customers will provide profitable referral business for the client and the hotel.

13. *Fund-raising events.*   Fund-raisers and other types of good-cause events are becoming more popular. Oftentimes the hotel property is a partner in these events, in that it contributes all or part of the products and/or services needed to hold them.

Some of these functions are multifaceted events. For instance, a fund-raiser may include a reception, dinner, silent auction, and dance.

Fund-raisers can be very profitable over the long run. You may not earn a fair profit on each one, but if you develop a reputation for taking the many disparate interests involved with a particular charity and organizing them into a successful affair, eventually you should generate profitable repeat and referral catering business.

14. *Other events.*   Holiday, costume, farewell, and other similar parties represent potential catering business. Sometimes they will be held in conjunction with another event. For instance, a company-awards banquet could double as a farewell, retirement party for recent retirees.

MARKET SUBGROUP

A market subgroup is the term used to describe an ancillary or auxiliary market that "piggy backs" on another market. For instance, if you have a large wedding booked for a weekend, some of the guests may take the opportunity to celebrate a reunion. Hence, the reunion function "piggy backs" on the wedding event. Catering salespersons are taught to seek out this type of auxiliary business and attempt to book it.

Most hotels generally expend a lot of effort courting the market subgroups that are part of large conventions. For instance, the Consumer Electronics Show (CES) is a major convention that will generate considerable catering business of its own. However, companies that attend this show, such as IBM and SONY, are subgroups that will be in the market for some private parties, hospitality suites, awards dinners, and so forth, that they would like to hold in conjunction with the major show.

In this example, the hotel that books the CES-sponsored functions is apt to have the advantage in attracting and booking market-subgroup business. This is especially true if the hotel is the major on-site headquarters for CES officials, as the subgroups will tend to locate as close as possible to the hub of activity.

The local convention bureau in your area normally publishes periodically a booklet listing the names and particulars of all conventions coming to town in the future. The catering sales representative should contact these conventions and ask for their exhibitor list (program and exhibitor guides). Every exhibitor (that is, market subgroup) noted on these lists represents potential catering business.

CLIENT DECISION MAKERS

Who makes the purchase decision? This is one of the first things to find out when soliciting catering business. In some instances, it could be a company secretary. In other cases, the chief executive officer (CEO) may be the decision maker.

Usually the type of function dictates who will make the purchase decision. A secretary may plan the office Christmas party, whereas the CEO might plan the annual Board of Directors meeting.

Some companies employ a meeting planner. Meeting planners, depending on the size of the company and the amount of meeting/training/convention activity, may or may not have other job responsibilities. The meeting planner who concentrates exclusively on this activity is usually much more professional than the one who has other job duties to perform. The professional is easier to work with because the planner with other company responsibilities often treats meeting planning as a side line.

Some very large companies employ a corporate meeting planner to plan and organize functions for all company-owned satellite locations. The corporate meeting planner is normally based at the corporate headquarters; for instance, Coca Cola's corporate meeting planner is based in Atlanta. However, even though the planner resides in Atlanta, this person may have the responsibility for planning and organizing events for all regional Coca Cola distributors.

Many associations have professional meeting planners on staff. Some associations are too small to afford this type of support. Consequently, they tend to hire independent or contract meeting planners to help them. If the association cannot afford to support an office and an office staff, it may use an independent contractor to handle all of its affairs, including its meetings and conventions needs. In fact, there are many multimanagement contract companies that manage several associations.

Association meeting planners on the national level are concentrated in a few cities. They move their meetings around the country, but are based at the association's national headquarters.

Most national associations are based in Washington, DC, because lobbying is one of their main activities. New York, Chicago, Atlanta, and San Francisco also have high concentrations of associations' headquarters staffs.

The American Society of Association Executives, an association for association executives, publishes a membership directory. Usually the reference section of the local public library will have this directory on its shelves.

The regional, state, and local chapters of national associations also have catering needs. Regional and state chapters usually have one or two functions per year. The meeting planner at the national level oftentimes will help the regional and state groups plan and organize their events.

Local chapters usually have monthly meetings where association business is discussed. These functions usually include a meal or reception as well as a guest speaker. For instance, the National Association of Catering Executives (NACE) has several chapters that plan and organize these types of monthly events.

Local chapter meeting planners are usually volunteers. The hotel catering department will experience a great deal of variety with the local chapters; some volunteers are well versed in planning and organizing events, whereas many are willing to work, but require considerable care and attention.

The local chapters often have some influence on the national office's meeting and convention plans. They often make their desires known before locations are selected for the national events.

Oftentimes a local chapter bids for the opportunity to host a national function. This is especially true with the national convention. The hotel caterer who gets involved with this arrangement usually will be working with the local volunteers as well as with the national's professional meeting planner.

Travel agencies are planning more meetings and conventions today. Companies and associations feel that it is good business practice to use travel agents since, theoretically, it is much more efficient to deal with one person for travel, catering, and sleeping-rooms needs. Unfortunately, some travel agents do not understand the meetings and conventions market. They usually do not comprehend the unique, subtle differences between planning a meeting and planning a tour. For instance, the typical travel agent may be unaware of the difference between meal couponing and meal guarantees and could therefore, be placed in an embarrassing position.

Under the meal-couponing procedure, when a travel agent books a catered function, he or she will presell event tickets to the guests and reimburse the hotel for each ticket redeemed. If some guests do not use their tickets, the travel agent keeps the "breakage," that is, the money paid by guests to the travel agent but not given to the hotel.

With meal guarantees though, there is no breakage. The hotel must be paid a guaranteed total price. The travel agent must pay regardless of the number of guests who attend the catered function. This is troublesome for the travel agent who is accustomed to earning considerable breakage income. It is even more disturbing to the travel agent who books a great deal of breakfast business as there is usually a very large no-show factor for this meal.

Another major problem with travel agents is their concept of professional compensation for their services. They have a commission orientation, whereas meeting planners do not. For instance, a travel agent usually receives a 10 percent commission for sleeping-rooms business booked for the hotel.

If a travel agent books sleeping rooms for a group, along with a meal function or two, he or she will expect a commission for each type of sale. If your hotel's policy forbids commissions for meal-function bookings, at the very least a travel agent will want a larger percentage commission for the sleeping-rooms business booked.

The client decision maker in the social and special events markets is not always easy to identify. For instance, just because the father of the bride may be the first one to make contact with the hotel catering department does not necessarily imply that he is empowered to make the decision. The hotel caterer must ensure that he or she does not waste valuable time with the wrong person.

Some special events market segments employ event managers and/or event coordinators. For instance, sports leagues usually have hospitality and special-events coordinators—some are employed full time at league headquarters, with other local independent coordinators hired to handle temporary assignments on location.

Sports leagues represent profitable catering opportunities. For example, the hospitality coordinator for the U.S. Open Championship arranges about 100 parties during each tournament; the director of special events for Major League Baseball plans several banquets throughout the year, some as large as 3,500 persons.

3

Marketing

Catering is the culinary equivalent of show business entertainment.
You are paid to perform and your audience expects an award winning
performance. Always strive for a return engagement.

John Caruso, CCE
Caruso Diplomat
Saugus, Massachusetts

In the past, most persons in the food and beverage industry paid less attention to marketing than they do today. At that time, the industry was growing rapidly. Many who entered the business then concentrated almost exclusively on production management and customer service. We assumed customers would always be there when the doors opened. During the 1960s and 1970s, this assumption was justified.

The good old days, though, are not with us any longer. The food-service industry in the United States is a battleground. Likewise with the U.S. hotel industry. These industries have entered the mature stage of the product life cycle. Large hospitality companies are finding that the majority of their current growth is attributed to expansion efforts in foreign markets. Growth in the U.S. market comes almost entirely from luring away a competitor's customers.

As we noted in Chapter 2, potential catering clients have a myriad of choices. Some clients feel one caterer is as good as another. To dispel this image and stand out in a crowded field, the successful hotel catering department must develop a competitive edge.

Clients do not buy a meal; they buy an experience . . . fantasy . . . as well as fun, service, ambience, entertainment, and memories. They buy food and beverage, but only incidentally.

As a result, much of what a caterer sells is intangible. The client cannot touch or feel an event before it occurs. The caterer is selling something that has yet to be produced and delivered. It cannot be resold, restocked, or returned. Clients purchase what they "think" will happen. It is a gamble for them. They are understandably nervous and need to be reassured that they have made the correct decision.

Caterers who consistently achieve their revenue and profit goals are those who understand their clients and what they are buying. They develop marketing procedures that meet their clients' needs.

In today's business environment, a strong price/value relationship must prevail in order to attract a profitable share of the market. The hotel's services must be equal to or better than the competition's. The sales staff must be very familiar with the services offered, their costs and benefits, and their impact on the hotel's overall performance.

In most hotels, revenue from sleeping rooms is the major contributor to sales and profits. Catering often is next in profitability. However, without a competitive edge, the hotel will be hard pressed to earn an adequate share of the catering market.

It is said that the "sizzle" sells the steak, and for many hotels the sizzle may be their excellent banquet and convention facilities. Statistics show that the type and quality of cuisine offered, ability to accommodate large groups, entertainment attractions, and variety of services offered are the major factors a client considers when selecting a hotel caterer. The successful hotel catering department will ensure that these aspects are clearly defined and articulated to potential clients.

THE MARKETING PLAN

Michael Roman, Director of Education at CaterSource, notes that the successful caterer develops a well-defined marketing plan and follows it closely. He feels that the marketing plan must include three major aspects: (1) Getting the job; (2) performing well; and (3) following up.

Getting the Job

Before the hotel can solicit catering business, it first must define clearly the market(s) it wants to service. The typical hotel is large enough to mix and match several markets. This affords the opportunity to maximize revenue and profit. However, specialization can lead to increased efficiency as well as a unique reputation and image in the market place.

The desired market(s) should be examined closely to determine the extent of their catering needs. For example, if a hotel wishes to cater the business market, it should examine closely and quantify the supply (i.e., other competing caterers) and the demand (i.e., potential business clients) to see if it is economically feasible to concentrate on this segment.

After determining the desired market(s), the next step is to set financial goals. There should be revenue and profit goals. There also should be some attention paid to other income that can be generated indirectly from catering; for instance, a wedding party could generate sleeping-rooms business as well as gift-shop and parking revenue.

Catering functions may also increase the business of the concessionaires located in the hotel. If the auto rental and travel agency concessionaires earn more, usually the hotel will earn more because it normally receives a percentage of their revenues.

Revenue and profit goals must be reasonable. It is useless to set unrealistically high goals because the certain failure to attain them can deplete employee morale. However, the catering executive must be willing to take some risks when setting these goals. He or she should not be overly conservative or else the hotel's overall performance will suffer.

Getting the job, that is, booking business, also includes the need to create a particular image. If, for example, the hotel wants to specialize in weddings, it should develop logos, menus, decorations, room layouts and designs, employee uniforms, and so forth to complement and enhance this image.

The hotel catering department needs to note standard procedures that sales representatives should use to solicit business. These procedures must be consistent with the desired image. For example, the caterer seeking clients in the deep end of the business market must tailor its sales solicitation efforts accordingly.

It is important to develop standardized procedures that should be used to: (1) canvass for new clients; (2) qualify leads; (3) make sales calls; (4) advise clients; (5) develop contracts; and (6) provide required products and services. A complete description of all catering policies and procedures must be prepared and distributed to the catering staff and all other relevant hotel operating departments.

Performing Well

Once bookings are obtained, the emphasis shifts from sales to service. Clients and their guests want to be treated with care. They want to be handled in a professional manner. Function hosts want the caterer to enhance their image.

Performing well involves standardized procedures designed to ensure that: (1) service is punctual; (2) foods, beverages, presentations, sanitation, cleanliness, and ambience meet established quality standards; (3) professional attention will be paid to all details; (4) the function host will be made to feel like a guest at his or her event; and (5) all last-minute requests and/or crises will be handled calmly, professionally, and to everyone's satisfaction.

Performing well is the bottom line for clients. They have entrusted their events to outsiders. They have relinquished control. Consequently, they will be understandably nervous and anxious.

The caterer who can satisfy clients and make them look good will enjoy several benefits. Referral business is an obvious benefit, as is repeat patronage. It is much harder and much more expensive to get new customers than it is to keep old ones. Referral and repeat business lead to a profitable catering operation. They are the organization's life blood.

Following Up

Following up is another very important part of the marketing plan. Standardized procedures must be developed to ensure that: (1) thank-you calls are made; (2) individual, personalized follow-up letters are sent; (3) event assessments are performed, one with the client and one with the catering staff, wherein all aspects of the function are evaluated and critiqued; (4) referral business is solicited; (5) appropriate souvenir gifts are presented to clients; and (6) accounts are settled.

Many industry experts feel that the follow-up stage is the most critical part of the marketing plan. The caterer and client have been working together for some time. It is inappropriate to just give the client an invoice at the end of the event and say, "goodbye." The relationship should not be ended abruptly; it must be continued. The time spent with clients during the follow-up stage will pay huge dividends.

This is the time when the caterer can learn something from the client that can be used to improve future functions. It is also the time when long-term relationships are cemented. The seeds of referral and repeat business are planted and cultivated during the follow-up period.

THE MARKETING BUDGET

Marketing expenses usually represent a significant percentage of expected sales revenue. For instance, a U.S. food-service operation will spend about 2 to 5 percent of sales revenue for marketing expenses such as advertising, promotion, public relations, franchising fees, royalties, and other fees and commissions.

Some hospitality operations allocate a set percentage of expected annual sales revenue to the marketing department at the beginning of the year. The department is expected to use these funds to accomplish the stated objectives. There may be some flexibility with these funds, whereby the department head can shift monies from one marketing expense to another. Other properties assign a "line-item" budget, giving the department head no flexibility; he or she cannot spend less money, say, for promotional materials, and shift the savings to radio advertising.

Some hotel catering departments are allocated a specific dollar amount for marketing expenses, not a set percentage of expected sales revenue. Prior to the beginning of a fiscal year, the director of catering, in conjunction with top management, will prepare an annual budget for the catering department. This budget will include all anticipated departmental incomes and expenses.

As a general rule, the sales forecast is based on tangible factors, such as business already booked, and major expenses, such as food, beverage, and payroll costs, are expected to maintain a certain percentage of these projected sales. If estimated sales increase or decrease, most expenses (except those that are completely fixed) must follow the curve and stay within their allocated percentage. If there are any cost variances, you do not change the budget. You document them, pay the extra costs (if necessary), and learn from them so that the next budget does not suffer the same fate.

Some hotels revise their annual budgets periodically within the year. For instance, after three or four months, the director of catering and top management may agree to shift funds from one expense category to another if business warrants. Alternatively, these executives may decide to allocate additional funds, say, to advertising, in order to combat a new competitor who plans to open soon.

When allocating the marketing budget, management considers historical trends as well as new business opportunities. As a general rule, past performance is the key variable influencing the budget. An analysis of previous revenues and expenses will reveal future trends.

Sales Analysis

The marketing budget's accuracy depends primarily on effective sales analyses. A thorough sales analysis will include:

1. *Total revenue.* Monthly revenue totals should be evaluated with an eye toward establishing trends. This can help ensure

that marketing dollars are directed to the seasons with the most sales potential.

2. *Average revenue per function.*   This statistic will reveal average productivity per function. If there is a consistent shortfall between the actual average revenue and the potential average revenue, marketing dollars can be devoted to reconciling this inequity.

3. *Average revenue per type of function.*   This figure will indicate which functions carry the greatest sales potential; marketing funds can therefore be allocated appropriately.

4. *Average guest count per function.*   Some functions have few guests. Unless they are paying a large amount per guest, it may be more profitable to concentrate on larger groups. More guests mean more exposure for the hotel.

5. *Average check.*   The per person price for different types of functions is a good measure of labor productivity. It also can reveal opportunities where marketing dollars can be spent in an effort to increase the average revenue per guest.

6. *Average contribution margin.*   This is similar to the average check. The difference is that it is the amount of money available from the average check after the hotel pays the cost of food and beverage used to serve a guest. Most food-service experts feel that the average contribution margin per guest (sometimes referred to as the menu score) is more important than the average check because it represents the amount of money left to cover all other expenses and a fair profit.

7. *Number of functions.*   A monthly analysis can indicate how well the hotel manages and sells its available space. Trends will reveal where marketing dollars should be used; for instance, if February is a slow month, perhaps a slight change in the marketing plan can improve significantly sales and profits during this time period.

8. *Space utilization percentages.*   This analysis can indicate periods of time when certain function space is underutilized. For example, if a particular meeting room is vacant every Wednesday and Thursday, some change in the marketing plan should be considered to locate functions for this time and space.

9. *Popularity of different types of functions.*   These statistics can indicate the hotel catering department's strengths and weaknesses. If, for instance, weddings are the most frequently scheduled function, clients must view the hotel as a good place to hold weddings. This gives the hotel a competitive edge for this type of business, but it may eliminate the hotel from consideration for other types of events. The event mix is important to full utilization of the property.

10. *Percentage of repeat business.* It takes much more time, money, and effort to create a new customer than it does to retain an old one. Turning a customer into a repeat patron is a significant goal.

11. *Percentage of referral business.* You know a product is good when you can recommend it to your friends. The hotel catering department that receives a considerable percentage of referral business is obviously doing something right.

The primary purpose for performing this type of sales analysis is to determine the success rate of the current marketing plan. If the results of the analysis suggest that changes should be made, then future marketing efforts will need to be altered to reflect a new direction.

For instance, the catering department may find that there has been a steady decline in the amount of weddings business handled by the hotel. If weddings are not a profitable sales item, marketing dollars might be wasted trying to increase this particular segment of business. This is especially true if there have been fewer weddings overall in the hotel's trading area. On the other hand, a bit of research into the weddings market might indicate that there is a good deal of potential and that a few adjustments in the marketing plan could make the hotel very competitive in this segment.

If the marketing plan requires significant alterations, the director of catering should ensure that the hotel can accommodate the changes. An analysis will reveal feasible opportunities and suggest profitable changes that should be considered. This analysis should include an evaluation of: (1) the hotel's capabilities, (2) the types of markets available, (3) potential sales trends in these markets, (4) number and types of competitors, (5) the hotel's strengths and weaknesses as compared to its competitors, and (6) trends in sales solicitation efforts.

Marketing plan alterations should never be made hastily. Once a plan has been established, it should be given a fair chance to work. Just as we would not dig up the earth every few days to see how seeds we have planted are doing, we should not make a habit of second guessing our marketing efforts.

Changes in the marketing plan should be considered only after evaluating past trends and future opportunities. They should be made only if there is a reasonable expectation of increasing sales revenue and profits.

MARKETING RESEARCH

Marketing research is an on-going activity. It involves a continuing analysis of the potential clients and competitors that reside in the hotel catering department's trading area.

The hotel catering department's trading area is not easy to define. Theoretically, it could be the world; realistically, it is a lot closer to home.

Food-service operations sometimes separate their trading areas into primary trading areas and secondary trading areas. The primary area generates at least 50 percent of the food service's business, with the remainder coming from the secondary area.

Restaurants also segregate their trading areas into meal segments, such as lunch-market areas and dinner-market areas. It is commonly believed that lunch customers will not travel more than 10 minutes to a preferred restaurant, whereas dinner guests generally will travel up to 30 minutes.

Hotel caterers do not have such neat rules of thumb to guide their marketing research efforts. However, maintaining adequate records will help determine as accurately as possible the sales revenues and profits the caterer can expect to earn in the future. The major records are: (1) group-history files, (2) lost-business files, (3) tracer files, and (4) market and competition surveys.

Group-History File

A group-history file is created whenever initial contact is made with a prospective client. Eventually this file will include all facets of the client's business relationship with the hotel. To a certain extent, the file involves a "cradle to grave" synopsis of all relevant aspects of the catered event, from initial inquiry, to final disposition.

Usually the hotel catering department uses a predetermined, standardized format to record client information. When a potential client calls the caterer for price quotations and space availability, the important details are recorded. A sales representative follows up on the inquiry after studying these details. If the initial inquiry results in a booked event, the appropriate entries are made in the function book and also in the group-history file.

A group-history file is also created when a sales representative solicits catering business from a prospective client. In some instances, there may be preliminary group-history files created for potential clients; for instance, sales representatives may develop open files of potential clients whose names and group affiliations are obtained from mailing lists, directories, and/or referrals.

The group-history file should be complete if it is to be useful. It should contain all relevant information, such as correspondence, client decision maker, attendance figures, contracts, potential for future business, credit history, business referrals, testimonial letters, and other relevant data.

Group-history files help the marketing effort because they reveal consumer desires, trends, and price sensitivity. They usually contain information that, when analyzed carefully, can indicate future business opportunities. For instance, the referrals noted in the files can lead directly to additional catering business, while the testimonial letters can lead indirectly to future catering business.

Group-history files represent the hotel's major source of repeat patronage. The wise director of catering will ensure that the client decision makers noted in these files are not forgotten. He or she will personally maintain some sort of communication link with them, or assign this responsibility to another member of the catering staff. For instance, birthday cards, direct mail flyers, and/or holiday greeting cards should be sent to these individuals.

Lost-Business File

If client inquiries or sales solicitations do not lead to booked business, the group-history file will be transformed into a lost-business file. These files must be evaluated periodically in order to determine why potential business did not materialize. If certain patterns, such as space unavailability, high prices, or inadequate menu offerings, are discovered, perhaps the hotel can do something to ameliorate the underlying problems. For instance, if there is a consistent problem with space availability, the hotel could use this information to support a proposal to construct additional function rooms. Future marketing plans, highlighting the additional space, could lead to a significant increase in business.

Some lost-business files will be created after the catering event is booked. For instance, the event could be scheduled, but the client may cancel at the last minute. The director of catering would want to know why the client canceled. It is inappropriate merely to retain the client's deposit; some further contact with the client must be made to determine if the cancellation was due to any action of the hotel management or staff.

A lost-business file created after the event is over is probably the most unfortunate one as far as the hotel caterer is concerned. This generally occurs if there was some dissatisfaction with the quality of food, beverage, service, and so forth. In this situation, the client's final billing usually must be credited.

The major problem created by this unhappy incident is not so much the loss of revenue, but the fact that an upset client is liable to share his or her disappointment with others who are potential clients. The director of catering must do whatever is reasonable to minimize any negative publicity.

Tracer File

Tracer files (sometimes referred to as tickler files) are similar to a manager's personal list of "things to do today." For instance, if a current client books catering business on a fairly regular basis, the manager's tracer file will include this information. The file will also note when the client should be contacted, how he or she should be approached, any special considerations that must be offered, and so forth.

A tracer file should be established for tentative bookings so that space is not held more than, say, two weeks without a deposit or definite option.

Similarly, a tracer file can be developed that will trace the number of bookings per market segment. A market segment that provides 5 percent or more of the hotel's total catering business should be monitored closely for trends and other indicators of future business. Furthermore, if the hotel has, say, 18 separate market segments, it should consider developing a specific marketing plan for each one.

Lost-business files should be part of the hotel's tracer filing system. Lost business should be coded according to the reason why it was lost. Perhaps the business was lost because you did not have a function room available.

The individual lost-business events should be tickled, that is, they should be put into a time frame in such a way that a catering sales representative will be able to go back to the file the same time next year and attempt to solicit the client's future business.

Catering sales representatives usually check and update the tracer files daily. They will add pertinent information to them as it is obtained. They also will use a system whereby the group-history files will be traced and reviewed a few days before client decision makers are contacted.

Some catering departments employ a part-time secretary whose only responsibility is to monitor the tracer filing system. He or she is responsible for planning part of the catering sales representatives' work day.

Market and Competition Surveys

Market and competition surveys consist of detailed descriptions of potential clients and current and potential competitors.

Sales representatives are expected to canvass for new clients, that is, they are responsible for "sourcing" new clients. The typical sourcing procedure usually involves studying consumer trends, client desires, and other similar data. The best way to obtain these data is to conduct a market and competition survey.

A market survey can be a simple questionnaire sent to potential clients asking them about their catering needs and the amount of money they would be willing to pay for these services. More elaborate surveys are very costly, but they do reveal considerably more information.

Food and beverage trade associations, such as the National Restaurant Association (NRA), usually conduct market surveys that may be useful to the hotel director of catering. For instance, the NRA sponsors consumer surveys conducted by the Gallup organization, and similar research performed by Technomic Inc.

A competition survey should be an on-going effort. Catering executives must know as much as they can about the competition. The hotel caterer's marketing plan cannot be completed without some knowledge of competing products and services.

A competition survey should include the following information for each competitor:

1. Competitor name and address
2. Space available
3. Guest capacity
4. Major markets serviced
5. Franchise affiliation
6. Chain affiliation
7. Number of catering employees
8. Average checks or other similar data
9. Main products and services offered
10. Daily analysis of its reader boards, that is, the daily list of functions (usually located in a hotel's front-office area) hosted at the competing property.

When gathering data on competitors, you must be careful not to violate the pertinent federal, state, and local antitrust laws. For instance, you cannot get together with a competitor and discuss your pricing strategies. Nor can you agree to charge the same prices that a competitor charges. You should unearth and utilize only those nonproprietary data available to the general public.

The competition survey will reveal any unmet market "niches." For instance, if the director of catering learns that no one seems to be specializing in the civic-events market segments, he or she may decide to explore the possibility of targeting this pool of potential business.

The competition survey also lets the catering executive know what he or she is up against. In today's competitive hospitality business, it is necessary to carve out a unique reputation, image, and/or specialty. Any attempts to do this though, should be initiated only after analyzing the competitive environment.

THE FOUR Ps OF MARKETING

An effective marketing plan includes a description of the hotel's four Ps: (1) place, (2) products and services offered, (3) prices charged, and (4) promotion policies and procedures. The director of catering, either alone or in conjunction with other management personnel, must develop and implement these four Ps of marketing.

Place

Place refers to the hotel's location, amount of space available, and the type of environment and ambience provided.

Clients are very interested in the number of persons that can be accommodated as well as the speed with which they can be served. They also are interested in other space issues. For instance, meeting planners want to know how long it takes for, say, 1,000 conventioneers to ride the elevators from the lobby to the four-teenth floor during normal meal hours. Detailed information such as this should be readily accessible.

A hotel property's environment and ambience include its sanitation, cleanliness, decor, view, and other related factors. The director of catering cannot do anything about the hotel's location, but he or she can ensure that the controllable variables meet established quality-control standards.

Products and Services

The hotel's products and services are probably the most flexible part of the marketing plan. The large hotel usually has the ability to provide an unlimited number of food and beverage menus, meal service styles, and other ancillary services. The property that offers clients a one-stop shopping opportunity will usually have a significant competitive edge in the marketplace.

Price

Price is perhaps one of the most important and troublesome parts of the marketing plan. It is a major concern to clients and it can present several problems for hotel caterers, particularly because it is risky to quote prices too far in advance.

Food costs fluctuate widely. They tend to undergo seasonal price changes. Some hotels have long-term contracts with some of their suppliers, so a certain amount of long-term predictability can be achieved. However, many suppliers are just as unwilling as catering directors to offer long-term price guarantees.

The hotel catering department has several costs that must be covered. In addition to food and beverage costs, it will incur costs for payroll, payroll benefits, direct operating supplies, music and entertainment, advertising and promotion, utilities, administrative and general, repairs and maintenance, rents, property taxes, property insurance, interest, depreciation, other taxes, and miscellaneous deductions.

Appropriate prices must be charged in order to cover the fixed and variable costs, as well as leave a fair profit for the hotel company. The director of catering also must ensure that prices are competitive. It is a delicate balancing act.

Usually the total price quoted for a catered event is the sum of several prices for individual client needs. For instance, a convention's total price could include charges for food and beverage, room rentals, deposits, security, set-ups, audiovisual (AV), lighting, entertainment, and printing. With so many aspects to consider, there is ample room for negotiations between clients and the hotel caterer.

Computing the total price can be somewhat complicated. Fortunately, the catering executive can tap the resources offered by the hotel controller's office when confronted with this task.

The catering executive must have a good understanding of costs in order to compute competitive and profitable prices. For instance, when computing food menu prices, the manager must: (1) precost the menu; (2) factor in other variable costs—such as payroll, payroll benefits, and direct operating supplies; and (3) factor in an allowance for overhead and profit.

Menu precosting involves costing out each food item recipe in order to compute the food cost per serving. This cost is then multiplied by the number of servings needed. The amount of other variable costs needed to service the particular type and size of event must be added, as well as the additional charge needed to cover overhead and profit. If applicable, charges for room rental, security, set-ups, and so forth must be included. The total price can then be divided by the number of attendees to obtain a per-person price quotation, or the manager can quote the total price for the event.

If applicable, the director of catering also must determine room rental rates and other similar charges. The basic pricing format is the same as the one used for setting menu prices. The total price is a compilation of variable costs, fixed costs, and profit. For instance, when setting room rental rates, one would consider the variable costs (such as utilities, set-up, cleaning, and security) and the fixed costs (such as insurance, depreciation, and taxes). A profit margin then would be added.

Usually the fixed-cost portion of any price is calculated only once in a while. For instance, the director of catering generally will have a good idea of the amount of fixed charges he or she will incur whenever a particular banquet room must be opened and readied for service. When calculating, say, a price quotation for a meal function, the catering sales representative will divide these fixed charges by the number of guests to get a per-person overhead charge. To this charge, he or she will add the variable costs needed per person to determine a tentative price quotation.

The same pricing strategy can also be used when determining menu prices for a standardized menu. You can compute the variable costs for one serving and add to it the standard set charge to cover overhead and profit. For example, some menu items' prices are set to reflect a 25 to 30 percent food cost. The remaining 70 to 75 percent (referred to as the contribution margin, or gross profit) usually is sufficient to cover all other costs plus leave a fair profit for the hotel company.

Before quoting a tentative price to a potential client, you may want to revise it in light of competitive pressures. For instance, if your direct competitors are selling the same product for one dollar less than your price estimate, you may need to meet this competitive price, or alternatively, convince the client that you provide additional value to justify the extra dollar.

Experience shows that competition may be the most important element in the pricing formula. Often it is the major influence on the final price quoted.

One way to address competitors' prices is to use your price quotation as your competitive bid subject to negotiations. For instance, you could give potential clients several price/quality options and let them mix and match according to their needs.

There are times when the hotel catering department prices its goods and services to break even or to incur a loss. For instance, catered events for celebrities in a large hotel may be provided free of charge to the clients; or they may be priced to cover only the "prime cost" (that is, food, beverage, and payroll expenses). This loss-leader pricing strategy is a typical procedure used whenever customers are solicited for other types of profitable business.

Deposits, guarantees, cancellation fees, gratuities, tips, and refund policies also need to be detailed by the director of catering and reviewed by senior management. Usually these rates are influenced by the season, opportunity costs associated with last-minute cancellations, employee union contract provisions, and the hotel company's credit policies.

The profit margins for catered events generally are greater than are those in the typical restaurant operation. However, the catering department has many more slow days—even days when there is no business—with which to contend. As a result, even though the director of catering may sympathize with clients' budgetary constraints, the fact remains that there is only so much he or she can do to accommodate them.

Yield Management

Some hotels use computerized yield management procedures to calculate suggested prices for meal functions, beverage functions, function-room rentals, and so forth. A computerized system codifies and systematizes the intuitive process an experienced catering executive would use to calculate prices. While the catering manager could personally take into account several cost and market demand factors when preparing a competitive price quotation, he or she could accomplish the same feat electronically by feeding these data into a computerized yield management system and letting the system perform the necessary data analysis.

Computerized yield management incorporates artificial intelligence or "expert systems" as they are sometimes called. Expert systems imitate the kinds of decisions a team of experienced managers would make. The computer speeds up the decision-making process. It renders the process more consistent. And, since a great deal of the skill needed to do the work is computerized and readily available, less experienced supervisors and managers can tap into the system and obtain expert analyses immediately.

Yield management, whether computerized or manual, seeks to maximize total profits by manipulating suggested prices based on perceived demand for the goods and/or services. It is a demand-oriented process, in that the price charged will be higher if the demand is high, and lower if demand is weak. The food-service manager who discounts prices during the early evening hours in order to spur demand during this normally slow period is practicing yield management. Likewise the hotel property that discounts its sleeping rooms on the weekends in order to increase weekend occupancy.

The director of catering also applies yield management principles when he or she reduces prices during the slow seasons or discounts the function-room rental rates in order to book profitable food and beverage business.

Performing yield management manually is a time-consuming process. It also can be somewhat risky and incomplete unless the manager doing the work is very skilled. Computerizing the process ensures that all relevant data are considered and the best decisions made. For instance, once a computerized system is set up correctly, it can automatically restrict the prices and availabilities of sleeping rooms and function rooms the way an expert manager would do. The person booking this type of business can input the client's requests and within a few moments the computer will determine an appropriate price quotation. The person working with this client does not have to be an expert because he or she can access an expert "advisor" with a few keystrokes.

Computerized yield management is not a new concept. It has been used extensively over the years in the airline and rental-car industries. Several large hotels, especially chain properties, use it to calculate sleeping-room prices. It has been so successful in pricing sleeping-room accommodations and smoothing out demand fluctuations that recently the technology has been extended to the catering department.

Several yield management software packages have been developed that specifically address the needs of the hotel catering department. These electronic systems can manipulate prices for new bookings according to variations and fluctuations in demand patterns by different markets. The end result is maximum revenue and profit as well as more predictable, consistent business.

Many hotels are very happy with their computerized yield management systems. It is not unusual for a hotel to increase its profits substantially after it computerizes the yield management function. And, at least in the case of sleeping-room rates and availabilities, the incremental profits far exceed the initial and ongoing costs of the computerized system.

Catering is just now beginning to enjoy the fruits of this technology. There now exist a sufficient number of software packages to satisfy most operation's needs. However, while there is an unlimited upside to computerized yield management, there are a few disadvantages that must be considered.

We are familiar with one software package written exclusively for hotel catering applications that costs approximately $8,000. It is designed to be installed on a personal computer in the catering office. Its potential is unlimited. For instance, it can tell you if the menu items desired by a client are in season; if the projected cost of meats six months hence will increase; what your food order size should be; and a whole host of other characteristics. It takes a comprehensive look at all variables impacting a catered event. It even allows you to "test drive," that is, try out, several price/availability combinations before preparing your final competitive price quotation.

Unfortunately, with this program, the learning curve is very steep. College students in advanced computer classes have a great deal of difficulty mastering it. And, like many computer applications, it is not overly friendly to users.

Another disadvantage we find with this program and several others is the tremendous amount of time that must be expended to input the start-up data. Most software packages require similar types of start-up data. To operate any computerized yield management system, you must input historical demand information for each market served. These data must be categorized according to time of year, day of week, time of day, and so forth.

In addition to inputting historical data, you must maintain the data files consistently. Without proper data management, the computerized system cannot function effectively and you run the risk of obtaining erroneous conclusions. Remember, the program is only as good as the data you input.

The computerized yield management systems that handle group-history files, tracer files, competitor profiles, recipe costing, and other related functions also require considerable start-up data as well as continual data revision. For instance, to maintain current recipe costs, you need to load all recipe formulas, inventory data, and current purchase prices into the system. As purchase prices change, you must update them. Once updated, all recipes will be recosted by the computer, thereby ensuring that you always have the most current food and beverage costs. Again though, if you fail to maintain the data files, your conclusions will be based on inaccurate information.

Some hotel catering departments using computerized yield

management systems report substantial increases in revenues and profits with minimum investments in time, money, and effort. If all employees are committed to the system, a hotel can earn significantly more income while simultaneously providing clients and guests consistent value for their money.

Promotion

Promotion includes the cost of advertising in newspapers, magazines, telephone directories, and trade media; outdoor billboards and other signage; radio and television advertising; fees paid to advertising and promotional agencies; entertaining business clients (such as hosting a customer-appreciation party for meeting planners); memberships in professional associations, civic, and other business groups; and promotional materials, such as sales brochures, menus, photographs, videotapes, direct mail pieces, and written solicitations for catering business.

If the hotel is a franchisee, or is part of a referral group, the franchising and/or referral fees, and royalty payments that must be paid to the parent company, are part of promotion expenses.

Public relations and publicity fees are another type of promotional effort. The cost of preparing press releases that will be sent to food editors, writing books, columns, and articles about the catering industry, and hosting charity and media events are considered part of promotion expenses.

Salespersons' salaries and commissions are also included in the promotional budget. In many cases, the typical catering salesperson earns no salary, or a minimum salary; commissions make up the bulk of his or her paycheck. Under this income arrangement, the hotel usually expects the salesperson to concentrate solely on selling directly to one or more market segments.

Salespersons may also be paid commissions for developing leads. For instance, they may be hired to generate interest among potential corporate clients. Once a lead is established, it would be turned over to a catering manager, who will then handle proposals, planning, contracts, and so forth.

The most effective and efficient type of promotional plan the hotel catering department can use should include: (1) brochures, (2) menus, (3) videotapes and photos, (4) proposals, (5) word-of-mouth advertising, and (6) soliciting future business at a current event.

These promotions are not listed in order of effectiveness. For instance, you cannot say that a brochure is always more effective than word-of-mouth advertising. It would be if you were using a mass-mailer campaign, but it would be much less effective than word-of-mouth advertising if you wanted to solicit specific local civic events.

Sales brochures generally include a considerable amount of information that potential clients can evaluate. The brochure notes the hotel's logo, slogan, catering policies, room availabilities, suggested menus, prices, credit information, and service procedures.

Since the brochure might be the potential client's first contact with the hotel catering department, it must be professionally prepared. It is an invitation to potential clients that will create a lasting impression. It should be complete and attractive; this is especially true if the hotel caterer is soliciting the deep segment of the business market. And, if it is mailed, it must be sent to a specific person, not to "occupant."

Many hotels use direct mail efforts to solicit catering business. Specific names, titles, and addresses can be obtained from several database sources that can be used to develop mailing lists.

Mailing lists are the key to an effective direct-mail campaign. Hotel executives are active in many local associations and fraternal organizations; their membership rolls can be excellent mailing lists. Lists also are available from the chamber of commerce, economic development authorities, and local charitable groups and foundations. Local department stores also have mailing lists; for instance, some of them have bridal registries that they might be willing to share.

Mailing lists also can be obtained from companies that specialize in developing them. For instance, American Business Lists, Inc., a division of American Business Information, Inc., prepares and sells business mailing lists and mailing labels encompassing just about any type of group, industry, or profession the catering executive may wish to solicit.

Direct mail is an effective marketing tool. It can be personalized, a specific audience can be targeted, and the results of a direct-mail campaign are readily measurable. However, it is an expensive marketing tactic; the cost of the brochure, other inserts (such as a cover letter, response card, and/or promotional flyer), envelope, postage, labor, and other ancillary expenses can be quite high.

Standardized banquet menus may be included in the sales brochures. If so, they should be attractively presented. The wise catering executive will resist the temptation to note a laundry list of menu items; he or she will note one or more examples of menu formats that clients can select for their functions. (See Figure 3.1.)

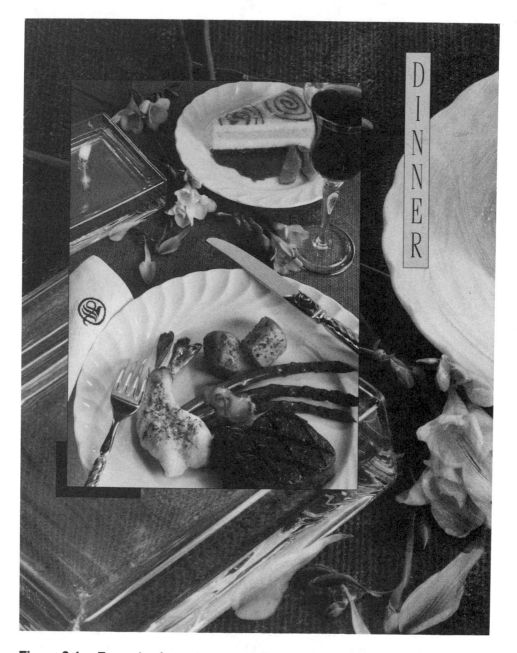

Figure 3.1.   Example of standardized banquet menus. (Courtesy John Steinmetz, The Westin Bonaventure, Los Angeles, CA.)

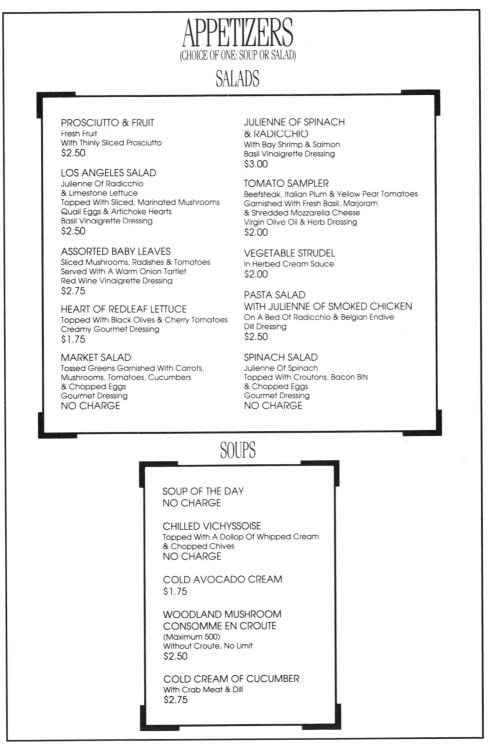

APPETIZERS
(CHOICE OF ONE: SOUP OR SALAD)

SALADS

PROSCIUTTO & FRUIT
Fresh Fruit
With Thinly Sliced Prosciutto
$2.50

LOS ANGELES SALAD
Julienne Of Radicchio
& Limestone Lettuce
Topped With Sliced, Marinated Mushrooms
Quail Eggs & Artichoke Hearts
Basil Vinaigrette Dressing
$2.50

ASSORTED BABY LEAVES
Sliced Mushrooms, Radishes & Tomatoes
Served With A Warm Onion Tartlet
Red Wine Vinaigrette Dressing
$2.75

HEART OF REDLEAF LETTUCE
Topped With Black Olives & Cherry Tomatoes
Creamy Gourmet Dressing
$1.75

MARKET SALAD
Tossed Greens Garnished With Carrots,
Mushrooms, Tomatoes, Cucumbers
& Chopped Eggs
Gourmet Dressing
NO CHARGE

JULIENNE OF SPINACH
& RADICCHIO
With Bay Shrimp & Salmon
Basil Vinaigrette Dressing
$3.00

TOMATO SAMPLER
Beefsteak, Italian Plum & Yellow Pear Tomatoes
Garnished With Fresh Basil, Marjoram
& Shredded Mozzarella Cheese
Virgin Olive Oil & Herb Dressing
$2.00

VEGETABLE STRUDEL
In Herbed Cream Sauce
$2.00

PASTA SALAD
WITH JULIENNE OF SMOKED CHICKEN
On A Bed Of Radicchio & Belgian Endive
Dill Dressing
$2.50

SPINACH SALAD
Julienne Of Spinach
Topped With Croutons, Bacon Bits
& Chopped Eggs
Gourmet Dressing
NO CHARGE

SOUPS

SOUP OF THE DAY
NO CHARGE

CHILLED VICHYSSOISE
Topped With A Dollop Of Whipped Cream
& Chopped Chives
NO CHARGE

COLD AVOCADO CREAM
$1.75

WOODLAND MUSHROOM
CONSOMME EN CROUTE
(Maximum 500)
Without Croute, No Limit
$2.50

COLD CREAM OF CUCUMBER
With Crab Meat & Dill
$2.75

Figure 3.1.   (continued)

ENTREES

CALIFORNIA CHICKEN
Poached Double Breast Of Chicken
Served With Green, Yellow & Red Pepper Strips
In Pernod Sauce
$24.00

LEMON BROILED CHICKEN
Marinated In Lime & Lemon, Sherry & Herbs
Served With Lemon Butter
$23.50

LEMON BROILED CHICKEN
& TIGER PRAWN
Marinated In Lime & Lemon Juice
Accompanied By A Baked Tiger Prawn
Topped With Herb Butter
$28.50

ROAST PRIME RIB OF BEEF AU JUS
10 Oz. Prime Cut
Served With Creamed Horseradish
$31.75

BROILED FILET MIGNON
With Woodland Mushrooms
Topped With A Creamy Bordelaise Sauce
$35.00

TWIN MEDALLIONS OF BEEF & VEAL
With Madeira & Green Peppercorn Sauces
$34.50

BROILED SALMON STEAK
Served With Tomato Relish & Dill Sauce
$32.00

BROILED SWORDFISH STEAK
& CAJUN STYLE HALIBUT
$32.50

CAJUN STYLE RED SNAPPER
Red Snapper Filet
Lightly Dusted With Mild Spices & Herbs
$23.25

CHICKEN BREAST TERIYAKI
Double Breast Of Chicken
Marinated In Teriyaki Soy Sauce
Garnished With A Pineapple Ring
$24.25

CHICKEN BROCHETTE
& TIGER PRAWN
Morsels Of Chicken Marinated In Lemon Juice
& Tiger Prawn Topped With Herb Butter
$29.50

CHICKEN & BEEF COMBINATION
Broiled Chicken Breast
Petite Filet Mignon
With Dijon Mustard Seed Sauce
$31.00

TOURNEDOS OF BEEF
Twin Tournedos
With Green Peppercorn Sauce
$29.00

BROILED NEW YORK STEAK
Served With Sauce Choron, Bordelaise
Or Chili-Flavored Madeira Sauce
With Red, Green & Yellow Peppers
$33.50

SONOMA VEAL CHOP
With Wild Mushroom Sauce
$43.00

FILET & TIGER PRAWN
Broiled Filet
& Baked Butterflied Tiger Prawn
Served Respectively With Green Peppercorn
Sauce & Herb Butter
$38.50

BROILED LAMB CHOP
& STUFFED LAMB CHOP COMBINATION
Jalapeno Jelly & Herbed Butter Sauce
$43.00

The Chef will select for you the finest Fresh Vegetables and Rice or Potatoes. All entrees served with French Rolls and Butter. All dinners are served with Coffee, Tea, Brewed Decaffeinated Coffee or Milk. Prices do not include service, administrative charges and sales tax.

Figure 3.1.   (continued)

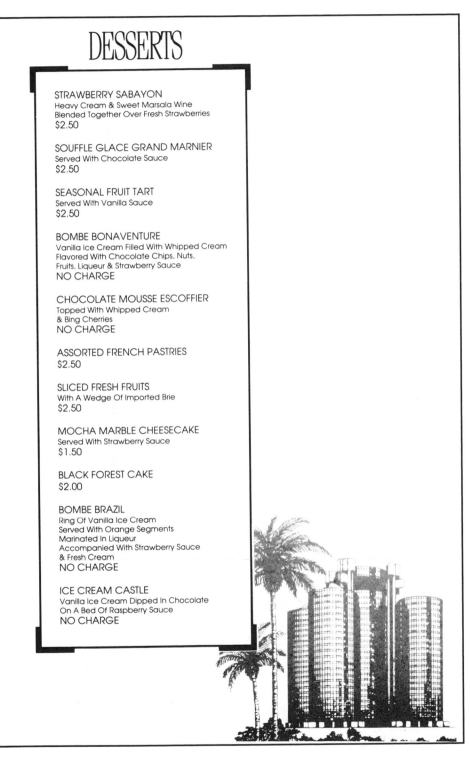

DESSERTS

STRAWBERRY SABAYON
Heavy Cream & Sweet Marsala Wine
Blended Together Over Fresh Strawberries
$2.50

SOUFFLE GLACE GRAND MARNIER
Served With Chocolate Sauce
$2.50

SEASONAL FRUIT TART
Served With Vanilla Sauce
$2.50

BOMBE BONAVENTURE
Vanilla Ice Cream Filled With Whipped Cream
Flavored With Chocolate Chips, Nuts,
Fruits, Liqueur & Strawberry Sauce
NO CHARGE

CHOCOLATE MOUSSE ESCOFFIER
Topped With Whipped Cream
& Bing Cherries
NO CHARGE

ASSORTED FRENCH PASTRIES
$2.50

SLICED FRESH FRUITS
With A Wedge Of Imported Brie
$2.50

MOCHA MARBLE CHEESECAKE
Served With Strawberry Sauce
$1.50

BLACK FOREST CAKE
$2.00

BOMBE BRAZIL
Ring Of Vanilla Ice Cream
Served With Orange Segments
Marinated In Liqueur
Accompanied With Strawberry Sauce
& Fresh Cream
NO CHARGE

ICE CREAM CASTLE
Vanilla Ice Cream Dipped In Chocolate
On A Bed Of Raspberry Sauce
NO CHARGE

Figure 3.1.   (continued)

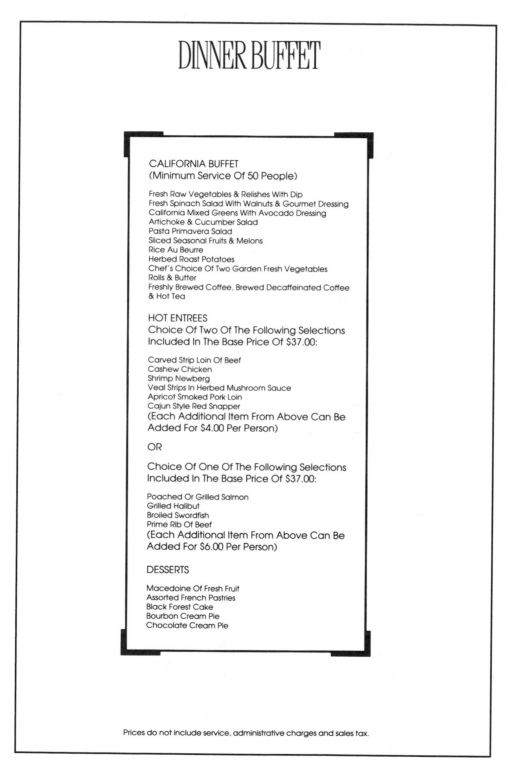

DINNER BUFFET

CALIFORNIA BUFFET
(Minimum Service Of 50 People)

Fresh Raw Vegetables & Relishes With Dip
Fresh Spinach Salad With Walnuts & Gourmet Dressing
California Mixed Greens With Avocado Dressing
Artichoke & Cucumber Salad
Pasta Primavera Salad
Sliced Seasonal Fruits & Melons
Rice Au Beurre
Herbed Roast Potatoes
Chef's Choice Of Two Garden Fresh Vegetables
Rolls & Butter
Freshly Brewed Coffee, Brewed Decaffeinated Coffee
& Hot Tea

HOT ENTREES
Choice Of Two Of The Following Selections
Included In The Base Price Of $37.00:

Carved Strip Loin Of Beef
Cashew Chicken
Shrimp Newberg
Veal Strips In Herbed Mushroom Sauce
Apricot Smoked Pork Loin
Cajun Style Red Snapper
(Each Additional Item From Above Can Be
Added For $4.00 Per Person)

OR

Choice Of One Of The Following Selections
Included In The Base Price Of $37.00:

Poached Or Grilled Salmon
Grilled Halibut
Broiled Swordfish
Prime Rib Of Beef
(Each Additional Item From Above Can Be
Added For $6.00 Per Person)

DESSERTS

Macedoine Of Fresh Fruit
Assorted French Pastries
Black Forest Cake
Bourbon Cream Pie
Chocolate Cream Pie

Prices do not include service, administrative charges and sales tax.

Figure 3.1.   (continued)

The menus should also include mention of the hotel's ability and willingness to create a personalized menu. The successful, competitive caterer is one who can accommodate specific client needs.

The hotel's restaurant menus can also be used as an effective marketing tool. For instance, a creative menu in the hotel's gourmet room can impress meeting planners who are on a fact-finding visit. Restaurant menus also can carry discreet notations that advertise the hotel's catering services.

Videotapes and photos are excellent promotional materials that should be part of all sales representatives' sales kits. Though they are expensive to produce, they are exceptionally useful marketing tools. They could also be used in direct-mail campaigns.

Videotaping is becoming more popular. Many catering clients are willing to spend a considerable amount of money to tape their functions; this is especially true for weddings, bridal showers, and other similar events. The hotel caterer should consider taping some of these functions and using them to show potential clients. For instance, if a videotaping company is hired to tape a wedding hosted in the hotel, the catering executive could make some arrangement with the camera operator to prepare a short version of the final tape for the hotel's use.

The hotel also should consider developing a video sales presentation. For example, a video walk through of the hotel's facilities can be a very persuasive part of the marketing plan. If a videotape is too expensive, a short slide or photo presentation with an accompanying audiotape might be an acceptable compromise.

Glossy, color photos are another very effective marketing tool. The photos should include some food items, especially the hotel's specialty products. They should also highlight the property's function space and other amenities.

As much as possible, people should be included in these photos because clients will identify more closely with them. Photos that do not include people are said to be "cold," whereas those with people are dubbed "warm." Presumably, the warmer the photo, the more positive its effect will be on the intended audience.

The director of catering should see to it that a folder or binder is maintained for sales use that includes photos of suggested plate presentations, lavish parties that were previously served, and other pictorial materials. The binder also should include testimonial letters. A copy of this binder should always be on display in the catering sales department's waiting room.

Proposals may be part of the sales solicitation efforts. They could include sales brochures, menus, and photos. A videotape or audiotape might also be included, which could include sales presentations, previous and/or suggested plate presentations, function-room set ups, and so forth.

Generally, a proposal is a direct response to a client inquiry. Sales brochures and other similar materials normally are sent to persons who represent potential business, but have not actively sought out the hotel's catering department.

A proposal is the first serious written understanding of a client's desires. It typically will include one or more options that the client can consider. For instance, if a qualified client is in the market for a company holiday party, the catering sales representative may prepare one or more competitive bids for his or her perusal. If the client selects one of the options, there usually is a confirmation notice included in the proposal that can be signed by the client and returned to the hotel.

Proposals usually are prepared only when there is serious client interest. Normally a sales representative will not prepare and send one to a client until both parties have met once or twice to explore possibilities.

The proposal is the first major step toward a signed catering contract. Consequently, it must include all relevant information. Nothing should be left to chance. There should be no verbal side agreements; if it is worth negotiating, it is worth writing down. This will prevent misunderstandings that can cause unhappy clients and a cloud on the hotel's reputation.

Word-of-mouth advertising is by far the most effective form of advertising. Many food-service operations, especially table-service restaurants, rely exclusively on this type of advertising.

Word-of-mouth advertising is the prelude to referral business. Most catering clients put a great deal of stock into current and previous customers' recommendations. This is especially true if the client knows the customer and trusts his or her opinion. No other marketing efforts will carry as much weight as will the opinions and recommendations of a trusted colleague and/or friend.

Soliciting future business at a current event is a controversial promotion technique that should be done very discreetly and, of course, only if the current client approves.

Statistics show that about 5 percent of the guests at a current event are likely to have a catering need in the near future. The temptation to exploit this latent need is overwhelming; catering executives must find some acceptable way to do it. For instance, the director of catering's business cards can be left unobtrusively on a side table. Tasteful signage can be displayed. Or a catering sales representative can attempt to obtain the current event's guest list and incorporate it into the hotel's mailing lists.

SALES PROCEDURES

One of the nice things about the restaurant business is that, once a guest enters an establishment, he or she most likely will buy something. Other retailers would love to be in this enviable position. Many of them, especially department stores, have a great number of casual shoppers who are just browsing and are not interested in buying anything.

Many potential catering clients are also casual shoppers. This is understandable because you cannot assume a person is apt to purchase a catered event just because he or she walked in the door seeking information. Unlike the restaurant patron who is willing to risk money to try out a new food-service operation, the potential catering client cannot afford to do this. A potential client feels obligated to perform a bit of research. And, before the final contract is signed, he or she must be sold.

Client Inquiry

Rarely a day goes by without a potential client seeking information about the hotel catering department's products and services. Most of these clients will be categorized as off-the-street business, while the remainder usually will be referral business.

The director of catering should develop a standardized procedure that catering staff members should follow when handling these inquiries. This procedure should be based on the assumption that a booked event will be the result.

Sometimes potential clients inquire about dates, meals, and other services the hotel is unable to accommodate. The word "no" is probably the hardest one to utter when dealing with potential clients. You do not want to lose *any* type of business. The skillful catering executive should be able to negotiate with the potential client to the satisfaction of all parties.

There are three ways a potential client can contact a caterer: (1) by letter, (2) by phone, and (3) in person.

If a potential client inquires with a letter, the caterer should always respond with a phone call. If other caterers have also been contacted by this client, you want to get back as soon as possible in order to avoid being upstaged by a competitor.

A phone call follow-up also is necessary because additional

information will be needed in order to prepare a proper proposal. For instance, the client's objective, budgetary constraints, dietary restrictions, and so forth must be considered before advancing to the proposal stage.

A phone call follow-up gives the catering executive the opportunity to invite the potential client to visit the hotel. You should make every effort to get the potential client to make a site visit. Experience shows that your selling task is much, much easier if you have potential clients on site where you can control the presentation and eliminate interruptions. While there, they can be treated to lunch, given a facility tour, and allowed to visit with other catering-staff members. If you visit potential clients at their homes or places of business, you do not enjoy this selling advantage.

If a potential client inquires by phone, ideally the receptionist will answer it before the third ring. Furthermore, you should ensure that whoever answers the phone is able to answer questions. At the very least, the receptionist must be able to route the call to the right person as quickly as possible.

There should always be someone in the office who can handle these calls adequately. A knowledgeable person should always be present. Too often the lowest paid, least knowledgeable person answers the phone. This person may be unable to answer questions because he or she has not been trained to do so. Many times the caller is not even asked to leave a message or number when the person he or she is trying to reach is unavailable. Consequently, a considerable amount of business may be lost. The wise director of catering ensures that a manager is assigned to each shift who is able to process these inquiries properly.

If a potential client inquires in person, it is imperative that someone see this person as soon as possible. The inquirer should be made comfortable. He or she should be offered coffee, soda, or other refreshment. An accurate estimate of waiting time should be indicated. A binder with photos, suggested menus, catering policies, testimonial letters, and so forth, should be available for the potential client to peruse while waiting. And the receptionist should be instructed to take some preliminary information from the inquirer, such as type of function, date needed, and number of guests. This activity gets the client involved—a positive step toward consummating a sale.

Client Solicitation

Some hotel caterers are in the position of not having to solicit business. For example, The Mirage Hotel in Las Vegas and the

Perimeter Marriott Hotel in Atlanta do not use outside sales representatives. They currently have all the incoming calls they can handle. In fact, they usually have to turn away potential business.

Most catering executives though, cannot wait for business to walk in off the street. Nor, for that matter, should the hotel that has all the business it can handle rest on its laurels. It should always plan ahead and have a system ready to use for those times when its business cycle bottoms out.

There will always be a certain amount of off-the-street, referral, and repeat business. However, in order to maximize the catering department's profit potential, customer solicitation is usually needed. It is especially necessary if you want to book business during the shoulder (that is, slow) periods.

Many hotels assign sales quotas to their sales representatives that cannot be satisfied with walk-in business. Generally speaking, there should always be a certain amount of solicited business because this ensures that you continue to get the business you want, not just the groups that walk in the door.

Client solicitation takes many forms. Sales representatives canvass for new business with telephone solicitation, direct mail, cold calling, and sales blitz techniques.

Direct mailing with telephone follow-ups, sales blitzes (where the catering staff works the phones once or twice a year in marathon solicitation efforts), and cold calling (where a sales representative personally calls on potential clients unannounced) are the most common forms of client solicitation efforts.

A direct mailing involves sending out a stock information kit (such as a sales brochure with menus, prices, photos, and so forth) to potential clients whose names were obtained from a mailing list.

The most effective type of mailing is the personalized one. A sales representative should not send out the information kit until he or she finds out something about the potential client so that the mailing can be personalized. This tends to generate more positive responses. It also enhances the hotel caterer's image and reputation, which is certain to pay dividends in the future.

The direct mail piece should have some unique physical characteristics to distinguish it from those sent by competing hotels. For instance, printed material could be inserted in an attractive, uniquely colored folder that will stand out in a potential client's files.

Some direct mailing efforts are aimed at previous clients who have not visited the hotel lately. For instance, a tracer file might be kept that shows customers who have not held an event at the hotel for over a year. An information kit with telephone follow-up can be sent as a courtesy so that these old friends do not forget that the hotel remains ready to satisfy their needs.

Some repeat customers may not receive a direct mailing, but they should receive an occasional telephone solicitation. For instance, if the hotel is in the process of booking next year's Christmas party business, it can call old customers to let them know that space is filling up fast and that the catering staff looks forward to booking space for them and servicing their events.

Sales blitzes and cold calls can yield considerable catering business if they are handled correctly. The most important aspect of these sales techniques is to use a process whereby you can identify quickly potential business. You do not want to waste anyone's time, but to be successful, you need to ask the right questions. For instance, you need to know: (1) Who is the decision maker? (2) How often are events planned? (3) Is hotel space ever booked? (4) What is the size, type, and budget of the typical event? (5) How are events planned? This information will help streamline selling efforts and make them more productive.

Canvassing will result in a certain percentage of prospects all with varying degrees of potential. Off-the-street and referral business will generate a similar list of prospects.

A major part of canvassing is to qualify these leads. One way this can be done is to run a credit check on them. For instance, the large hotel company usually belongs to a credit reporting service, such as Credit Bureau/Equifax, Dun & Bradstreet, TransUnion, and/or TRW. A call to these organizations will reveal a potential client's credit worthiness as well as other useful information.

In addition to running a credit check, the sales representative may ask the potential client to complete a credit application. Most hotels have standardized credit applications that they use to uncover important credit data, such as the credit applicant's bank branch and the name of a financial official who can provide a credit reference.

Credit verification is an important part of the selling effort. As soon as possible, you should ask the potential client for permission to verify credit. If he or she refuses to grant permission, you must be certain the potential client understands that the hotel will expect payment in advance for any catering services booked. In some cases, if permission is denied, you might want to terminate contact with these potential clients and remove them from your list of prospects.

The sales representative can also cull prospects from the list by checking references. For example, if a potential client's name was drawn from the membership list of a local civic association, someone in the hotel probably knows something about this group, as well as who in the group should be contacted for a reference.

Once qualified, the sales representative will set an appointment to meet with the potential client. Ideally, the appointment would be at the hotel so that the client can tour the facilities, visit a restaurant, and personally witness the hotel's capabilities to handle the proposed event.

After the initial appointment, the sales representative may have enough information to prepare a formal proposal. If necessary, there may need to be one or more additional meetings before a competitive bid can be submitted to the potential client.

When submitting proposals, it is important to recognize that the presentation is in itself a major part of the hotel caterer's promotional efforts. The "packaging" is critical. According to Michael Roman, the catering executive should:

1. Use an overnight service to deliver the proposal, even if the client is in the same city.
2. Avoid folding the proposal document.
3. Offer a home telephone number so that the potential client can get in touch quickly and efficiently.
4. Show a copyright statement on the proposal document.
5. Use stamps in lieu of a postage metering machine.
6. Send a hand-written thank-you note before the potential client receives the proposal.
7. Send a copy of photos or videotapes that show recent functions that are similar to the one desired by the potential client.
8. Print the proposals on legal-sized paper.
9. Consider hand delivering the proposal instead of sending it in the mail or faxing it.
10. Create a sense of urgency by indicating the proposal's expiration date.
11. Put a line in your proposal that states:

    Event planning . . . $50.00 per hour . . . no charge.

    Potential clients now know that your time is valuable and is worth something to them. They will then appreciate your efforts much more.

Once the proposal is presented, the next step is to commence negotiations. If all goes well, a formal contract that is mutually acceptable to all parties will be signed.

Client Contact

Serious contact with potential clients usually begins with a general discussion of the event. Specific details are then uncovered, such as prices, times, room availabilities, and other customer requirements. Eventually, there will be a meeting of the minds and a signed contract will be prepared.

For this process to become reality, sales representatives must be knowledgeable. They must be able to answer clients' questions. They cannot afford to lose face. A stumbling, bumbling answer leaves a terrible impression.

Sales representatives must be very familiar with food and beverage production and service. They also must know and understand the hotel property's limitations, especially those restricting the types of functions that can be hosted properly.

Sales representatives also must be enthusiastic and likable. They must be polite and friendly. And they should exude the proper amount of sophistication consistent with the hotel's competitive position.

Sales representatives sell benefits to the client. They should not wait for the client to ask about them. Rather, they must take the high ground and see to it that clients know that, for example, parking is free, that there are special prices available for some functions, or that the hotel has a unique view.

Clients want to know that they are being handled correctly and professionally. They want to trust someone to do a good job and make them look good in the eyes of their guests. They expect to pay a reasonable price for the catered event, but they must be satisfied with the results. Consequently, the wise sales representative will ensure that he or she knows exactly what the client wants. This is no time to guess.

A checklist of things to ask the client is an essential part of the sales representative's sales kit. (See Figure 3.2.) The list should contain the obvious questions, such as the number of guests, the event's starting and ending times, and the required room set-up. It also should contain unique questions, such as dietary and religious restrictions, entertainment needs, and the number and type of outside contractors that will be used.

A sales representative must find out as much as possible about the potential client before advancing to the negotiating and proposal stages. This information will indicate the potential for upselling, how many other competing caterers the client is considering, and any unusual needs that must be accommodated.

Reception Checklist

Type of Reception: Before Dinner _____ No Planned Dinner to Follow _____

Time Allowed for Reception _____

Local and State Laws _____

Open Bar _____ Charge by the Drink _____

House Brands _____

Call Brands _____

Cash Bar
    Tickets _____

    Bartender Fee _____

Drink Costs   Special Preference Drinks
    Mixed Drink _____   Non-Caffeine _____

    Beer _____   Diet Soda _____

    Wine _____   Mineral Waters _____

    Soda _____   VIP Call Brands _____

Service Charge _____ Tax _____ Set-Up Fee _____ Bartender Fee _____

Hors d'oeuvres and Snacks
    Number of Attendees _____

    Selection and Volume _____

    _____

    Duration _____

    Served Butler Style _____ Served at Tables or Stations _____

    Custom Cooking/Carving _____

    Pricing
        Per Person _____

        Per Piece _____

        Tax and Service Charge _____

Decorations _____

Hotel Guarantee Policy _____

Program
    Background Music _____   Favors _____

    Entertainment _____   Photographer _____

    VIP Arrangements _____   Microphone _____

    Honors _____

Setup
    Standing _____ Cabaret _____ Lounge _____ Perimeter Seating _____

Figure 3.2. Example reception checklist.

4

Client Relations

The most exciting challenge catering offers is to capture a client's vision and make it a reality.

Judy Cantu
President
JC Catering
Coronado, California

The initial client contact sets into motion a series of events that one hopes will lead to a completed, and successful, catered function. The catering executive will be involved throughout this process.

When a potential client indicates a serious interest in purchasing catering services, the catering staff should find out as much as it can about the client's needs before proposing various alternatives. The staff also must have some idea of the client's minimum and maximum spending limits. Usually this type of information is obtained during an initial meeting with the potential client.

Once these preliminaries are taken care of, the client-relations cycle shifts into high gear. Generally, the major aspects of this cycle are: (1) client negotiations; (2) communications with the client; and (3) problem resolution. Woven throughout this cycle are protocols to which catering staff members must adhere in order to please the client while simultaneously achieving the hotel's goals.

CLIENT NEGOTIATIONS

Before entering into serious negotiations, the catering sales representative must evaluate the client's needs. According to the Professional Convention Management Association (PCMA), the catering executive should determine for each function:

1. Estimated attendance
2. Audiovisual (AV) needs
3. Meal service requirements
4. Ceremonies performed during the event
5. Lighting needs
6. Sound needs
7. Flags and other displays included
8. Entertainment requirements
9. Required platform and table setups
10. Decorations needed
11. Timing of events
12. Rehearsal time needed
13. Special diets and other unique requests
14. Head table requirements
15. Budget constraints.

Before, during, or just after gathering this information, the catering executive must see to it that the client is informed about the hotel's production and service capabilities.

All potential clients need some amount of education. A catering executive expects to provide a different kind of learning experience to, say, the parents of the bride planning a wedding reception than to the professional meeting planner. However, all clients must understand early on what types of services the hotel can provide, and the size of functions it is able to accommodate.

The catering executive must also educate clients to prevent them from making any obvious mistakes. According to Barbara Nichols, editor of *Professional Meeting Management,* the most common mistakes made by function planners that you should caution them to avoid are:

1. Selecting heavy foods for breakfast and lunch. Sink-to-the-bottom entrees will make guests drowsy and unable to appreciate fully the program to follow.
2. Not taking into account some guests' special dietary restrictions.
3. Failing to accommodate guests who prefer a wide selection of nonalcoholic beverages.
4. Scheduling an excessively lengthy reception before a dinner function. Guests are liable to become exhausted and/or inebriated if the reception stretches on too long.

5. Booking inadequate room space.

6. Paying scant attention to room ambience, comfort, attractiveness, and suitability for the event.

7. Failing to rehearse the event. This can cause unnecessary problems that are apt to embarrass the client as well as the hotel.

8. Saving money by skimping on sound and lighting. For instance, if the speaker cannot be heard, guests will become anxious and are liable to embarrass the function host.

9. Lack of familiarity with the audience. Function planners must know their guests or else they will be unable to select appropriate food, beverage, entertainment, and other services.

10. Failing to include head table guests in the guest count. For instance, it is sometimes easy to overlook guest speakers and presenters as well as VIPs who are not processed through regular channels.

Once this ground work is settled, the catering sales representative can begin negotiating the major aspects all catering functions share. These are: (1) prices; (2) special needs; and (3) guarantees.

Prices

Potential clients must be aware of all relevant charges. They should be quoted the total charge for all products and services purchased. For instance, some hotels quote separate prices for meal and beverage functions, room rentals, room set-ups, taxes, gratuities, union minimums, costs for continuing service beyond the scheduled cut-off time, license fees, insurance costs, and outside contract services. The sales representative must ensure that the price quotation lists all these separate charges as well as the grand total; last-minute surprises will seriously harm the hotel's professional image.

The typical hotel is willing to quote prices three to six months in advance. Since the hotel's costs of doing business tend to fluctuate (particularly food costs), anything over the three-month period usually calls for a price-range quotation. For example, the hotel caterer may agree to quote a tentative price, subject to a range of percentages that will be used to increase or decrease the final price.

The short-term booking puts the hotel in the driver's seat. The short period of time usually precludes the client from pulling out of the deal. The hotel therefore, does not have to make too many concessions. It is too late for most clients, especially conventions, to pull out. A client would have to pay a cancellation fee and take the chance of finding another suitable hotel for the function. Furthermore, the client may have printed publicity items, such as registration materials, convention programs, shopping bags, and hats, with the hotel's name and logo prominently displayed. These convention materials would be wasted if the location was changed.

Most large functions, such as major conventions, are planned one, five, or even as many as ten years in advance. The meeting planner obviously is interested in a long-term, firm price quotation, and will usually press the hotel caterer to comply with this request. However, the director of catering must ensure that long-term price quotes are tentative. There must be some built-in adjustment alternatives; for instance, the hotel should have the option of increasing prices or decreasing food portion sizes if it encounters supply problems.

Sometimes a hotel can get a short-term, firm price commitment from clients if it is willing to make concessions in other areas. For instance, a popular strategy many hotels follow is to exchange complimentary coffee breaks, free parking, and/or reduced-rate sleeping-room accommodations for these price commitments.

Food and beverage revenue generally is the hotel's second largest source of income. To clients though, catering is usually the largest expense in their budgets. The hotel caterer should assume that price will be most client decision makers' primary concern.

While price is a key consideration, statistics show that the quality of food and beverage is another very important criterion evaluated by a client when deciding which caterer to use. On the one hand, clients are very price sensitive. But on the other hand, they want good quality food and beverage products. In effect, they want to maximize the price-value relationships received. The successful director of catering must be able to walk this competitive tightrope.

Clients with unlimited budgets are the most fun to work with. In this case, price negotiations may consist of nothing more than weighing the pros and cons of French service.

Many clients though, want filet mignon at peanut-butter-and-jelly prices. This is particularly true of the social, military, education, religious, and fraternal (SMERF) market.

The SMERF market is the most price-conscious market. The catering sales representative must expect to work with these groups very closely as they typically are on tight budgets. They need to "sell" the events to their members and guests. And if the person negotiating with you cannot make a commitment without checking with others in the organization, negotiations could drag on indefinitely.

The hotel caterer will rarely have to grant concessions during the high (i.e., busy) seasons. Generally though, catering executives must be willing to negotiate and be somewhat flexible.

Sleeping-room sales is the hotel's main source of profits. If a group books a large number of sleeping rooms, usually the catering executive must be willing to work within the client's budget for meal and beverage functions. The types and number of sleeping rooms available are major selling points and are usually the most important considerations to large conventions. Consequently, while food and beverage prices are important, a hotel may want to concentrate primarily on sleeping-room profits and only secondarily on catering revenue.

Price negotiation is a game. Clients do not haggle over prices when they shop for products in a supermarket or department store. However, they do expect to negotiate with caterers. There are many options a sales representative can offer clients. If the hotel caterer and client choose wisely, the catered event will be profitable for the hotel and memorable for the client. The successful catering manager will try to find some common ground whereby the hotel and the client can achieve their personal objectives.

For example, the sales representative can ask the client to allow the hotel to be creative. Instead of haggling over a lower price for something on a standardized food menu, maybe it would be better for everyone if the client allows the sales representative to work with the chef and create something unique within the client's budget.

A client also might save money if there are any promotions currently offered in other areas of the hotel for which he or she might qualify. For example, the hotel's restaurant outlets might be holding a Strawberry Festival in June; clients therefore, may be able to participate indirectly in this event and save money by using promotion-priced strawberries on their menus.

A sales representative could suggest food items that are in season as well as those that are not labor intensive; the client willing to make a few minor menu changes can earn a lower price.

If the client is willing to move the event to another function room, or hold it on an alternate date (thereby freeing up the space for another more profitable event), he or she might be granted a price concession. Clients that have this type of flexibility generally have the most negotiating power. For instance, if the function is held during the off season, the catering sales representative usually is empowered to, and is eager to, negotiate an across-the-board percentage reduction.

If there are other similar events in the hotel that day, perhaps the client would be willing to accept the same menu as another group (a process known as "ganging menus"). This option can reduce production costs and increase labor productivity. A client willing to do this may be rewarded with a lower price quotation.

Since payroll, employee benefits, and payroll-related administrative costs can exceed 40 percent of revenue, a client could save money by selecting a menu that is easy to produce and serve. For instance, you may be able to reduce the number of servers if guests would be satisfied with self-service options or with standard American service, where foods are preplated in the kitchen and served quickly and efficiently to guests.

Payroll can also be reduced if the client allows you to preset some courses, such as salad and dessert, on the dining tables. Preplated and preset food is a very functional and quick type of table service.

Savings also can accrue if a client hosts a larger function. For instance, even though meeting-room expenses incurred by the hotel are based on set-up, servicing, tear-down, and cleaning costs, the price charged for the function room will be influenced primarily by the number of sleeping rooms used, the type and number of meal and beverage functions, the number of guests, and the amount of other revenue generated by the group. As revenues in one area increase, the hotel will usually reduce the price of the meeting room; if there is sufficient other revenue, the meeting-room price may be waived. If there is no other revenue, the meeting-room price may be prohibitive because it must compensate for other business lost to the hotel.

If beverage is a major part of the catered event, there are some money-saving ideas that the catering sales representative could suggest to the function host. For instance:

1. Bars could be wedded toward the end of the event. Wedding a bar means closing one or more portable bars down about half an hour before the end of the function and using the partial bottles at those bars remaining open. Alternatively, if your banquet rooms have permanent bars, you could offer to close one early. Under both strategies, the client should be able to reduce labor expenses.

Wedding bars usually is a viable alternative only when clients purchase liquor by the bottle. However, in some parts of the country, purchasing full bottles for on-premises consumption may be prohibited by local liquor codes. Furthermore, the codes may not allow you to move beverage from one bar to another during a catering function. You must ensure that your local liquor code allows you to offer these forms of cost-saving alternatives.

2. Avoid letting guests prepare their own alcoholic drinks. If all drinks are prepared and served by bartenders, or prepared by bartenders and passed by cocktail servers, liquor consumption will decrease significantly. People tend to drink much less when they are served. Even though there is a higher labor cost when liquor preparation and service is controlled by the hotel, the product-cost savings obtained with reduced consumption could more than offset the extra payroll charges.

3. Use low-cost house brands instead of premium brands.

4. Serve large quantities of food. The more people eat, generally the less they drink. Cheese is particularly filling. Minimize salty foods though; thirsty guests will tend to compensate by drinking more.

5. Reduce the time of the event by about 15 to 20 minutes. This will make a big difference in the amount of food and beverage served, and few guests will mind the early cut off.

6. Limit "landing space." If there is no place to set a drink, it is less likely to be lost and replaced when half empty. This can reduce significantly beverage costs.

7. Schedule the event on a week night. Most guests will consume more beverages on the weekends.

8. Consider using a no-host bar. A no-host bar (sometimes referred to as a cash bar) requires each guest to pay for his or her drinks; beverages are not included in the price of the function. It is the opposite of a host bar (or open bar), where the function price includes both food and beverage.

The no-host strategy usually works well with, for example, a civic organization's monthly meeting. It may not work as well with, say, a wedding reception; however, a compromise usually acceptable to wedding guests is to provide hosted beer and wine with guests purchasing their own distilled spirits.

9. Price the function with the understanding that the first two drinks per person are included in the price, with the attendee expected to pay for additional beverages. In this case, the function host pays for the first two drinks, and all attendees receive two drink tickets. If they want more beverage, they must purchase additional drink tickets from the function cashier. Under this arrangement, a client agrees to a fixed function price; he or she does not have to worry about inheriting a huge bar bill.

Alternatively, a function host could host the bar for a limited amount of time, after which the bar reverts to a cash-bar arrangement. This strategy could backfire though, if guests are unaware of it and are suddenly put into an embarrassing position when the time comes to pay for their drinks. It also could backfire if guests, being aware of the time limit, decide to load up on drinks during the hosted time period.

The most difficult client is the one who has to have a certain menu on a certain day for a certain price. Generally the only way to negotiate a reduced price on a fixed menu is to go off menu with substitute items. For example, ice cream can be substituted for chocolate mousse cake; a 6-ounce luncheon steak can be substituted for the 10-ounce dinner steak; sliced roast tenderloin can take the place of broiled filet mignon; and so forth. In most instances, these types of food substitutions offer clients the best opportunities to reduce prices.

The list of substitution options, particularly food-substitution options, is endless. It is important though, to ensure that substitutes offer comparable quality to guests. For instance, it is better to suggest a reduction in portion size rather than suggest the use of a lower quality grade of meat. The catering sales representative must have a solid background in food and beverage production and service capabilities before engaging in this sort of give and take.

Some price-reduction alternatives can be very risky for the hotel. For instance, it is not a good idea to allow clients to eliminate courses from a set menu. Removing the salad course to save money for the function host can leave guests with the wrong impression. They may assume that the hotel is in the habit of cheating its customers.

The hotel also is vulnerable if it allows the client to tinker with the hotel's standardized buffet and/or beverage service. For instance, to save money, a client may want you to pour inexpensive liquor, open the bars late, delay replenishing some near-empty chafing dishes, and/or close some food stations a little early. These strategies can reduce significantly the guests' price-value perceptions. Furthermore, with a buffet meal and/or host bar, the caterer is usually committed to providing enough food and beverage for the guaranteed number of guests.

Another risky money-saving proposition is allowing clients to use their group members as volunteer labor. For instance, many associations use their own paid staff, or member volunteers, to handle things such as ticket collections, name badge preparation, and recordkeeping. This is a very common occurrence in the meetings and conventions trade. However, the hotel must ensure that union regulations are not violated, its insurance will cover this arrangement, and that proper procedures are used to collect, count, package, and present for verification and documentation all tickets and other pertinent records.

Some clients want to use their own food and beverage in order to save money. This practice should be prohibited. The hotel has no quality control over these items, yet it may still be liable for any problems they cause. Furthermore, the use of personal food and beverage may violate local liquor laws or the local health district's sanitation regulations.

Another risky venture is allowing a client to save the luncheon dessert for the afternoon refreshment break. This could harm the hotel's reputation as guests might think that service was terrible because the staff forgot to serve the dessert. Or worse, guests might think that the hotel cheated the function host and the attendees. If a client insists on leaving the dessert for later in the day, the wise director of catering will see to it that place cards are set at each table informing the guests that luncheon dessert will be served during the refreshment break in order to keep the luncheon light and less filling.

Sometimes the catering executive must help clients juggle their budgets. A client could be asked to permit the hotel to manipulate his or her budget in order to gain maximum satisfaction and productivity. For example, the catering sales representative could suggest that the client change a sit-down breakfast to a continental breakfast and redirect the savings to the dinner meal function. If the client budgeted, say, $15.00 for breakfast, you could recommend a $12.50 breakfast and add $2.50 to the dinner, thereby resulting in a more memorable dinner event instead of two mediocre meals.

There are an unlimited number of price-cutting opportunities, but the catering sales representative should be leery of shaving the price so much that guests are dissatisfied. The sweetness of a low price never offsets the bitterness of poor quality and/or service. The memory of a disappointing function will linger long after clients have forgotten the low price.

Special Needs

Clients who have special needs may be more concerned with nonprice issues than with prices. The fact that they have special requests and unique demands indicates that they are prepared to pay more to ensure satisfaction. However, as with all price negotiations, the need for something special does not mean a client has an unlimited budget.

Some clients may need the hotel to carry out a specific theme. For instance, corporate functions normally require the caterer to work with company officials to ensure that the corporation's logos, trade marks, and other similar trappings are interwoven throughout the event. Business clients are particularly fond of ice carvings that display these messages. This usually means that the catering department will be forced to work a little longer and a little harder to ensure success.

Similarly, some clients may have special entertainment needs. For instance, a high school reunion may want to include a beach party as part of its event. This could require an outside decorator or in some cases the hotel to truck in sand, green plants, and other necessary materials, as well as break them down and take them out when the function ends. Once again, more logistics, more work, more trouble; however, there is more potential profit as well as satisfied guests who are sure to remember fondly the hotel who handled their requests so graciously and expeditiously.

Another special need hotels must be able to handle these days is the request for nonsmoking areas. For instance, a banquet room may need to be sectioned in such a way that smokers and nonsmokers will be satisfied. Special equipment, such as technologically superior venting systems, and additional administrative time, such as processing guests' reserved-seating requests, will add to the hotel's costs of doing business. Unfortunately, it would appear that the hotel caterer cannot expect to charge more for this service because people view it as a given; to remain competitive, the hotel will need to accommodate this need.

Transportation is yet another type of special need. For example, a client may want the hotel to use its limousine to transport VIPs. Normally though, the hotel expects the client to use an outside independent contractor to provide this service.

Even in those cases where clients use outside transport companies, the hotel will be involved somehow, either directly or indirectly. For instance, the hotel may be asked to recommend a service. At the very least, the hotel will need to provide reserved parking space for buses, limousines, and/or shuttle vans. And, if the outside service contractors do not satisfy clients, some of the blame may be laid at the hotel's door.

Some special needs may be too risky for the hotel to accommodate. For instance, a client may want the chef to prepare a special meal using the client's personal recipes. This type of request will require the chef to work closely with the client to test the recipes.

Unfortunately, if the recipes are not suitable for quantity-cooking procedures, the catering manager will need to confer diplomatically with the client and suggest acceptable alternatives. If a client's personal recipes cannot be prepared properly in large quantities, guests will notice the dilution in quality and may be quick to assign culpability to the hotel.

Probably the most common type of special need is the client who has one or more diet restrictions. Some guests will have medical restrictions, while others may have religious restrictions or health and life-style concerns.

The typical medical restrictions are fat-restricted, sugar-restricted, and sodium-restricted diets. Occasionally there will be a guest who is allergic to one or more food groups; for example, many people are allergic to shrimp, peanuts, and/or strawberries. You also might encounter guests who bring their own food; for instance, some dieters are on a programmed dietary regimen—such as Nutri/Systems®, Opti-Fast®, and Weight Watchers®—where they must consume products made specifically by the diet firm.

There are several types of religious diet restrictions that the hotel may be asked to honor. For instance, some clients may request kosher food service. Some may require meatless meals. And some may need a specific type of food and/or beverage as part of a religious ceremony.

Some clients have one or more health and life-style concerns that may tax the hotel's ability to run a smooth function. For instance, a party may have a few vegetarian guests. There may be some guests who refuse to eat fried foods. Some guests may want to avoid politically unpopular foods, such as veal raised inhumanely or tuna that is harvested with dolphins. Or some guests may insist on frozen yogurt instead of ice cream.

Hotel catering departments will usually bend over backwards to honor special requests. But unless they are processed correctly, they can cause problems. For instance, most chefs are willing to offer a choice of fried, baked, or broiled chicken. However, if the majority of guests are receiving fried, the banquet staff must not serve the broiled alternative until all the fried products have been delivered to the other guests. If you do not serve the unusual item last, a few other guests will want it. Result: an unhappy kitchen staff and some confused and/or disgruntled guests.

If special requests are made by clients, the hotel first must determine if it is able to accommodate them. While no sales representative wants to say no, sometimes it cannot be avoided.

If the hotel is able to honor special requests, and if it agrees to do so, the catering executive should document that special needs were handled correctly. For instance, if a client requests that a special type of meat, oil, or condiment be used to prepare the meal, the wise catering executive will see to it that suppliers provide special certificates or invoices attesting to the fact that these items were ordered and delivered. Or if a client requests a low-sodium, low-fat meal, pertinent recipes approved by a registered dietician (RD) should be available for inspection.

It is important to point out that when, for example, meat is ground or otherwise processed, its origins cannot be determined easily or with any degree of certainty. Even a laboratory analysis cannot ensure that the origins will be uncovered. Consequently, it is very important to keep appropriate records in case a dispute arises.

Some disputes may result in legal action. For instance, in the book, *Convention and Banquet Management,* Falkner noted a caterer once served a banquet where a client of Indian ancestry specifically requested that the meal be prepared with lamb instead of beef. During the meal, some guests commented that the meat was beef and so no one ate the meal. The client refused to pay, noting that the catering contract had not been honored by the hotel. The resulting legal battle was very unpleasant, time consuming, and costly. But in the end the hotel won its case primarily because adequate records were maintained and credible witnesses presented verbal evidence in court.

Guarantees

The hotel catering department must have an accurate estimate of the number of guests expected at the catered event. To ensure as much as possible an accurate estimate, the typical catering executive expects the client to provide a guaranteed number.

Setting guarantees though, is oftentimes a treacherous activity. There is a natural reluctance on the part of clients to commit themselves. Likewise, the sales representative wants to minimize the hotel's risk.

The typical hotel requires a written guarantee at least 48 hours prior to the event. Some hotels expect a 72-hour guarantee if a weekend is included in the time period. While this amount of time may seem excessive to the average client, actually it is very short given the amount of work and effort that goes into preparing the normal function.

For instance, the hotel purchasing department will need to purchase food, beverage, and supplies for the event. The kitchen staff will need to schedule production and labor. The banquet-setup crew must be scheduled. And the banquet captain must go over the A-list and B-list for food servers, cocktail servers, buspersons, bar backs, and bartenders.

Experienced meeting planners will try to negotiate a 24-hour guarantee. They also tend to "low ball" their estimates, especially for breakfast functions. This is especially true in the association market.

Guarantees are more troublesome with associations because they have to market the functions to members. The typical association meeting planner never knows in advance exactly how many members will attend; for instance, several members may decide on the spur of the moment to attend only because their busy calendars were cleared at the last minute.

A 24-hour guarantee generally is too short. It places an onerous burden on the kitchen and catering staffs, not to mention the other hotel departments involved with the event. About the only time you can live with such a short time period is when the client is ordering standard food and beverage items that are offered on other hotel restaurant menus. Anything more complex or unique must be implemented at least 48 hours in advance.

At times you may need to consider a compromise guarantee. For instance, when negotiating with a client who wants a 24-hour guarantee, you could suggest a 48-hour minimum guarantee with the option to add (but not subtract) guests 24 hours later. This gives the hotel a firm basis for planning, and also allows the client a bit of flexibility.

Another form of compromise is to negotiate for a 48-hour guarantee time period while allowing the client to guarantee a range of guests. For instance, a meeting planner may estimate 90 to 110 attendees. The hotel may agree to this if, in return, it enjoys a sufficient guarantee time period.

A similar situation arises when a meeting planner, for example, is willing to guarantee 100 customers 48 hours in advance, with the understanding that the catering staff will be able to serve, say, 125. The hotel usually can do this if it is willing to set up open seating.

Open seating essentially means that the catering staff will set up two or three extra tables to handle any last-minute needs. These tables should not be set completely, otherwise guests will spread out and use all available space. Rather, if the guest count suddenly jumps at the last minute, a server or busperson can quickly set a few place settings and serve the extra guests.

Serving these additional guests the same menu though, could be impossible in some situations. If the menu is standardized, and the items are used in the hotel's restaurant outlets, it is not difficult to handle a few extra guests. But if the banquet menu is unique, the additional guests may have to make do with off-menu items. This can harm the hotel's reputation unless the client sees to it that guests are apprised of the situation in advance. Generally though, most clients and guests will accept this trade off.

Quite often the catering sales representative will be working with inexperienced clients who will typically overestimate the guest count. When confronted with this problem, the sales representative will need to educate them.

The sales representative and client must consider several variables that could impact guest counts. The major variables that can influence the number of guests are:

1. *Attendance records of previous years' events.* You are especially concerned with the historical pattern of preregistrations, local ticket sales, arrival/departure patterns on sleeping-room blocks, number of cancellations, number of no-shows, number of paid attendees, number of other authorized attendees (such as spouses), guarantees, excess over guarantees, and percentage of attendees at a particular meal function to total attendees at the event. According to Gary Budge, past president of the National Association of Catering Executives (NACE), accurate guarantees are based primarily on a thorough, competent analysis of historical as well as current information.

2. *The type of event.* For instance, it might be easier to estimate guest count for a wedding than for a customer-appreciation party.

3. *The number and type of speakers and celebrities who will attend.* Incidentally, it is easy to forget to count these guests. Or, conversely, you may inadvertently double count these head-table guests—once when tallying the registrations, and once again when checking the VIP list.

4. *The number and types of competing events.* For instance, other similar functions, major sporting competitions, and political events will tend to reduce guest counts.

5. *The event in relation to the rest of the day's program.* For instance, people attending a three-day convention will tend to miss at least one lunch; many of them will be occupied with convention business and will either skip the meal or will eat somewhere else.

6. *The cost of the function.* It is safe to assume that a high cost will have a negative impact on guest counts, especially if guests are paying their own way.

7. *Purpose of the event.* If it is a command performance, say, a retirement party, you can expect all invited guests to attend.

8. *Who pays for the event.* If the client is paying, chances are the guest count will be high; vice versa may be true if attendees pay their own way.

9. *The type of meal.* Breakfast tends to attract fewer guests than does a luncheon or dinner. For example, conventioneers who attended a late-night hospitality suite the night before may prefer an extra hour's sleep instead. Moreover, usually about half of those attending a breakfast will settle for coffee or another beverage and will bypass the food courses.

The luncheon guest count is heavily influenced by the event's location, if there is a speaker, the popularity and/or relevance of the speaker, the weather, and other events competing for the attendees' time.

Cocktail receptions at the end of a long day tend to be packed if the client schedules some type of entertainment, such as a raffle, music, or celebrity attendees. They will also be well attended if they are offered during the normal meal hour and are intended to take the place of a meal. If they are routine, premeal affairs, they will probably be under attended.

Dinner functions draw the most convention guests. Theme parties, ice-breaker parties, dinner dances, or any similar type of event tends to be well attended.

10. *Timing of the event.* If an event is planned, say, just prior to a three-day weekend, attendance at some events should be enhanced, while other types of events may be poorly attended. For instance, convention attendance may improve if attendees can package it around a minivacation; conversely, a professional association meeting on Friday may attract fewer members if the following Monday is a holiday.

11. *The client's attendance policies.* A client may require compulsory attendance of all guests. For instance, the corporate client typically expects all attendees to attend each function. Under these conditions, it may be a bit easier to forecast guest counts for each catered event.

12. *Expense-account policies for attendees.* In some cases, guests are expected to attend and pay for the catered event, save their receipts, and turn them in for reimbursement. For instance, a corporation may reimburse its managers whenever they attend an association convention. Usually though, the corporation in this case will reimburse the employee only if he or she attends the entire convention, not just one or two events. Consequently, you might have a situation where there are several preregistrations, but much less participation at all functions, because the attendees who want to attend only one or two events will still purchase the entire convention package because that is the only way they can get their money back. The astute catering sales representative will consider this possibility when estimating guest counts and negotiating guarantees.

13. *Length of the event.*   If a guest suspects that the catered function will last four or five hours, he or she may be very reluctant to attend, especially if a long day of work beckons tomorrow. For example, a long dinner meeting with several speakers will tend to discourage attendance.

14. *Length of the convention.*   If a convention lasts more than three days, chances are some attendees will need to leave before it ends. Undoubtedly personal or business problems will crop up for a few attendees who will then need to leave abruptly. Boredom may also take its toll. As a result, guest counts at catered functions during the convention's last day or two may be significantly less than those experienced earlier on.

COMMUNICATIONS WITH THE CLIENT

The catering staff must maintain an open line of communication with each client. Generally there is a considerable amount of lead time between the point when an event is booked and when it transpires. An astute catering executive usually uses tracer files to schedule the number and types of client contacts.

Pre-Event (Pre-Function) Meetings

During the lead-time period, the client and catering sales representative should touch base periodically to discuss the event's progress. Some of these meetings will be "romance" meetings, where pleasantries and other social discussion are exchanged. While these may be a necessary preliminary, you are more interested in the "detail" meetings because this is where anticipated changes will be discussed and early, tentative decisions will be firmed up prior to the event.

Typical issues that are discussed during the "detail" pre-event meetings include:

1. *Timetable.*   For example, the client may need to alter the scheduled wedding ceremony time in order to accommodate the celebrant's schedule.

2. *Guarantees.*   If the tentative booking calls for a price-range guarantee, this will need to be solidified and confirmed. A firm guest guarantee must be established at least 48 hours prior to the event.

3. *Other confirmations.* A client must confirm that association members will be able to handle, for example, ticket collections, display set-ups, and the distribution of program materials.

4. *Use of outside service contractors.* If clients want to use outside independent contractors, such as florists, decorators, and/ or audiovisual (AV) companies, they must hire them personally and inform the catering executive so that the appropriate accommodations can be made.

5. *Space release.* Specific space may not be assigned to a function at the time it is booked. Tentative function-room space usually is allocated based on the client's agenda. As time goes by, any necessary changes are made. When the event date approaches, space is released and function rooms assigned. When this occurs, it is necessary to inform the client and any other relevant persons, such as outside contractors.

6. *Recommendations.* A catering sales representative may want to contact a budget-conscious client if, for example, the hotel recently was offered exceptionally low purchase prices for some foods. If frozen shrimp costs suddenly plummet, the sales representative might suggest a menu change to take advantage of this price reduction.

7. *Uncontrollable acts.* If, for instance, the menu calls for fresh asparagus, and the hotel finds out that none will be available due to inclement weather conditions, the client will need to be contacted as soon as possible so that a suitable substitution can be determined. Likewise if an unforeseen circumstance requires you to move the event to another function room.

8. *Upgrades.* Clients may wish to upgrade their events after the initial booking has been made. A face-to-face meeting should be scheduled to handle the revisions.

Sometimes the hotel has a last-minute cancellation that could benefit a client. For instance, a bigger function room may be available at a discounted rate. The client should be contacted to see if he or she might be interested in pursuing this change.

9. *Conditions not met.* For example, a charity ball may require a business license. The hotel must receive notification that the license has been approved. If the notification is not forthcoming by the agreed-upon date, the catering executive will need to contact the client.

10. *Moving the function off-property.*   Unfortunately, this problem may arise through no fault of the hotel. For instance, a fire could preclude the hotel's ability to provide sleeping rooms to all convention attendees. Consequently, those who cannot be accommodated must be contacted and alternative arrangements made.

11. *Tastings and sample meals.*   If clients have special food and beverage requests, it is advisable to schedule a pre-event sample dinner. Production and service problems can be aired, discussed, and rectified. The menu can then be finalized.

Post-Event (Post-Function) Meetings

All clients should be contacted after the events so that the completed functions can be evaluated. These meetings give the hotel an opportunity to rectify any shortcomings. It also allows the catering executive to solicit referral business, repeat business, and testimonial letters.

Post-event meetings can be excellent learning experiences. To maximize the benefits generated by these meetings, it is recommended that clients be contacted personally. Telephone and questionnaire responses generally do not disclose as much information. For instance, the catering executive wants to see the client's facial expressions when he or she is commenting on the event. Many persons never disclose their unhappiness over the phone or on a survey response card, but body language is most revealing.

Statistics show that in the United States, the typical business never hears from over 95 percent of its dissatisfied customers. For every complaint registered, 25 go unreported. Furthermore, the guest who does not complain to the business will relate his or her unhappiness to a number of other persons.

Statistics also suggest that in the United States, about 10 percent of persons who buy an identical item will be unhappy with the purchase to some extent. You cannot expect this ten percent to speak up. Many of them vote with their feet, that is, they say nothing: they just never return. Face-to-face post-event meetings will help ensure that all complaints and compliments are mentioned.

Most caterers feel that, with enough prodding, the typical client will reveal the one little thing he or she did not like. Talking about it has a tendency to comfort clients and leave them with positive feelings about the hotel. They are more likely to do business with the hotel again, and will more than likely relate this positive encounter to other people. According to many industry experts, the unofficial rule of thumb is that one satisfied client generates nine potential clients.

We in the industry are too close to our businesses: we are unable to view them objectively. The wise catering executive will listen intently to his or her clients and use the information to improve future guest satisfaction. This type of client feedback is invaluable.

The catering department should construct an event evaluation form that can be used to guide the discussion during a post-event meeting. Typically you are interested in the client's satisfaction with the following key areas:

1. *Food and beverage.*   You should consider taste, textures, temperatures, presentations, and portion sizes.

2. *Service.*   Major considerations are speed, accuracy, and server courtesy.

3. *Decor.*   Was it appropriate for the event?

4. *Space.*   Some potential issues to ponder are: function-room size, layout and design, and display set-ups.

5. *Ancillary services.*   You should consider guest satisfaction with restrooms, cloak rooms, shuttle vans, and other relevant similar features.

6. *Outside contractors.*   The client should be queried about his or her satisfaction with outside service contractors. This is important if you maintain a list of recommended contractors that needs to be revised periodically.

7. *Last-minute requests.*   Clients should be asked if they were pleased with the hotel's handling of last-minute requests.

8. *Sleeping-room accommodations.*   If applicable, you might want to involve the hotel's rooms division manager to sit in on your post-event meetings.

9. *Timing of the event.*   Would the client do anything differently? Would he or she alter the starting time? Ending time? If so, why?

10. *General satisfaction.*   An overall satisfaction rating should be solicited from the client. An excellent way to gauge this feeling is to ask the client if he or she would recommend the hotel and the hotel catering department to a friend. If the answer is yes, it would be appropriate to solicit a testimonial letter and business referrals.

If personal post-event meetings with clients are infeasible, the hotel should use the outline noted above to construct a questionnaire, copies of which could be sent to a random sample of guests who attended the catered event as well as to the client. The results of these questionnaires should then be sent to the director of catering and/or the food and beverage director and used where necessary to revise operating procedures.

One of the benefits questionnaires have over personal interviews is that you can send them to several guests as well as to clients. They are an efficient data-gathering technique. Furthermore, the questionnaires could include a section where respondents can list potential catering clients, thereby expanding the pool of potential catering business.

Thank-You Letters

A formal thank-you letter should be sent after the post-event meeting. It should include the normal expressions of appreciation and thanks. In addition, it should be personalized and address specific concerns raised at the post-event meeting.

It would be appropriate to include a small gift with the thank-you letter unless you know the client cannot accept it. For instance, government meeting planners cannot accept gifts. If they receive one, they must send it back. You should learn about these types of restrictions in advance in order to avoid a potentially embarrassing situation.

Token gifts are a bit more common in the international market than they are in the United States. However, if handled correctly, they are sure to generate warm responses from your customers.

Many caterers usually send a "signature" gift to each client. Typical signature gifts are paper weights, calendars, and note books. These gifts usually are adorned with the hotel's logo.

A complimentary meal at one of the hotel's restaurant outlets is another popular gift. Like the signature gift, a free dinner or two at one of the hotel's restaurants is big enough to be meaningful, yet small enough to avoid any conflicts of interest.

One form of noncontroversial gift giving is the customer-appreciation party. These usually are theme parties, with "Christmas in July," "Octoberfest," "Monte Carlo Night," and "Las Vegas Night" being the most popular themes. For instance, a hotel in Atlanta managed by a person of German ancestry always hosts an Octoberfest party each year for current and potential clients.

Oftentimes customer-appreciation parties are used to solicit future business. For example, a Christmas-in-July party is an excellent opportunity for a hotel to display its collection of holiday decorations and holiday foods. This can encourage current and potential clients to consider booking Christmas party business early instead of waiting until the last minute. Moreover, these clients may provide referral business opportunities.

PROBLEM RESOLUTION

Into each life some rain must fall. The catering executive must see to it that the occasional drizzle does not turn into an uncontrollable thunderstorm.

While it is not a good idea to harbor negative thoughts, the sad fact remains that you will sometimes encounter problems with an event. There is no way to avoid it because some clients will almost guarantee that they, and the hotel, will get wet.

Some clients cannot resist the temptation to tell the catering staff what to do. These persons would never consider directing the automobile manufacturer. But since they are there when the catering product is produced and served, some of them like to tell you how to do everything. Or worse yet, they want to change things at the last minute.

Excessive Worrying

Experience shows that the major problem encountered by catering executives is the worry-wart client. Many clients cannot help second guessing everything. This is understandable because many clients have never hosted a major function. So, they worry, fidget, and foresee all sorts of disasters.

The catering executive must prevent these clients from worrying too much. To do this, he or she must work very hard to gain their confidence. The catering staff must convince clients that their events will go smoothly and that guests will be very happy.

The best way to gain a client's confidence is to dissipate the typical customer's major fear, which is: will the event start and end on schedule? Many catered functions include nonfood and nonbeverage activities. For instance, a breakfast absolutely must end on time so that attendees can board the tour busses on schedule; the dessert course must be cleared before 9:00 PM or the program speaker may be reluctant to begin; or the luncheon meal must be timed accurately around the guest speaker's remarks or else the speech will be poorly received.

Some clients are born to worry. They are a major challenge. If the challenge is met though, these satisfied clients will most likely become some of the hotel's most loyal customers.

Typical Problems

Inevitably, the catering executive and client will encounter some rough spots along the way. The problems that tend to crop up most often are:

- *No shows.* Clients want to wait forever if there are any late guests. Keeping a plate "warm" for late-arriving guests is so common for some types of events that it is no longer correct to refer to this as a problem; in many cases, it is standard operating procedure.

- *Unanticipated increase in number of attendees.* Even though you have set guarantees and are prepared to accommodate a few extra guests, every so often you and the client will be overwhelmed with more people than you can handle comfortably. For instance, wedding guests who failed to RSVP may decide at the last minute to show up. You will encounter a similar problem with conventions that allow attendees to purchase separate meal tickets at the last minute instead of buying convention booklets that contain tickets for all events.

- *Lost and found.* The housekeeping department generally handles lost and found articles. However, the catering executive will certainly hear from the client whose guests have suffered a loss.

- *Tentative clients.* Some clients want to put off confirmations and guarantees until the very last moment. This causes a few headaches for the kitchen and catering staffs. Sometimes you have to force clients to make a decision.

- *Underperforming outside contractors.* While it is true that clients must make their own arrangements with outside contractors, the catering executive realizes that he or she may be drawn into any difficulty that arises between them. For instance, if an outside contractor is not paid, the hotel may be asked to mediate the dispute and play the peacemaker role.

  In a similar vein, the catering executive may run into difficulty working with outside contractors and coordinating their work. You do not want clients to use contractors you know cannot be trusted to do a good job. However, you need to be careful not to give the impression that you are steering clients to a few favored outside contractors.

- *Invoice disputes.* Occasionally billing problems will crop up. The catering executive will need to reconcile any differences of opinion that arise between the client and the hotel credit department.

- *Fights and other disruptions.* There is always the slim possibility that a medical emergency will occur. A fire could break out. Or one or more guests may create a disturbance. If these troubles interfere with the success of the catered event, the catering executive may need to make some adjustments in the client's final billing.

  While the hotel normally is not liable if two guests try to harm each other, it should have a professional security department standing ready to handle these problems and keep them under control so that innocent bystanders are not injured.

- *Outside construction.* Some clients do not like to see signs that say, "pardon our dust." More importantly, they do not want to experience construction noise pollution that negatively affects an event's success. If these types of situations arise, the catering executive will need to make some concessions in order to satisfy clients and their guests.

- *Interference from other catered events.* At times you might encounter a situation where two catered events overlap to the extent that they bump into one another, causing temporary inconveniences. Likewise, one catered event could generate considerable noise pollution that spills over to another occupied function room. Proper planning and scheduling of events should minimize this problem.

- *Outside demonstrations.* It is possible that a catered function will generate some sort of political discomfort. For instance, a furrier convention may attract animal-rights groups that might organize a mass protest outside the hotel. Once again, the hotel's licensed security department must be briefed so that it can plan its efforts accordingly.

- *Last-minute changes.* At times, the hotel may encounter a problem at the last minute that precludes it from honoring exactly its contract with a client. For example, a fire at the meat supplier's warehouse may cause a last-minute menu change. Clients understandably will not take kindly to these occurrences. These types of problems will test the catering executive's patience, skill, and negotiating abilities.

- *Moving the client off-property.* Or alternatively, asking the client to switch from a confirmed date to another open date. This is a drastic situation and should only be considered if there is no other alternative. In other words, we do not subscribe to the theory that it is acceptable to dump a client if another more profitable event can be booked in that time slot. If there is a legitimate reason to move the client, such as fire damage, then naturally it cannot be avoided. Also, changes are permissible if clients agree and are given some financial inducements to alter their plans.

- *Timing difficulties.* The catering executive is not unlike the movie director. He or she must see to it that all event activities take place as scheduled. A successful event must have more than adequate food, beverage, and service. It also must follow a programmed timetable.

  In some cases, a client actually may overlook some shortcomings in, say, one of the food courses, but he or she will not forgive, say, the breakfast that did not end on time. The rest of the day's events are dependent on this meal ending as scheduled; the catering and kitchen staffs absolutely must honor the meal's production and service schedules.

Handling Customer Complaints

One of the best ways to reduce client and guest dissatisfaction is to anticipate potential difficulties and allow for their occurrence when planning the catered events. For instance, many of the typical problems noted above may be reduced or eliminated by setting forth clear, precise instructions in the catering contract. Unhappily though, it is infeasible to wave a contract in front of a dissatisfied person; in some cases, this may backfire and cause additional grief.

According to the results of a recent survey reported in the *Cornell H.R.A. Quarterly,* the ten most common customer complaints heard by hotels are: (1) price of rooms, meals, and other services; (2) speed of service; (3) quality of service; (4) availability of parking; (5) employee knowledge and service; (6) quietness of surroundings; (7) availability of accommodations requested; (8) checkout time; (9) cleanliness of establishment; and (10) adequacy of credit.

This study also revealed that the ten most frequent customer complaints received by restaurants are: (1) availability of parking; (2) traffic congestion in establishment; (3) quality of service; (4) price of drinks, meals, and other services; (5) noise level; (6) helpful attitude of employees; (7) food quality and method of preparation; (8) spaciousness of establishment; (9) hours of operation; and (10) quantity of service.

The catering department will most likely encounter a combination of these types of customer complaints since it bridges the hotel's sleeping rooms and food and beverage departments. For instance, a mixture of the most frequently encountered hotel customer complaint (price) and the fifth most common restaurant customer complaint (noise) can cause strained relations between clients and the catering executive even though catering has little control over these events.

Handling customer complaints is a very sensitive undertaking. Ellsworth Statler once suggested that, "the customer is always right." Since we are in the service business, we must adopt this attitude. At the very least, while we may not agree that the customer is always right, we must recognize that he or she pays for satisfaction.

Catering professional Catherine Campani Messmer notes that an irritated guest who is handled correctly can become one of the hotel's most loyal patrons. Adroit handling can lead to increased referral business. Statistics show that the customer whose complaint is resolved satisfactorily will discuss this positive experience with about five different persons.

Ms. Messmer suggests that the catering executive follow a select few rules of thumb when working with the dissatisfied client. These are:

1. The most important thing to do is listen to the client. Most disgruntled guests need a way to unload. This catharsis will usually soothe a few ruffled feathers. The idea is to let the client get rid of his or her anger by running out of things to say. Once this happens, you can gain his or her attention and then move on to resolving the situation.

2. When listening to irate guests, try to determine if they are angry or hostile. The hostile guest will want you to suffer. He or she will want to heap abuse on the catering staff. On the other hand, the angry guest is not interested in making everyone else suffer. He or she wants to resolve the problem.

Normally you must listen longer to hostile guests. They need more time to calm down before they and the catering executive can draft possible solutions. Sometimes they merely want to yell and scream and feel superior. If so, the best way to get them back on track is to mention their names; for instance, you might respond by telling the guest that, "perhaps, Mr. Client, this is not a good time to discuss this. I can come back later."

Angry guests usually are interested in moving quickly to the problem-solving stage and are not eager to prolong unpleasant situations. They want to work immediately toward one goal, and that is: solve the problem and move on.

3. When listening to guests complain, do not tell them to calm down. This will backfire and make guests angrier.

4. When a guest is complaining, the listener must remain calm. However, you should not respond with an overly calm, reassuring, gentle voice. This will make you appear condescending, patronizing, and aloof, traits that are sure to aggravate the already-upset client. It is best to let the guest work through the frustration while encouraging him or her to move as quickly as possible to the problem-solving stage.

5. While you must agree with the guest that there is a problem and that it needs to be rectified, do not dwell on the negative. Try to move as quickly as possible to outlining mutually agreeable solutions.

6. While you should express regret, do not offer a long-winded apology. Avoid excessive, overly sorrowful dialogue.

7. When you have the client's attention, it is time to discuss possible solutions.

8. Any alternative solutions should include the one or two that, hopefully, the disgruntled guest suggested when he or she was letting off steam.

9. When settling on a solution, make sure to note a definite plan of action. Do not say merely that you "will take care of it." Tell the client exactly what will be done, and when. The client is more likely to be satisfied if you make a definite commitment.

10. Do not let company rules and regulations inhibit problem resolution. The catering staff member who is handling a disgruntled client must have the power to do whatever is legal and moral to satisfy the guest. One of the worst things you can do is tell the guest that you have to follow the "rules."

11. Do not promise anything you cannot do. This will exacerbate an already difficult situation.

12. Thank the client for bringing the problem to your attention.

13. Follow up. Call or drop a note or letter to the client. Again, thank him or her for telling you about the problem and giving you a chance to take care of it.

14. Above all, be polite. Courtesy is doubly important when dealing with irate customers.

PROTOCOLS

In addition to being polite, catering-staff members also must be professional at all times. The professional, competent catering executive empathizes with clients and treats them as he or she would want to be treated. For instance, it is unprofessional to: ask a customer's name five times; shuffle clients from one department to another; make a potential client repeat what he or she wants to umpteen unseen employees while being transferred around the property by the telephone operator; have unknowledgeable employees answering client telephone inquiries; make it difficult for a client to contact the catering staff when questions and/or problems arise that must be handled.

Telephone Courtesy

A good deal of catering business is transacted over the phone. Most of the time, a potential client's first impression of the hotel is the one formed during the initial telephone inquiry. If you have the lowest paid, least experienced person answering the phone, a good deal of business and/or goodwill can be lost.

Persons handling telephone inquiries must be trained. They must be able to answer pertinent questions, or know immediately who can. The catering executive must either train the catering receptionists or else assign managers to take incoming calls.

The phone also must be answered before it rings off the hook. A good rule of thumb is to insist that the phone be answered before the second or third ring.

Do not put clients on hold unless it is absolutely necessary. Persons on hold tend to become restless and may hang up. And all too often, this results in a client being cut off and having to call back. In some cases, he or she may decide to call a competitor instead.

If you must put clients on hold, do it as pleasantly as possible. Ask them if they will please hold, and give them a chance to say something. If you merely say hurriedly to "please hold," and then cut off the caller, he or she may interpret this as a lack of respect and courtesy.

When you answer the phone, state your name first. For instance, say that, "this is John Doe, how may I help you?" You also should thank people up front for calling instead of waiting until the conversation ends.

When a caller asks to speak to another person, usually the receptionist will respond, "may I say who is calling, please?" If catering staff members are trained to follow this procedure, they must be very careful how they recite the phrase to callers. Sometimes when this is said, a caller may get the impression that he or she is being slighted. This can easily occur if the call comes in at the end of a hectic day. While it may be very courteous to avoid screening calls, it may be impossible in a busy office where time is precious and selectivity is needed.

When no one is available to answer the phone, a recorder can be used to take incoming messages. Or a recorded message can relay to potential clients the hotel's fax number, a catering sales representative's cellular phone number, and/or other methods by which the catering staff can be contacted.

Whenever a catering-staff member receives a message or an inquiry, he or she should call back as soon as possible. This is true even if a potential client made the initial inquiry by letter. A customer who is kept waiting may find a more attentive reception at a competitor's property.

When returning calls or cold calling, the professional catering executive also follows proper telephone etiquette. For instance, when making a sales call, it is appropriate to begin by saying, "Ms. Jones, is this a good time to talk?"

When you need to leave a message, or if customers will need to return your call, make them feel special. For example, give them your direct or private phone number. And inform them that they will not have to go through the hotel switchboard. Alternatively, you can give them your private cellular line, or telephone paging number.

Personal Contact

When interacting personally with people, there is always the slight possibility of offending them unknowingly. In international business, for example, protocol is extremely important. In some countries, a limp handshake is preferable to a firm one, direct eye contact is considered rude and disrespectful, and back slapping is taboo.

Generally speaking, catering-staff members understand the standard protocols that must be followed in the United States. The international client though, is another story.

The most universally recognized personal gesture is the smile. It is never misunderstood. All cultures appreciate it and will respond positively. Catering-staff members though, cannot rely strictly on the smile to shepherd them through the many personal customer contacts that are unavoidable in the catering industry.

Private Protocol, a company specializing in dealing with the international client, suggests that the following list of topics should be considered when planning an event with or for guests from foreign cultures.

1. Food restrictions (for religious or cultural reasons)
2. Toasting etiquette
3. Traditions regarding gift giving/receiving
4. Conversational suggestions/topics to avoid
5. Attitude and traditions toward women
6. Holidays (religious and national)/current events
7. Gestures
8. Dress
9. Color and floral restrictions/preferences
10. Flag etiquette
11. Smoking.

Dr. Sondra Thiederman advises meeting planners and catering executives to adhere to the following rules when dealing with the foreign client.

1. *Shaking hands.*   Arabs, Hispanics, and Greeks tend to shake hands several times during a meeting. The French will shake hands very lightly and quickly; they also will not shake hands with a superior. Germans tend to shake hands with everyone upon arrival and departure. And, generally speaking, you should offer your hand to women only after offering it to the men and elders in the group.

2. *Distance.*   Most Americans will stand about $1\frac{1}{2}$ to 3 feet away from each other when conversing. Hispanics and most Middle Eastern nationalities like to stand close together, while Asians and Africans prefer standing farther apart. Many foreigners tend to stand far apart when conversing with members of the opposite sex.

3. *Language barriers.*   Many foreigners can understand English if you speak slowly and coherently. However, they are usually able to read and understand English much better than when they must simultaneously listen and understand. Body language, such as nervous smiling, indicates that the client does not quite understand the conversation, but is afraid to say so.

4. *Touching.*   Generally speaking, avoid touching any client. Most international guests will be uncomfortable with this type of familiarity. In some cases it can be insulting. For instance, Moslems

consider the left hand to be dirty and will be upset if they are touched with it.

5. *Eye contact.*   Hispanics, Middle Easterners, and Europeans prefer direct eye contact. Asians, especially the Japanese, consider it rude and offensive.

In his book, *Do's and Taboos Around the World,* Axtell cautions us that certain gestures we take for granted in the United States can be very offensive, rude, or meaningless in the international market. Some particularly troublesome gestures are:

1. *Finger pointing.*   This is insulting to Middle Easterners and Far Easterners. The open hand is preferred.

2. *Thumbs-up sign.*   Considered rude in Australia.

3. *Crossing legs.*   Arabs abhor the sight of shoe soles. Feet must be kept flat on the ground.

4. *The OK sign.*   Making this sign with the thumb and forefinger in Latin countries is comparable to extending the middle finger in the U.S. In Japan it indicates "money." In France, it means "worthless."

5. *Business cards.*   Do not use abbreviations. The back side of your card should have the other side's information printed in the foreign language. Titles are impressive. Never present your card with the left hand. In Japan, present it with both hands.

6. *Social chit chat.*   This usually precedes a business meeting. Japanese customers especially like to have tea and get better acquainted before they discuss business.

7. *Slang.*   Do not refer to the international customer as a "foreigner" or "alien." Also, do not use disparaging language when referring to the country.

8. *Hugging.*   This is common in Latin American and Slavic cultures: men hug men, women hug women. It is a form of greeting, similar to the hand shake. However, you must be very certain that this gesture is appropriate in a particular situation before engaging in it; if there is any doubt, it should not be done.

MAKING THE TRANSITION FROM SALES TO SERVICE

Historically, prior to the explosion of the meetings and conventions market and the subsequent development of mega-hotels, hotel sales executives were responsible for selling to and servicing the clients. It is still this way in smaller hotel properties where the size of the market does not warrant a division of labor.

Smaller hotel properties tend to employ combination catering sales and service representatives. While this type of organizational structure may spread catering employees too thin, clients may feel more comfortable with this arrangement. They may appreciate the opportunity of working with one person while enjoying the pleasures of "one-stop" shopping.

With the advent of the larger properties, the catering departments began employing sales specialists and service specialists. The salesperson concentrates on sales, while the service representative concentrates exclusively on servicing the group after the sales manager finalizes the contract.

In a mega-hotel, eventually clients booked by sales are turned over to a service coordinator. The coordinator works in the catering department or in a department usually referred to as convention service. All aspects of the event—from implementation to completion and billing—are supervised by this person. He or she also is the client's major contact.

When, for example, a convention is booked ten years in advance, the sales manager will not turn over the booking to convention service and/or catering until it is definite. A definite booking is usually turned over to convention service and/or catering about twelve to eighteen months before the group is scheduled to arrive. The manager then tentatively allocates function-room space and makes initial contact with the client.

The 12- to 18-month period may seem excessive, but in reality it is a very short time frame. It can take weeks or months for a large convention to solidify its plans and activities. This is especially true if several persons located throughout the country or the world need to approve changes and/or additions to the tentative convention program. For instance, if specific meeting rooms were not determined when the business was booked, this must be arranged so that the meeting program can be developed. Themes, menus, and decor need to be discussed and confirmed. And information on VIP needs, outside contractors, and guest count must be obtained from the client.

Large hotel companies feel that people who are good at sales should have the freedom to sell. They should not be tied down to the property in order to service groups. Also, an excellent salesperson may be only marginally effective when trying to service groups. Furthermore, the dawn to midnight work schedule needed to both sell and service quickly leads to burnout and employee turnover.

As discussed in Chapter 1, the role of catering and convention service varies among hotel companies. For example, in some properties, such as the Flamingo Hilton in Las Vegas, there is no convention-service department. Since there is very little local catering business handled by the hotel, sales and catering can handle all logistics for each function.

In other properties though, such as the Westin Peachtree Plaza in Atlanta, sales handles the selling function, convention service handles food and beverage functions for groups that use 20 sleeping rooms or more, and the catering department services the local/ social functions as well as any group that books less than 20 sleeping rooms. This organizational structure is more appropriate for this property because it handles a considerable amount of local catering business.

Another type of organizational structure exists at the Atlanta Marriott Marquis, where sales takes care of the selling effort, the catering department handles all food and beverage functions, and convention service handles all non-food and non-beverage logistics, such as meeting-room setup and tear down.

No matter how the sales and service functions are organized, one thing is very clear: it is the responsibility of the catering and/or convention-service department to provide excellent service, create a worry-free environment for the client, and satisfy the guests. If these objectives are accomplished, catering sales representatives can look forward to repeat patronage and referral business.

5

Working with Other Hotel Departments

Communication with your support departments is critical to maintaining an efficient operation—only then can you provide superior service to your guests.

Daniel H. Dodson
Banquet Manager
Scottsdale Princess Hotel
Scottsdale, AZ

The hotel catering department does not operate in a vacuum. While it often is the only one visible to the client, it depends on many other hotel departments for its success.

The catering department cannot perform *all* of the necessary tasks; it must have the cooperation of other hotel departments. One could think of the catering department as the orchestra leader. It assembles the players, develops the music, and supervises the performance. A successful catering event, like a pleasing musical performance, comes about when all participants play their roles well.

The purpose of this chapter is to note the other hotel departments that contribute to the catering department's success and to discuss the major relationships that exist between them and the catering staff.

KITCHEN

It is extremely important to have a good working relationship with the chef and his or her staff. These food experts are perhaps the most important players in the catering orchestra. At times, they will be your salvation.

The chef must know as soon as possible the menu, the number of guests, the timing, and all other relevant aspects of booked functions. He or she must be sure that the proper amount and type of foods are ordered, production is scheduled properly, and an adequate and appropriate workforce is retained for each event.

The chef also must be privy to any and all budgetary constraints. He or she has the last word in costing the menu. If, for example, the catering sales representative is preparing a competitive bid for a corporate meeting planner, the chef's food cost estimates must be obtained.

The chef can work with you in combating budgetary constraints, planning heart-healthy meals, outlining theme parties, and developing other pertinent customer-pleasing suggestions. He or she usually knows what will be in season, menu trends, typical customer likes and dislikes, cost trends, quality trends, and product availability. Chefs usually love the opportunity to contribute. Many of them enjoy being creative.

In most hotels, the catering staff participates with the chef in developing standardized catering menus. Usually the food and beverage director and purchasing agent are also part of the menu-planning team. The menus prepared by this group become one of the catering sales representative's major tools in his or her sales kit.

It is essential to check with the chef before committing to any off-the-menu selections. Many clients want something special and disdain the standardized menus. While you may want to accommodate them, you cannot do so without checking with the chef or the sous chef in charge of banquet functions.

Some off-the-menu selections may be infeasible because they cannot be prepared in bulk. For instance, usually it is futile to ask the chef to prepare individual chocolate souffles for 1,000 guests, club sandwiches for 750, or Maine lobsters for a group of 500. These food items usually are impossible to produce correctly for large groups.

Some menu items also may be impossible to produce and serve because the hotel does not own the necessary equipment. For instance, is there enough broiler and oven space to prepare 2,000 New York steak dinners? Are there enough slow-cook ovens to cook and hold roast sirloin for 1,500 guests? Can the kitchen prepare country-fried potatoes for 1,000 guests with the available griddle and steam-table space?

A menu item may not be feasible because the hotel does not have the appropriate labor to do the work. There may be an insufficient supply of labor or there may be a lack of labor skills needed to prepare a specific recipe. For instance, is there enough quantity and quality of labor to produce an ice carving, a five-tiered wedding cake, or fancy carved vegetable garnishes?

According to John Steinmetz, to have the best possible working relationship with the chef, you should adhere to the following rules:

1. Consult with the chef *before* promising a special menu or any changes to a standardized menu.
2. Make certain that the chef receives the menus well in advance of the events (at least ten days in advance).
3. Ensure that the chef receives timely updates of guarantee changes, special needs, and other major alterations. Do not wait until the last minute.
4. Do not spring any surprises on the chef.
5. Do not make it difficult, or impossible, for the chef to achieve his or her budgeted food, payroll, and other operating costs.

BEVERAGE

Large hotels employ a beverage manager who reports to the food and beverage director. His or her job description is similar to the chef's in that they both administer departments that produce finished menu products and serve them to guests.

The beverage manager usually oversees the hotel's main bars, service bars, special events bars (such as banquet bars), room-service beverage deliveries, hospitality-suite bars, and individual-access bars (for example, locked bar cabinets located in each sleeping room).

Catering typically works with the beverage manager when developing beverage functions, planning beverage menus, and evaluating product and service options. The beverage manager may also help catering managers schedule the appropriate number of bartenders, bar backs, cocktail servers, and buspersons.

PURCHASING

Most large hotels employ a full-time purchasing agent. His or her primary responsibilities are to prepare product specifications for all foods, beverages, and supplies, select appropriate suppliers, maintain adequate inventories, obtain the best possible purchase values, and ensure that product quality meets the hotel's standards.

The purchasing agent normally works very closely with the kitchen and beverage departments. He or she needs to be apprised of all catering events booked by the hotel in order to purchase the necessary stock.

On a day-to-day basis, the purchasing agent orders sufficient merchandise to satisfy the hotel's normal business needs. Catering though, is additional business and must be handled separately. For instance, if there is a party scheduled requiring 2,500 chicken breasts, the purchasing agent must order enough to satisfy the hotel restaurant outlets' chicken-breast needs as well as the additional 2,500 needed for the party.

Standard catering menu items are usually readily available from local purveyors. In fact, a menu item may be standardized primarily because it is easy to obtain. If a catering sales representative is negotiating for off-the-menu item selections though, the purchasing agent should be consulted to see if the products are available, what they cost, and how long it will take to deliver them to the hotel.

If the catering executive is considering a menu revision, he or she will also need to check with the purchasing agent to see if the planned changes are feasible. Cost and availability trends must be evaluated very carefully in order to avoid menu-planning mistakes.

RECEIVING AND STOREROOM

All but the smallest hotel properties have a central warehouse storeroom (sometimes referred to as the commissary) where all food, beverage, and supplies are kept under lock and key. Only authorized persons are allowed to enter the storage areas and/or obtain products from the storeroom manager.

Storeroom personnel work closely with the receiving department. In some hotels, both functions are housed in one department. Receiving agents check in deliveries and storeroom clerks help them move shipments from the receiving dock to the warehouse. The merchandise remains in the storeroom areas until hotel department heads requisition them.

In order to obtain these products, a department head must fill out a stock requisition form and hand it to a storeroom clerk. These requisitions establish the fact that the department head is now responsible for these items.

Once the requisition is processed, the department head can pick up the products or, alternatively, have them delivered by a storeroom attendant.

Most of the products needed to service a catered event are requisitioned by production and service departments that are handling the booked event. For instance, the kitchen will requisition food and the beverage department will requisition beverage. The catering staff though, also will need to requisition other things such as paper products, decorations, and office supplies.

HOUSEKEEPING

The hotel's housekeeping department's primary responsibilities are to clean sleeping rooms, function rooms, and all public areas. It also works with maintenance to ensure that the property is kept in good repair.

In some hotels, housekeeping is responsible for selecting replacement carpeting, upholstery, and fabrics. If you are involved with these decisions, be sure to avoid light colors and materials that do not have a pattern. Stains and spills show up quickly on light-colored materials. Cigarette burns are quite obvious in unpatterned carpets. Incidentally, repeating patterns on carpeting are excellent guides for setting out tables and chairs symmetrically.

The housekeeping department, especially the linen room, is the source of table linen, employee uniforms and costumes, laundry and dry cleaning, and valet services. The catering staff must see to it that the linen room manager has sufficient lead time to ensure that all necessary supplies are available.

In many hotels, housekeeping is responsible for precleaning function rooms and other public areas as outlined in the catering department's instructions or in the convention service department's directives. Housekeeping also is involved with cleaning up after functions. Housekeeping must be apprised of special functions well in advance so that the necessary work can be scheduled and carried out properly.

Function rooms must be cleaned in plenty of time to avoid any embarrassing situations. For example, you do not want last-minute furniture moving going on as guests are arriving.

Function rooms need to be torn down and cleaned immediately after guests depart. If you wait too long to do this, stains have time to set in upholstery or carpets and vermin will be attracted to the debris. Immediately after the catering or convention-service staff strip the tables, housekeeping should come in and clean the walls, carpets, and furniture. Any items needing repair should be reported to the maintenance department.

Lobbies around function rooms (sometimes referred to as pre-function space if receptions are held there before the main event) require continuous attention from housekeeping. Attendees will leave soiled ash trays, cups, newspapers, and so forth lying about and these should be removed as quickly and unobtrusively as possible. Routine dusting, polishing, trash removal, and vacuuming should be done when guests are not present.

Public restrooms are in need of constant attention. Most people lose respect for management if a dirty restroom is encountered. At the very minimum, restrooms must be cleaned thoroughly twice a day. They must be checked constantly for quick clean ups and restocking of tissue, seat covers, towels, and toiletries. Attendants also need to check periodically for equipment failure and, if found, must report the problem to the maintenance department.

To reduce confusion and increase efficiency, some hotels assign several, or perhaps all, function-room housekeeping chores to the convention-service department. This is particularly true for mega-hotels.

Some hotels use an outside contract cleaning service to handle certain housekeeping tasks. For instance, if you do not have the proper equipment and/or employee talent, you may not want to try cleaning large chandeliers, outside windows, or copper facades.

CONVENTION SERVICE

Some hotels have a convention-service department to handle banquet setup and banquet service. The banquet-setup division is responsible primarily for setting up function rooms, tearing them down, and putting away the furniture and equipment.

Banquet setup works closely with banquet-service. The banquet-service division is responsible primarily for providing meal service. It may also be responsible for providing beverage service.

In lieu of a convention-service department, banquet-setup and banquet-service activities may be performed by the catering staff, or by the catering staff in cooperation with other departments. For instance, catering may share this work with the kitchen and housekeeping staffs.

Usually smaller hotels do not have separate convention-service departments. Their small size usually requires them to allocate the necessary duties to other hotel departments.

Convention-service activities can be housed in various departments and can also have many names. Banquet setup, banquet service, and convention porters or housemen are just a few of the titles used to describe these important jobs.

Convention service is the backbone of the catering and convention departments. Function-room setup and tear down, room maintenance and cleaning, transporting furniture and equipment throughout the function-room areas, and other related duties must be performed quickly and efficiently. All catered functions depend on the swift completion of these critical activities.

The major activity of convention service is function-room setup. This involves many aspects, the most critical of which is the need for all furniture and equipment to be in place by a certain time. Foremost in function-room setup is receiving the proper information from the catering/convention coordinator. He or she must have a good working knowledge of the type, amount, and capabilities of the furniture, equipment, staff, and facilities so that clients can be advised correctly when they are planning their events.

Function-room setup begins with information obtained from the client. This information must be complete and conform to the hotel property's physical constraints. Table sizes, exhibit booths, registration needs, and so forth require physical setups. Someone has to obtain the proper furniture and equipment, transport it to the correct location, and install it properly. Before this can be done, convention-service employees must know and understand the client's needs.

There are usually three types of banquet-setup employees. The first is the regular or full-time employee. This employee is scheduled for a full work week or is the first person called when a function room must be set up.

The second type of employee is the steady extra. This person is on call, but is considered a permanent employee. Although this type of employee does not receive full employee benefits, he or she usually receives prorated benefits based on the number of hours worked. The primary advantages steady-extra employees provide to the employer is that the hotel can use them only when they are needed, but when they are called to work, they are as productive as full-time employees because they are familiar with the job, property, furniture, and equipment.

The third type of employee is the one-time recruit hired temporarily to help set up an unusually large function, or to assist regular employees temporarily overburdened with large and/or several back-to-back catered functions that require quick turnarounds. These types of employees usually receive limited training and are not employed long enough to become familiar with your property. Consequently, they are used primarily to move furniture and equipment and perform other manual labor.

Convention service requires an adequate storage facility to house all necessary furniture and equipment. Storage of these items though, involves more than just the housing of tables, chairs, portable dance floors, risers, meeting equipment, and convention materials when not in use. The storage area must be large enough as well as convenient to the function rooms to facilitate the constant movement of furniture and equipment in and out of the function rooms. Unfortunately, adequate storage in the convention-service department is sometimes overlooked in hotel design and construction. This can cause continual problems and frustration.

A proper storage area allows you to store all furniture and equipment as well as transport equipment needed to move these items. For instance, you need enough room to store table and chair carts, which are used to transport several tables and chairs at one time, thereby allowing quick and efficient movement to and from function rooms.

The storage area should be large enough to house and organize an inventory of spare parts. For instance, if a houseman loses a piece of portable dance-floor trim and cannot find another one in storage, you increase the risk of someone tripping on an improperly installed dance floor. If you lose one section of a portable dance floor, it decreases the size of the floor and increases the risk of guest dissatisfaction. Adequate storage space and proper storage procedures can prevent problems associated with missing, lost, or stolen pieces.

The storage area also must allow you to store furniture and equipment as close as possible to the function rooms. For instance, a portable dance floor should be stored near the function rooms because it is too heavy to transport easily.

Dance floor movement is a major concern. Heavy duty carts are typically used to transport the 3 feet by 3 feet squares of wood and metal. Each full cart can weigh over 500 pounds. Damage can be done to walls, doors, and employees by improper movement and handling. The probability of damage increases if this heavy load must be transported a great distance.

If applicable, the storage area must be able to accommodate meeting equipment such as blackboards, easels, podiums, water pitchers, glasses, ashtrays, pads, and pencils. It also may need to house audiovisual (AV) and lighting equipment. In some hotels, some or all of this equipment is stored in other departments. Convenience, though, quickly overrides departmental lines and convention service typically finds it necessary to store many items that were originally intended to be stored elsewhere in the hotel.

The storage area also must be able to accommodate the temporary storage and movement of clients' convention materials. Some clients send convention materials, such as registration packets, machinery, and sample products, to the hotel via independent carrier services. These materials are extremely important to clients and their attendees. A lost or misplaced package can be devastating to a meeting planner.

Convention service is responsible for the safe delivery of convention materials to the function rooms. Although receiving convention materials may be the responsibility of other departments, such as the receiving or storeroom departments, convention service accepts responsibility when taking the goods out of the warehouse.

Generally speaking, hotel receiving and storeroom departments do not want to store convention materials. The primary reason is that their facilities are not designed to hold the varying types and amounts of materials that arrive for different groups. Due to the nature of the receiving activity though, it is logical that these departments be the ones to maintain an accurate accounting of all packages sent to the hotel.

All delivered convention materials must be signed-in, counted, and inspected for damage at the point of transfer from the independent freight company. Hotels assume a liability in the form of a bailment when they take possession of items they do not own so it behooves them to ensure that all shipments meet client standards.

It is important to maintain clear records of all client shipments. Clients must ensure that their instructions are communicated to the hotel. This is very important because often receiving clerks are not allowed to accept a client's shipment unless they know in advance when it will be delivered and what inspection procedures they must follow. If clerks refuse to accept shipments, they can create tremendous difficulties for the unsuspecting clients.

A clear audit trail must exist in order to track any client property delivered to the hotel. The hotel that denies receiving a client's shipment loses that client's respect when the independent carrier service can show a copy of the packing slip signed by a hotel employee who received and took possession of the shipment. Liability exposure increases if the convention materials are misplaced internally and this misplacement causes the client embarrassment and/or monetary losses. A hotel risks losing future business if clients suspect it will mishandle their convention materials.

Housemen or convention porters must sign for convention materials when they obtain them from the receiving or storeroom department. The materials must then be taken directly to the appropriate function-room areas.

A secure and central location must be provided in the function-room areas to store convention materials. Employees must then ensure that the materials are delivered to the appropriate person at the right time and place. Additionally, they must have the client, or client representative, sign for the delivery so that the hotel is relieved of the responsibility for lost materials.

When the function is completed, convention service usually is involved with shipping unused convention materials back to the client's home or place of business. When shipping materials, the hotel must be apprised of the client's shipping and payment instructions. Nothing can be shipped without this information.

Usually the hotel will comply with the client's shipping and payment instructions, with the exception of cash-on-delivery (COD) shipments. Most hotels do not want to ship anything COD. If a COD shipment is refused by the addressee for any reason, it will be returned to the hotel and the hotel will be billed by the independent carrier service for the shipping costs. It may then be very difficult, or impossible, for the hotel to secure reimbursement from the client.

Banquet setup and banquet service are two of the most visible activities—all of the work is witnessed first hand by the clients and their guests. These departments are responsible for the staffing, service, and successful completion of each catered event. They are usually only second to the kitchen and beverage departments in terms of their ability to influence client and guest satisfaction.

MAINTENANCE

The maintenance department is in charge of all property maintenance and repairs. Its employees perform routine maintenance, such as calibrating oven thermostats, oiling motors, and changing filters. They also are responsible for repairs, such as fixing broken water pipes, changing burnt-out light bulbs, and reconditioning worn equipment.

If the catering department has a repair need, normally it must fill out a repair requisition and send it to the maintenance department supervisor. The supervisor then prioritizes these requisitions and prepares work orders for maintenance employees. The employees work their way through the prioritized stack of work orders. If you are under a time constraint and need work done quickly, you will need to note URGENT! on your requisition. This will move you up on the priority list, but the hotel may have a policy of charging a department's budget a little extra for express service since usually it will disrupt the normal work schedule and could require some employees to work overtime.

ENGINEERING

The hotel engineer generally is responsible for all major property systems, such as heating, ventilation, and air conditioning (HVAC), refrigeration, electrical, plumbing, and sewer. He or she also supervises the property's energy-management systems. Furthermore, the department usually works closely with maintenance to ensure complete, coordinated control of the physical plant.

The catering staff must see to it that the engineer is contacted whenever a booked function requires sound systems, such as microphone, recorder, and speaker hookups. While the audiovisual department normally handles the delivery and set up of this equipment, the engineering staff typically is responsible for hooking them up and unhooking them correctly.

The engineering department will need to know each function's energy requirements so that it can accommodate them. For instance, if a banquet needs several buffet stations, it may be necessary to install several electrical drop cords when the room is being set up by the banquet-setup crew. In addition, if there are any unique lighting needs, the engineer must see to it that the appropriate power is available and that the systems are set up and torn down properly.

Engineering also must be aware of each function's beginning and ending times, as well as the expected number of guests, so that the proper amount of heating or cooling can be directed to the meeting and banquet rooms. Most function rooms are closed a good deal of the time and are usually not heated or cooled during these periods. The engineer must have advance notice when the rooms will be used because it takes anywhere from 20 minutes to one hour to adjust a room's temperature.

When determining room temperature needs, the engineer will take into account the size of the room, number of attendees, time of day, the "solar load" (that is, the heat that the building absorbs from the sun), the type of HVAC system, ceiling height, the amount of heat given off by appliances, amount of insulation, outside weather conditions, the amount of body heat given off by employees and guests, and type of function. For instance, a large room requires more heating or cooling. However, a large group of people will quickly raise the temperature of a room.

PROPERTY MANAGER

The hotel property manager is responsible for all outside areas. Normally he or she supervises landscaping, snow removal, pool and spa maintenance, and parking lot and sidewalk maintenance.

In some mega-hotels, there may be a separate property management department working independently and reporting directly to the hotel general manager. In other mega-hotels and in most smaller properties, property management functions usually are housed in the engineering or maintenance departments.

In some small hotels, part or all of outside groundskeeping may be handled by an independent service contractor. For instance, maintenance may handle the pool-maintenance and cleaning chores, while an independent gardener may stop by once or twice a week to take care of landscaping needs.

Occasionally a catering sales representative will book a function to be held on the hotel grounds. For instance, many weddings are held outside, including the ceremony, reception, dinner, and entertainment. To service these events properly, the catering staff will need to coordinate its efforts with the grounds crew to make sure that any needed tents are erected, sprinkler systems shut off, parking lots roped off, portable heaters installed, portable lights erected, and so forth.

STEWARD

The typical hotel employs an executive steward whose major responsibilities include supervising kitchen sanitation and supervising the china, glass, and silver stockroom. He or she provides one of the key links connecting the kitchen and other food and beverage production areas to the point of guest service.

The catering staff must work with the executive steward to ensure that sufficient employees are scheduled to clean the dirty dishes, pots, pans, silverware, and utensils generated by catered events. Adequate manpower must be scheduled to perform the necessary kitchen, bar, and pantry clean up after the functions end. If specialized china, glass, and/or silver is needed, the catering staff usually must requisition it formally from the executive steward.

Some hotels employ kitchen stewards. Their responsibilities are similar to those of the executive stewards, except they also have food purchasing duties. Normally the smaller hotels use kitchen stewards to oversee the kitchen sanitation crew, handle the chef's and bar manager's food and beverage orders, check in shipments, and monitor all storeroom facilities. Being relatively small, these properties do not have separate purchasing agents, receiving supervisors, and storeroom supervisors. In this case, it may be easier to coordinate your efforts with only one person instead of several.

PRINT SHOP

Many hotels have a central copying center to handle their most common printing needs and a contract with an outside printer to handle all unique requirements, or jobs that cannot be done in house. For instance, the central copying center may have computerized desk-top publishing capabilities to print standardized menus, but its equipment may be insufficient to produce 4-color, glossy convention programs.

A few large hotels do all of their printing in house. This allows them to maximize quality control. It also gives them maximum flexibility since they do not need to accept an outside printer's scheduling requirements. Furthermore, an on-site print shop might be the most economical option.

The catering department uses a lot of printed materials. Many catered functions call for printed programs, menus, name plates, personalized match books, signage, and accounting records. While clients can opt to select their own printers, the convenience of an on-site print shop is a much-appreciated benefit.

When the catering staff has a printing need, it usually must fill out a work requisition form and give it to the print shop or central copying center manager. He or she then prioritizes the work and assigns it to the appropriate employee(s) or, if necessary, subcontracts the order to an outside printer.

ROOM SERVICE

The hotel room-service department usually handles all guest-room food and beverage service. It is responsible for delivering food and beverage menu items, and retrieving leftovers, soiled tableware and linen, tables, and equipment.

Generally speaking, catering does not get involved with guest-room functions. However, occasionally the catering staff may need to coordinate with the room-service crew to handle hospitality suites or small, intimate meal and beverage functions held in a hotel suite. For instance, a major corporate convention may host several hospitality suites during the cocktail hour. Alternatively, it may decide to hold a board of directors luncheon in the president's suite instead of in a function room.

HUMAN RESOURCES

The human-resources department's primary responsibility is recruiting, developing, and maintaining an effective employee staff. It is also responsible for administering many personnel-related matters. For instance, it must process all relevant government paperwork, handle grievances, work with union representatives, and supervise employee-compensation packages.

The director of catering will work with human resources whenever there are job openings in the catering department that must be filled. The typical human-resources department has an employment manager whose main activities include helping department supervisors develop job specifications and job descriptions, and developing and implementing recruiting programs, job application procedures, interviewing procedures, and methods used to process new hires.

When the catering department needs a new employee, the director of catering may need to fill out a job-opening form listing the position, work hours, skills required, and other pertinent job information.

For entry-level, nonmanagement catering jobs, the employment manager conducts prescreening interviews of job applicants, develops a list of one or more qualified job candidates, and sends it to the catering department. The catering manager then makes the final hiring decision, usually after personally interviewing qualified applicants.

For supervisory and management catering positions, the director of catering often finds a qualified candidate and sends him or her to the human-resources department for processing. For instance, a catering executive may find an appropriate supervisory candidate through his or her membership in the National Association of Catering Executives (NACE). In fact, this professional organization publishes several employment openings in the job-bank section of its bimonthly magazine, *NACE News*.

The director of catering also may uncover viable managerial job candidates through his or her memberships in other professional organizations and other contacts in the food-service and food-supply industries. For example, a few telephone calls to respected food suppliers in your local area can quickly reveal qualified people who are looking to make a career move.

Occasionally the catering executive may find a potential job candidate to fill an hourly position. For instance, a current staff member may recommend a friend to fill a job opening. If so, the catering executive would send this person to the human-resources department so that all necessary processing can be performed. As a general rule though, hourly personnel are located solely by the human-resources department.

Once a person is hired, he or she is processed by the employment manager. Generally speaking, this process involves an employee orientation, uniform fitting (if applicable), ID preparation, and assignment of a payroll authorization number, parking place, and employee locker.

The employment process may be shortened a bit for part-time catering employees. For instance, employees on the A-list and B-list may be scheduled temporarily at the discretion of the catering director. However, the employment manager must process their applications initially before they can be placed on these "on-call" lists.

The employment manager may also provide a bit of training to new employees. Usually though, the human resources department employs a director of training who manages this responsibility.

The director of training usually will provide some basic training as part of the orientation process. Job-related training, though, usually is an effort shared by the training director and catering director.

The director of catering also will be involved with human resources whenever employee problems arise. Usually the human resources department employs an employee-relations manager to handle these situations. However, if, for example, there is a problem with a catering employee's paycheck, usually the catering director must be part of the solution. This is also true if there is an employee-benefits dispute, disciplinary problem, accident, insurance claim, union contract dispute, or employee grievance.

CONTROLLER

The hotel controller is responsible for securing all company assets. He or she normally supervises all cost-control activities, payroll processing, accounts payable, accounts receivable, data processing, night auditing, and cashiering.

The catering department's major relationships with the hotel controller involve report preparation, cashiering, and accounts receivable.

All hotel departments prepare reports. Many of them are coordinated and printed by the controller's office. For instance, budgets, profit and loss statements, and activity reports are usually prepared in final format by the controller's management information system (MIS) data-processing center based upon information provided by the departments.

Many catered events have cash bars. The controller's office will assign cashiers to sell drink tickets to the guests. Guests will then exchange these tickets for beverages. At the end of the function, the cash collection will be compared to the ticket count and the amount of missing beverage inventory. If everything goes according to plan, these three totals will be consistent with each other.

With open bars and some meal functions, drink and meal tickets may be purchased in advance by the client and distributed to the guests. Guests then exchange them for food and beverages. The controller's office will ensure that used tickets are consistent with the amount of missing food and beverage inventory.

At times, a client will be billed at the end of the function for all food and beverage consumed by guests. For instance, an open bar at a wedding could be set up in such a way that bartenders keep track of each drink or bottle served. When preparing the final billing, the number of drinks or bottles served will be multiplied by the agreed-upon selling price. This total will then be added to the other bill charges.

When a potential client is shopping for catering services, he or she may need to put up a modest deposit to hold space. The catering sales representative will then enter a tentative booking in the master catering book and, after obtaining the potential client's permission, ask the credit manager to run a credit check on the client. It is important to obtain this permission in advance because many clients will not agree to a credit check until after the functions are booked and billing is requested.

If credit is denied, usually the catering sales representative contacts the client and tries to resolve the problem and salvage the event. In this situation, the client will need to prepay unless the credit manager is willing to change his or her mind and make other arrangements.

As noted earlier, most hotels are not in the habit of granting clients long-term, favorable credit terms and conditions. For instance, political functions and social events, such as weddings, are seldom granted the luxury of post-event billing.

If credit is approved, or if the client has indicated that prepayment will not be a problem, the sales representative will contact him or her to confirm the event and outline billing arrangements. When confirmed, the event is changed from a tentative booking to a permanent one after the client has signed the agreement.

The controller's office prepares final billings and sends invoice statements to the clients. It handles collections and processes payments. If there are any problems, such as invoice disputes, late payments, or bounced checks, the catering department may need to help the credit manager resolve them.

SECURITY

This is the least visible hotel department, but by far *not* the least important. You know it is doing an effective job when guests do not recognize its presence.

Catered events present unique security challenges. Large groups may need someone to control foot traffic. Some groups may have considerable personal property that must be protected. Some of them may include VIPs who require additional attention. Some groups may attract disruptive protestors. And some groups have the seeds of potential disruption; for instance, proms and fraternity parties must have security guards to prevent underage drinking and rowdy behavior.

The catering department must keep the security department apprised of all special functions because there may be some potential security problems it can spot that may go unrecognized by the catering sales representative and client. If so, the chief of security would have an opportunity to reconcile them beforehand.

Usually the chief of security receives copies of all banquet event orders (BEO) in advance. This allows him or her to schedule the appropriate amount and type of security. It also gives the security chief sufficient lead time to process special needs, such as hiring temporary security guards, renting special equipment, and/or setting up perimeter barriers.

SALES

In most hotels, the sales director is responsible for selling, advertising, promotion, public relations, marketing research, and other relevant marketing efforts. Usually the hotel's sales department handles all local business on its own, but is backed up by a corporate sales and marketing staff that solicits and coordinates regional and national business.

Recall from the discussion in Chapter 1 that in some hotels, the catering department is part of the sales staff. In this situation, catering sales and service employees report to the sales director, while kitchen and bar staffs report to a banquet manager employed by the food and beverage director. In this type of organizational structure, some or all catering services may be provided by a convention-service staff housed in the sales department.

Catering must work closely with the sales staff. At times, their efforts may even overlap. For example, a convention sales representative may be trying to sell sleeping rooms, function space, and meal functions to a meeting planner while at the same time, the meeting planner may be working with a catering sales representative to schedule a trial event, such as a small luncheon or reception. A great deal of coordination and cooperation must exist in order to avoid any duplication of efforts and to ensure that the more profitable business is booked first, thereby maximizing function-room space utilization and sales revenue.

FRONT OFFICE

The front office is considered to be the heart of the hotel. It is the hub of activity. It is usually the second contact (reservations being the first) guests make with the hotel. And it tends to be the place that influences customers' first, and most-lasting, impressions of the property.

The front office normally includes the reservations, PBX (Private Branch Exchange), registration, cashier, and guest-services sections.

The catering department will need to work closely with reservations whenever conventions are booked into the hotel. Reservations will keep a running tally of sleeping rooms blocked and sleeping rooms booked. This information will be used by the catering staff to forecast attendance at the various catering events scheduled by convention clients.

PBX is the hotel's communications hub. Catering will cross paths with this front-office section whenever telephone calls are routed to its department, messages are taken and delivered, and clients request specialized communications service.

A catered event may require extraordinary communications service or equipment. If so, PBX may be part of the team handling these needs. If, for example, a large convention requires several phones in the reception areas, PBX may deliver and retrieve them, engineering may hook them up and tear them down, and PBX may provide an operator or two to monitor incoming and outgoing calls.

The registration desk is the source of sleeping-room occupancy statistics. If, for example, a large convention is checking into the property, the catering director will want to be kept up to date on the numbers of registrants so that accurate guest-count estimates can be computed for each catered event.

The front-desk cashier handles guest check out. Normally this involves guests paying sleeping-room, room-service, gift shop, restaurant, lounge, and other incidental charges. At times though, the costs of catered events may be part of a departing guest's final accounting. If so, the catering staff must make sure that accurate data are made available to the front-desk clerks and cashiers so that guest folios can be posted correctly and the proper accounting prepared in the time-frame required.

Guest services includes the bell desk, valet parking attendants, door attendants, concierge, and property hosts.

Bell desk employees are trained to promote the property's amenities, especially the hotel's restaurant and lounge outlets. They also can put in a good word for the hotel's catering staff.

At times, bell-desk personnel may be involved more directly with catered functions. For instance, some of them may serve as ushers, tour leaders, or airport-shuttle drivers for convention attendees.

Many hotels provide valet-parking services. Usually these services are under the direction of a parking supervisor (or garage manager).

The typical guest usually must pay for reserved parking-lot space and valet-attendant services. An extra daily charge normally is added to the guest's folio since the standard sleeping-room rate does not normally include this amenity.

If a guest is part of a catered event, he or she may not have to pay separately for parking; it might be part of the total package price quoted by the catering sales representative for the entire function.

Parking charges might be waived by the catering sales representative if the event booked generates considerable other income for the hotel. If parking charges are typically very high, you may not be allowed to waive them; however, usually you can discount them for large groups.

If the parking facility is operated by an outside parking concession, the parking charges usually cannot be waived. In some cases though, the concession agreement may grant the hotel some discount privileges that can be passed on to some catering clients and their guests. Absent such an agreement, either the client or the catering department must pay the concessionaire.

The concierge is an important part of the hotel's guest-services team. This person specializes in providing information to guests about hotel activities, amenities, and off-property attractions, such as where the best shopping, restaurants, and tourist attractions are located. Some catering clients and their guests undoubtedly will be influenced by this person's advice.

A few hotels employ property hosts to service their high-spending clients. For instance, in Las Vegas, most properties employ casino hosts to cultivate high rollers.

To some extent, catering sales and service representatives are similar to property hosts in that they try to cultivate long-term relationships with profitable clients. For instance, a professional association may be so pleased with a particular catering executive that the group is liable to stick with this person even if he or she moves to another hotel property.

AUDIOVISUAL

Some large hotels, and almost all conference centers, have audio-visual (AV) departments that are responsible for maintaining an inventory of AV equipment. In-house AV departments are also commonly found in large, rural resorts that do a considerable amount of convention business.

The AV department may own the equipment or rent it from an outside service as needed to accommodate an event. It may also be involved with delivering the equipment to function rooms and retrieving it when guests are finished. It may also be responsible for providing AV technicians.

Many hotels do not want to operate an AV department. The equipment inventory needed is very expensive. The repair and maintenance is quite costly. And the equipment can quickly become obsolete and need to be replaced well before its useful life expires.

While hotels are reluctant to operate their own AV departments, they do want to make this convenience available to the guest. This is absolutely necessary if you want to offer clients one-stop shopping opportunities.

One way to provide in-house AV services economically is to grant an outside AV company an exclusive concession inside the hotel property. For instance, Nevada Audio Visual Services, a private company, has an exclusive contract to provide AV services at The Mirage Hotel in Las Vegas. Ideally, the concessionaire will have adequate in-house storage space so that services can be provided quickly and efficiently.

Catering clients can opt to use their own outside AV services. For instance, a major convention client may have a long-term, national contract with Greyhound Exposition Creative Services Division, a large, national firm that provides a wide array of meetings and conventions services. In this case, a client will save money because of the quantity discounts available with national contracts. An added benefit is that over time, the national firm will learn and understand the group's unique needs and personalities and tailor its services accordingly.

Experience shows that most catering clients will not use off-premises AV companies unless the hotel's AV equipment is priced exorbitantly. They prefer the convenience of an on-site department. For instance, when the department is located in the hotel, a client can examine the equipment beforehand, back-up equipment can be retrieved quickly, equipment can be secured on-site, and qualified technicians are on site and can respond immediately if problems arise.

Catering must see to it that the AV manager is kept apprised of all client AV needs. The equipment, its delivery and pick up, and any necessary technicians must be scheduled well in advance. Sometimes the hotel is so busy that the AV manager must use and reuse a particular piece of equipment several times during the day, for several functions. During the high season, close communications are necessary in order to pull off these scheduling miracles.

RECREATION

Many hotels offer several types of guest-recreation activities. Several properties have swimming pools, health clubs, and spas. Some have additional recreation amenities, such as golfing, tennis, beaches, trail riding, and boating.

Hotel salespersons may use the hotel's recreation offerings as a loss leader when trying to influence a meeting planner's property-selection decision. For instance, a meeting planner could be offered free use of the spa for all convention attendees. If this complimentary amenity is used to secure a booking, it is imperative that the spa manager knows about it well in advance so that he or she can be ready to handle the extra guests properly.

Providing complimentary recreation amenities sounds like it might be an expensive giveaway, but in reality it costs the hotel very little. For example, many attendees will not use the spa facilities;

however, they will be favorably impressed with the perceived value offered. Also, the hotel does not incur an out-of-pocket cost by promising clients preferred tee times or tennis-court times.

ENTERTAINMENT

A few hotels employ entertainment directors. These executives are responsible for dealing with agents and booking entertainment acts. They also are responsible for dealing with entertainment licensing authorities. For instance, the American Society of Composers, Authors, and Publishers (ASCAP) and Broadcast Music Incorporated (BMI) collect fees from businesses that provide musical entertainment to their guests for profit-making purposes.

If a catered event requires some sort of entertainment, the hotel entertainment director may be involved with the decision. If a client books his or her own entertainment, the hotel entertainment director may still be involved; for example, he or she might provide a list of available acts to the meeting planner, help the meeting planner contact a speaker's bureau, or help schedule the events.

The entertainment director must always be made aware of catering activity in the hotel because this could influence his or her selection of acts. For instance, if a western-wear association convention is booked, the entertainment director would want to arrange to have a country-and-western act performing in the hotel lounge.

BUSINESS SERVICES

Business services are clerical and secretarial services provided by the hotel to its guests. Hotels that accommodate business travelers and the meetings and conventions business typically make them available to all guests for an additional charge.

Many catered events require some business services. For instance, a convention may need copying and typing services. It may need someone to take minutes, collate reports, or handle incoming and outgoing fax or telex messages. Some clients might need slides or photographs coordinated for a presentation.

As with guest-recreation activities, a few hotels may provide a modest amount of complimentary business services to clients who book a large amount of catering business with the hotel.

The business-services manager must know as soon as possible the types and amounts of business services clients will need. This is very important because most employees working in this department are on-call, temporary employees who usually have full-time jobs elsewhere. They will need advance notice so that they can adjust their schedules accordingly.

GOVERNMENT AGENCIES

While government regulators are not housed in the hotel, nevertheless they play an important role in achieving your business objectives. In some cases, you may need to work closely with one or more of them when planning a special catering event.

For instance, you may need to inform the fire department if you are putting together an outdoor pyrotechnics display. The fire department may also need to oversee and inspect any portable electrical-power setup to ensure it is grounded properly and safe to use in a public area.

If the event requires the use of some unique live plants or other greenery, the state agriculture department may need to grant approval before you can use them. The local health district's approval also may be required.

Experience shows that the local health district is the government agency that catering executives must work with more often than any other regulator. Usually any time you need to set up portable, temporary tents, cooking lines, serving lines, and so forth, a sanitarian must approve your plans. He or she must ensure that you do not violate health guidelines.

RENTAL COMPANIES

Rental companies, like all suppliers, technically are not part of the hotel. However, they may be used so much that they become de facto hotel departments.

Many hotels do not wish to own and store equipment that is used sparingly. It is too expensive and inconvenient to do this. Generally, when specialized equipment is required, it is more economical to rent it. The catering executive should ask the purchasing department to seek out approved rental companies that can fill these needs.

Hotels do not have to limit their renting to specialized equipment. Conceivably, anything can be rented. However, usually only those items that are needed to help produce a unique and/or unusually large catered function will be rented and the cost passed on to the client; everything else will be owned.

Hotels typically will rent the following types of equipment:

1. Audiovisual (AV)
2. Refrigerated storage
3. Freezer storage
4. Transportation
5. Tableware
6. Service utensils
7. Lighting
8. Off-site production facility.

SUBCONTRACTORS

The decade of the 1990s is the age of the subcontractor. Many clients today want services that the hotel may be unable to provide itself because it lacks the equipment, labor, and/or expertise to handle the requests properly. Normally it is too expensive to have all resources available if they are used sparingly.

You can satisfy these clients though, by cultivating an approved list of outside subcontractors who meet your quality standards and who agree to handle special requests on a per-job basis. For instance, if a client wants a Japanese theme, you may be able to subcontract the sushi bar to a local Japanese restaurant. The same strategy can be used to provide other unique attractions, such as ethnic foods, traditional barbecues, and on-site ice cream production.

In addition to providing client and guest satisfaction, subcontracting can be very profitable for the hotel. As a general rule, when a hotel subcontracts, it will add a profit markup of about 20 percent to the subcontractor's charge. Furthermore, since the subcontractor usually provides only one aspect of the catered event, you retain the other profit-making aspects. For instance, you might subcontract only the unique entree and provide the rest of the meal yourself.

If you book a very large catered function, subcontracting may be the logical way to handle it. For instance, when the Democratic National Convention held in Atlanta had to feed 35,000 people, a catering executive subcontracted different parts of the meal and coordinated the final production and service.

You can also subcontract nonfood and nonbeverage activities. For instance, you can engage a service contractor to handle exhibit-hall setup. The firm can provide furniture, carpet, pipe and drape, labor, freight, and so forth, and relieve you of this burden as well as the need to stock expensive assets.

Some large, full-service contractors can handle everything except meal and beverage functions. If desired, you can engage a full-service firm, such as Greyhound Exposition, The Freeman Company, or United Exposition, to perform all nonfood and non-beverage activities, everything from menu printing to function-room setup and tear down.

COOPERATING WITH OTHER HOTELS

Some catered events are so large that two or more hotels must cooperate in servicing them. For example, it is common in Las Vegas for large conventions to book meeting and exhibition space at two or three hotels. Delegates usually are shuttled back and forth. And the catering departments normally take turns hosting catered functions.

If you are involved in this sort of "co-op" venture, someone will need to coordinate and direct it. The client will usually handle a great deal of the organization needed, but the individual catering executives must go beyond this. They will need to get together a few times to ensure that everything runs smoothly. For instance, if there will be several meal functions, menu planning should be a community effort. If all hotels do not communicate, chances are guests will not receive sufficient menu variety.

6

Meal Functions

Catering is the backbone of the food and beverage profession. You find lasting friendships and satisfying rewards.

Helen Roberts
Special Catering Representative
Radisson Hotel Atlanta
Atlanta, Georgia

Exceptional food and service is a major marketing advantage. While all aspects of a catered function are important, it is reasonable to assume that the quality of food and guest service makes the deepest and most-lasting impression on attendees.

The hotel that strives for a competitive advantage would do well to emphasize consistent-quality food because this consistency is something some hotels cannot offer. While it may be easy for most properties to offer clients similar function space, meeting times, and number of sleeping rooms, this is not the case with food.

Other factors may initially attract clients, but food is the key variable influencing return patronage. This is especially true if you offer one or more "signature" menu items, that is, items that you have created, or were created for you, that customers cannot obtain elsewhere.

Service is just as important as food quality. In most consumer surveys, restaurant patrons usually rank service a close second after food quality. While it may be a bit easier to provide consistent service than it is to ensure consistent food quality, it is by no means a simple accomplishment.

Service and food go hand-in-hand. The successful catering department will use both to attract and retain profitable business.

PURPOSE OF THE MEAL FUNCTION

One of the first things to consider when planning a meal function is the client's reason for scheduling it. Does the client want a meal function primarily to:

Satisfy hunger?

Create an image?

Provide an opportunity for social interaction and networking?

Showcase a person, product, and/or idea?

Present awards?

Honor dignitaries?

Refresh convention attendees and sharpen their attention?

Provide a receptive audience to program speakers?

Keep people interested in other nonfood activities?

Increase attendance at conventions?

The list of reasons is endless. The catering executive though, should query the client about his or her particular reason(s) so that the appropriate menu and production and service plans can be formulated. For example, many meeting planners plan group meals, especially group luncheons, because they do not feel that the hotel's restaurant outlets can handle large numbers of people in the short time allotted. Also, a group-meal function tends to keep people at the meeting; if they go out of the hotel to eat, they may never return for the other business sessions. If the catering executive knows about these considerations and concerns, he or she will tailor the function around the time constraints while simultaneously making it attractive to convention attendees so that they will not go elsewhere.

MENU PLANNING

As mentioned earlier, the director of catering is responsible for developing standardized menus as well as unique menus customized for particular clients. He or she also must see to it that the standardized menus are revised periodically in order to keep them current with changing consumer trends.

All menu planning must be done in cooperation with the chef. It also is a good idea to get input from other department heads, such as the purchasing agent, food and beverage director, and hotel sales director. Since people are more concerned with nutritional issues these days, a registered dietitian on a consulting basis might be a good addition to the menu-planning team.

The types of menu items a hotel can offer its guests depends on several factors. Before adding a menu item to a standardized menu, or before offering to accommodate a client's peculiar menu needs, the menu planner needs to evaluate all relevant considerations that will affect the hotel's ability to offer it and the guest's desire to eat it.

Food Cost

Ideally, the catering department will offer a variety of menu prices to suit its target markets. These prices must be consistent with the target markets' needs and desires. For instance, the budget-conscious market usually will respond positively only if the hotel offers excellent price/value options. Consequently, it would be foolhardy to develop menus for budget-conscious groups that contain too many high-cost ingredients.

Many clients appreciate the opportunity to work with several price options when allocating their meal budgets. This is especially true for those who are in charge of planning all meal, beverage, and nonfood functions. These clients tend to shuffle their budgetary dollars back and forth among these events; this routine is easier to accomplish if the catering department cooperates by offering several price variations.

Guest Background

A menu planner should consider the demographics of the group ordering the meal function. Average age, sex, ethnic backgrounds, socioeconomic levels, diet restrictions, where the guests come from, employment and fraternal affiliations, and political leanings can indicate the types of menu items that might be most acceptable to the group. Psychographics, such as guests' life styles and the ways in which they perceive themselves, are also useful indicators.

Age is often an excellent indicator. For example, senior citizens usually do not want exotic foods or heavy, spicy foods. In this case, you should try to avoid excessive use of garlic, hot spices, and onions. You would want to avoid other distress-causing foods, such as herbal teas, monosodium glutamate (MSG), cabbage-family vegetables, and beans. You also should not overdo it when serving cheese. It is high in fat and calories, very filling, and hard to digest.

Guests with special diets will influence the types of foods served. For instance, some persons cannot tolerate MSG (allergic reactions), onions and garlic (digestive problems), spices (allergic reactions), sugar (diabetics), salt (high blood pressure, heart problems), fat (weight problems, triglycerides, high cholesterol), and/or milk products (allergic problems, butterfat, digestive problems).

Some guests consume special diets for religious or life-style reasons. For example, Moslems and Jews will not eat pork. Orthodox Jews require kosher-prepared foods. Some persons will not eat red meat, but will eat poultry and seafood. Some vegetarians (referred to as "vegans") will not eat anything from any animal source. And some vegetarians (referred to as "lacto-ovo" vegetarians) will not eat animal flesh, but will eat eggs and dairy products.

If a group is coming from a previous function where heavy, filling hors d'oeuvres were served, the meal should be lighter. If guests are coming from a liquor-only reception, then the meal could be heavier.

If a group will be going to a business meeting immediately after the meal, you need to serve foods that will keep attendees awake. Protein foods, such as seafood, lean beef, and skinless chicken, will keep guests alert. Carbohydrates, such as rice, bread, and pasta, tend to relax guests and put them to sleep. Fats, such as butter, whipped cream, and heavy salad dressings, also tend to make guests sluggish and inattentive.

If a group is affiliated with, say, the National Cattlemen's Association, Overeaters Anonymous, or Pickle Packers International, then the menu should reflect these affiliations. In fact, usually these types of groups will insist that the catering department use a particular ingredient in as many menu items as possible.

Politics can play an important role in menu planning. Some groups will not consume certain types of foods. The catering department and the function planner must see to it that politically and healthfully correct foods are made available. For example, serving veal at banquets for animal-rights organizations can embarrass the hotel as well as the clients and their guests because these groups believe that veal is raised and processed under inhumane conditions.

Politically active groups may insist that the hotel purchase and serve politically correct products. For instance, you may be prohibited from purchasing beef raised on recently deforested tropical rain forest land. You may not be allowed to purchase tuna from countries that allow the use of drift nets that trap and kill dolphins indiscriminately. And you may be prohibited from packaging finished food products in disposable containers; you may need to use reusable containers and not charge a premium for this service.

Nutrition Concerns

Nutrition is a serious consideration whenever the group members expect to be at the hotel for several days during a convention. Since virtually all meals during their stay will be consumed on your premises, special attention must be paid to nutritional requirements when planning menus.

The healthy diet must include the four basic food groups. The menu planner should strive to provide foods from the:

1. Milk group—such as milk, cheese, ice cream, and yogurt.
2. Protein group—such as meat, seafood, poultry, and eggs.
3. Cereal group—such as bread, rice, corn, and oatmeal.
4. Fruit and vegetable group—such as citrus fruit, green leafy vegetables, carrots, and apples.

Preparation and service procedures can impact the healthy diet. For instance, many customers will appreciate it very much if the hotel:

1. Serves some low-fat, low-calorie, high-protein meal options.
2. Uses the four Bs when preparing foods (broil, bake, barbecue, and boil).
3. Trims fat from meats.
4. Minimizes (or avoids) frying, grilling, and deep frying.
5. Serves broth-based soups instead of heavy cream-based soups.
6. Serves green salads with vinaigrette dressing instead of with heavy fat-based salad dressings.
7. Avoids serving potato salads and pasta salads that have a high concentration of fat-based mayonnaise.
8. Serves sauces and dressings on the side so that guests can control their own portion sizes.
9. Limits the serving of alcoholic beverages.
10. Provides half-sized portion options.
11. Uses fresh ingredients instead of processed foods to prepare finished menu items. Today's consumers want some fresh choices. They also are becoming more adept at recognizing preprepared, processed foods.
12. Provides some menu options that are approved by the American Heart Association (AHA), American Diabetes Association (ADA), and/or the American Cancer Society (ACS).

13. Provides some menu options that are prepared in accordance with the nationally sponsored Project Lean program. This program aims to reduce fat in the diet to the point where 30 percent, or less, of a person's calories come from fat.

While there is a trend toward healthier, more nutritious foods, recently food-service operators have noticed a resurgence of "comfort" foods, or "Haute Grandma" cuisine. For instance, meat loaf, chicken pot pie, hot turkey sandwiches and gravy, strawberry shortcake, and chicken-fried steak appeal to some people because they tend to rekindle warm memories of happier days.

Similarly, food-service managers notice that many guests are loathe to give up their dessert course. Ironically, when people are "good" they like to reward themselves with a rich dessert.

In spite of the fact that people are becoming more health conscious, fancy desserts are expected at a food function. The typical guest feels cheated if the meal ends without a dessert, or if the dessert offered is viewed as mediocre.

The dessert creates the last impression of the meal and should be spectacular. A small portion of a rich dessert is sufficient if the presentation is very artistic. For instance, desserts can be very impressive if served on a large plate, on special tableware (such as ice cream served in chocolate cups), and/or prepared at table side.

Special service presentations can be very effective. For instance, a Baked Alaska parade, where the lights are dimmed and the servers carry in the flaming dishes, is a pleasant sight.

Action stations (such as exhibition cooking) are certain crowd pleasers that are guaranteed to have a favorable impact on guests. Chefs working at these stations can prepare hot crepes with different sauces. Or they can prepare bananas foster, fruit beignets, and/or cherries jubilee to order.

Dessert buffets are also a nice touch, especially when served with champagne, flavored coffees and teas, liqueurs, and/or brandies. This type of service allows the guests an opportunity to stretch, a good idea if you expect the meal function to be more than one and one-half to two hours.

If you provide dessert buffets or dessert action stations, you should prepare bite-sized "taster" dessert items. Guests will appreciate this because many of them will have a hard time choosing. You do not want them to take two or three full desserts because this will increase waste and food costs.

When stocking a dessert buffet, a good idea is to display full-sized desserts on an upper tier of the table, then on the lower tier, place duplicate miniature versions of the showcased ones. This type of presentation is especially effective if the dessert tasters are placed on mirrored platters. Experience shows that cheesecake, tarts, tortes, cakes, baklava, cannoli, butter cookies, chocolate leaves, and fresh fruit are especially attractive and inviting when presented like this.

Hard-to-Produce Foods

Certain delicate items cannot be produced and served in quantity without sacrificing culinary quality. For example, lobster, souffle, rare roast beef, rack of lamb, and roast duckling are almost impossible to prepare and serve satisfactorily for more than a handful of guests.

If a client insists on receiving these types of items, the hotel may need to implement a creative and costly procedure to accommodate the request. For instance, flaming desserts do not lend themselves easily to quantity production. However, a hotel could install an action station on an elevated platform safely away from tableside. Guests can view the flaming displays without worrying about getting burned. And servers can retrieve the finished desserts when the chefs are done.

Standardized Menu Offerings

The catering sales representative should encourage clients to order menu items also offered in the hotel's restaurant outlets. This will keep food costs under control since banquet leftovers can be utilized elsewhere.

Usually the hotel will prepare enough foods to serve more than the guaranteed guest count. This overproduction is necessary to avoid stockouts, that is, running out of food and disappointing guests. Unfortunately, if the menu includes unusual foods that cannot be used in the restaurant outlets, a client will need to pay a higher price to defray the extra food costs. With a standardized menu, clients may not have to worry about paying for overproduction.

Length of Convention

If guests will be at the hotel for several days, and if they will be eating mostly catered meals, you must be careful not to repeat food items from meal to meal and from day to day. For instance, you would not want to serve carrot cake for dessert if you served a carrot and raisin salad and/or glazed carrots last night, serve chicken for dinner if you served it yesterday for lunch, or serve beef two nights in a row.

Similarly, you should not use the same ingredients in more than one course unless the meal is specifically designed for this. For instance, a convention group visiting Atlanta may be pleased if some courses include Georgia peaches. Likewise with the group visiting Seattle, where the creative director of catering might be able to include Pacific salmon in two or three courses.

The most important consideration is to provide variety and nutrition options. The longer the meeting, the more critical these factors become.

If guests are not eating every meal in your hotel, you should try to find out what they are scheduled to eat the meal before they come to your function. This will prevent your using too many of the same ingredients. For example, when Prince Charles visited Los Angeles a few years ago, he was taken to several meals at different locations. Each one served him a veal dish, which caused the Prince to wonder aloud if veal was the only product Americans eat.

Seasonality

A catering sales representative should always try to recommend seasonal foods. The quality of food items is greatly enhanced when they are in season. In-season foods also are less expensive. Lower food costs will increase hotel profitability. Moreover, the lower food costs will allow you to pass on some of the savings to the client in the form of lower price quotations, thereby possibly capturing catering clients who would not purchase standard-priced meal functions.

Easy-to-Produce Foods

The director of catering should resist the temptation of emphasizing only easy-to-prepare foods. Clients may think that these menus lack creativity and flair and may have doubts about the hotel catering department's capabilities.

Chicken is a very common item served on banquet menus primarily because it is easy to prepare, and can be prepared and served in so many ways.

Beef is another very common menu offering for at least three reasons. One, it is usually a safe choice for meeting planners; most people will eat beef at least once in a while. Two, a tremendous variety of cuts are consistently available. And three, it can be prepared and served in many ways.

Seafood is not a universally accepted food item, so many clients are reluctant to offer it to their guests. However, you could suggest a "surf and turf" entree that is easy to produce, such as crab legs and broiled chicken breast, which will bridge the gap between the familiar and the unique.

In general, catering executives tend to favor poultry, beef, and other similar items that lend themselves to assembly-line production and service. If nothing else, the menu offers no disastrous surprises, and usually it can be prepared and served very efficiently.

Some clients will be satisfied with these tried-and-true menu options. For instance, a recent survey conducted by the Marriott Corporation revealed that association meeting planners prefer familiar products. However, this same survey indicated that corporate meeting planners are more adventurous when they develop menus for meal functions and are more receptive to unique cuisine.

Product Shelf Life

Since catered events do not always run on time, it pays to have foods that will hold up well during service. This is also an important consideration whenever a banquet is scheduled for a large group and you anticipate a few minor logistics problems.

Large pieces of food hold heat or cold longer than small pieces. Solid meats hold temperature better than sliced meats. Lettuce wedges stay fresher and colder than tossed salad. Whole fruit and muffins stay fresher longer than sliced fruits or sliced cake. Whole vegetables hold better than julienne cuts. Generally speaking, cold foods retain the cold temperature longer than hot foods hold heat. And cold foods will stay cold longer if they are served on cold plates, and hot foods will stay hot longer if they are served on warm plates.

Sauces tend to extend a hot food product's holding capacity. They can keep foods from drying out. And they can add color to finished dishes. However, if not used properly, a sauce could run all over the plate, skin over, and/or pick up flavors and odors from other foods or heating fuels.

Examples of hot foods that will stay fresh over an extended period of time are:

1. Chicken
2. Oven-browned potatoes
3. Link sausage
4. Green beans
5. Filet mignon

6. Medallions of beef

7. Pork tenderloin in sauce

8. Swiss steak

9. Rice

10. Steamed carrots

11. Sauces

12. Scrambled eggs.

Market Availability

Before committing to a specific menu item, the catering executive must ensure that the food is available. It is especially imperative to check the availability of ethnic products before preparing a client proposal.

At times, there are seasonal restrictions, product shortages, and/or distribution shortcomings that interfere with acquiring some products. For instance, while vine-ripened tomatoes may be in season, there may be a temporary shortage and local purveyors may be unable to satisfy your needs.

Menu Balance

The menu planner should try to balance flavors, textures, shapes, colors, temperatures, and so forth. Appetites are stimulated by all senses. You should not plan meals that tend to overpower one of them.

Color is pleasing to the eye. How appetizing would it be if you prepared a plate of sliced, white-meat turkey, mashed potatoes, and cauliflower? Customers will be turned off by the lack of color contrast.

Be leery of flavors that clash. For instance, you would not want to serve broccoli, cabbage, cauliflower, or brussels sprouts at the same meal. They are all strong-flavored vegetables and are in the same vegetable family. You need more variety and contrast. You should strive to have something bland, something sweet, something salty, something bitter, and/or something sour on the menu.

Textures also are very important. Ideally, you would have a pleasing combination of crisp, firm, and soft foods.

Product forms, shapes, and sizes should be mixed and matched. You should offer as much variety as possible. For instance, a menu could include a combination of flat, round, long, chopped, shredded, heaped, tubular, and square foods.

A temperature contrast will also appeal to most guests. A menu should offer both hot- and cold-food options.

The type of preparation offers an opportunity to provide several pleasing contrasts. For instance, an appropriate combination of sauteed, broiled, baked, roasted, steamed, sauced, and pickled foods will be more pleasing to customers than will foods prepared only one or two ways.

The menu planner also should offer several types and varieties of food courses. A client should be able to select an appropriate combination of entree, starch, vegetable, salad, soup, appetizer, dessert, bread, and beverage from the standardized menu offerings. Ideally, the catering sales representative would be able to offer more than one combination within a specific price range.

Equipment Limitations

Certain foods require special equipment to prepare and/or serve properly. For instance, a standing-rib roast dinner for 2,500 people usually requires a battery of cook-and-hold ovens. Buffets cannot be set up properly unless sufficient steam-table space and/or chafing dishes are on hand. And a large banquet that requires several hundred deep-fried appetizers cannot be serviced adequately unless you have sufficient deep-fryer capacity.

The size of your food and beverage production and service facilities and their layout and design also impact menu-planning decisions. For instance, while you may have a sufficient number of cook-and-hold ovens, if they are not located correctly, your ability to serve large numbers of guests could be severely limited.

Experience suggests that if there is any question about equipment capacity, an equipment specialist can usually provide the correct answer. An equipment manufacturer, dealer, designer, sales representative, or leasing company usually is able to help you estimate your facility's capacity and recommend minor, inexpensive changes that can increase it significantly. The chef and hotel engineer may also be able to offer useful suggestions.

Labor

Some menu items are very labor intensive, especially those made from scratch in the hotel's kitchens. It is not unusual for payroll costs to be as much as one-third, or more, of a meal function's total price.

Payroll is expensive in the food-service industry. There are many hidden labor costs that are not readily apparent. For instance, in the typical restaurant, for every dollar paid in salaries and wages, the National Restaurant Association (NRA) estimates that payroll taxes, employee benefits, and personnel-related administrative expenses add another forty cents to that dollar. As a result, the cook who earns $10 per hour actually costs the house $14 per hour.

To say the least, there is a great deal of pressure in our industry to hold the line on payroll costs. Unfortunately, this puts you in a very awkward position when planning the menu. To control payroll, you may need to purchase more convenience foods, reduce menu options, eliminate menu items that require a great deal of expensive expertise to prepare and serve, charge the client more, schedule fewer servers, and/or compromise on other services.

The director of catering must stay within his or her payroll budget, but it is equally important to avoid alienating guests. Instead of cutting labor to the bone, and possibly incurring the guest's wrath, it is much better to try to convince the client to pay a modest labor surcharge so that the meal can be prepared and served professionally. If you feel that a labor surcharge is a client's best option, you should suggest it and plan for it in advance; it should not be a last-minute consideration.

Family Recipes

Not only do some clients have preconceived menus, they also have their own recipes that they want the hotel to use when producing them. As mentioned earlier, this is a risky, controversial procedure that can generate a bit of difficulty and unhappiness if the final result is unacceptable to guests.

While the typical hotel does not like to veer from its standardized production and service plans, it will always try to satisfy its clients whenever possible. In this situation, the catering staff will need to work with a client or his or her representative to test the recipes. As this requires additional time and effort, an extra charge would be appropriate.

Matching Food and Wine

Generally speaking, delicate, less-flavorful foods should be served with white wines. Red meats, pastas with meat and tomato sauce, and other strong-flavored foods should be served with red wines.

Some wine lists are not based on color. A list could note wines according to their degree of sweetness, lightness, alcoholic strength, or other relevant factors. In fact, it is a good idea to have many wine options available for client selection.

The catering sales representative should be prepared to suggest food and wine combinations to clients. Since many clients are unsure of these selections, it is important to help them make the right choices. Many wine companies provide a service to food-service professionals whereby a company representative will come to your establishment and help you pair all of your wines and foods. These purveyors usually will pair all wines, not just those you purchase from them.

Figure 6.1 includes a list of recommended food-and-wine pairings that catering sales representatives and clients can use when developing their menus.

Some clients have personal preferences that could interfere with selecting appropriate wines for the meal. For instance, a client may want to serve red wine with fish. If so, the catering executive should convince him or her to have alternative wines available or else some guests will think that the hotel catering department is incompetent. Furthermore, some guests cannot tolerate the histamines and tannins in red wine (they can upset some guests' stomachs); they will appreciate having a choice.

Promotion Value

A menu may be put together in such a way that it promotes certain types of foods. For instance, most large processed-food manufacturers hold parties at hotels to introduce new food products. The catering staff is expected to produce a menu that incorporates these items, highlights them, and shows the many, varied ways they can be produced and served.

Some clients may overdo it when they insist that every menu item contain a specific ingredient. The idea may backfire and cause guests to poke fun at the product. For instance, the California Olive Growers Association once sponsored a luncheon at which every menu item included olives. By the time the dessert was served, guests were beside themselves with laughter. The astute catering executive will not allow a client to be put into this potentially embarrassing position.

In some instances, the hotel purchasing agent may negotiate with a food-service supplier for a promotional discount that can be passed on to the cost-conscious client if he or she is willing to abide by the rules of the promotion. For instance, a meat company may offer a reduced purchase price for beef if the client agrees to allow the firm to display some signage in the banquet room, table tents on the tables, and/or product brochures on the buffet lines. Since some guests may find these types of promotions tacky, you should

Foods	Compatible Wines
Asparagus with hollandaise	Pouilly-Fuisse, Pouilly-Fume, blush wines
Capon	Montrachet, white Burgundy
Cheeses:	
Blue, gorgonzola	Claret, Burgundy, Port, Brandy, Chianti, Champagne
Brick	Rose, white wines, Cream Sherry
Brie	Dry port, Cognac, Calvados, Burgundy, Champagne, Riesling
Camembert	All ports, red wine, pink Champagne, Champagne, Cognac, Riesling
Cheddar	Ports, Sherry, Madeira, Claret, Burgundy, Italian reds, St. Emilion
Colby	Ports, Sherry, Madeira, Claret, Burgundy
Cream	Sparkling wines, Rose, sweet wines
Edam	Tokay, Cold Duck, Claret, Muscatel
Gouda	Tokay, Cold Duck, Rose
Gruyere	Sancerre, Beaujolais
Liederkranz	Dry red wines
Limburger	Dry red wines
Monterey Jack	Rose, white wines, Cream Sherry
Muenster	Rose, white wines, Cream Sherry
Neufchatel	Sparkling wines, Rose, white wines
Port du Salut	Light, dry, fruity wines
Provolone	Dry red wines, dry white wines
Roquefort	Chateauneuf du Pape
Stilton	Fruit wines, Port, Burgundy, Cognac, Sherry
Swiss	Sauternes, Brut Champagne, dry or sweet white wines, Sparkling Burgundy
Chicken, veal	Dry white Bordeaux, very light red Bordeaux, dry whites
Clear soups, consommes	Dry or medium sherries
Cold meats	Dry Alsatian whites
Coq au vin	Volnay, red Graves, light reds
Fish with white sauces	Dry Alsatian whites
Heavy pate	Red Bordeaux
Lamb, beef, roast chicken	Light dry reds
Leg of lamb	Heavy reds, Cabernet Savignon
Light pate	Soave, Alsatian, light reds
Lobster	Mersault, Muscadet, dry whites
Nuts	Ports, light red Bordeaux
Oysters	Chablis, dry Riesling, Pouilly-Fuisse
Roast pork	Valpolicella, Beaujolais
Roast veal	Red or white Beaujolais
Salmon	Dry whites
Shrimp	White Burgundies, Muscadet
Steak, beef	Chianti, Bordeaux, Burgundy, Pinot Noir, Merlot
Turbot, trout, bass, sole	White Burgundies, dry whites
Turkey	Light, dry reds or whites, blush wines
Veal scallopini	Beaujolais, fruity reds
Vegetable soups	Soave, dry whites

Figure 6.1. Example food and wine pairings.

be very careful when suggesting this cost-saving strategy. For example, you might suggest this option only if the client is a food manufacturer or some other type of related food company or trade association.

Entertainment Value

Some menu items lend themselves to entertaining displays in the dining room. For instance, action stations are very popular. Seafood bars and other similar food stations are attractive and tend to generate enthusiasm among guests. And flaming dishes, when prepared safely, are always well received by the dining public.

Any form of entertainment is bound to be expensive. For instance, the examples just noted can be very costly. There is considerable set-up and tear-down work, labor hours, and labor expertise involved that can strain a client's budget.

On the other hand, special touches may promote attendance. For example, the association meeting planner who wants to attract the maximum number of member attendees, and spouse attendees, must be willing to provide an extra incentive. Special foods, prepared and served in an entertaining, exciting way, are sure to enhance attendance. Furthermore, this form of entertainment may be the least expensive way to motivate guests to attend the event.

Menu Trends

It is important to keep up with trends, but it is equally important to be able to differentiate between a trend and a fad (or "craze"). Trends seem to be more permanent. They are like roads, providing direction—a way to go. Fads, on the other hand, are like highway rest stops which come and go along the way.

The move to a healthier diet is a trend. Significant numbers of people want less fat, salt, and sugar in their diets.

Chocolate is a trend. Many persons who eat healthy all week reward themselves on the weekend with rich, gooey chocolate desserts.

Nouvelle, cajun, southwest, and spa cuisines were fads. Mesquite grilling was another fad. Unlike most fads though, it was a very expensive endeavor for those properties that adopted it. They went to great expense to remodel the facilities and put in the grilling equipment, only to see the fad die in short order.

Is the resurgence of nostalgic comfort foods—such as meat loaf, mashed potatoes, gravy, puddings, and short cakes—a trend or a fad? It is often difficult to tell. Complicating matters is the possibility that it can be popular in one part of the country and disdained in others.

The menu planner can assume a risk by trying to lead the pack. For instance, someone had to get on the cutting edge and introduce goat-cheese pizza with dried tomatoes. On the other extreme, if you are risk averse, you could be classified as a laggard or someone woefully behind the times. It would appear that most properties take the middle ground by staying close behind the leader.

Style of Service

Often the style of service clients want will influence the types and varieties of foods the menu planner can offer. For instance, foods that will be passed on trays by servers during an afternoon reception must be easy to handle and able to hold up well. In this case, sauced items that could drip should not be served, but easy-to-eat finger foods would be appropriate.

The service styles that can be used for a catered meal function are:

- *Buffet.* Foods are arranged on tables, or placed on a movable carousel. Guests usually move along the buffet line and serve themselves or, in the case of a movable carousel, they stand still and wait for the foods to come around to them. When plates are filled, guests take them to a dining table to eat. Servers usually provide beverage service at tableside.

- *Reception.* Light foods are served buffet-style or are put on trays in the kitchen and passed by servers. Guests usually stand and serve themselves. They normally do not sit down to eat.

- *Butler.* Foods are presented on trays by servers with utensils available for guests to serve themselves. Typical style of service used for up-scale dinners.

- *Action station.* Similar to buffet. Chefs prepare and serve foods at the buffet. Foods that lend themselves well to action-station service include pastas, grilled meats, omelets, crepes, sushi, flaming desserts, and spinning salad bowls.

- *Cafeteria.* Similar to buffet. Guests stand in line, but do not help themselves. They are served by chefs and/or servers and often use trays to carry their food selections to the dining tables.

- *Family-style (English).* Guests are seated. Large serving platters and bowls are filled with foods in the kitchen and placed on the dining tables by servers. Guests help themselves and pass the foods to each other. Caterers usually try to avoid this type of service because it has a higher food cost due to excess foods placed on the table. For instance, if there are six guests, you must put more than six pieces of meat on the platter.

- *Plated (American).* Guests are seated. Foods are preportioned in the kitchen, put on plates, and served by servers from the left. The meat is placed in front of the guest. Beverages are served from the right. This is the most functional, common, economical, controllable, and efficient type of service. However, if foods are plated too far in advance, they could run together, discolor, or otherwise lose culinary quality.

- *Plated buffet.* Selection of preplated foods, such as entrees, sandwich plates, and salad plates, set on a buffet table. They may also be placed on a roll-in (such as a rolling cart) and then moved into the function room at the designated time.

- *Preset.* Foods are already on the dining tables when guests are seated. Since preset foods will be on the tables for a few minutes before they are consumed, you must preset only those that will retain sanitary and culinary qualities at room temperatures. Water, butter, bread, salad, and cold appetizers are the most common types of preset items.

- *Russian (Silver).* Guests are seated. Foods are cooked tableside on a rechaud (portable cooking stove) that is on a gueridon (tableside cart with wheels). Servers put the foods on platters and then pass the platters at tableside. Guests help themselves to the foods and assemble their own plates. Service is from the left.

- *French.* In the most common form of French service, guests are seated. Platters of foods are assembled in the kitchen. Servers take platters to the table. Guests select foods and the server, using two large silver forks in his or her serving hand (or silver salad tongs if the forks cannot be coordinated with one hand), places them on the guests' plates. Each food item is served by the server from platters to individual plates. Service is from the left.

  Cart service is another less commonly used form of French service. It is the type of French service used in fine-dining restaurants or at upscale catered events of no more than 30 to 40 guests. Guests are seated. Foods are prepared tableside. Hot foods are cooked on a rechaud that is on a gueridon. Cold foods are assembled on the gueridon. Servers plate the finished foods and serve them to guests. Foods and beverages are served from the right. Some foods, such as desserts, are already prepared. They are displayed on a cart, the cart is rolled to tableside, and guests are served after making their selections.

- *Hand.* Guests are seated. There is one server for every two guests. Servers wear white gloves. Foods are preplated. Each server carries two servings from the kitchen and stands behind the two guests assigned to him or her. At the direction of the captain or maitre d' hotel, all servings are set in front of all guests at precisely the same time. This procedure is followed for all courses. This is a very elegant style of service that is sometimes used for small gourmet-meal functions.

- *Wave.* A method of serving where all servers start at one end of the function room and work straight across to the other end. Servers are not assigned work stations. In effect, all servers are on one team and the entire function room is the team's work station. The wave is typically used in conjunction with plated and preset service styles. Large numbers of guests can be served very quickly. This is an excellent style of service to use if your servers are inexperienced.

If clients are not knowledgeable about service styles, the catering sales representative may wish to explain some of them so that they can make informed choices. You should describe only those service styles your staff is equipped and trained to execute properly. Moreover, when pointing out service options, clients must be made aware of any extra labor charges associated with them.

Service styles play an important role in the success of a catered event. Clients can choose those that may be less expensive (such as preset), or can splurge with French or Russian service. Furthermore, some service styles (such as action station) are very entertaining and can contribute significantly to guest satisfaction.

For variety, you can mix service styles during a single meal function. For instance, you might begin with reception service for appetizers, move into the banquet room where the tables are preset with salads, rolls, and butter, use French service for the soup course, use Russian service for the entree, and end the meal with a dessert buffet.

TRUTH-IN-MENU GUIDELINES

The menu planner must ensure that he or she does not inadvertently misrepresent menu items. Printed menus, photos, illustrations, signage, verbal descriptions, and other media presentations must not deceive or mislead clients.

The National Restaurant Association (NRA) recognized the problem of menu misrepresentation as early as 1923 when it issued a report entitled, *Standards Of Business Practices*. In 1977, it published the *Accuracy in Menus* report that reaffirmed its position decrying menu misrepresentation.

In some parts of the country, local governments have enacted truth-in-menu legislation. For instance, in Southern California, health district sanitarians are empowered to inspect a restaurant's menu items and determine if customers are receiving the advertised value.

The NRA identifies eleven potential menu misrepresentations. The menu planner must see to it that menu offerings adhere to these guidelines. By doing so, ambiguity will be eliminated and guests will not be unpleasantly surprised.

Misrepresentation of Quantity

If portion sizes are listed on the menu, they must also be noted on the standardized recipes. The sizes noted must be as-served sizes. Alternatively, a size can be noted with a qualifier, such as: "one-pound steak, weight before cooking."

You may get into trouble if you use terms that are recognized sizes. For instance, you cannot use the term "large egg" if in fact you are serving the medium size. According to federal government guidelines, large eggs must weigh 24 ounces per dozen, while medium eggs must weigh 21 ounces per dozen. Anyone using the description "large egg" must serve a 2-ounce egg.

Some terminology, such as jumbo tossed salad, can be misleading. There is no established government standard for these types of marketing qualifiers, so you must be careful when using such language.

Some terms have implied meanings. For instance, when a customer notices that you offer a cup of soup and a bowl of soup, he or she has the right to assume that the bowl contains the larger portion. Likewise when you list the terms small, medium, and large soft drinks.

Qualifiers, such as "mile-high pie," "world-famous strawberry shortcake," and "our special, secret sauce," usually do not mislead consumers because they tend to view these terms as a permissible form of trade puffery. However, the menu planner may want to avoid even the appearance of impropriety and not use any term that cannot be supported.

Misrepresentation of Quality

The federal government, through the United States Department of Agriculture (USDA) and the Food and Drug Administration (FDA), has established quality-grading procedures for many foods. For instance, meats, poultry, and fresh produce have standardized quality grades that can be noted on the menu only if you purchase and use products that have received these grade designations from a government inspector. You cannot, for example, note that you serve U.S. Grade AA butter unless you can prove you are purchasing and using this type of item.

Misrepresentation of Price

You will run into problems if you do not disclose all relevant charges. For instance, if there will be an extra charge for each cook at an action station, all-white-meat chicken, no-ice drinks, and so forth, the client must know about it before he or she signs the catering contract.

Misrepresentation of Brand Name

You cannot advertise that you serve a particular brand if in fact you do not offer it. For instance, you cannot say that you offer Sanka coffee if you serve another brand of decaffeinated coffee.

Sometimes we are guilty of using brand names as generic terms. For example, we tend to use casually the terms "Coke," "Ry-Krisp," "Tabasco Sauce," and "Jell-O," not realizing they are proprietary brand names. One major food-service company was sued and eventually had to pay considerable monetary damages because guests were not informed when generic cola was served instead of the Coke product requested.

Misrepresentation of Product Identification

The standard of identity defines what a food product is. The federal government has established standards of identity for over 300 foods. For example, maple syrup is not the same as maple-flavored syrup, beef liver differs from calf liver, and ice milk cannot be served if ice cream is noted on the menu.

Misrepresentation of Point of Origin

Some menu items traditionally note specific points of origin, that is, areas of the world where the foods were harvested and/or produced. For instance, some seafood menu items are often preceded by their point of origin—Maine lobster, Alaska crab, and Colorado trout. You cannot make these claims unless you can prove you are purchasing these items from appropriate suppliers and serving them in your dining rooms.

Sometimes a misunderstanding can arise if you use a geographic term that describes a method of preparation. For instance, Manhattan clam chowder indicates that the chowder is tomato-based, not milk-based or cream-based. A naive client though, could misinterpret this designation; it is up to the menu planner to foresee problems of this type and, if necessary, explain the situation to the client beforehand.

Obviously, french fries do not come from France, russian dressing does not come from Russia, and swiss steak does not come from Switzerland. The typical consumer realizes these terms reflect a method of production and/or service. However, some qualifiers are too close to call and could confuse some guests. For instance, some customers may wonder about the origin of "imported cheddar cheese" while others will not give it a second thought. The astute menu planner should not flirt with these types of potential problems.

Misrepresentation of Merchandising Terms

Sometimes you can get into trouble if you use too much trade puffery when describing menu items. For instance, saying that you serve "only the best meat" implies that you serve the highest government quality grades.

You must avoid using terms such as "fresh daily," "home made," "center-cut portions," and so forth unless you can substantiate these claims.

You need to be careful when using any descriptive terminology to market foods. Words such as "silky," "crusty," and "creamy" can place you in an awkward position if the finished menu items do not live up to guests' interpretations of these descriptions.

Misrepresentation of Means of Preservation

The biggest problem in this example is when you say something is fresh when in reality it is fresh frozen, canned, bottled, or dried. The word "fresh" is probably the most overworked and incorrect term on the typical menu. For example, some people react negatively to the words "fresh orange juice" when in fact the product was made from frozen concentrate. Some eyebrows will rise when customers read "fresh shrimp cocktail" on the menu when in reality the shrimp were previously frozen. Even though some guests will ignore strict definitions, you cannot indicate freshness on the menu if the foods you purchase and use to make these menu items were preprepared, processed products.

Misrepresentation of Means of Preparation

Guests consider several things when selecting items from a menu, but it is felt that the way a dish is prepared is one of the most important determinants in the selection process.

When a guest orders a broiled food, he or she will not be happy with oven-fried, pan-fried, or baked food. Likewise if the customer orders deep-fried food; roasted, barbecued, or sauteed are unacceptable.

Sometimes we encounter difficulty when we book a party for 2,000 broiled steaks, which necessitates browning them on a broiler and then finishing them in a convection oven. Some customers will be able to identify the browned, baked steaks, and may be unhappy with the result.

Food preparation terms can also be used indiscriminately. For instance, it is tempting to note on the menu the words, "made from scratch." The prudent menu planner will avoid this description because it may be impossible to obtain raw food ingredients consistently. If a processed substitute must be used once in awhile, some guests may notice it and be disappointed.

Misrepresentation of Verbal and Visual Presentations

A catering sales representative must be careful when describing menu offerings to clients. If there is any doubt, he or she should contact the chef. At no time should you promise something that cannot be delivered.

Photos are a major part of the hotel catering department's sales effort. But since they always display subjects at their very best, the difference between a picture and the real thing can sometimes be as great as the difference between lightning and a lightning bug.

Even when you try to live up to a pictorial representation, there may be times when it is impossible. For instance, a picture may show seven different vegetables in an oriental dish. But if one of them is temporarily unavailable, a few guests may notice it and cause you an embarrassing moment or two.

Misrepresentation of Dietary or Nutritional Claims

No dietary or nutritional claim can be made unless you can prove the menu item meets the prescribed standards. In addition to being deceptive, false claims can be dangerous for your guests. For instance, if you note "salt free" or "free of preservatives" on the menu, persons on salt-free and/or preservative-free diets can be harmed if they consume an item that does not live up to expectations.

MENU PRICING

A menu price must cover the cost of food, payroll, and other variable and fixed costs, plus a fair profit for the hotel. As a general rule though, the price charged for a particular menu item is based primarily on its food cost.

Generally speaking, if the food cost for a catered event is estimated to be $9.00 per person, the menu price for this function will range between $27.00 per person (that is, a 33 percent food cost) to $36.00 per person (that is, a 25 percent food cost), plus applicable consumption taxes, gratuities, and/or service charges.

There are other, less-common menu-pricing procedures that can be used. For instance, some restaurant operators like to estimate their total annual expenses (except food costs), add in a fair annual profit, and divide this amount by the estimated number of customers expected during the year. This figure is the average amount of contribution margin (CM) needed from each customer. A menu price for any particular menu item then, is the food cost for one serving plus the average CM.

For example, assume the director of catering needs to earn an annual profit of $250,000, the forecasted annual expenses (except food costs) are $1,500,000, and 125,000 guests are expected during the year. In this case, the total amount of CM needed is $1,750,000 ($250,000 + $1,500,000) and the average CM is $14.00 ($1,750,000/125,000). A menu item with a food cost of $4.50 would be priced at $18.50 ($4.50 + $14.00) plus applicable consumption taxes, gratuities, and/or service charges.

When using this type of pricing procedure, the menu planner assumes that all costs of doing business, except food costs, are fixed. Realistically, food is not the only variable cost incurred by the typical food-service operation; for instance, labor cost is at least a semi-variable cost. However, the conservative menu planner realizes that semi-variable costs are more fixed than variable. To open the doors, a certain critical mass of labor, utilities, and so forth, must be made available; and this critical mass is quite expensive.

A catering sales representative could use this type of pricing procedure when computing competitive price quotations and preparing proposals. Alternatively, he or she could use a variation of it. For instance, a CM could be calculated that does not include food costs or labor costs. The average CM then can be added to the estimate of payroll and food costs needed to serve one guest.

For instance, assume a client wants to book a party for 100 persons and that the catering sales representative knows from experience that the average CM per person must be $5.00. Initially then, we know that the function must earn a total CM of $500 (100 × $5.00). Next, we determine that we will need about 6 servers and food production workers, which is priced out at, say, $460. If the menu desired is precosted at $6.00 per serving, the total food cost is $600 (100 × $6.00). The price quotation then, will be $15.60 per person (($500 + $460 + $600)/100) plus applicable consumption taxes, gratuities, and/or service charges.

Another way to price a meal function is to charge one price for the meal, one for labor, one for room rental, one for utilities, and so forth. This type of pricing is more common with off-premises caterers than it is with hotels. As a general rule, hotels do not use this pricing strategy primarily because it is too cumbersome. The typical client does not want to be burdened with an itemized list of charges even though it tends to be less expensive to negotiate for each charge separately. He or she prefers a price-per-person bottom line. It is more convenient, and it makes it easier for him or her to compare price quotations from several caterers.

It is important to note the required amount of applicable consumption taxes, gratuities, and/or service charges when quoting prices to potential clients.

Consumption taxes usually include local and state sales taxes. Some parts of the country also levy an entertainment tax, cabaret tax, and/or luxury tax on commercial food-service meals. These taxes are usually equal to a set percentage of a catered function's net price. (The net price does not include consumption taxes or gratuities.)

Though consumption taxes are usually a set percentage of a function's net price, there are some states and local municipalities that require you to charge taxes on the net price plus the gratuity. Generally, if a gratuity is noted separately on the final bill, and if it is dispensed entirely to employees, you will not have to charge consumption taxes on it. But if you note a service charge on the bill, and if you use this money to pay all employees a flat rate of compensation, then chances are you will need to charge consumption taxes on the function's net price plus the service charge.

In most states, if a commercial food-service operation extracts a service charge from each guest, in lieu of a voluntary tip, the restaurant must charge consumption taxes on it. In effect, the service charge becomes part of the net price, whereas the tip or gratuity does not.

The variations in taxing procedures between states and local municipalities can cause a great deal of confusion for clients, especially those who book events in several parts of the country. For instance, in some parts of Florida, the gratuity is taxed, whereas in Las Vegas it is not.

It can also be confusing for the catering executive because some events may have gratuities while others may have built-in service charges. For instance, with a convention, you might have one meal served by employees who receive a flat rate of compensation while the other meals will be handled by servers who receive gratuities. In this situation, you may need to calculate consumption taxes on the service charges, but not on the gratuities. You may need to calculate the taxes differently for each set of catered events before preparing competitive price quotations for potential clients.

It is also conceivable that a specific meal might include both flat-rate employees and gratuity-earning employees. For instance, employees on the A-list usually receive gratuities, whereas B-list employees usually work for a flat rate. The client may be paying a bit more consumption taxes than he or she might have to pay if the event was booked at another hotel in another state or local municipality.

In the restaurant industry, the terms "tips" and "gratuities" are used interchangeably. They have the same meaning. However, in the catering business, gratuities are mandatory charges, whereas tips are discretionary. Gratuities are usually equal to a mandatory 15 to 19 percent of the catered function's net price.

The gratuity is divided among various hotel employees. Usually hotel politics and traditions dictate who receives a share, and what the value of the shares will be. In some hotels, catering managers receive a share, while in other properties managerial personnel are excluded. Servers and sometimes set-up staff usually are the primary beneficiaries.

In some parts of the United States, state laws govern the distribution of gratuities. For instance, in California, gratuities are "owned" by the service staff. Hotels and restaurants can keep service charges, but cannot retain any portion of gratuities. You should check with the local state restaurant association to determine the pertinent regulations in effect in your area.

A client may wish to award voluntarily a tip to one or more catering employees because some additional service, or exceptionally good service, was provided. Some clients may also wish to reward noncatering employees because of their help in making the function an especially memorable one.

Professional meeting planners recommend that convention clients consider tipping several "unseen" hotel employees who do not participate in the gratuity pool, yet whose services can sometimes make or break a function.

Generally, convention clients are advised to budget 1 to 3 percent of their master or total bill for voluntary tips. For example, if the convention costs $100,000, a client should expect to award approximately $1,000 to $3,000 to other employees, especially the "heart-of-the-house" employees (such as technicians, PBX operators, and so forth) if their services were particularly timely and beneficial.

In ITT Sheraton's *A Guide for Meeting Planning,* the suggested basic tip guidelines are:

> The total tip should be 1 to 3 percent of the total master bill. The suggested distribution is: (Each area will vary depending on the size of the meeting and complexity of responsibilities.)
>
> 20 to 25 percent of the tip: convention coordinator
>
> 20 to 25 percent of the tip: sales manager (if active during the meeting)
>
> 10 to 15 percent of the tip: house set-up crew
>
> 5 to 10 percent of the tip: telephone center personnel
>
> 5 to 10 percent of the tip: front desk
>
> 5 to 10 percent of the tip: reservations
>
> 5 to 10 percent of the tip: audiovisual technician
>
> 5 to 10 percent of the tip: housekeeping (for VIP suites, staff rooms, and public areas)
>
> 3 to 5 percent of the tip: receiving department
>
> 2 to 5 percent of the tip: bell staff (for movement of convention materials, deliveries, and so forth)
>
> 20 percent of the tip: miscellaneous.

Convention clients are also encouraged to distribute these tips after the function ends, not before. This is the traditional procedure. Giving money or gifts ahead of time can smack of bribery. Furthermore, once the tip is given, there may be less incentive for employees to provide above-average service.

A client can give money, gifts, or both. For example, he or she can see to it that when tip money is distributed, employees also receive a small memento.

In addition to tips, the client should write a letter to the hotel general manager praising the employees' special efforts. In most cases, these types of letters can be the most valuable "tips" employees receive.

Some hotels require tips to be pooled and then distributed to members of the pool, while other properties allow the individual recipient to keep the entire amount. All tips received must be declared by staff members so that management can withhold the appropriate amount of income and social security taxes from the tip earners' pay checks.

Service charges are not gratuities. Nor are they tips. In restaurants, they are added to the customer's guest check in lieu of tips. In catering though, they would represent a separate charge for labor and would typically be part of an itemized price quotation. For instance, a service charge for extra servers would be added to a client's bill if he or she requested special service, or additional service, for some VIP guests. And, as noted above, the appropriate consumption taxes must be charged on them.

Usually when a catering sales representative quotes a price, he or she will note a "price, plus, plus." The price is the menu price per person, while the plus, plus represents the taxes and gratuity. For instance, a price quotation of "$20.00++" in Las Vegas tells the client that the total price per person will be $24.80 ($20.00 menu price, plus 7 percent sales tax ($1.40), plus 17 percent gratuity ($3.40)).

Many receptions are priced a la carte, that is, clients select the types and amounts of foods they want, and pay only for what they choose. For instance, a client may want to order coffee by the gallon, hors d'oeuvres by the piece, deli meats by the platter, and salads by the pound, and pay accordingly.

The prices charged for typical food functions usually include all the necessary labor and other overhead charges. About the only time extras are added is when the function is very small (in which case a room charge may be added) or it requires extra-special service (in which case a labor surcharge will be added).

Many hotels have "bingo" menus where the client orders, for example, B-5 (breakfast number 5), L-10 (luncheon number 10), or D-15 (dinner number 15), with prices usually listed on a separate sheet. Separate sheets are used so that the expensive standardized menus do not have to be reprinted whenever management decides to revise the menu prices. However, from a guest-satisfaction point of view, it is much better to have the prices next to the respective menu items so that the client does not have to bother flipping back and forth to match menus with prices.

Regardless of the type of pricing procedure used, you need to remember that your prices must be in line with your competitors' prices. You can charge more, but only if you give more. Clients seek overall value. They are willing to pay more if the quality and/or service justify a higher price. Conversely, they expect to pay less if the quality and/or service are marginal.

Usually a catering executive, under the guidance of senior management, will develop menu prices based on his or her costs of doing business. Once these are computed though, the manager will compare them to competitors' prices. He or she must "shop" the competition and determine if the calculated prices are competitive. If they are not, they may be revised or, if that is impossible, the recipes, quality, portion sizes, and/or service must be adjusted to allow for lower menu prices.

MENU DESIGN

The typical hotel catering department generally designs two types of menus: standardized and customized.

The standardized menu usually is a very lengthy presentation. It covers several pages of suggested appetizers, entrees, desserts, and so forth, along with current prices for each one. It also includes several suggested complete meal packages and their respective prices. Most potential clients pore over these listings when planning their functions.

The standardized menu is one of the catering sales representative's main sales tools. It is a major part of the catering department's brochure. It is perhaps the keystone of the department's marketing plan. Consequently, the hotel usually spends a great deal of time, money, and effort designing an attractive package. The format, layout, colors, pictures, paper stock, illustrations, graphics, copy, and fonts are normally first-rate.

The customized menu is primarily designed for those clients who want something different. For instance, a client may want to assemble a unique set of menu items and print a souvenir or commemorative menu. Some clients request menus printed on souvenir napkins or plates. This is typical with awards dinners, anniversaries, and weddings.

Customizing menus also allows the catering sales representative to work within a client's specific budgetary constraints.

A client may want to develop a specialized menu to include a certain logo, advertising, and/or style. For instance, a computer convention may want menus printed in the shape of personal computers.

If you are asked to print a customized menu, you should have all menu items listed in the center of the page, not on one side or the other. You want to avoid a "laundry-list" type of presentation. If possible, try to distribute the menu items on the page in such a way that they create an attractive visual presentation.

Convention clients who book several meals may want to communicate the menus to attendees ahead of time. For instance, a professional association convention may last several days. The convention announcements and registration booklets could list each day's menus so that attendees will know in advance what to expect and, if necessary, have enough time to make alternate plans.

TYPES OF MEAL FUNCTIONS

Each type of meal presents a unique set of challenges and opportunities. When planning a meal, the catering sales representative must know and understand the meal planner's objectives so that the appropriate menu, room setup, service, and timing can be provided.

Breakfast

Speed and efficiency are extremely important to breakfast meal planners. This is especially true if the attendees are conventioneers who will be going to business meetings, seminars, or other events immediately after the meal. The last thing a client wants is to start the day's activities late and throw off the whole day's schedule. Everything must be ready at the appointed time in order to avoid this problem.

Many conventioneers will skip the breakfast meal. Some of them traditionally do not eat breakfast. A few may be in the habit of engaging in early-morning exercise workouts and cannot make the scheduled breakfast time. And others may have been out late the night before and would rather sleep than eat.

Breakfast is a functional meal. Guests need to energize the brain cells. If they skip breakfast, chances are their attention spans will decrease and they will become irritable by 10:00 AM.

The menu should contain energizer foods, such as fresh fruits, whole grain cereals, whole grain breads, and yogurt. As a general rule, a person should try to start the day with these types of foods because, in addition to providing a bit of energy, they are much easier to digest than fatty foods. This will keep attendees awake and ready to tackle the morning's business needs.

There is a trend away from sweet rolls toward whole-grain, blueberry, and oat-bran muffins and fruit breads, such as banana or date breads. Sugary and fatty sweets, such as Danish, doughnuts, and pecan rolls, give only a temporary lift.

There must be some variety though, at breakfast. While many persons will not eat sugary, fatty foods, they may want to have at least a little taste of one. As much as possible, the menu should accommodate all guest preferences. For instance, you can offer bite-sized portions of several types of foods on a breakfast buffet table.

A buffet is the best type of service to have for breakfast functions because it can accommodate very easily both the early and late risers. In some cases it may cost less than sit-down service. And it can be just the thing for guests who are in a hurry because, if there are enough food and beverage stations, a breakfast buffet can be over in less than one hour.

The traditional breakfast buffet includes two or three types of breakfast meats, three to six varieties of pastries, two styles of eggs, one potato dish, and several selections of cereals, fresh fruits, cold beverages, hot beverages, and condiments.

An English-style breakfast buffet usually includes the traditional offerings along with one or more action stations. For instance, an action station, where chefs are preparing Belgian waffles, crepes, and eggs to order, is very popular with guests. This type of service though, can increase significantly the food and labor costs so it can only be offered if clients are willing to pay an extra charge.

For the cost-conscious client, the more economical continental breakfast buffet is appropriate. The traditional continental breakfast includes coffee, tea, fruit juice, and some type of bread. A deluxe version offers more varieties of juices, breads, and pastries, as well as fresh fruits, yogurt, and cereals.

If a breakfast buffet is planned, you should separate the food and beverage stations so that persons who want their coffee quickly, or do not want a full meal, will not have to stand in line behind those who are deciding which omelet to order. You also should separate condiments, such as cream, sugar, and lemons, and flatware from the coffee-urn areas. Since it usually takes a guest about twice as long to add cream and sugar as it does to draw a cup of coffee, this type of layout will prevent traffic congestion. If separate beverage stations are not feasible, you should have food servers serve beverages to guests at the dining tables.

Conventional sit-down breakfast service usually includes a combination of preset and plated services. This is an appropriate procedure if the guests have more time and want to savor the meal function a little longer. Served breakfasts though, make greater demands on the catering and kitchen staffs. More servers are needed and more food handlers are required to dish up the food in the kitchen. However, unlike buffet service, food costs are more controllable because you, not the guest, control portion sizes.

Many clients, especially corporate clients, want some added luxury touches at breakfast. For instance, they often appreciate things such as mimosa cocktails, virgin marys, exotic coffees, puff pastries, and fresh fruit in season.

Many people are not very sociable at breakfast. Also, if the guests trickle in a few at a time, they might spread out in the banquet room so that they can be alone with their thoughts, or with their last-minute work. The catering department might want to make available newspapers, such as *The Wall Street Journal* and/or *USA Today,* to those who do not wish to socialize so early in the day.

Refreshment Break

A refreshment break is an energy break. It is intended to refresh and sharpen attention. It also helps alleviate boredom that tends to develop when guests are engaged in tedious business activities during the day.

Refreshment breaks are typically scheduled at midmorning and midafternoon. They are usually located near the meeting and conference rooms. And they usually offer various types of "mood" foods, that is, foods that increase guests' enthusiasm to tackle the rest of the day's work schedule.

Ideally, the refreshment break station would include hot and cold beverages, whole fruits, raw vegetables with dip, yogurt, muffins, and other types of breads and pastries that will hold up well and will not dry out. Chewy foods, such as peanuts, dried fruits, and sunflower seeds, should also be available because these types of products are thought to relieve boredom.

The catering manager must ensure that cold beverages are available for each refreshment break, no matter what time of day the break is scheduled. Many guests prefer cold beverages throughout the day. And most of those that do prefer diet beverages. In fact, experience shows that over 75 percent of guests selecting cold beverages will choose a sugarless drink, such as diet soda, sparkling water, or club soda.

Some refreshment breaks include only beverages. This is especially true with the midmorning coffee break. A beverage-only break does not distract convention attendees as much as one where several foods are available. Guests get a beverage and are apt to return to business quickly, whereas foods take longer to select and consume, thereby slowing down service and possibly throwing off the rest of the day's schedule.

Speed is a major consideration for some refreshment breaks. If so, the menu should not offer any foods that will slow down service and cause attendees to arrive late at their next business activity. For instance, when you have a short break, you would not want to offer sliced fruit on a tray. Instead, you should offer fruit kabobs, which can be picked up quickly and easily.

Another major consideration is to locate the refreshment break station so that it serves the client's needs. Ideally, it should be placed in a separate room or in the prefunction space. It should not be located at the back of a meeting room. If it is, a speaker will have a hard time getting started if attendees are lingering too long around the food and beverage stations. The speaker also cannot compete easily with the food and beverage stations; guests are liable to sneak a quick trip to the back of the room and disrupt the proceedings. Furthermore, there may be a lot of noise pollution when tables are replenished.

Be sure to provide trash receptacles for waste and trays for dirty tableware. A server should check the refreshment setup periodically and replenish foods and beverages as needed. He or she should remove trash and soiled tableware and not let them stack up. Someone also needs to be responsible for tidying up the break area regularly. Few things are as unattractive as finding, for example, a half-eaten pastry on a pastry tray next to whole, untouched ones.

Many clients, especially meeting planners, want refreshment breaks available all day. In effect, they want permanent refreshment centers.

Meeting planners who are accustomed to conference centers expect permanent refreshment centers. The permanent refreshment center was introduced to our industry by conference centers. If the hotel wants to compete effectively with these properties, it must offer similar amenities.

Clients reap many advantages with permanent refreshment centers. For one thing, clients feel this will keep attendees around all day. If attendees go off to a restaurant outlet for a cold drink, they may never return for the business activities.

Permanent refreshment centers also provide additional flexibility. For instance, clients do not have to schedule a break at, say, 3:00 PM sharp. A break can be taken a little before or a little after 3:00 PM, that is, whenever there is a natural break in the business activities. Attendees do not have to break at an inconvenient or inappropriate time in order to get a quick snack or drink.

A permanent refreshment center usually stocks coffee, tea, and cold soft drinks all day, with foods being offered only at certain times, say at 10:00 AM and 3:00 PM. (If foods are kept out all day, make sure to serve items that will not dry out—muffins, for example, instead of sliced breads.) All-day nonalcoholic beverage service provides an attractive, comfortable social atmosphere for attendees to congregate and discuss the day's activities.

Some clients prefer nonfood and nonbeverage refreshment breaks. For instance, many conventions are beginning to schedule exercise breaks during the day. Instead of eating and drinking, they adjourn to the hotel's health club, spa, tennis court, or other athletic area and spend a few minutes getting their juices flowing.

Some clients want the traditional refreshment breaks, but they also want them to be preceded by exercise periods. For instance, just before the midmorning refreshment break, a corporate client may schedule an exercise leader to come in and lead attendees in a few stretching exercises.

Luncheon

Often luncheons are very similar to breakfasts in that they are intended to provide a convenience to convention attendees and to ensure that they will not roam away and neglect the afternoon's business activities.

If a luncheon is intended solely to provide a refueling stop for attendees, the menu should not include an overabundance of sink-to-the-bottom foods. If attendees eat too much of these foods they will most likely become drowsy and inattentive later in the day.

Sink-to-the-bottom foods are greasy, fatty foods, such as cheese omelets, and carbohydrate foods, such as pasta dishes. These products take a long time to digest; for instance, fats can sit in the stomach several hours. Conversely, fruits and vegetables are digested more quickly. Carbohydrates are somewhere in between, in that they digest more rapidly than fats, but not as quickly as fruits and vegetables.

"Working" luncheons usually rely quite a bit on white meats and salad greens. Breads, pastas, heavy sauces, and so forth are usually de-emphasized. If served, they usually are served on the side so that guests can take a small taste. Serving these products on the side will tend to discourage guests from consuming too much.

You should have some fatty foods on the menu. Some guests will be disappointed if, for example, they cannot have a few french fries or butter pats. The wise director of catering will see to it that options are available to satisfy everyone. For instance, if the main course is chicken, if feasible, you may want to offer a choice of fried, baked, or broiled. Another crowd pleaser is the deli buffet. It serves the dieter, the manhandler, and everyone else in between.

Whatever strategy followed by the working luncheon meal planner, it is important to remember that attendees may be eating several luncheons during their stay at the hotel. In this situation, variety is mandatory.

Most guests are satisfied with the few traditional breakfast selections. But they normally seek greater variety when selecting luncheon menu items. If they do not get it from you, they will go to a restaurant or bar for lunch and be late getting back to the afternoon's business sessions. In some cases, they may get side tracked and not come back at all.

Many luncheons are not working luncheons, where refueling and keeping attendees on the property are the major objectives. The "nonworking" type of luncheon usually involves some sort of ceremony. For instance, many luncheons have speakers, audiovisual displays, fashion shows, awards, announcements, and so forth that may overshadow other objectives

When you have a ceremonial type of luncheon booked in your hotel, the logistics are more complicated. For instance, you must ensure that head tables and reserved tables are noted correctly, name badges prepared, audiovisual installed and ready to go, all lighting synchronized properly, and printed materials, if any, set at each guest's place. You also need to ensure that sufficient labor is scheduled to handle the food and nonfood service demands adequately.

Buffet, preset, and plated services are the typical service styles used for luncheon meals. In most cases, luncheon service is similar to breakfast service. Speed is usually a major concern. Consequently, menus and service styles are usually selected with quickness and efficiency in mind.

Reception

Receptions are often predinner functions designed primarily to encourage people to get to know one another. For instance, most conventions schedule an opening reception, that is, ice-breaker party, to allow attendees to make new friends and renew old acquaintances. If an ice-breaker reception is not scheduled, but a dinner is, an attendee usually will meet only the handful of people sitting at his or her dining table.

Some receptions are not predinner functions. For instance, many conventions have hospitality suites that are open late in the evening. Hospitality suites are similar to ice-breaker parties in that they encourage participants to mingle. They also can be used by sponsors to introduce new products and/or build goodwill. For example, a book publisher at a book-sellers convention may sponsor a hospitality suite to introduce new authors, or to allow guests to meet established authors.

Some receptions are held during the standard dinner hours and are intended to take the place of dinner. For instance, a museum may host an evening reception to unveil a new collection and, incidentally, solicit membership for the local museum society. The function allows people to eat and get to know one another, while at the same time giving the museum an opportunity to gain favorable publicity.

One thing that most receptions have in common is that they usually include alcoholic beverage service in addition to food. Another common trait is the fact that rarely are they scheduled during business-day hours; normally a reception begins after 5:00 PM.

When planning a reception, it is best to locate several food buffet stations around the room, each with a different type of food. This encourages guests to move around and socialize. If possible, you should include one or two action stations. You also should have a server at each station to replenish foods, bus soiled tableware, remove trash, and be a psychological deterrent to curb guests' tendencies to heap their plates and/or return several times.

If beverages are served, the bars and nonalcoholic-beverage stations should also be spaced around the room. You should place them a sufficient distance from the food stations so that people have to change locations in order to get a drink. This further increases guest participation and mingling.

If the reception is intended to take the place of dinner, you should offer a complete balance of food type, color, temperature, preparation methods, and so forth, to suit every taste. And, since this type of reception normally extends for a longer period of time than the predinner one, and people will in effect be consuming the equivalent of dinner, sufficient backup food and beverage supplies must be available to prevent stockouts.

The selection of foods offered should have broad appeal. You should be careful when serving exotic foods some guests may not recognize. For instance, if you are serving unusual fish items on a buffet table, you might want to identify them with name cards. Similarly if unusual foods are passed by servers; the servers should be able to answer any questions posed by guests.

Menu items should be bite-sized. This allows guests to sample a wide variety of foods without wasting too much of it. It also ensures that the foods will be easy to consume. Ease of consumption is very important since most guests must balance plates and glassware while moving around.

Menu items must be easy for guests to hold and to eat. For instance, while kabobs are popular items served at receptions, if they are not prepared and assembled properly, guests will have a frustrating experience trying to eat them. If you serve kabobs, you should put the food ingredients only on the bottom half of the skewer. Otherwise, guests will be unable to get all the food off the skewer without making a mess.

Foods also should not be messy or greasy. Nor should they leave stains on clothes or teeth. For instance, you should avoid sauced foods, such as barbecued chicken wings, that might drip when guests are eating them. Instead, you should offer chicken tenders with a stiff sauce served on the side.

Be certain not to use dinner-sized plates for receptions. These encourage overeating. It also encourages excessive waste because a guest may fill the plate, eat some of the food, set the plate down somewhere, forget it, and then go back for another plate of food. Furthermore, guests with large plates of food will tend to sit down to eat and will not mingle and network very much, if at all.

Seating should be minimized at receptions. You do not want to encourage guests to sit and eat; remember, you want to promote mingling and networking. Seating should not exceed 25 to 30 percent of the guest count. Cabaret-style seating, or park benches, both of which have little or no table space, are suitable.

To encourage mingling, and to control food costs, you should consider having servers pass foods in addition to, or instead of, placing food buffet stations throughout the room. Guests tend to eat less if the foods are passed. Generally, if the foods are displayed on a buffet table where guests can help themselves, they will eat twice as much as they would if all foods were passed butler-style by servers.

You should not have all foods passed. You should have at least one or two food stations and/or action stations to enhance the visual appearance of the function room.

If you offer passed foods, you should only place one type of food on a tray, otherwise guests will take too long to make their selections. If they cannot decide easily what to take, they may take one of each. This will slow down service because the servers will not be able to work the room quickly and efficiently. It also might encourage overconsumption and food waste.

Unfortunately with passed foods, the client's labor charge will be a bit higher. However, this should be offset with a lower food cost. As noted, guests will consume less if foods are passed. You also can control the pace of service. For instance, you can stagger service by sending out servers with trays every fifteen minutes instead of taking all the food out at one time. Furthermore, the catering sales representative should remind clients that passed foods lend an air of elegance to the reception that many guests will appreciate.

Receptions can be tailored to any budget. Unlike other meal functions, the clients have more flexibility. There are many opportunities to be extravagant or frugal. For example, clients can control the time allocated for the reception; they can offer a seafood bar with a few shrimp and a lot of inexpensive mussels arranged on crushed ice; or they can start with expensive hors d'oeuvres and back them up with less expensive cheese and dry snacks. The breakfast, luncheon, and dinner planner generally does not enjoy such a wide array of options.

Generally, if you are charging clients according to the amount of foods consumed, you would opt for buffet tables, dinner-sized plates, and self service. On the other extreme, passed foods are appropriate if the client is paying a per-person charge for unlimited consumption. Since many clients prefer paying a per-person charge for foods, your service strategies will tend toward passed foods. However, usually you and your clients can find several mutually agreeable positions between these two extremes to satisfy everyone's quality and cost requirements.

Dinner

Dinner is the most typical catered meal. While it shares many similarities with breakfast and luncheon, usually it is a longer, more elaborate affair.

Unlike breakfast or luncheon, a client will be more adventurous when booking a dinner function because he or she usually has more money and time to work with. For example, Russian and French service styles are more likely at dinner than at other meals. Even the buffet, preset, and preplated service styles are enhanced. Furthermore, entertainment is more common at dinner.

Many dinners are part of a theme, ceremony, or other type of major production where food service is only one part of the event. Rarely are dinners scheduled merely for refueling purposes.

Dinner guests usually are not on a tight time schedule. They normally do not have to be at a business meeting or any other sort of activity later on in the evening. As a result, some tend to wander in late, while others tend to linger well after the function ends. Catering staff must be aware of these tendencies and plan accordingly.

The catering sales representative should be prepared to work closely with the client in developing the dinner event. Many clients do not have sufficient background or expertise to plan a major function. Nor do they have the creative talents necessary to plan an unforgettable experience.

For instance, most conventions reserve one night for an awards banquet. Clients and catering executives need to find ways to take the boredom out of awards presentations without sacrificing the recognition that winners deserve.

An awards banquet is often part of a grand banquet given on the convention's last night. Unfortunately, this approach has several drawbacks. For one thing, attendees have just survived an intense few days of meetings and other business activities and are ready to party. Most of them have probably been to one or more receptions earlier in the evening and have consumed a few alcoholic beverages. And if wine is served with the meal, the group may become boisterous.

The catering sales representative should suggest ways to avoid these problems. For example, there is a trend in the industry to present awards early in the convention, say on the first day. This ensures greater attention from attendees. It also allows the recipients to bask in the limelight throughout the convention.

Awards can also be given at breakfasts or luncheons. Guests are a bit more alert during these times. Furthermore, they then can have the last night free to have fun and unwind.

If there are several awards to be given, another tactic is to spread the presentations throughout the convention. You should begin with the minor awards and save the most important, prestigious one for the last night.

If a client insists on the traditional final-night awards banquet, you should suggest that the presentations be staggered between courses instead of scheduling them at the end of the meal. Since dinner meals tend to run overtime, if all awards are presented at the end, chances are the program will have to begin before or during dessert. Some guests may not be paying attention and embarrassing conversation may continue throughout the program.

The catering sales representative also must be aware of the protocols, seating arrangements, and other similar considerations associated with various ceremonies so that the client can be advised correctly.

The catering sales representative also should be prepared to suggest themes that can be used by clients to increase interest in their dinner functions.

Theme parties will promote dinner attendance. For instance, some convention attendees may be motivated to register because one or two theme parties are being offered. Furthermore, convention attendees' spouses are also more anxious to go to the convention if this type of entertainment is offered.

Theme parties are in vogue. They add interest and provide a good deal of fun for the guests. You do not need to spend a great deal of money to throw a theme party. Carnival, circus, state fair, drive-in, fifties, sixties, and halloween are easy themes to incorporate into the dinner function. For instance, a successful halloween party needs only a costume contest, harvest buffet, and a few magic props.

Some clients want to design themes that will enhance the image of the group booking the dinner. For example, a dairy convention may want to hold an ice-cream-social theme party to introduce new frozen dairy products. The catering sales representative will need to work closely with the client to ensure that this party runs smoothly.

A dinner usually is much, much more than a meal. Food and beverage is only one part of it. The catering executive must be able to juggle many attractions when helping clients plan these major events.

Off-Premises Catering

Some hotels go beyond the traditional on-premises meal functions and offer off-premises options. However, there are only a few properties that offer this option. Usually the typical hotel is unable to perform this service adequately.

Off-premises catering is a very-involved business that is much different than on-premises catering. It requires a very different form of management. To do it correctly, you must have a considerable amount of unique, specialized equipment that the typical hotel does not have.

For example, the off-premises caterer needs on-site preparation and service equipment, and transport equipment. The full-service off-premises caterer also needs power generators, fresh-water and brown-water wagons, portable furniture, and tents.

Some hotels will not solicit off-premises catering business because they do not want to be put into the unpleasant position of being unable to get maximum use from expensive fixed assets. To perform adequately, you need to invest a great deal of money in transport equipment, especially trucks and vans. Portable hot-holding and cold-holding equipment that can be transported off-site are also very expensive. Unless these assets can be rented for a reasonable price, it could be economically disastrous to own them if they are going to be used sparingly.

In addition to investment considerations, the off-premises caterer encounters many problems foreign to the typical hotel director of catering. For instance, the off-premises caterer must pre-visit the site and check the layout and design, see what utilities are available, determine what, if any, type of cooking can be performed on site, have a back-up plan in the event of inclement weather, hire qualified drivers, secure communications equipment (such as cellular phones), obtain the appropriate insurance rider, obtain union permission to use on-site employees off-site, and a whole host of additional related details.

The off-premises caterer also encounters many sanitation and safety problems that do not afflict the hotel catering department. For example, the off-premises caterer cannot reuse any leftovers (except sealed condiments), whereas the hotel may be able to salvage some. Only foods that transport well can be used. The off-premises caterer does not have complete control over the function site, so his or her product liability insurance will be very expensive. The hotel usually is not set up to remove finished foods safely from the kitchen, to the back door, and onto a waiting vehicle. It may be difficult to secure a potable water source. Garbage and trash removal are more difficult to handle at off-site venues. In addition, equipment used to transport finished foods usually cannot be used as serving containers on a buffet line; the foods must be removed from the transport containers and put into serving bowls, trays, and/or pans designed for service.

Other operational problems unique to the off-premises caterer include: tying up the hotel's loading dock and receiving area when stocking the catering vehicle(s); prepreparing products in-house, transporting them, and handling final preparation and service on location; making sure all employees get to the right place at the right time; transporting, setting up, and tearing down all furniture and equipment; controlling shoplifting; setting up and tearing down tents; installing and removing portable heating or cooling equipment; installing and operating electrical power generators; packing items very carefully to eliminate breakage; and qualifying for the relevant business licenses, liquor licenses, and health permits.

Usually the biggest barrier facing the hotel that wants to get involved with off-premises catering is the lack of adequate vehicles. One way to get around this stumbling block is to borrow another hotel department's truck or van. Another method used is to rent or purchase old UPS vans, milk trucks, or hotel laundry trucks; they work well because they back up readily to loading docks and equipment can be rolled in very easily. The only problem with these strategies though, is unless the vehicles meet local health district codes, you cannot use them to transport foods.

If a regular client requests off-premises catering, it is not smart to refuse the request. If the hotel cannot handle the request, at the very least you should refer the client to a reputable off-premises caterer whose standards and reputation parallel yours. It is a mistake to refer the client to an unknown off-premises caterer who does not share your views.

Even though off-premises projects may be minimally profitable for some hotels, a few may be willing to get involved with them in order to satisfy good clients. These properties also may decide to maintain vending machines, prepare box lunches, cater an off-site picnic, stock the sleeping rooms' in-room bar cabinets, and so forth, rather than divert this business to competitors.

One form of off-premises catering provided by many hotels is the box-lunch option. For instance, a convention may request individual box lunches for a day when the attendees will be taking a bus tour. Alternatively, a catering and/or kitchen employee could pack a few foods and beverages, ride with the group, and set up a small picnic-style buffet at a rest stop location.

Another type of off-premises catering provided by many hotels involves a food or beverage function held outside the banquet areas, but within the hotel property. For instance, a client may want to book a pool-side party, garden wedding, or picnic barbecue.

Most hotel catering departments are usually able to handle the out-door function so long as it is on hotel property. For instance, if there are many requests for picnic barbecues, the hotel may build a permanent out-door grill and shelter, complete with hot and cold running water, refrigeration, and storage space.

Another form of off-premises catering that may be thrust upon the catering department is the type that starts out being an on-premises function and eventually ends up being a combination of on-premises and off-premises. For instance, a major banquet may suddenly require more floor space than the hotel has available. To accommodate it though, a tent and other related equipment can be rented.

In lieu of renting, hotels may wish to purchase one or more tents so that they have them readily available to handle space crunches. Tents are aesthetically pleasing and come in all shapes and sizes. They can be used solely to shelter the foods, or they can house the entire party. Some can be heated, air conditioned, and floored with wood or astroturf. They also can be used indoors to enhance decor.

It would appear that sooner or later, the director of catering will get involved with some type of off-premises catering function. You must be prepared to handle the occasional request or else risk losing current and future business.

7

Beverage Functions

When love and skill work together, expect a masterpiece.

John Ruskin

Beverage functions almost always include food today. It is very unusual for a beverage function to offer only alcoholic and non-alcoholic drinks. At the very least, clients want to include a few hors d' oeuvres or dry snacks.

In view of increasing host and host-property liability, the wise catering executive will not book events that offer only alcoholic beverages. For instance, all-evening drinking parties, such as fraternity bashes and bachelor parties, are inappropriate.

This chapter will highlight those catered events where alcoholic beverages are served. Since alcohol is often served at meal functions, the reader should read Chapter 6 before continuing with this chapter because much of that discussion is pertinent to Chapter 7.

By necessity, Chapters 6 and 7 overlap. Our intent is to highlight the beverage-service aspects of the hotel catering business. To that end, Chapter 7 should be considered a supplement to Chapter 6, and vice versa.

PURPOSE OF THE BEVERAGE FUNCTION

The purpose of the beverage function will give the catering sales representative an insight into the client's wishes. This information is invaluable when working with the client to create an exciting, memorable event.

There are many reasons why clients schedule beverage functions. However, unlike meal functions, there tends to be at least one common thread appearing in all of them: the fact that these events usually serve as a way for guests to socialize and practice networking.

A beverage function is not a refueling stop. It is not scheduled primarily to give guests the opportunity to recharge their batteries. After all, no one needs to consume alcoholic beverages to survive.

Rather, beverage functions offer guests a chance to visit with other guests in a relaxed, leisurely setting. New acquaintances are made and old ones rekindled. Job openings are circulated. Hot tips are exchanged. And the seeds of many successful business dealings are planted.

Another common thread that most beverage functions share is the time of day they are offered. Usually they are scheduled after 5:00 PM. Every once in a while you will be asked to offer poured-wine service, and/or specialty drinks such as bloody marys, at a luncheon meal function. However, it is less common today for a client to request liquor service before the end of the normal business day.

Still another interesting common thread found among beverage functions is that many of them are scheduled before a meal. Premeal cocktail receptions, such as an ice-breaker reception, allow strangers the opportunity to get acquainted. For instance, if a guest is invited to a meal function where he or she knows very few of the other guests, it is much easier to meet them while strolling through a reception area than it is by sitting at one dining table for the whole evening.

Some receptions are intended to take the place of a meal. For instance, a cocktail reception scheduled from 5:00 PM to 8:00 PM usually must offer a reasonable variety of foods so that guests can select enough of them to create a meal. Even if these guests expect to go out to dinner later, the client usually must see to it that sufficient foods are offered to satisfy those guests who will not make alternate dining plans.

A client may schedule a short reception in order to provide some sort of transition period from a long work day to an enjoyable meal function. For instance, the convention client realizes that some attendees who were working very hard during the day may not stick around for a dinner function scheduled to begin at 8:30 PM. However, if a short cocktail reception precedes the dinner, many of the attendees who do not expect to go to dinner may show up for the reception. Once at the reception, some of them may stay for the dinner. This bit of uncertainty could cause difficulty with guarantees and seating arrangements, but proper advance planning should minimize the problem.

Even though there are several commonalities found in each beverage function, the catering sales representative still must query clients regarding their perceived primary objectives for scheduling them. By knowing as much as possible about clients' needs, desires, and objectives, the catering executive can suggest the types of functions that will satisfy them.

MENU PLANNING

It is relatively easy to develop a drink menu. If the client wants a particular type of drink, you usually can provide it. If you do not have the necessary ingredients in stock, you usually can get them before the date booked for the function. And if you have sufficient production and service equipment to handle a standard drink menu, you essentially have enough equipment to prepare and serve just about any type of drink clients and guests might request.

Most clients are satisfied with the standard drink menu. This menu usually includes a red, white, and blush wine, a domestic light beer and domestic regular beer, a few soft drink brands, drink mixers, and at least one brand each of scotch, gin, vodka, bourbon, rum, tequila, and Canadian whisky.

A more elaborate drink menu usually includes the standard offerings plus one brand each of blended whisky, rye, brandy, champagne, and imported beer. It also may offer some specialty drinks, such as margaritas, frozen daiquiris, and/or grasshoppers.

The top-of-the-line drink menu offers a wide selection of liquor brands, both imported and domestic. For instance, a guest who wants a gin and tonic does not have to settle for the one brand offered on the standard drink menu (that is, the hotel's "well" brand"). Chances are he or she can choose from among two or three brands of gin. In other words, guests are offered the choice of several "call" brands.

Some clients may want to specify each brand of liquor and nonalcoholic beverage offered during the beverage function. However, when shopping for beverage service, most clients will not want to select all brands. Usually some of them will choose only those few that absolutely must be offered in order to satisfy guests. For instance, some clients may want to specify the exact brand names of wines served at upcoming catered meal functions, but not those liquors served during the premeal receptions.

Instead of specifying each brand name of beverage that must be served at the catered event, most clients would rather concentrate on the price per drink, price per bottle, labor charges, specific needs (such as a particular style of cocktail service), and/or the price charged for each hour the bar is open. This does not mean though, you should ignore the subject of well liquor versus call or premium liquor.

You will need to broach this subject with potential clients. One way to do this is to develop a drink menu that notes all brand names and the prices charged per container. For instance, you might note that a well brand costs $20.00 per liter, plus, plus, and that a call brand costs $25.00 per liter, plus, plus. If a client desires, he or she can then mix and match well brands and call brands and create a unique drink menu.

Occasionally you will encounter clients, or guests, who have personal drink recipes they want your bartenders to prepare. For example, a guest may prefer a unique type of martini made in a special way.

Usually it is no problem for you to honor these requests if you know about them in advance so that you can stock the necessary ingredients. If guests request off-menu selections at the last minute though, you may not be able to accommodate them. While a bartender could run off to one of the hotel's permanent bar outlets to service a special request, unfortunately this could slow down service drastically and disappoint the other guests.

MENU PRICING

Beverage functions can be priced several ways. The catering sales representative usually can offer a few alternatives to clients. However, before discussing pricing procedures with clients, it is important to determine if the beverage function will be offered as a: (1) cash bar; (2) open bar; or (3) a combination of cash bar and open bar.

Cash Bar

A cash bar is sometimes referred to as a no-host bar. In order to get drinks at a cash bar, guests will need to pay for them personally. The guests typically must purchase drink tickets from a separate cashier and give them to the bartenders in exchange for drinks. At a small beverage function, the bartenders may take cash and prepare and serve drinks, thereby eliminating the cashier position.

Open Bar

An open bar is sometimes referred to as a host bar. Guests do not pay for their drinks. The client (that is, host) or a sponsor is paying for them. Guests usually can drink as much as they want and what they want during the beverage function without having to pay.

In some cases, the open bar may have a limited amount of stock of each type of beverage. When one brand runs out, guests will need to select another brand or another type of beverage product.

The catering sales representative must warn the client that some of his or her guests may not take kindly to the open bar that stocks a very limited amount of merchandise. While guests usually will go along with limiting the amount of wine served at a sit-down meal, they may get upset if they must wait in line at a portable bar only to find that their favorite type of beverage is gone. The gin drinker can live with an off brand of gin, but he or she will not be happy if bourbon or rye are the only alternatives left.

Combination Bar

A combination bar includes elements of both the cash bar and the open bar. The typical combination bar arrangement involves the client paying for each guest's first two drinks, with the guests then paying for any subsequent ones. For instance, the client may purchase the first two drink tickets and issue them to each guest in convention-registration packets. After that, guests are on their own. If they want more drinks, they will need to purchase their own drink tickets.

The combination bar is the logical solution for the client who does not want to provide a limited stock of liquor at an open bar, yet cannot afford to allow guests unlimited consumption. Most guests would rather pay for one or two drinks if that is what it takes to get the exact products they want. They will usually ignore the extra costs long before they forget the fact that they were unable to indulge their desires.

Beverage Charges

The way in which liquor charges are set varies somewhat from food-menu pricing procedures. Generally speaking, with food, the menu price offered to potential clients includes all relevant charges for food, labor, and direct and indirect operating expenses. With beverage though, potential clients usually can pick and choose how they want to pay these relevant charges. They usually can pay one price for everything, or they can opt for an itemized list of charges and pay for each one separately.

1. *Charge per drink.* This is the typical pricing procedure used for cash bars. Normally the price charged per drink is high enough to cover all relevant expenses.

Individual drink prices usually are set to yield a standard beverage cost percentage set by the hotel. For instance, mixed-drink prices usually are based on a beverage cost percentage ranging from approximately 12 percent to 18 percent; wines and beers usually are priced to yield a beverage cost percentage of approximately 25 percent. The prices will be lower only if a client pays separately for other relevant charges.

The client sometimes can negotiate away some of these extra charges if a certain level of sales is attained, unless he or she requests something special not normally provided by the hotel. For instance, the results of a recent survey reported in *Meeting News* noted that hotels will often waive bartender charges if the beverage sales are approximately $300 per hour.

The price-per-drink method can also be used for open bars. Bartenders can keep track of all drinks prepared and served by ringing up each one on a precheck machine. At the end of the beverage function, a total count will be computed and extended by multiplying the number of drinks consumed by the agreed-upon price per drink. Consumption taxes and gratuities are added, and the final accounting is presented to the client for payment.

Some clients may want the hotel to charge a relatively low price per drink at cash bars in order to minimize the financial impact on guests. The catering executive can accommodate these requests by charging clients separately for the bartenders, cocktail servers, cashiers, security personnel, and/or room rental. Alternatively, he or she could suggest that the client directly subsidize the drink prices by, for example, paying the hotel $1.00 for each drink served.

When charging per drink, the catering sales representative may offer a sliding scale of prices depending upon the size of the beverage function. For instance, you might charge $3.50 per drink for the first 500 drinks, and then $3.00 per drink for those served thereafter.

2. *Charge per bottle.* This is a common pricing procedure used for open bars. The charge-per-bottle pricing method also is typically used when poured-wine service is offered during a luncheon or dinner meal function.

A physical inventory of all liquor is made at the beginning and end of the beverage function in order to determine liquor usage. Many hotels will charge the client for each opened bottle even though all the liquor is not used. In this situation, the remaining liquor often is sent to the client's suite or to a hospitality suite. If a client has booked several catering events during the convention, the leftover opened liquor could be used at the next function. Before doing this though, check any liquor codes that may apply.

A hotel might charge for partial bottles, though this is an unusual practice. For instance, it could charge the client for each tenth of a container of nonperishable liquor consumed. However, if a container of perishable liquor, such as draft beer and some wines, is opened, the client is usually charged for the whole container even if some product is left over. This liquor could be sent to the client's suite, or to a hospitality suite; generally though, anything that is past its peak of quality is discarded.

If the client pays for each bottle, instead of per drink, he or she may save a bit of money in the long run, though it is usually more difficult to calculate costs and monitor consumption. For instance, if a liter of gin yields 15 drinks at a price of $3.00 each, the expected revenue is $45.00 per liter, plus, plus. Generally though, a hotel catering department will not charge this amount if the client purchases the gin on a per-bottle basis. Usually the per-bottle charge in this case will be a little less. However, it cannot be significantly lower unless the client is willing to pay separately for other relevant charges.

3. *Charge per person.*   This pricing option usually is available to clients who want to offer open bars to their guests. Since the open bar reduces the hotel's control over liquor consumption, the price per person usually is set fairly high to ensure profitability.

The amount charged per guest may include a charge for food in addition to beverage. If so, the client's final billing usually is based on the type and amount of foods and liquors desired and the amount of time the bar must remain open. For instance, if a client wants specialized, expensive canapes, quite a few call brands, and/or wants the bar to remain open longer than normal, the catering executive will charge much more per person than if the client settles for standard offerings. This method is often more attractive to clients because they know up front the charges; there are no surprises.

4. *Charge per hour.*   This is similar to the charge-per-person pricing procedure. The major difference is that usually this pricing method includes a sliding scale of charges. For instance, for 150 guests, a client may have to pay $1,500 for the first hour of standard bar service and $1,000 for the second hour. Since most guest consumption takes place in the first hour, the hotel can offer a lower price for the second hour and still earn a fair profit.

When using this pricing procedure, the catering executive must consider the number of guests expected. For instance, you might charge $1,500 for the first hour if there are 150 guests or less. If you do not consider the number of guests, you have no control over the number of people who can show up at the event. You must have a guaranteed number of maximum guests expected before quoting a specific charge per hour.

To some extent then, the charge-per-hour pricing strategy must be combined with the charge-per-person pricing strategy. For instance, you might charge $15.00 per person for the first hour, $10.00 per person for the second hour, and so forth. This combination strategy will usually satisfy those clients who prefer a fixed charge per hour. It also ensures the hotel will retain control over sales, expenses, and profits. However, if you pursue this strategy, make sure all guests arrive at the first hour.

5. *Flat-rate charge.*   This is similar to the price-per-guest pricing procedure. With this pricing method though, the client pays one bottom-line charge for the beverage function.

The flat-rate charge is usually based on the assumption that guests will consume an average of 2 drinks apiece during the first hour, and 1 drink apiece per hour thereafter. The charge usually varies according to the number of guests expected and the amount of call liquor requested by clients.

Some clients prefer the flat-rate charge to other pricing methods since it is the easiest way to purchase a beverage function. And, no matter how much guests consume, clients know in advance what the price will be. They do not have to worry about exceeding their budgets. And there is no need for the client to bother with inventorying empty liquor containers or auditing the number of drinks prepared and served.

Labor Charges

Clients can usually opt to pay separately for liquor and labor charges. Some clients prefer the convenience of one all-inclusive charge. However, many of them would gladly do some extra work if the potential savings are worthwhile.

When labor charges are segregated from food and beverage product charges, in effect you are giving clients an opportunity to save money. For instance, a client may be able to reduce the meal price if he or she is willing to accept a style of service, such as preset, preplated service, that is not very labor intensive. Similarly, the client who agrees to reduce the number of bartenders and let some guests help themselves to wine and beer can also cut labor costs.

Unfortunately, since these options can sometimes compromise food and beverage quality- and cost-control standards, you should not offer them indiscriminately unless clients understand the potential trade-offs.

Sometimes labor charges are waived by the catering sales representative. For instance, a very large party that generates considerable food, beverage, and sleeping-room revenues may receive complimentary bartenders and cocktail servers.

Labor charges may also be waived if the beverage function generates a specified amount of business. For instance, the catering sales representative may charge the client for three bartenders to staff a cash bar, but note in the catering contract that half of the charge will be rebated if 300 drinks are consumed, and all of the charge will be rebated if 500 drinks are consumed.

1. *Charge for bartenders.* Usually clients must hire a minimum number of bartenders for a minimum number of hours. For example, a hotel may have a policy that all beverage functions must have at least one bartender working a four-hour shift. This minimum is particularly common in union properties.

Often the labor charge for bartenders is based on a sliding scale. For instance, if two bartenders are scheduled, the client may have to pay $125.00 for the first hour, $75.00 for the second hour, and $50.00 for every hour thereafter.

2. *Charge for bar backs.* Generally speaking, there is no separate charge for bar backs. Their cost is normally included in the charge assessed for bartenders. For instance, if two bartenders are purchased by a client, their cost will normally include the cost of one bar back needed to assist them.

3. *Charge for cocktail servers.* Cocktail servers can cost almost as much as bartenders. For instance, if a client wants a few cocktail servers to pass trays of filled wine glasses, this little touch of luxury will add significantly to his or her final bill.

Some clients view cocktail servers as an unnecessary cost. If a beverage function has two or three portable bars set up throughout the room, it may be more convenient to let guests give their orders directly to bartenders instead of to cocktail servers. In fact, in some cases the additional layer of service imposed by cocktail servers can slow down service as well as add unnecessarily to a client's costs.

4. *Charge for cashiers.* Most hotels will not allow clients to schedule cash bars unless they agree to employ at least one cashier. They usually will not let bartenders handle cash since this extra work will slow down beverage production and service significantly.

Bartenders handling cash also creates additional security problems. Separate cashiers are an excellent form of financial checks and balances and must be used if tight cost control is desired.

Clients may be able to have cash bars without cashiers though, if state and local liquor codes allow them to purchase the drink tickets in advance and resell them to their guests. Unfortunately, this could backfire if guests want to purchase more drink tickets during the function and there is no cashier available to accommodate their needs.

If you allow clients to purchase drink tickets for resale to guests, you should exert some control over the resale prices. If local laws allow, a client may decide to add a personal profit markup to the prices you charge, thereby leaving the impression with guests that the hotel's prices are too high when in reality the client is dictating the excessive prices. You should ensure that resale prices are not exorbitant or, if they are, make certain the client informs his or her guests that the hotel is not responsible for them. As an aside, if a client decides to engage in this repricing strategy, he or she may need a temporary business license.

5. *Charge for security.* It is unusual for a catered function to have extra security assigned to it. However, if a large beverage function has a cash-bar arrangement, and/or there are minors expected at the event, a client may feel more comfortable if the hotel provides an extra margin of safety.

Since in this situation the hotel may be at risk, a client may expect the hotel catering department to absorb the added security costs. However, since the typical hotel employs a standard, in-house, licensed security service to patrol the entire property, usually the client will need to pay for anything beyond this.

Some clients may be more than willing to pay a few extra dollars to hire additional security so that they have one less thing to worry about. The catering sales representative should broach this subject with clients because some of them may be unaware that they can employ additional plain-clothes and/or uniformed security and, thereby, gain some peace of mind.

6. *Charge for corkage.* Some clients may want to purchase liquor from a liquor store, or have it donated, and have it served at their beverage functions. In some cases, the clients wish to do this because they think they will save money by avoiding the higher prices necessarily charged by the hotel. In other cases, clients are not concerned about cost, but are motivated strictly by the desire to serve something special that only they are able to obtain.

Some hotels have policies prohibiting guests from bringing in and serving their own food and beverage products. And some state and local government agencies, especially health districts, may prohibit this type of thing. However, if there are no restrictions, and the hotel is willing to allow clients to use their own liquor, usually a corkage fee is charged.

The corkage fee charged is typically based on the hotel's estimated labor cost needed to handle the products. For instance, you may need labor to receive a special delivery, store it, and deliver it to the portable bar. You also may need labor to set up a clean drink area, keep it clean, maintain clean glassware and sufficient ice, and so forth. The more expense involved, the higher the corkage fee must be.

Part of the corkage fee may represent a type of "luxury" or "privilege" tax assessed on clients. For instance, you may want to charge something for the "privilege" of bringing personal liquor into your licensed establishment. You also want to charge the clients because you lose the opportunity to serve profitable beverages yourself.

Clients who want to bring in and serve their own liquor usually will only do so when serving wines. For instance, it is not unusual for a convention to have a few corporate sponsors, one of which might be a winery. Naturally the winery will want its wines served at one of the catered events. And, to keep the peace and accommodate a good client, the hotel usually will make arrangements to honor this request.

A corkage fee is usually quoted on a per-bottle basis. For instance, you might charge $4.50 for each outside wine bottle brought in by the client and served by your staff.

A corkage fee might also be extracted from clients in the form of "drink set-up" charges. For example, if a client brings in a very special, very old brandy that is unavailable locally, you may agree to handle it only if you can charge $1.50 per set up, that is, $1.50 every time you use the liquor to make a finished drink.

TYPES OF BEVERAGE FUNCTIONS

As with meal functions, each type of beverage function presents unique challenges. In some cases, the number of challenges increases considerably if the beverage function must be arranged around a meal function. For instance, not only must a predinner cocktail reception go off without a hitch, it also must set the stage for the dinner that follows it. Any guest dissatisfaction erupting during the reception may carry over to the banquet service and cause additional unhappiness.

Cocktail Reception

The cocktail reception is one of the most common types of beverage functions. Those held during the work week usually are scheduled during the early evening hours, just after the end of the normal business day. On weekends, there is more flexibility, but as a general rule, cocktail receptions are usually scheduled after 5:00 PM.

Cocktail receptions oftentimes precede a dinner event. They usually are scheduled for only about forty-five minutes to one hour. And in almost all instances, at least a few foods are served along with the liquor.

Hospitality Suite

These functions are usually set up in a client's hotel suite. Sometimes they are set up in two or more hotel sleeping rooms that have connecting doors, and that can be stripped of their beds and other guest amenities in order to accommodate the reception's production and service equipment, supplies, employees, and guests.

In some cases, a hospitality suite is set up in a public area. For instance, a small meeting room may be converted to a hospitality suite. This may be less expensive for the client than reserving a hotel suite. In addition, it may be more convenient for guests to locate.

If a hospitality suite is held in a hotel suite, usually the hotel's room-service department handles the event. Private hospitality suites are not usually serviced by the catering staff. Generally speaking, catering is involved only when selling the event and/or when the hospitality suite is held in a public area.

Some hotels have designated employees in the catering department whose primary function is to market hospitality suites to major conventions. The food and beverage service may be handled by the room-service department, but the selling, planning, and coordinating activities in these hotels are the responsibility of the catering department.

Hospitality suites are an inextricable part of the convention business. Conventions have sponsors and/or attendees who want to hold "open houses" so to speak. These affairs are primarily social events. However, to some extent, they also present opportunities for guests to network and discuss business.

Hospitality suites are normally open only in the evening, after the regular convention business day is over. Attendees who wish to expand their social horizons like to make the rounds of these hospitality suites in order to meet friends, acquaintances, and business associates, and to cast their networking webs as wide as possible.

Some hospitality suites are ongoing affairs. For instance, a convention sponsor may have an open house around the clock. During the evening, the open house serves liquor, but during the rest of the day it resembles a refreshment break. In this case, the sponsor is competing for attendees with other refreshment breaks and other attractions located in the convention area.

A sensitive issue that tends to arise with hospitality suites is the convention attendee who wants to offer surreptitiously his or her own hospitality suite. It is not uncommon for attendees to go out to the local supermarket/liquor store and purchase a few wines, beers, spirits, paper and plastic supplies, and dry snacks. Not only does the hotel lose this revenue, the underground hospitality suite puts a big dent in the hotel's complimentary ice stock. Furthermore, these clients and guests can increase the hotel's liability exposure.

Poured-Wine Service

This type of beverage service is part of a meal function. Many dinner events include one or two wines. In some instances, the wines are opened and preset on the dining tables. Guests may serve themselves, or the food servers may be responsible for serving the wine.

At more elaborate meals, cocktail servers, supervised by a sommelier, may be in charge of wine service. This is especially true if guests are offered a choice of wines. It is also more common when a rare and/or expensive wine is served with each course.

Special Events

Alcoholic beverages, especially wines, are oftentimes the stalwarts of special functions. For instance, many fund-raising events are centered around wine-and-cheese tastings, meet-the-winemaker dinners, and introductions of new wineries and new wine products.

Unique alcoholic-beverage presentations are also used by convention clients to generate excitement and enthusiasm at one of their catered events. For example, you may encounter a client who wants to book a dinner where the first beaujolais of the season is served. Or there may be some clients requesting unique selections, such as bloody mary breakfasts and champagne parties.

LIQUOR LAWS

Of all the products and services sold by hotel caterers, none are subject to more governmental control and regulation than liquor sales and service. The hotel must adhere to liquor laws enacted by the federal, state, and local governments. While there is some similarity in liquor laws throughout the nation, usually each state, and particularly each local municipality, have unique liquor codes.

Illegal Liquor Sales

No matter where the hotel is located in the United States, there are at least four types of illegal liquor sales that must be avoided by the hotel catering department.

1. *Sales to minors.*   In most parts of the U.S., it is illegal to sell alcoholic beverages to anyone under 21 years of age. There are a few exceptions to this, though. For instance, in some states, it is legal to serve a minor if his or her parents are present, or if his or her majority-age spouse is present.

Usually the law allows you to refuse liquor service to anyone you suspect is under age. This is true even if someone shows you what appears to be a true and correct identification card that indicates legal drinking age.

Most parts of the country also prohibit minors from being inside a tavern or liquor store. The catering staff must ensure that minors are not allowed near the portable-bar areas.

Admittedly it is very difficult to police guests' movements during a catered function. While hotel bars and gift shops are ever vigilant, there is a tendency to relax normal crowd-control procedures when serving a private party, especially if there is the feeling that clients will get upset if you adhere strictly to the letter of the law. However, the catering executive must not surrender to this temptation to relax standards. If you are caught serving minors, you can rest assured that the private-party defense will receive a cold reception from the legal authorities. Furthermore, the client will usually be one of the first persons to complain that you failed to exercise reasonable care.

2. *Sales to intoxicated persons.*   It is illegal to serve alcohol to a person who is legally intoxicated. In fact, usually the law stipulates that you cannot serve alcohol to anyone who appears to be intoxicated.

In most states, a person is legally intoxicated if his or her blood alcohol concentration (BAC) is one-tenth of 1 percent, or 0.10. In some parts of the country (such as California and Utah), a person is legally intoxicated if his or her BAC is 0.08.

It is impossible for you to predict accurately each guest's BAC. For instance, after consuming one drink, a young person may appear stoned, whereas an older guest having several drinks who has considerable drinking experience may be legally intoxicated yet show no outward signs of intoxication.

One way to solve this problem is to keep track of the number of drinks each guest consumes and slow down service whenever a guest has had approximately enough liquor to cause legal intoxication. The average person's liver needs about one hour to eliminate the alcohol in one drink. If he or she has more than one drink per hour, the BAC will increase quickly. For instance, if a person weighing 125 pounds consumes three average drinks (that is, a drink that contains approximately one-half ounce of alcohol) in one hour, his or her BAC could be 0.10 or above. Unless this person reduces his or her liquor consumption significantly, or refrains from drinking during the rest of the catered function, the liver will not have enough time to reduce the BAC to a legal level before the function ends.

Some hotels use other strategies to prevent overconsumption. For instance, instead of dictating the number of drinks a guest can consume, you could offer "minidrinks," low-alcohol frozen drinks, and/or use low-alcohol liquors in all prepared drinks.

There is a budding trend in the beverage industry of offering smaller drinks at lower prices. For instance, if you normally charge $3.75 for a highball with $1^1/_2$ ounces of liquor and 6 ounces of mixer, you might offer one with $3/_4$ ounces of liquor and 5 ounces of mixer and charge only $2.75. In the long run, guests will probably spend just as much money. By altering the consumption pattern though, the guest is more likely to remain sober.

Another trend is for bars to offer frozen concoctions that have only a hint of alcoholic beverage. When frozen, the guest is less able to determine the amount of alcohol present. Furthermore, many guests seem to love these types of drinks. Unfortunately, they are much harder to prepare and serve, so you may have to charge more to cover the additional expense. They also take longer to drink, as the typical guest cannot take too much cold too fast. Consequently, since you serve fewer frozen drinks, you will need to charge more for each one in order to compensate for this revenue shortfall.

Some states and local municipalities allow the sale of low-alcohol products. For instance, instead of using an 86-proof bourbon, you might be able to purchase a 56-proof product in your area.

Even though this product has less alcohol, it is a better choice than merely adding more mixer to the 86-proof product. Excess mixer tends to give the finished drink a "washed out" character. The low-alcohol alternative though, tends to retain the characteristic flavor of the original beverage even though it contains less alcohol.

If there is any doubt about a person's BAC, you must cut off that person. When this is necessary, try to use peer pressure to your advantage. Ask another guest, or the client, to help you handle the situation. Be courteous to the guest and minimize the confrontation. Note that you cannot serve any more alcohol, but you can offer food or nonalcoholic beverage alternatives. Or you could see to it that the guest gets a safe ride home. Retain a professional demeanor and do not prolong guest contact any longer than necessary.

Some hotels participate in the designated-driver program, where at least one guest in a small group consumes no alcohol so that he or she will be able to drive everyone home safely. Unfortunately, this concept has backfired on some occasions. For instance, if you cut off a guest who is part of a designated-driver group, he or she may become quite agitated. After all, the guest may assume that the designated-driver program allows him or her to get completely sloshed. The fact that it is illegal to serve visibly intoxicated persons is at odds with the customer who has arranged ahead of time for a safe ride.

You may encounter a similar problem with conventioneers who do not plan to leave the hotel after the catered function. Instead, they plan to go directly to their rooms and go straight to bed after a long night of partying. They feel that they should receive special consideration since they will not be driving that evening.

Our liquor laws are sometimes contradictory, as are some of the solutions we have developed over the years to combat drunk driving. But that does not alter the fact that you cannot serve liquor to an intoxicated guest, even if that person is chained to a table and cannot drive. To do so puts your liquor license, not to mention your career, in jeopardy.

3. *Hours of operation.*   Most local municipalities restrict the hours during which liquor can be served in a commercial beverage establishment. For instance, you may be unable to accommodate a client's request for a champagne brunch because no liquor can be served before noon.

You will need to check the local codes to determine if these restrictions apply to private parties. If they do, you must ensure that catering sales representatives do not book beverage functions during the prohibited hours.

4. *Liquor license.*   To serve liquor, you must hold the appropriate liquor license. For instance, a full tavern license, or hard-liquor license, is usually needed to serve spirits, wines, and beers for consumption on premises. The typical hotel usually holds this type of liquor license.

If the hotel holds only a soft-liquor license, that is, a wine-and-beer license, it cannot serve distilled spirits. To say the least, this puts a large crimp in your ability to sell full-service catering functions. It is possible though, that under these conditions, the clients may be able to bring in their own spirits, in which case you can earn your revenue by charging corkage fees or drink set-up charges.

In some parts of the country, a hotel or conference center may be unable to serve liquor unless it holds a private-club license. In this case, you cannot serve anyone who is not a member, or member's guest. Usually though, you are able to grant memberships to any qualified clients and their guests. But since this adds to your administrative burden, you may need to charge a bit more for catered beverage events.

You may be in an area where the hotel cannot purchase its own liquor. In this case, usually you must have a private-club license, or similar license, in order to prepare and serve liquor brought in by the client. For instance, in some parts of the country, the guest must buy liquor at a state-operated liquor store and bring it to the hotel. The guest then pays a drink set-up charge for each drink prepared and served. At the end of the function, the guest carries home the leftover product.

Potential Liquor-Code Violations

The catering executive must ensure that all local liquor laws are obeyed when booking and serving group functions. While the illegal sales noted above are common throughout the United States, each local municipality usually has one or two unique regulations that place additional controls on the local liquor licensees. Those that usually affect the hotel catering department are:

1. *Food served with beverage.*   In some parts of the country, the local Alcohol Beverage Commission (ABC) may prohibit beverage functions that do not offer foods. In these areas, a person applying for a liquor license to sell and serve alcoholic beverages for on-premises consumption must show that he or she intends to serve foods as well.

Alcohol should never be consumed on an empty stomach. Without food to slow down the rate at which alcohol is absorbed into the blood stream, guests run the risk of becoming intoxicated very quickly. If these guests leave the function and drive away in their cars, unfortunate, preventable traffic accidents may occur. By requiring you to serve foods at all beverage functions, the local government authorities are giving society one more weapon to fight these tragic situations.

2. *Bring your own bottle.*   Before allowing clients to bring in their own liquor, you need to check with the local ABC to see if the liquor code permits this. In some parts of the United States, you are not allowed to use liquor purchased from a retail liquor store in a bar operation that serves liquor by the drink for on-premises consumption. You must purchase all liquor from licensed liquor wholesale distributors or, in control states, from the authorized state liquor agency.

3. *Free liquor.*   You may be prohibited from giving away any liquor during a catered function. Usually you must sell the beverages for a fair market price.

Similarly, you may be prohibited from offering sliding-scale price ranges to your catering clients. For instance, you may be unable to offer the first 250 drinks for $3.00 apiece and anything over that amount for $2.00 apiece.

In some parts of the country, you are prohibited from offering any other types of sale-price promotions. For instance, happy hours, drink-and-drown nights, two-for-one specials, and so forth, are quickly disappearing from our industry.

Free liquor or reduced-price liquor tends to encourage over-consumption. By outlawing these types of pricing practices, the local ABC keeps a tight rein on the irresponsible sale and purchase of alcoholic beverages.

4. *Self service.*   To control further overconsumption of alcohol, some local municipalities may prohibit guests from preparing their own drinks at group functions. If this restriction exists in your area, usually it does not infringe upon the hospitality-suite host's ability to allow guests to mix their own beverages.

5. *Alcoholic content of liquor used.*   There may be a regulation prohibiting the purchase and use of closed containers of liquors that have exceptionally high alcoholic contents. Some parts of the country prohibit the use of any distilled spirit that exceeds 100 proof.

Some clients may be unaware of this type of restriction, so it is up to you to inform them. This is especially true for conventions that attract attendees from all over the country. You should let these clients know that some drinks, such as a traditional Zombie, cannot be prepared and served.

Similarly, if an out-of-town client wants to bring his or her personal liquor, and assuming the liquor code and your hotel policy permit this, you must ensure that anything brought in does not violate alcoholic-content restrictions.

6. *Amount of alcohol per drink.*   Some local municipalities may restrict the amount of alcohol you can put into each drink. For instance, doubles, boiler makers, and pitchers of beer may be outlawed because they can cause overconsumption of alcohol. Likewise for drinks that contain more than one type of liquor. For instance, you may not be allowed to prepare and serve drinks such as traditional mud slides, Long Island teas, and scorpions because they contain multiple liquors.

The major problem with a multiple-liquor drink is that one of them can have the same clinical effect on a person's central nervous system as two or three average drinks. Recall that the average person's liver can eliminate alcohol from the body only at the rate of about one average drink per hour. Also recall that the average drink contains about one-half ounce of alcohol. A typical highball contains about one-half ounce of alcohol, but a traditional mud slide contains approximately one and one-half ounces of alcohol. If a guest consumes two mudslides in one hour, his or her BAC may exceed 0.10.

7. *Leftover liquor.*   The local ABC may prohibit letting clients or guests take home any leftover liquor. If a client books a beverage function and agrees to pay for each bottle served as well as each bottle opened, you must let him or her know up front that no leftovers can leave the hotel.

If you face this situation, you could charge clients the standard price for each full container consumed, and a prorated amount for each partial container used. This probably will satisfy all clients except those who order something special that cannot be reused at one of the hotel's regular bars. If these clients want something special, but are unwilling to leave any of it behind, one way to solve the problem is to underorder the product from the liquor wholesaler so that there will be none left over.

Recall that another acceptable alternative is to charge the client for each opened container and send partial containers to the hospitality suite at the end of the catered beverage function. This may not be a complete solution because, unless guests consume it all at the hotel, the leftovers must stay behind. In this situation, you may find it necessary to grant the client at least a token credit on the final billing. This may be good strategy if you intend to solicit the client for future and referral business.

Alcohol-Awareness Training

Some local municipalities require anyone who sells, serves, distributes, or gives away alcoholic beverages to take an approved server-awareness training course before they are allowed to work in a licensed alcohol beverage establishment. These courses are similar in concept to the sanitation courses that some local health districts require all food handlers to take before they can work in a public food-service establishment.

The typical server-awareness training involves instruction in the following areas:

1. Dealing with minors
2. The tell-tale signs of intoxication
3. Dealing with intoxicated guests
4. Clinical effects of alcohol on the human body
5. Local liquor codes.

Server-awareness training courses offered throughout the United States vary from about 4 hours of instruction to 20 hours. They usually follow the format initially established by the TAM (Techniques of Alcohol Management) course, or the Serving Alcohol with Care course developed by the American Hotel & Motel Association (AH & MA).

Before hiring a permanent beverage-staff member, or putting anyone on the A-list or B-list, the catering executive must ensure that the job candidates have the appropriate training. Usually they receive a pocket card after taking the course that they can show to potential employers to prove they have been certified.

THIRD-PARTY LIABILITY

If you serve an intoxicated guest, or a minor, and he or she goes out and hurts an innocent third party, the hotel, server, and client may be liable for damages to the injured person.

Some states have passed dram-shop laws that specify exactly your liability in these instances. Under dram-shop legislation, if it is proved that you served a minor or legally intoxicated person who causes damage to a third party, you usually will be held at least partially responsible. For example, if a minor you served gets into a traffic accident and injures someone, the injured party can sue the driver, server, hotel, and even the client. Chances are the minor does not have the same financial resources as the hotel. Consequently, the hotel stands to lose a great deal since it has the "deep pockets" that a judge or jury can tap for huge financial awards.

In a dram-shop state, usually the hotel cannot defend itself if it is proved that its employees served a minor or legally intoxicated guest. You cannot, for example, tell the judge that the minor presented what looked like a legitimate ID card. Nor can you plead that, "Your Honor, the person appeared to be 30 years old." Such defenses usually are not permitted where absolute liability has been legislated. As a result, if you serve a minor or legally intoxicated person who causes damage to an innocent third party, you can count on being held responsible, period.

It is important for clients to realize that some states have passed social-host laws. Social-host laws hold function hosts liable for private functions hosted in their homes or at other locations. For instance, if a minor served at a private party held at a hotel inflicted damage on an innocent third party, the function host and the hotel could share responsibility for the accident.

Most states do not have dram-shop or social-host laws. However, the hotel, server, and client still could be held liable under common law.

Under common law, an injured third party can sue you for damages. However, it is up to him or her to prove you were negligent in serving the person who caused the accident. For instance, if you can prove that a minor who you served proved his or her age by showing what appeared to be a legitimate ID, chances are you would be absolved from liability, especially if you can also show that the minor appeared to be older than 21.

Unlike dram-shop or social-host laws, under common law, the burden of proof shifts to the plaintiff. He or she must prove you were negligent and did not exercise reasonable care. As long as you followed generally accepted beverage-service principles and practices, usually you can mount an adequate defense.

In addition to the hotel and the person causing the accident, clients and servers can also be named parties to a lawsuit under common law. Clients with deep pockets can rest assured that, one way or another, they will be defendants.

It is imperative that clients realize the types of risks they incur when booking beverage functions. In some cases, they may need to be reminded of this if they expect you to cater a wild affair, such as a stag party. A few minutes spent discussing liability problems faced by our industry should dispel these requests quickly.

8

Function Room Selection and Setup

Just Say Yes! is the only attitude for a successful company. You find the best way to match the client's needs to your services, and then you deliver!

Jane Jaeger
Director of Sales & Marketing
Foodservices by MGR
Georgia World Congress Center
Atlanta, Georgia

The catering sales representative must select an appropriate function room to house the event. Along with the client, he or she needs to consider several things when making this selection. The major factors influencing the selection process are a function room's appearance, location, utilities, and amount of floor space.

APPEARANCE

Often the function room's appearance is high on most clients' priority lists. In fact, frequently a potential client is attracted to the hotel primarily because of the ambience provided. For instance, a function room in Caesars Palace in Las Vegas overlooks the Las Vegas Strip. At night, the view is phenomenal. To say the least, many clients want to book this room regardless of any other advantages or disadvantages it offers.

Room dimensions, ceiling height, columns, exits, entrances, the number and quality of restroom facilities, the colors and types of floor and wall coverings, sound insulation, and lighting are also important, especially for those hotels whose function rooms do not enjoy breath-taking views.

Usually most room dimensions are acceptable to the client so long as he or she can avoid the "bowling-alley" effect. Clients will be turned off by a function room that is long and narrow. This type of dimension precludes guest mingling, participation, and networking. It also harms service because many guests will tend to gravitate toward one end of the room; for instance, the bar at one end may be very busy, with the others having only a few guests.

The typical ceiling height in function rooms is approximately eleven feet. In many local municipalities, the building code may require a higher ceiling. For instance, many building codes stipulate 14-foot ceilings in public areas, such as restaurants, theaters, and shops.

Clients tend to be turned off by columns, especially if they have guest speakers and/or a considerable amount of AV services scheduled (such as films). A few are acceptable, but too many will detract from the catered event unless the catering sales representative can suggest a room setup that will minimize their negative effects. For instance, buffet tables can be arranged between some decorated columns that may enhance the room's appearance. Or the columns can be decorated to enhance a wedding theme.

Usually a function room has a sufficient number of entrances and exits if for no other reason than the local fire code requires them. Many clients will take this factor for granted; for instance, they will assume that there will be a sufficient number of crash doors (that is, emergency exit doors equipped with panel bar opening devices that sound an alarm when opened).

Other clients though, will be very concerned with entrance and exit doors. For instance, some luncheon clients that have speakers and visual aids scheduled will want to know how easy or difficult it will be to transport their convention materials to and from the function room.

Doors should not be near a speaker's stand, head table, or display table. You do not want late-comers disrupting the event. For instance, if a movie or slide presentation is part of the event, if possible, have the room set up so that the doors are on the side of the room. By so doing, a late-comer does not have to walk in front of the projector and interrupt the presentation.

As with the number of entrances and exits, many clients will not evaluate the number and quality of restroom facilities when booking their functions. However, the director of catering will ensure that the facilities are well-maintained and easy for guests to locate. Many guests' lasting impressions of the hotel will be based solely on these factors.

The colors and types of floor and wall coverings are usually the first thing a client sees when viewing a function room. In addition to meeting building-code requirements, they should be free from stains and in good repair. They also should be in good taste and executed with style.

If you have any choice in selecting floor and wall coverings before the hotel is developed, or before it undergoes remodeling, you should choose those that are fire retardant, easy to maintain, and durable. The colors and types of materials used to make these coverings should be consistent with the types of functions booked in the room and the type of lighting used.

Carpeting also needs to be consistent with the hotel's architectural style. For instance, an old hotel with traditional architecture, layout, and design would lose some of its atmosphere if a contemporary design carpet was installed throughout the property.

With carpeting, you are especially concerned with obtaining the proper cushioning, installation procedures, traffic rating (that is, medium, heavy, or extra heavy), and maintenance costs. You do not want guests to feel uneven padding, or see ragged seams and/or carpeting that is excessively worn in the traffic areas. Moreover, the carpet selected should be easy to clean and repair.

Unsophisticated clients may not consider a function room's sound and lighting capabilities when selecting a room. However, if there are any inadequacies, they will be noticed during the event and cause guest dissatisfaction. For instance, if platform speakers are scheduled during the meal function, the room used cannot have any dead space, that is, area(s) in the room where sound is absent or unintelligible.

If the function room is too close to the kitchen, hallways, and service corridors, the setup crew must ensure that sufficient air walls, room dividers, or other types of baffles are installed to prevent unwanted noises from seeping into the function room. Hotel employees moving about in these behind-the-scenes areas may occasionally cause distractions. For instance, some guests may be unable to hear a platform speaker if employees are overheard shouting, laughing, or talking. Employees should be trained to tread lightly in these areas in order to minimize noise pollution.

A similar type of installation will also be needed if you have to minimize the amount of ambient light (that is, unavoidable light seeping into a darkened room from around doors, draped windows, or production and service areas).

LOCATION

Ideally, the function room should be located next to the production and service areas. This will increase the efficiency of the catering and banquet staffs. It also ensures that foods will be much more attractive and will retain their culinary quality better since there is a shorter road from kitchen to guest.

In some hotels, the kitchen is on one floor level and the function rooms are on other levels. If there are not enough service elevators, it can be a nightmare transporting finished menu items. It can be especially difficult if you need to share the inadequate service elevators with housekeeping, convention service, and other hotel departments. For instance, if there is a meal function in the hotel, housekeeping may be prohibited from using the service elevators to stock linen closets during the function period. In this situation, the catering manager will need to coordinate very carefully the use of the service elevators with other hotel departments.

Unfortunately in our industry, all too often you encounter this type of design flaw. The production and service flow patterns are not always given high priority by architects and designers, especially when they are constrained with a tight property-development budget. Even if the construction budget is ample, an architect or designer may not have enough familiarity with the catering department's needs to plan the production, service, and function areas properly. For example, we are familiar with some hotels where the only elevator connecting the central kitchen with restaurant outlets and function rooms on other floors is the one used by hotel guests. Most guests do not want to share a ride with a food cart.

If the function room is a great distance from the kitchen, the menu planner may be limited to only those foods that hold up well. The banquet staff also will need to use hot-and cold-transport equipment in order to preserve the foods' culinary quality en route. Without this equipment, food costs could increase because finished food items are more vulnerable to quality deterioration when they must be preplated in advance and transported long distances. The extra effort also could increase labor costs.

UTILITIES

The meetings and conventions clients are concerned about the function room's utility capabilities. Usually the catering sales representative has room schematic drawings that illustrate them. These drawings should be included in any mailed sales solicitation because these clients will book functions that tend to tax a function room's utilities.

The catering sales representative must be conversant with each function room's utilities. Clients will be concerned with:

1. Types of electricity available in house
2. Types of electricity that can be brought in
3. Maximum wattage available
4. Maximum lighting available
5. Number of separate lighting controls. For example, if a client will be using rear-screen projection, you will need to darken the area behind the screen while leaving the rest of the room light.
6. Heating, ventilation, and air conditioning (HVAC) capacity
7. Closed-circuit TV, radio, and VCR system
8. Closed-circuit, audiovisual (AV) system
9. Paging system
10. Number, types, and locations of:
    a. electrical outlets
    b. electrical floor, wall, and ceiling strips
    c. phone jacks
    d. dimmer switches
    e. vents and ducts
    f. built-in speakers
11. If the function will be held in an exhibit hall, the client will also be concerned with the number, types, and locations of:
    a. gas hookups
    b. exhaust fans
    c. floor sinks (i.e., drains)
    d. water connections.

SPACE REQUIREMENTS

The amount of floor space available is perhaps the function room's most critical feature. The catering sales representative must shoulder the responsibility for determining the amount of square footage needed. He or she cannot expect the client to make this calculation.

Several factors influence the amount of space needed. The most critical ones are:

1. *Number of guests.*   The local fire code will dictate the maximum number of people who can be legally housed in a function room. This maximum usually is an excellent guide when planning a stand-up function, such as a cocktail reception. It can also be a good guide when planning theater or auditorium setups. However, some events, such as banquet or classroom setups, will accommodate fewer persons.

Generally speaking, for most meal and beverage functions, you would be unable to accommodate the maximum number of persons allowed by the local fire code. The room setups required for these types of events will usually reduce significantly the number of guests that can be handled efficiently and comfortably.

2. *Type of dining table used.*   You need to allocate about 10 square feet per guest if seating is at rectangular banquet tables. If round tables are used, you will need about $12^1/_2$ square feet per guest. These estimates will suffice if you are using standard chairs whose chair seats measure 20 inches by 20 inches. You should adjust your estimates if you use smaller chairs (seats measuring 18 inches by 18 inches) or larger armchairs (which usually have a minimum width of 24 inches).

3. *Aisle space.*   Aisles are needed for server access and customer maneuverability. Aisles between tables and around food and beverage stations should be a minimum 36 inches wide. For some events, aisles should be 48 to 54 inches wide. For instance, weddings usually prefer wider aisles to accommodate the lavish gowns worn by the bride and some guests. (See Figure 8.1.)

When planning aisle space, remember to leave enough entry and exit room for guests. You should plan to allocate sufficient cross-aisle space, that is, aisles used for guests to collect and funnel in and out of the function areas. A cross-aisle should be approximately 6 feet wide.

Cross-aisle space is very important when setting large functions. For instance, for a function requiring 100 tables, you cannot set a square layout of 10 tables by 10 tables without allowing some additional space for guests to maneuver comfortably to the middle tables from the outside perimeter. As a general rule of thumb, if you need 100 tables, you should set up four blocks of 25 tables. Within the 25-table block, 36-inch aisle space is sufficient.

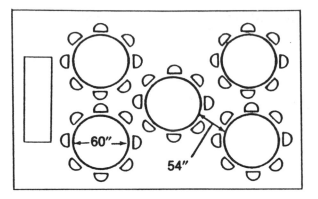

Figure 8.1. Recommended aisle-space allotment for weddings and other similar functions.

However, there should be a 6-foot-wide cross aisle surrounding each block of 25 tables.

Before making any final decisions regarding aisle space, you must check the local fire code for specific requirements.

4. *Dance-floor space.* If the function includes dancing, you need about 3 square feet of dance floor per guest. A few hotels use roll-up dance floors. If you use lay-out squares though, most of these types of portable dance floors come in 3 feet by 3 feet (that is, 9 square feet) sections; plan on using one section for every three guests. (See Figure 8.2.)

As a general rule, if a dance floor is required, the typical setup will measure approximately 24 feet by 24 feet. If using standard 9-square-foot sections, you will need 64 pieces of dance floor, 24 pieces of regular trim, 8 pieces of corner trim, and 256 set screws. The typical total setup covers approximately 600 square feet of floor space.

You usually will need to increase your estimate of dance-floor space if you intend to set up two dance floors instead of one. For very large functions, a second dance floor is very convenient. Guests at the back of the room will not have to negotiate the long trail leading to the front where the single dance floor normally is located. On the other hand, this arrangement may divide the group into two subgroups unless you connect two diamond-shaped dance floors. If the function room is big enough though, you should present this option to the client, along with the pros and cons, and let him or her consider it. Chances are, the client will appreciate the choice.

5. *Bandstand.* You should estimate about 10 square feet per band member. Drum sets usually require about 20 square feet. Large pianos, synthesizers, runways, and so forth also need

SICO
SICO INCORPORATED   OAK PORTABLE DANCE FLOOR   ALSO IN STOCK IN THAI TEAK

Figure 8.2.   Typical dance floor installation. (Courtesy Sico Incorporated.)

additional space. Disc jockeys also may need considerably more space to hold their equipment and tape collection. You should check the entertainment contract as it may set forth the floor-space specifications.

Bandstands and other similar attractions are sometimes elevated on risers. Stage risers come in many shapes and sizes. Their purpose is to elevate speakers, other entertainers, or audiovisual equipment so that a large audience can see what is taking place at one end of the function room.

Some risers are nothing more than 4 feet by 8 feet by 6 inch wooden boxes that can be moved from room to room. The most common ones though, are the 4 feet by 4 feet and 4 feet by 8 feet folding risers that can be adjusted to several heights.

Risers may require steps. If so, you should provide steps that have attached hand rails and a mechanism that allows them to be connected securely. A lawsuit can occur if a guest falls from an improperly set stage.

A lawsuit can also occur if someone falls from a riser. To minimize this possibility, risers should always be placed against a wall so that a guest cannot step back and fall off.

6. *Other entertainment.*   You may need to allocate additional floor space for speakers, strolling musicians, and other similar entertainment. For instance, if the function includes a speaker or two, you may need space to house a podium, platform, audiovisual equipment, and wider aisles throughout the function room to allow the speaker to interact with the audience. Once again, you should check the entertainers' contracts for exact space requirements.

7. *Head table(s).*   Head tables usually need about 25 percent to 100 percent more floor space than regular dining tables. Furthermore, if the tables will be placed upon risers, you must increase your space estimate accordingly to accommodate the platform area, steps, and the need to spread the table-and-guest weight properly over the stage. For instance, if using typical platform sections measuring 4 feet by 4 feet and 4 feet by 8 feet, you would need to connect a 4 by 4 and a 4 by 8 to have enough space to accommodate a dining table measuring 3 feet by 8 feet. In other words, you will need about 48 square feet of platform space to accommodate approximately 24 square feet of dining-table space. The 48 square feet will accommodate four guests seated at 24-inch intervals. The 12 square feet per person is usually the minimum amount needed for head-table guests seated on a platform.

If you have head tables reserved for speakers, dignitaries, and other VIPs who will be addressing the guests after the meal, you may be asked to set up extra dining tables on the floor for these guests, near the head tables, so they can eat without feeling like they are in a fishbowl. Some guests do not want to sit at an elevated table and eat. If there is enough space in the function room, they can eat at regular dining tables, and then move up to the head tables just before the program begins.

Setting up extra dining tables allows you to maximize the number of VIPs who can be accommodated at the head tables. For instance, if you have 10 VIPs and 10 spouses, you can set up 20 place settings (that is, covers) at regular dining tables. And, if the client agrees, instead of setting up a head table for 20, you can set one for only the 10 VIPs. The spouses can remain at the dining tables after the meal.

This table arrangement may reduce your floor-space needs and increase the banquet-service staff's efficiency. However, you must gain the client's permission to do this because he or she may assume all spouses will be seated at the head table. You do not want to risk alienating guests or placing them in an embarrassing position.

8. *Bank maze.*   A bank maze consists of posts (stanchions) and ropes set up to control guest traffic. You may want to use bank mazes to control traffic around cashier and ticket-taker stations. If they are necessary, you will need to allocate more floor space to accommodate them.

9. *Reception needs.*   If the function room is used to house a reception and a meal, you will need enough space to handle both phases of the catered event. In most cases, you will be unable to reset the reception area in order to accommodate meal guests. There usually is insufficient time to do this. Furthermore, it is aesthetically unattractive.

To accommodate a reception adequately, you will need about 6 to 10 square feet of floor space per guest.

With 6 square feet, guests will feel a bit claustrophobic; they also will have a bit more trouble getting to the food and beverage stations. Consequently, they may eat and drink less. If a cost-conscious client is paying on a per-person basis, where guests can eat and drink as much as they want for one price, you might consider allocating only about 6 square feet per person to keep the price low and your food and beverage costs under control. However, since some guests may perceive this arrangement negatively, you should use it only if other cost-reducing options cannot be pursued.

Seven and one-half square feet is considered to be a "comfortably crowded" arrangement. It is thought to be the ideal amount of floor space per guest for receptions and other similar functions.

Ten square feet provides more than ample space for guests to mingle and visit easily the food and beverage stations. It is an appropriate amount of floor space for an upscale reception. It is also an appropriate setup if the client is paying according to the amount of food and beverage consumed. You want guests to have enough room to eat and drink as much as they want so that your revenues are maximized.

As a general rule, a director of catering will try to allocate for receptions, 10 square feet per guest after taking into account space needs for equipment, tables, and employees. He or she will allocate more space if it is available. The typical hotel catering department strives to maintain a reputation for high quality food, beverage, and service. It will provide as much luxury as it can within its budget, regardless of how the event is sold.

10. *Buffet table.*   All food stations need enough floor space for the tables and aisles. For instance, an 8-foot-long rectangular banquet table needs about 24 square feet for the table, and about 60 square feet for aisle space (if the table is against the wall); about 100 square feet for aisle space is needed if the table is accessible from all sides.

When determining the number of buffet tables needed, as well as the number of buffet lines required, you need to consider:

a. Number of guests expected

b. Length of dining time

c. Amount of service equipment required

d. Type of service equipment required

e. Type of menu

f. Style of service

g. Amount of decor desired on the buffet line

h. Amount of total floor space available in the function room.

Generally speaking, you must allocate approximately two running feet of buffet table for each food container needed. For instance, if you have to display 3 hot offerings, 3 cold offerings, and a condiment basket, you should set up a buffet table about 14 to 16 feet long. If you use two standard 8-foot rectangular banquet tables, you will need about 48 square feet of floor space for the buffet table and approximately 150 square feet of standard 3-foot aisle space surrounding the buffet table. The total allocation for this setup then, is about 200 square feet.

11. *Beverage station.*   For self-service, nonalcoholic beverage stations, the setups are similar to buffet-table setups. For instance, a hot-beverage station will need about as much space as a buffet table laden with foods. Bars though, will need more floor space because you need room to store back-up stock, ice, and coolers to hold beer and some wines. You also need to allocate enough working space for bartenders, bar backs, and, if applicable, cocktail servers. Generally speaking, the smallest portable bar you can use measures approximately 6 feet by 7 feet, or about 42 square feet. However, when you take into account the aisle and other space needed, you will need to allocate at least 150 square feet for the typical portable banquet-bar setup.

If you are setting up portable bars for a large function, you may be able to reduce your space estimates if you can arrange to locate them in pairs. For instance, you may be able to locate two portable bars back-to-back in the middle of the function room so that the bars can share a common area where glassware, ice, wines, beers, and so forth are stored. This will eliminate duplicate storage areas and free up extra floor space.

12. *Side stand and bus cart.*   Similar to buffet table.

13. *Action station.*   Similar to buffet; however you must allocate a bit more floor space so that guests can congregate and view the chefs' performances. Your floor-space estimate also must be increased if the action station is elevated.

14. *Staging area.*   You may need to set up a temporary serving line in the function room. A band or disc jockey may need a place to store its shipping containers. A client may need space to store convention materials, party favors, and other similar items. You may need to allocate floor space to store temporarily lighting and sound equipment. Or you may need to set up a temporary service corridor on one end of the function room to store hot carts, cold carts, and gueridons. If you anticipate any of these needs, you will need to allocate sufficient space to accommodate them.

If you must allocate floor space for a staging area, you should block it off with pipe and draping so that it does not interfere with the appearance and ambience of the catered event.

15. *Cashier.*   Some functions, particularly beverage functions, may require floor space for one or more cashiers. For instance, the catered event might include a cash bar. If so, the typical hotel will require the client to use cashiers to sell drink tickets.

Generally speaking, you should allocate at least 25 to 30 square feet for one cashier station. If a security guard will be stationed at the cashier area, you will need additional floor space to accommodate this person.

16. *Display area.*   Sometimes clients need space to set up their own cashier stations, registration/information tables, kiosks, booths, and so forth. For instance, a client may need a cashier station in order to sell meal tickets to guests who have not prepaid, but who decided at the last minute to attend the event.

Selling individual event tickets is typical with convention clients. Most conventions give a book of event tickets (one ticket for each meal function) to each attendee who registers and pays in advance for the total convention. A few attendees though, may decide after the preregistration deadline passes to attend the convention. Some may not want to attend every event; instead, they may show up for only one or two preferred events and pay only for these functions. In some cases, you will have local ticket sales and tickets purchased for spouses and friends of attendees.

If guests need to use tickets to enter a function room, you will need to provide sufficient space for someone to collect the tickets. Usually the ticket taker has a spot reserved just inside or outside the function room's main entrance. This space is sometimes the same space used to house the client's registration/information station. Guests therefore, can check in and pay at one station. This is more convenient for guests. It also allows you to economize on your floor-space requirements.

If you set up an area to handle all of the client's cashiering and check-in procedures, you must ensure there is sufficient floor space to accommodate one or more cashiers, desks, tables, chairs, backdrops, service corridors, telephones, waste receptacles, lock boxes (to hold the used tickets and/or receipts to prevent reuse), and so forth. Some clients may have lists of their display needs along with exact dimensions. If not, you should question them carefully about these requirements so that you do not have to rearrange the function-room layouts at the last minute.

17. *Landing space.*   Recall that this is the area where guests can discard empty plates, glasses, soiled napery, and waste. Generally speaking, the amount of landing space needed can be computed by adopting the space-estimate standards used to forecast buffet-table space requirements.

You should set up a few empty tables to accommodate this need. If this is not possible, you can set up folding tray stands with empty trays on them.

Landing space should also be allocated on the buffet tables between and in front of food containers. Guests will need some place to set their drinks while putting food on their plates. They also will need room on the table to set their plates temporarily while deciding what foods to take.

18. *Meeting activity during the meal.*   A client may want to have a business meeting and the meal or reception in the same function room. For instance, an association chapter may want the function room divided into two sections: one section housing the reception, and the other housing an auditorium-style setup to accommodate the group's program.

The meeting activity can easily be accommodated if the function room is large enough to be divided appropriately. It cannot be accommodated as readily though, if the meeting and the meal or reception must share the same space.

One way to handle events where space must be shared is to use a conference-room, U-shaped, or hollow-square setup. For instance, with a U-shaped setup, guests can conduct their meeting and, when it is time to eat, roll-ins can be placed in the hollow section of the setup and foods arranged to allow self-service.

A conference-room setup usually requires no more space than the typical meal function; however, the U-shaped or hollow-square setups may need two to three times as much floor space. According to Coleman Finkel, the U-shaped setup is the least efficient use of floor space. It requires about 42 square feet per person.

19. *Style of service.*   This is important if you are planning to use French or Russian service, as these service styles require up to twice as much floor space than the others. Some buffets, especially those where beautiful displays and several tables are used, may also need extra space. For instance, instead of the typical buffet floor-space estimate, you may want to increase it by 50 to 100 percent if the function is very elaborate and you want to provide a luxury amount of space for all guests.

20. *Audience separation.*   If it is necessary to divide or separate the audience, you may need considerably more floor space. For instance, if you set up smoking and nonsmoking sections, you should set one or two extra tables in each section unless you know exactly how many smokers and nonsmokers to expect. In the worst case scenario, you will have several half-used tables in each section.

21. *Handicapped seating.*   If you expect to have a physically handicapped guest, you will need to allocate additional floor space. For instance, a wheelchair-bound guest will need a bit more space at the dining table as well as a wider aisle in which to navigate.

22. *Decor.*   Some decorative pieces take up considerable space. You can minimize the amount if the client will agree to use, for example, facades instead of the real items.

PLANNING THE FUNCTION-ROOM SETUP

Function-room setups must be established well in advance. Table locations, exhibits, displays, food-and-beverage-station locations, table sizes, head table, seating mix (that is, the number of each table size needed), table spacings, table settings, and preferred decor usually are planned by the catering sales representative and the client. Occasionally though, you may encounter a client who brings in his or her own drawings showing how the room should be set up. However, many clients do not want to be bothered with these details; they are much more interested in the menu, price, and decor.

Using hotel floor plans and other schematic drawings that show square footage, dimensions, doors, and other factors that may be important to the client, several visual plans can be developed.

The catering sales representative can obtain templates from Meeting Planners International to assist in developing suggested room setups. This professional meeting-planners organization also provides additional function-room space/guest count guidelines that can be used to plan the function-room arrangement. For instance, it provides a calculus you can use to determine the number of guests that can be seated comfortably, given a particular seating style and the available amount of square footage.

If your hotel can afford it, you can purchase computer software that will correlate the room's dimensions, location, doorways, service corridors, columns, protrusions, dead space, permanent service installations (such as a permanent bandstand, bar, and/or dance floor), and other limitations, with the client's desires and draw out several suggested layouts for consideration. (See Figure 8.3.) For instance, the typical software program will draw a layout using industry standards for such things as distances between rows of chairs or tables, aisle space needed, and the optimal angles that should be set to accommodate video presentations. Most of these software packages also will automatically generate standard seating styles. If you are unhappy with a computer-generated layout, you usually can alter the data and ask the computer to draw another layout. You can continue doing this until the client is satisfied with the result.

These exercises provide an opportunity to try out different room setups. The client and catering sales representative will then be in a good position to decide what will work best.

These exercises also help the hotel in many other ways. For instance, the preferred function-room setup will indicate the room utility demands that must be accommodated. It also will indicate if the desired menu can be produced and served efficiently.

Generated by MEETINGMATRIX

Facility Name: * Sample Facility *   Function Name: Banquet
Meeting Name: * Sample Meeting *   Function Date: 3/20/91
Room Name: Ballroom   Function Time: 11:30 am

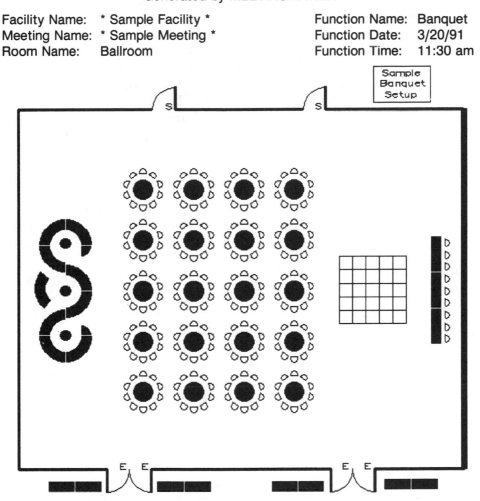

Figure 8.3. Example of computer-generated function-room layout. (Courtesy SCLM Software, Inc. MEETINGMATRIX is a trademark of SCLM Software, Inc. and is used with permission.)

It is advisable to get the client involved with this room-setup planning exercise. Experience shows that the client who is involved from the start is more satisfied with the result, primarily because he or she has a great deal of control over the final outcome. In addition, the involved client tends to be more sensitive to the hotel's needs and is more willing to consider the hotel's viewpoints.

Before developing the final function-room setup plan, it is important to estimate the amount of time needed to accomplish the client's layout and design objectives. When scheduling a function-room setup, many things must be considered. Some of these critical factors are:

1. *Function-room status.*   Function rooms used as temporary storage or those being repaired or remodeled cannot be used. If a function room has an existing setup, additional time must be scheduled so that it can be torn down. Furthermore, it is important to know how the room will be used after the catered event ends. Similar functions should be scheduled in the same room. Breaking down one setup only to reset it in another function room is a waste of time, money, and effort. When schedules permit and group sizes are similar, a basic setup can be used several times.

2. *Timing of events.*   If the function room will be empty several days before the catered event, its setup can be scheduled during slack-time periods. In this case, you have more flexibility. Moreover, usually you can maximize labor productivity.

On the other hand, if there is a meeting scheduled in a function room that ends at 5:00 PM, and you need to turn over the room for a 7:00 PM reception, time becomes your enemy. This type of scheduling demand can increase your payroll costs unless you plan very carefully.

3. *Setup difficulty.*   The amount of time needed to perform the final setup depends primarily on the type of setup required. For instance, a theater-style setup requires less time than a schoolroom-meeting setup and a reception can be set up quicker than a sit-down dinner.

4. *Function-room layout and design.*   Usually the catering manager or banquet manager is responsible for preparing the final function-room layout and design for all catered events. In some cases, exact locations of food stations, bars, seating, decor, and other requirements must be communicated to convention service well in advance of the functions' dates. Standardized and frequently used setups however, do not require complete instructions. Nor do they usually require a significant amount of advance notice. For instance, it is not necessary to draw a diagram of each schoolroom-meeting setup unless there is something unusual or distinct about the setup. Nor is it necessary to draw a complete layout if you use a system whereby each possible design is assigned a code number that is familiar to all staff members. (See Figure 8.4.)

5. *Decor.*   A theme party or similar function requires additional time to set up properly. Props, plants, flowers, lighting, and so forth must be delivered and located. The amount and type of decorations, where in the hotel they are stored, or if they must be

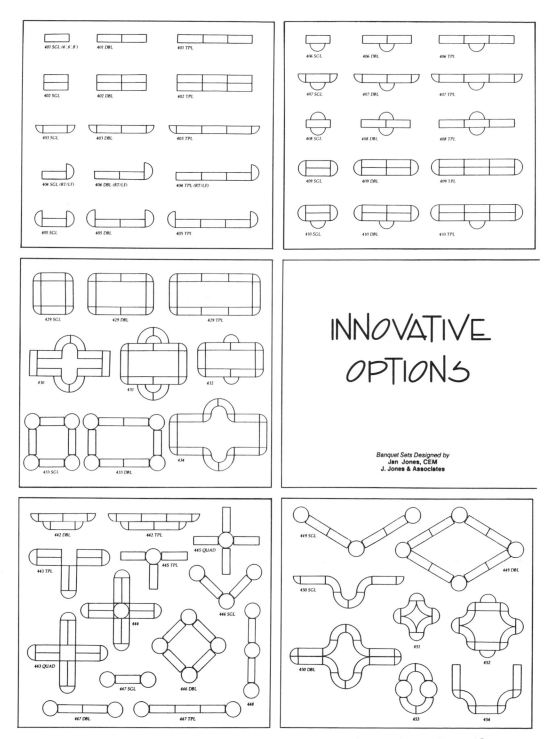

Figure 8.4. Example of banquet sets and corresponding code numbers. (Courtesy Jan Jones, CEM, J. Jones & Associates, Chicago, IL.)

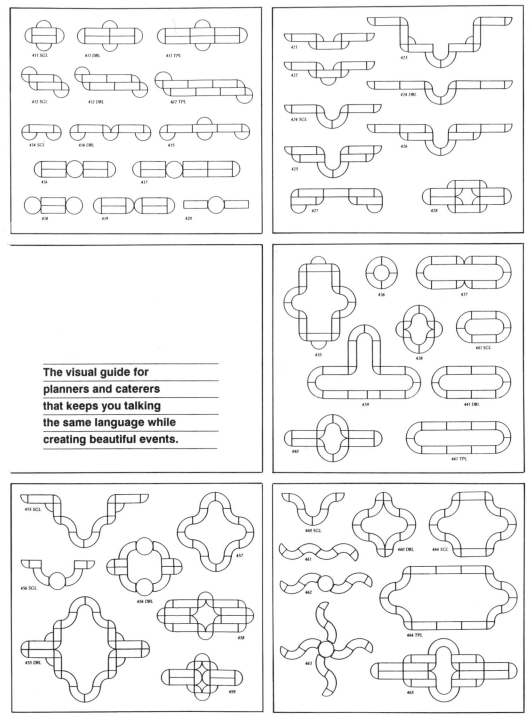

The visual guide for planners and caterers that keeps you talking the same language while creating beautiful events.

For permission to reprint, contact Jan Jones, CEM, J. Jones & Associates, Chicago, IL

Figure 8.4.   (continued)

delivered and set up by outside contractors, will determine when the function room can be set and how much of the function room can be set at one time. Larger props should be set first, furniture and equipment set next, with smaller props then set around the furniture and equipment.

6. *Premovement.*   Larger functions require additional planning primarily because it takes more time to transport the furniture and equipment. Premovement is necessary so that final room setups can proceed quickly. For instance, if a function requires 1,000 chairs, when convention service has some extra time available, it should move them as close to the function room as possible and store them temporarily. The final room setup can be handled quickly and efficiently if a good deal of furniture and equipment are preset this way.

Moving large quantities of furniture and equipment early allows time to handle any unforeseen delays that might occur. Forklift problems, employee sick calls, and equipment miscounts can derail the final setup schedule. Time is precious when setting up a function room for a large event. Presetting furniture and equipment will increase productivity, eliminate the need to rush at the last minute, and decrease the chances of an accident occurring when moving items.

7. *Tear down.*   When a function ends, convention service must dismantle the furniture and equipment and return it to storage. Efficient scheduling though, can reduce labor requirements and increase productivity. For instance, if the next setup in the function room requires chairs, you should leave the required amount in the room. The cycle of delivering, setting up, and tearing down furniture and equipment is similar to a chess game, with all pieces subject to constant movement.

8. *Lighting and audiovisual (AV).*   Meetings and meal functions sometimes require extensive lighting and/or AV services. Function-room setups that include these services usually require an additional setup time, usually referred to as a "rehearsal set." While complete furniture and equipment setup is not necessary for a rehearsal set, it can be if a band or keynote speaker wants to test the sound system with all other furniture and equipment in place. To say the least, rehearsal sets increase significantly the time and effort needed to set up a function room properly.

Communication is critical for a rehearsal set. When will it take place and how long will it last? Will other setup work continue during the rehearsal set or must it be postponed until after the rehearsal ends? Unplanned rehearsals can seriously interrupt the overall setup schedule. Productivity is compromised if convention porters or housemen must work in the dark or work while a band is checking sound levels.

9. *Outside service contractors.*   If clients are using outside service contractors, convention service must ensure that their work dovetails nicely with the hotel's standard operating procedures. For instance, if an outside service contractor is hired to handle all lighting installations and tear downs, convention service must coordinate closely with the crew to maximize productivity and eliminate unnecessary downtimes.

Dining-Room Layout

When you walk into the set-up banquet room, everything should be symmetrical. Round tables should be evenly spaced so that the eye can view attractive, neat rows. All of the table legs should face the same direction. And the points of square tablecloths should form V-shapes over the table legs. When the banquet room is completely set, the client should be able to look down a row of tables and see a consistent line of V-shapes surrounding each table leg.

The tables used should meet the height standard of 30 inches. The typical types used in catering are:

1. 60-inch round—called a round of 8, or 8-top. It is usually used to seat between 6 to 10 guests.

2. 72-inch round—called a round of 10, or 10-top. It is usually used to seat between 8 to 12 guests.

3. 66-inch round—a more recent compromise table size, it is designed to take the place of the 60-inch and the 72-inch rounds. It can seat between 8 to 10 guests. If it uses this table, the hotel may be able to minimize the different types of tables it carries in stock.

4. Banquet 6—a rectangular table, measuring approximately 30 inches by 6 feet. These tables are the typical dining tables used in restaurant banquet rooms since these types of restaurants normally do not own rounds. Hotels usually use rectangular tables only for buffet tables or display tables.

    Some clients may specifically ask for rectangular dining tables because they want picnic-style seating. Generally though, hotels do not normally use them for dining tables, except where U-shaped, hollow-square, or conference-room setups are required. For instance, a small luncheon with a guest speaker can be more readily accommodated with the

U-shaped arrangement. The platform, podium, and supporting props can be set up at the top of the U before the meal is served. The speaker can begin right after dessert. Guests will not have to change seat locations; they can remain in their present seats.

5. Banquet 8—similar to the banquet 6. It measures approximately 30 inches by 8 feet.

6. Schoolroom table—similar to the banquet 6 and banquet 8. It is 18 or 24 inches wide and 6 or 8 feet long. Used for business meetings where classroom presentations are made. Seating is usually on one side only. Can also be used as one-half of a buffet table.

7. Serpentine table—a crescent-shaped table. The typical size used is one-fourth of a hollowed-out round table. You also can purchase one that is one-fifth of a hollowed-out round table.

   Serpentines are used with banquet 6s and/or banquet 8s to make an oval-shaped buffet line. They also can be used to make a circular-shaped buffet line; for instance, four of them can be assembled to create a hollowed-out circle, where foods can be displayed on the tables and some sort of attraction (such as a floor-mounted fountain) can be displayed in the hollowed-out center.

8. Half-moon table—a half-round table. It is typically used to add another dimension to a buffet line. It can also be used by itself to hold, for example, a few dry snacks at a beverage function.

9. Quarter-moon table—a quarter-round table. It is generally used as part of a buffet line.

10. Cocktail table—a small, round table. Usually available in 18-inch, 24-inch, 30-inch, and 36-inch diameters. You can use regular heights (for sit-down service), short heights (for displays), and bar heights (for stand-up bar service).

11. Oval table—a table of varying proportions, used primarily as a dining table. The typical one used for catering measures 54 by 78 inches. It can be used to increase room capacity; for instance, you can fit 10 ovals in place of 8 rounds, thereby accommodating more people with approximately the same amount of seating. The oval table also allows a more elegant seating arrangement, in that a "host" can sit at its head.

   Oval tables do present some drawbacks. For instance, their shape makes it more difficult for servers to work around them efficiently. Guests seated on the narrow ends may feel cramped and crowded. There are wheels in the center (so that the tables can be folded up and rolled into storage) that can interfere with some guests' comfort. And, if a few foods are preset in the middle of the table, some guests may be unable to reach them easily.

When taking banquet tables from storage, opening them, and setting them up, be sure that the legs are locked properly. This will prevent unfortunate accidents that can occur if the tables are not set up and adequately secured. If locking bolts are exposed incorrectly, a guest could scratch his or her legs.

You also must ensure that the table legs lock properly when tearing down the tables and putting them away. And if the tables are stored on a dolly, they must be secured correctly to prevent accidents and damage.

The seats of the chairs used should measure 17 inches from the floor. The seat-cushion dimension should be 20 inches by 20 inches. The typical stack chair used meets these specifications. Folding chairs usually do not; they are usually too low and, hence, uncomfortable. Folding chairs should only be used for emergency backup or for outdoor picnic-type functions.

When setting up the tables and chairs, think in terms of blocks of no more than 250 seats (five 10-top tables by five 10-top tables). This arrangement, with normal aisle space within the block, and standard cross-aisle space on its perimeter, is an efficient floor design. This type of block layout, or one proportionately smaller, will usually accommodate any type of service.

Ultimately, the seating arrangement used will depend on the purpose of the catered event. For instance, awards banquets, celebrations, theme parties, and so forth will influence the dining-room layout as well as the type of tableware, props, napery, floral arrangements, centerpieces, and other decor used.

The purpose of the function also will indicate if a head table is appropriate. These days, fewer groups use head tables, believing that their absence contributes to a more egalitarian arrangement. It is sometimes felt that head tables create an unnecessary barrier between head-table guests and the other guests.

If there will be a head table, it is important to specify if it must be on a riser because the platform, just like a dining table, must be set up and dressed appropriately.

The appropriate platform height also must be determined. Platforms, or risers, usually have a minimum height of 6 inches. Using multilevel tiers, you can build them to a height of 36 inches.

Generally speaking, the bigger the room, the higher the platform must be so that head-table guests can be viewed easily by all guests.

Recall that the typical platform section is 4 feet by 4 feet. Another common dimension is 4 feet by 8 feet. A sufficient number must be assembled, connected properly, carpeted, and decorated or skirted. On the taller setups, lighted steps and hand rails must be installed. Furthermore, utilities usually must be adapted to accommodate a platform's location and other requirements.

Before the banquet set-up crew is finished, it must be certain that all ancillary tables, chairs, and equipment are set up. For instance, you may need to deliver and set up podiums, AV equipment, cashier stations, registration/information tables, kiosks, booths, and display attractions.

Finally, the dining room set-up is not complete until all outside service contractors, such as decorators and florists, finish their work. You will need to coordinate schedules with these service contractors to ensure that the dining room is ready for service at the scheduled time.

Bar Layout

Bar setups are easier to plan than food events. Unlike food, alcoholic-beverage service tends to be very standardized. Also, you do not normally set up portable bars with the wide array of equipment needed to prepare and serve a complete line of specialty drinks. Simple mixed drinks, wines, and beers are more commonly served; specialty drinks, such as pink ladys, Long Island teas, and frozen daiquiris, are not usually offered.

Bar setups are also a bit easier to plan because the hotel may have permanent, self-contained banquet-bar installations in some function rooms or banquet areas. These bars usually need only a bartender or two, a bar back, some inventory, and they are ready to go.

Even in function rooms that use portable bars, some hotels often have designated specific locations for them that are always used. These locations provide the appropriate utilities, space, and accessibility. When planning beverage service therefore, the catering sales representative and client need only to work around the preallocated space. In effect, you are working with semipermanent bars that tend to be almost as convenient as permanent ones.

A bar also does not pose the same quality-control problems as does food. The product is very standardized. It is a manufactured item, with standardized packaging, quality, and servable yields.

And, except for beer and some wines, the inventory has a virtually unlimited shelf life. You can set up bars well in advance of the functions without worrying about spoilage or quality deterioration.

If portable bars are used, and if you need to allocate space for them because there are no designated specific locations, the planning is a bit more challenging. You will need to ensure that they are set up to:

1. *Serve all function needs.*   For instance, if there is a reception with dinner following, the bars may have to accommodate both events. This implies that there must be enough room to allow guests to approach the bars during the reception, and also sufficient service-bar area to accommodate guest lines and cocktail servers who may need to handle poured-wine service.

2. *Provide sufficient working space.*   Normally you will need at least one bartender and one bar-back per bar. If you are catering an up-scale function, and are using a sommelier, you should allocate some working space so that he or she can handle wine service correctly. Depending on the type of function, you may also need cocktail servers.

3. *Provide sufficient storage space.*   A busy bar will need a back bar area in which to store additional in-process inventory. Portable refrigerators, portable ice carts, glassware, and paper supplies should be available so that service does not lag.

4. *Enhance cost-control procedures.*   There must be enough working space to eliminate bottlenecks, which can lead to overpouring and spillage. With cash bars, if there are no cashiers scheduled, the hotel will need to bring in cash registers for the bartenders to use to ring up sales and hold cash receipts. If drink tickets are sold by a separate cashier, the bar will need a lock box to store used drink tickets. Furthermore, sufficient standardized portion-control measuring devices, such as posi-pour, color-coded bottle pour spouts, and standardized glassware, must be used and appropriate space allocated.

5. *Prevent access to minors.*   A permanent or semipermanent bar installation usually is positioned to avoid this problem. Portable bars though, may not be so closely watched. However, local liquor codes usually demand that you provide some type of separation to prevent underage drinking.

6. *Allow adequate space for required cocktail tables and chairs, landing space, cashier(s), and ticket taker(s).*

7. *Accommodate special customer requests.*   For example, a client may want you to provide a separate draft-beer station, wine-tasting station, and spirits-and-mixed-drinks station. In this case, you will need to plan your setup very carefully in order to prevent overcrowding.

8. *Allow for a proper accounting of all drinks served.*   If the bar service is set up to charge the client for each drink consumed by his or her guests, you will need to allocate space for precheck cash register machines to record the number of drinks served. Alternatively, you could use disposable glassware, calculate total glassware usage at the end of the event, and charge the client for each disposable glass used.

9. *Enhance security.*   Liquor theft is all too common in our industry; tight security will minimize this problem. Usually you will transport all liquor stock in a wheeled, portable, locked cage made of cyclone fencing material. You will want to leave the cage nearby the portable bar so that, if the area must be unattended, the liquor stock can be secured. You also can have the portable bar and locked cage set up well before the catered event is scheduled to begin; when the bartenders and bar backs come on duty, they then can unload the liquor cage and set up the bar.

Buffet Layout

Buffets allow guests to choose their favorite menu items. Guests also have some personal control over the portion sizes. However, since the menu items will be handled by many different people, it is imperative to offer foods that hold up well.

Buffets are generally faster and more efficient than table-service procedures, assuming that there are enough buffet lines to accommodate the guests quickly and efficiently. One of the potential disadvantages of buffets though, is the possibility that some guests will be finished eating while others are still waiting in line.

If the purpose of the meal function is merely to refuel the guests, slower service may be acceptable. However, if there is a program following the meal, it will be almost impossible to retain everyone's attention and conduct a cohesive event. If you cannot provide enough buffet tables to prevent this problem, you should suggest that the client consider using some type of table service. For example, preset and plated service could be an acceptable alternative. This combination is very efficient primarily because you are able to time the courses.

Some clients prefer buffets because they are under the impression that buffets are less expensive to implement than table-service styles. However, buffets can be quite expensive unless you use acceptable techniques designed to reduce their costs.

For instance, low-cost food items, such as some salads and breads, can be placed first on the line so that the guests' plates will be full by the time they reach the entree stations. You can also save a bit of money by using a 9-inch plate instead of a 10-inch one.

Another cost-saving technique is to put small portion sizes on buffets. For instance, instead of serving whole chicken breasts, or even half-breasts, you should cut them into three or four pieces each. Guests who also want to eat another meat on the buffet, but want to sample the chicken, will not have to take a large piece of chicken, taste part of it, and throw the rest away.

Another cost-control procedure is to have a chef personally supervise the buffet tables. Psychologically, people will avoid loading up their plates if they are being watched.

Similarly, the chef could serve the meat course while simultaneously supervising the rest of the line. For instance, for cost-conscious groups, each guest could be issued a meat ticket that must be exchanged for a serving of roast beef. This eliminates second helpings. It also prevents a guest from taking a full serving, eating a little bit of it, and returning for another full serving because the rest of the original serving got cold when he or she was distracted while socializing with other guests.

While there are many similar types of cost-saving opportunities, the director of catering should not reduce the buffet experience to an institutional "chow line" atmosphere. A low-price, low-cost buffet may give some guests the wrong impression of the hotel's capabilities. It may be foolhardy to court catering clients who do not wish to purchase the quality and value you normally serve.

Regardless of a client's budget, buffets can provide many advantages to both the client and the hotel. For instance, they provide an acceptable level of customer service. They allow guests to control what and how much they eat. Chefs can use their creative talents to decorate the foods and buffet tables. And labor costs can be trimmed a bit if guests are satisfied with self-service and minimal food offerings.

When laying out the buffet stations, you should try not to put salads, entrees, and desserts on the same table. This will slow up service as the guests will try to take everything at once. Most guests cannot carry two plates, but this does not stop them from trying. The inevitable result: spillage and other food-wasting accidents.

Since guests will form a line anywhere they can, you should avoid setting up the buffet tables near doors or other entry ways where they can cause traffic jams. If this is impossible, you should consider using round buffet tables instead of rectangular ones as these will provide slightly better traffic flow.

If the buffet line will be longer than 16 feet, it should be two tables wide, that is, about 4 to 6 feet wide. A long, narrow line is unattractive. A wider line allows you to spread out the foods, create a more aesthetically pleasing depth perception, and enhance the set up with decorations and food displays.

If you must use long, narrow lines, you should use a combination of straight tables and curved ones to eliminate the "bowling alley" effect. Unfortunately though, curved lines require a bit more floor space.

If the buffet line will include an action station, you will need to allocate enough space to accommodate the in-process inventory of food, preparation and service equipment, the chef, and the guests who will want to congregate and watch the chef create the finished items.

If the action station will be put toward the center of the function room instead of up against a wall, you will need more floor space. An action station "in the round" usually is set up with several inside tables and outside tables to allow for maximum chef maneuverability and exposure and guest accessibility.

It is difficult to determine the number of action stations needed because it depends on the amount of time needed to prepare and serve the foods, and the estimated number of guests who will want them in lieu of the other foods displayed on the buffet line. At the very least, you should expect that half of the guests will want something from an action station.

Some buffets incorporate a bit of cafeteria service. If so, there must be enough room allocated so that food servers and chefs can maneuver adequately.

If floor space is at a premium, you should consider using double-sided buffet tables. They can save as much as 20 percent of your available floor space. They also tend to reduce leftovers because, when service slows near the end of the meal, you can close one side of the line and consolidate all foods on the open side.

The buffet should not have an attached self-service beverage station. Whenever possible, beverages, such as wine, hot coffee and tea, and soft drinks, should be served at the table. This provides a bit of personalized table service that guests appreciate. It also makes the overall service much quicker and more efficient. Experience shows that guests take a long time at beverage stations and that bottlenecks are inevitable.

Experience also indicates that you should not allow guests to walk across the room balancing two or three cups of hot coffee.

Hot drinks should always be served. Guests who have had a few glasses of wine are not prepared to negotiate the pathway to and from the beverage station. You do not want an unfortunate accident to mar the event and, incidentally, make the hotel liable for employee and guest injuries.

If possible, you should use small containers of food on the buffet line. Try to use containers that hold no more than 25 to 30 servings. In the long run, they will be more attractive than large, elaborately garnished containers. Keep in mind that only the first few guests through the line will see the beautifully garnished large presentations before they are disturbed. Furthermore, half- or quarter-full large bowls have a lot of food, but they are unattractive.

In lieu of decorating all food containers, it may be more efficient to decorate and embellish the tables and their surroundings. All guests therefore, will be able to see and appreciate the decor instead of the few lucky ones who get first crack at the food presentations.

Small containers will need more frequent replenishment, so you will incur a bit more payroll expense. However, experience shows that guests will take smaller portions from smaller containers, and larger servings from bigger containers. The result: you save more on food cost than you spend for the extra labor. Furthermore, smaller containers usually mean fresher, more attractive presentations.

Most meal buffets are usually set with one line for every 100 guests. The maximum amount you can serve efficiently with one line though, is 120 guests. The break point therefore, is 120 guests. Generally speaking, you should have one line for every 100 guests, but you should have two lines if the number of guests ranges from 120 to 200.

The general feeling in the industry is that you are courting disaster and customer dissatisfaction if you cannot maintain these standardized ratios. This is especially true for luncheon meal functions because guests usually arrive at once. In this case, speed is very critical.

If you set one buffet line for every 50 guests, you can feed the entire group in about 15 minutes. The first guest will take about 5 minutes to go through the line. After that, there will be about 4 guests passing through the line every minute. For some luncheons, it might be a good idea to set one line for every 50 guests.

If hors d'oeuvres are served buffet-style during a beverage function, some industry experts recommend setting one table for every 50 guests. Fewer, larger tables tend to interfere with bar traffic.

If you set one buffet table for every 50 guests though, you may need more labor to replenish food supplies. You will have more product-distribution problems unless you set up enough service corridors to handle replenishment. And you may have more leftovers with several small buffet tables unless you consolidate some tables toward the end of the event.

For breakfast functions, you may be able to get by with one buffet line for more than 100 guests. Unlike luncheon guests, breakfast guests tend to arrive a few at a time. For instance, many convention attendees will drift in throughout the meal. Even though the typical breakfast buffet will have a guest rush during the last 15 minutes of the meal period, usually enough guests will have already been served to prevent any service glitches.

Dinner buffets are usually more elaborate. There are many decorations and more lavish food displays. If you set this type of buffet, guests will usually take more time to serve themselves. They will want to savor the visual effects and not rush through. Generally speaking, for every hour it takes to serve a luncheon buffet, it will require about one and one-half hours to serve a dinner buffet.

Table Setting

All dining tables and buffet tables must be dressed and outfitted appropriately. The type of meal function, menu, and style of service will influence the quality and type of table decor used.

The table setting is the focus of a function room's decor. It is the one thing that guests see throughout the meal. Because it influences the mood in which the patron judges what he or she eats and drinks, you should spend as much time designing the right look as you spend developing the most appropriate menu.

Display tables will often need to be skirted, that is, their sides must be completely covered from the floor to the top of the table. Skirting is draped over the side of the table. It is connected on the table's edges and allowed to fall to just above the floor.

Up until a few years ago, skirting was attached with straight pins. Skirting today though, is easier to install, remove, and clean. Plastic clips and Velcro fasteners have made installation and removal much easier. Some clips have Velcro on the back. They come in two sizes, standard and angled. Standard is made to fit a three-quarter inch thick table top and angled is used for one-half inch thick table tops.

Some skirting have plastic clips attached that clip onto the table. Some skirting have Velcro bands intended to hook onto

Velcro-strip tapes that are attached to the table. To avoid sagging, clips are attached at intervals of two feet or less.

Table skirting is 29 inches high. Stage (that is, platform) skirting is readily available in lengths ranging from 6 inches to 36 inches. Longer skirting is available, but if the standard lengths do not meet your needs, you may want to use pipe and drape to dress anything higher.

For some skirting, you will need to use a skirting liner. For instance, if you plan to use an elegant lace skirting, you will need to line it so that the uncovered areas do not show through.

Usually all buffet tables, display tables, and platforms are skirted. Some dining tables may also be skirted. For instance, a head table usually is skirted on three sides. The skirting provides a vanity shield as well as an attractive presentation.

Hot- and cold-food delivery carts should also be skirted. For instance, a roll-in luncheon buffet on a 3-tier cart may be used to accommodate a small business meeting. The cart should be skirted from the top to the floor on three sides. The unskirted side, out of guest view, can be opened to remove the foods for service.

You may also want to skirt portable bars and related equipment, such as crushed-ice containers and wine and beer coolers. If you have any carts in the room holding back-up stock, you may want to skirt them so that they do not detract unnecessarily from the function's overall appeal.

Usually you must requisition skirting from the linen room. When calculating the amount needed, you must be very careful to compute the correct total. If, for example, you need enough skirting to cover a banquet-8 table, you will need about 22 running feet (that is, two, 8-foot sides and two, approximately 3-foot sides equals about 22 running feet).

Tables should be padded so that table noises are minimized. The typical dining table and buffet table usually have pad underliners placed underneath the tablecloths. This pad can be permanent; for example, you can buy a roll of padding, cut pieces to fit each table, and staple them to the table tops. Or the pad can be temporary; for example, the housekeeping department may issue one pad (which is similar to an ironing board pad) with each table cloth requisitioned.

You can purchase tables whose tops are prepadded. Generally though, these tables are much more expensive than unpadded ones.

All tables require napery. Buffet tables and display tables will need tablecloths. And dining tables will need tablecloths and napkins.

You will also need napery for your beverage stations. For instance, the alcoholic and nonalcoholic beverage stations will need tablecloths. And, while both types of stations need coasters and napkins, normally you will use disposable paper coasters and cocktail napkins instead of permanent, reusable napery.

Napery adds warmth and color. In the public's eye, cleanliness is its most important attribute. Crisp, clean, stain-free napery helps create a favorable impression.

White is the traditional color of napery used. Light colors are used when white does not provide the background desired. Darker colors can be used when a stark contrast is desired or for all-day functions (such as permanent refreshment centers) where the napery, which will get soiled during the day, cannot be changed easily. And darker colors (usually green) are used for schoolroom tables so that convention attendees can take notes without battling the glare that white napery gives off.

Sometimes you may want to use two or more colors to dress a table. For instance, a combination of white and mauve may be appropriate for a buffet table; white and gold may be just right for a table used to display door prizes; white and green is a good combination for landing space around beverage stations; and black tablecloths with bright-color napkins (such as fuchsia, gold, or white) provide a startling and crowd-pleasing visual effect.

Many hotels own their napery and launder it in house. The alternative is to use an outside laundry and linen supply firm that will deliver clean napery and pick up the soiled articles. In some cases, perhaps for a very large function, you may need to supplement the in-house supply with a temporary rental. There also may be times when specialty napery is needed for affairs that require colors or patterns you do not carry in house.

Ideally, the linen-room manager strives to maintain at least three sets of napery in house. One set should be clean, on the linen-room shelf, ready to use. One set should be in the laundry. And one set should be in use in the function rooms. Maintaining this 3-par stock ideal is a challenging task because napery has a rather unpredictable useful life.

If you have any choice in selecting the napery, you should choose products that are fire retardant, heavy-weight, soil-resistant, and nonshrinking. You also want no-iron napery that will hold folds readily, cling neatly to the table top, and not fade after a few washings.

When selecting napery, the three most important considerations are:

1. Durability—how long will it last? What is its expected useful life?

2. Laundry and maintenance cost—how much does it cost to wash? to repair?

3. Purchase price—more importantly, the purchase price spread out over the life of the napery. This "long-term" purchase price takes into account the cost of washing and repairing the napery. For instance, an expensive product that can be cleaned in cold water and withstand 300 washings is preferable to a less-expensive item that must be washed in hot water and can be washed only 150 times. Ultimately, it is the cost per use that influences napery's overall value.

When ordering linen, or requisitioning it from the linen room, you will need to specify the exact measurements needed. The standard tablecloth sizes normally used for banquets are 78-inch and 90-inch round tablecloths. Regardless of the type and size of table used, though, the size of the tablecloth should be approximately 18 inches wider than the table diameter so that about 9 inches of cloth will drape over the sides. If the table-top diameter is 36 inches, you should use a cloth 54 inches square. A 45-inch diameter table should be fitted with a 64-inch square cloth; a 54-inch diameter needs a 72-inch square cloth; and so forth.

If you use rectangular dining tables, the same rule of thumb prevails, that is, the tablecloth should drape about 9 inches over the table's sides.

Recall that the standard table's height is 30 inches and the standard chair's seat measures 17 inches from the floor. A tablecloth with a 9-inch hem will not quite touch the chair seats. If this tablecloth is fitted correctly on the dining table, it will not interfere with guest comfort.

In general, tablecloths should be large enough to cover the tables and leave some hem, but not so large that the hems lap the chair seats and cause guest discomfort. At most, hems should just barely touch the front edges of the chair seats.

There are times when you may want to use a round tablecloth whose diameter is double the table-top diameter. For instance, for an elegant reception, you may want to cover a 60-inch round to the floor with a 120-inch tablecloth instead of with a smaller tablecloth and skirting.

Some hotel properties have one set of napery for catering and another set for the restaurant outlets. In this case, instead of requisitioning tablecloths, you would need to specify "banquet" cloths. This allows you greater control over the use of these items. It also means you will receive the appropriate sizes and the exact items that will serve your purposes adequately.

When placing the tablecloths on the tables, you should be careful to keep the hemmed sides down and the creases up. For instance, on a rectangular table, all creases should be up. And, as much as possible, they should be centered on the tables. If the tablecloths were pressed incorrectly (that is, where the creases and hemmed sides are both in the same direction), you should keep the hemmed sides down even though the creases will look unattractive. In this case, you must select the lesser of two evils.

The napkins used must be laundered and handled correctly so that they will have enough strength to hold whatever fold you want to use. For instance, you can use the more common napkin folds, such as the pyramid, goblet fan, or Lady-Windermere's-fan, or you can use something more adventurous and unusual, such as the rosebud, bishop's-mitre, or candle folds. (See Figure 8.5.)

For more exotic folds, such as those used to decorate serving trays and buffet-line containers, you can use a thin-gauge metal foil insert to give added strength to the napery. For example, you may want to have two goose-neck shaped napkins adorning each side of a canape tray. The metal foil will give you enough tension to make these folds and ensure that they will hold up throughout the function.

A napkin must be placed at each cover, that is, at each dining-table place setting. The layout must be symmetrical and pleasing to the eye. If you are using a buffet-style service, you may opt to provide the napkins at the beginning or end of the buffet line. For speed and efficiency at casual events, you could roll the flatware inside the napkins.

To complete the dining table setup, you will need to requisition from the executive steward's office an assortment of china, glassware, and silver. Plates, cups, saucers, flatware, water glasses, wine goblets, roll baskets, condiment containers, wine coolers, carafes, show plates, and other appropriate items must be preset on the dining tables in a symmetrical pattern. As with napkins though, if you are using a buffet-style service, you could let the guests help themselves to some tableware on the buffet line.

There are many other types of tableware needed that usually are not preset on the dining tables. For instance, you will need tea pots, pitchers, mugs, serving platters, serving bowls, ramekins, casserolettes, and specialty utensils.

When selecting tableware, most hotels prefer vitrified china or some similar type of product. China retains heat or cold longer

How to fold the folds that hold with Visa° napery fabrics.

1. **THE CANDLE** Fold napkin in half diagonally (1). Fold down base 1/3 way (2). Turn napkin over and roll from bottom to top (3). Tuck corners inside cuff at base of fold and stand (4). Turn one layer of point down and set on base (5).

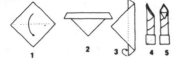

2. **BIRD OF PARADISE** Fold napkin in half and in half again (1). Then fold in half diagonally with points on the top and facing up (2). Fold left and right sides down along center line, turning their extended points under (3). Fold in half on long dimension with edges facing out (4). Pull up points and arrange on a fabric surface (5).

3. **THE ROSE** Fold all 4 corners of open napkin to center (1). Fold new corners to center (2). Turn napkin over and fold all 4 corners to center (3). Holding center firmly, reach under each corner and pull up flaps to form petals. Reach between petals and pull flaps from underneath (4).

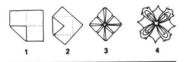

4. **THE GOBLET FAN** Fold napkin in half (1). Pleat from bottom to top (2). Turn napkin back 1/3 of the way on right (folded) end and place into goblet (3). Spread out pleats at top (4).

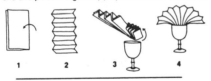

5. **ROSEBUD** Fold napkin in half diagonally (1). Fold corners to meet at top point (2). Turn napkin over and fold bottom 2/3 way up (3). Turn napkin around and bring corners together, tucking one into the other (4). Turn napkin around and stand on base (5).

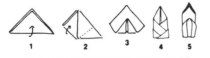

6. **LADY WINDERMERE'S FAN** Fold napkin in half (1). Starting at bottom, accordion pleat 2/3 way up (2). Fold in half with pleating on the outside (3). Fold upper right corner diagonally down to folded base of pleats and turn under edge (4). Place on table and release pleats to form fan (5).

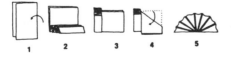

7. **CLOWN'S HAT** Fold napkin in half bringing bottom to top (1). Holding center of bottom with finger, take lower right corner and loosely roll around center (2), *matching corners*, until cone is formed (3). Turn napkin upside down, then turn up hem all around. Turn and stand on base (4).

8. **THE CARDINAL'S HAT** Fold napkin in half diagonally (1). Fold corners to meet at top point (2). Turn napkin over with points to the top, fold lower corner 2/3 way up (3). Fold back onto itself (4). Bring corners together tucking one into the other. Open base of fold and stand upright (5).

9. **PYRAMID** Fold napkin in half diagonally (1). Fold corners to meet at top point (2). Turn napkin over and fold in half (3). Pick up at center and stand on base of triangle (4).

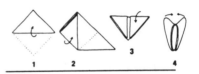

10. **THE ARUM LILY** Fold napkin bringing bottom up to top (1). Fold corners to top (2). Fold bottom point up to 1" below top (3). Fold point back onto itself (4). Fold each of points at top down and tuck under edge of folded-up bottom and fold down one layer of top point and tuck under base fold (5). Turn napkin over and tuck left and right sides into each other (6). Open base and stand (7).

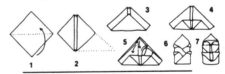

11. **THE CROWN** Fold napkin in half diagonally (1). Fold corners to meet at top point (2). Fold bottom point 2/3 way to top and fold back onto itself (3). Turn napkin over bringing corners together, tucking one into the other (4). Peel two top corners to make crown. Open base of fold and stand upright (5).

12. **BISHOP'S MITRE** Fold napkin bringing top to bottom (1). Fold corners to center line (2). Turn napkin over and rotate 1/4 turn (3). Fold bottom edge up to top edge and flip point out from under top fold (4). Turn left end into pleat at left forming a point on left side (5). Turn napkin over and turn right end into pleat forming a point on right side (6). Open base and stand upright (7).

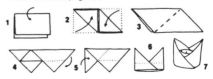

Figure 8.5. Standard napkin folds. (Courtesy Milliken & Company, Spartanburg, SC.)

228

than other materials. China is also impervious to salt, alkali, and acid, all of which attack and corrode metal. It can be produced with dishwasher-safe, lead-free glazes, and with oven-proof, freezer-proof bodies. In addition, china also resists scratches from knives and other utensils much better than other materials.

Glassware includes stemware, tumblers, goblets, parfaits, decanters, pony glasses, snifters, pilsners, bottles, ashtrays, punch bowls, and cake plates. Hotels usually purchase glassware that has been produced with a heat-treated, rapid-cooled process that ensures durability and long-term attractiveness.

Glassware is one of the most useful decorating tools you can use. It helps set a mood and carry out a theme. Furthermore, hotels can use specialty glassware as a signature; for instance, the Ritz Carlton is renowned for its cobalt-blue water goblets.

The standard cover includes plateware set in the center with flatware placed on either side. Forks are placed to the left, knifes and spoons to the right. Some dessert flatware may be placed above the center plate.

Flatware is placed in the order in which it will be used by the guest, from the outside in. For instance, the soup spoon would be on the outside, as soup is usually an early course. The knife would be closest to the center plate, with the blade edge facing the rim of the plate. The smaller salad fork would be set farther out than the dinner fork.

The exact place setting depends primarily on the menu and style of service selected by the client. Many catering executives have sample covers set out on credenzas in their offices that can be viewed by clients wishing to see what they are getting. Clients can also redesign the sample place settings in order to develop something unique.

Once the desired place setting is developed, pertinent information, such as the number of covers per table, is included in the banquet event order (BEO). Working with these specifications, the banquet captain usually sets a "Captain's Table," that is, a sample cover, as a guide for the servers to follow when setting the dining tables. (See Figure 8.6.)

Some clients want you to use unique types of tableware in order to complement the theme. For instance, they may want you to display a few antique bowls. If these bowls are used strictly for decorations, you can display them. However, if they will contain food, or be placed where they might come into contact with food, you cannot use them unless they are approved by the National Sanitation Foundation (NSF) and/or the local health district for use in food-service operations.

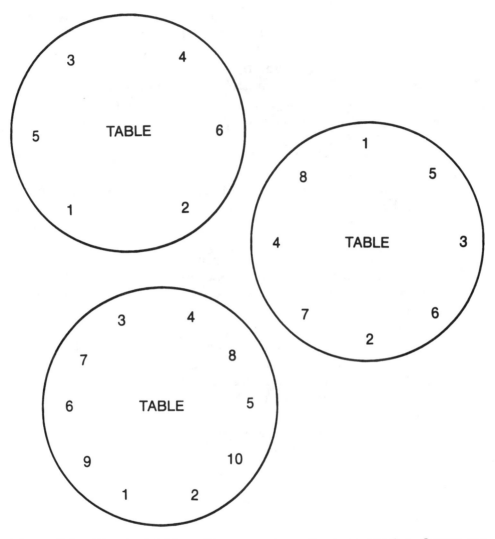

Figure 8.6. Standard table setting procedures for even spacing. Covers are placed according to numbered pattern.

If you own unique decorative items or serving containers, you must be careful to use only those intended to hold foods. For instance, an imported serving bowl could contain lead in its glaze. Care must be taken to ensure that these types of containers are used only to hold and/or display nonfood items.

Some dining tables may need nameplates and/or personalized menu cards. For instance, if you are setting a head table, you must see to it that the head-table guests are seated correctly. For the head table at a formal event, the first guest of honor should be seated on the host's or hostess's right with the second guest of honor seated on the left. If a third guest of honor is present, he or she should be seated to the right of the first guest of honor. If there are other dignitaries, they should be balanced back and forth according to rank or prominence.

For the head table at a wedding, the bride and groom should be seated at the center, with the bride sitting on the groom's left. On the bride's left will be the best man, followed by a bridesmaid, groomsman, bridesmaid, groomsman, and so forth. On the groom's right will be the maid of honor, followed by a groomsman, bridesmaid, groomsman, bridesmaid, and so forth. There should be enough room allocated at the head table to accommodate the entire formal wedding party, but if this is impossible, you should seat the most important members at the head table with the others seated at the dining tables closest to the head table.

Your table setting is not complete without some sort of additional decoration. Most catered events, especially dinners, have centerpieces on the dining tables. They also have similar attractions on the buffet tables.

Centerpieces should be attractive and appropriate for the type of function booked. Floral arrangements, candles, lights, and ice carvings are excellent centerpieces appropriate for any type of food or beverage function.

Generally speaking, you should avoid using edible centerpieces. They will be disturbed very early by the first two or three guests who touch them. Once deteriorated, they may detract from the overall beauty of the catered event. Guests may remember little else about the function save the unattractive centerpieces.

In some cases, you may be required to prepare an unusual centerpiece, or allow the client to prepare it. For instance, many conventions request fun centerpieces, such as pinatas, world globes, or scale models. Many conventions also request centerpieces that highlight their organizations. Oftentimes these types of unusual centerpieces are souvenirs in disguise, in that the client expects some guests to take them home.

Centerpieces on dining tables should not interfere with guests' normal sight lines. They should be placed under or over these sight lines. You do not want guests to feel uncomfortable peering under, over, or around them. Or, worse yet, you do not want the guests to place them on the floor where they will hinder traffic, or place them on the next table that is yet to be occupied, thereby ruining that table's setup.

If guests are expected to take home centerpieces after the catered event, you should suggest ways in which the function host can distribute them without playing favorites and offending some guests. For instance, if there is a floral arrangement on a dining table, you could select one cover at the table and code it with a gummed color dot under a preset plate. The function host can announce that the person finding the dot under his or her plate can take home the floral arrangement.

Before setting the tables, the banquet manager must specify the exact setup needed for regular dining tables, head tables, beverage stations, and buffet tables. It is a good idea to diagram in advance the required setup so that the setup crew does not have to scurry around at the last minute for directions. For instance, if special centerpieces must be placed on the head table, the setup crew must know about this before it goes to work.

The banquet-setup crew will need to know if some place settings must be set a bit differently than others. For instance, if a guest at the head table needs some props for a speech, his or her place must be identified so that it can be arranged correctly.

All head-table guests usually have assigned seating. Every once in a while the client may want to assign specific seats to all guests. Generally speaking though, guests may be assigned a specific table, but seat assignments are uncommon.

If a few guests will be having off-menu meals, their covers could be identified so that servers do not have to ask everyone who gets what. Usually though, these guests are told to inform their server when they sit down that they are having a special meal. The banquet captain informs the servers ahead of time about these special requests, so there usually is no need to mark their place settings.

The banquet-setup crew will also need to know if there will be a no-smoking section. If the client requests one, it is traditionally set on the left side of the room. The crew will need to set out ashtrays on the tables in the smoking section and "Thank You for Not Smoking" signs on those tables in the no-smoking section. (If you do not put these signs out, guests may think you merely forgot to put out ashtrays; they may just go ahead and light up without thinking.)

Dining-room layout, bar layout, buffet layout, required table settings, and other pertinent information will be listed on the banquet event order (BEO). Some BEOs also include a room diagram. However, experience shows that, while the typical BEO details very specifically the dining-room, bar, and buffet layouts, it does not always include an exact description of the required table settings. For instance, if the client wants menus, brochures, and handouts placed at each cover, this information must be noted on the BEO. Every detail, no matter how small, is important to the client. You cannot afford to let any get lost in the shuffle.

EMPLOYEE UNIFORM

A good deal of a food or beverage function's visual impact can be attributed to the type and style of employee uniforms and costumes used. The typical client does not think about this unless he or she requests a specific theme, in which case special uniforms and costumes will be needed to carry out the theme.

Usually the hotel uses a standard server uniform for breakfast and luncheon meal functions, with a slightly different server uniform used for evening affairs. Bartenders, cocktail servers, bar backs, and buspersons also wear a standard outfit. These standard uniforms are designed to suit most food and beverage functions adequately.

If the client is a bit more adventurous and has a bit more money to spend, the catering sales representative may wish to broach the subject of alternative employee attire if he or she thinks it would add significantly to the function's success. For instance, you could suggest renting unique garments specifically for the meal function. This little extra touch can be just the thing to make a good event a great event.

CLEANING AND MAINTAINING THE FUNCTION ROOM

Convention service (or housekeeping) is usually responsible for the cleanliness and routine maintenance of function rooms. Dirty windows, walls, or floors can reduce a function room's quality level and cause guest dissatisfaction.

Function rooms must be vacuumed before each function setup (when the room is empty), with one final sweep or vacuum just before the catered event is scheduled to begin. Post-function cleaning is equally vital. Trash and leftover convention materials must be discarded promptly.

The major cleanliness concern is the function-room loading door through which dirt can be tracked into the room area. Trucks, forklifts, and carts that must enter the function room will hasten carpet deterioration and generate a considerable amount of working dirt. Covering the floor near the loading entrance with old carpets and plastic sheeting can be an effective dirt catcher. Precleaning ramps and loading docks can also reduce the amount of dirt tracked into the room.

Trash-can and public-ashtray cleanliness and maintenance are also handled by convention service. Constant care during peak periods must be scheduled to ensure an attractive atmosphere.

Burnt-out light bulbs, torn wallpaper, torn carpet, and broken equipment must be replaced or repaired quickly so that the function rooms remain presentable and safe. Quick room turnarounds and constant movement of heavy furniture and equipment will cause damage to doors, floors, ceilings, and walls. Convention service must monitor these details consistently.

Frequent inspection and repair can reduce wear and tear of the facilities as well as create a favorable guest environment conducive to memorable, exciting catered events. Convention service (or housekeeping) must handle problems personally or, in many hotels, report the conditions to the hotel's maintenance department.

COMMUNICATION IN THE FUNCTION-ROOM AREAS

Hotel properties with several function rooms in various locations require coordination and control of convention-service staff. It is difficult to monitor employees who are constantly on the move. Managers must select an appropriate method to supervise and communicate quickly with all employees.

One basic, low-cost method of control is the call-back method. In this situation, an employee must contact a supervisor when his or her assigned task is completed. The supervisor will know how much time it normally takes to complete the task and can therefore, anticipate a pattern of calls from his or her employees. As calls come in, new tasks are assigned on a priority basis. Furthermore, if a last-minute request is received, the supervisor will be able to assign it to the first employee who calls in.

A medium-cost method of control is the beeper method. With this option, beepers are assigned to all convention-service employees or the employees are divided into groups with each group leader holding a beeper. This method allows the supervisor to assign a wide variety of tasks to each employee because the supervisor can quickly call all employees when emergencies arise.

Another advantage of using beepers is the ability to assign one to the client. Instead of trying to track down a client to verify a setup or time, information can be checked quickly.

The major disadvantage with beepers is the time it takes employees to respond when called. When an employee receives a call, he or she must cease working and locate a phone. This stop-and-go action can be time consuming and frustrating, especially if it is continuous. Phone availability is also a consideration; if the only available phone is in a back office, additional time will be lost and labor productivity will plummet.

The most expensive method of communication control is the walkie-talkie method. Walkie-talkies (or cellular phones) eliminate the need to stop what you are doing and locate a phone station. Although some systems can cost thousands of dollars to install, the time and efficiency gained can be well worth the expense.

Lead employees and supervisors can be assigned walkie-talkies and thereby, become instantly accessible. Last-minute changes can be communicated immediately. Clients are very impressed when their requirements change and employees respond to them instantaneously.

With walkie-talkies, supervisors can also monitor the conversation between employees and keep up to date on the movement of furniture, equipment, and labor. For instance, if a request is broadcast to one employee to locate some equipment, another employee monitoring the broadcast can break in with some new pertinent information.

As with beepers, a walkie-talkie can also be issued to a client. Unlike beepers though, the walkie-talkie ensures instant verification of all details.

EQUIPMENT INVENTORY

As can be seen, the catering department uses a considerable amount of specialized furniture and equipment to set up the function room and serve the catered event. The department should ensure that complete, up-to-date lists of these items are kept by convention service and other related departments so that the catering staff knows what is available and what will need to be obtained from a rental company.

These inventory lists should note all chairs, tables, easels, tripods, stanchions, dance floor, audiovisual equipment, gueridons, rechauds, china, glass, flatware, linen, skirting, serving utensils, side stands, trays, bus carts, hot carts, cold carts, permanent centerpieces and other decorations, portable bars, and other furniture items kept in house.

The equipment lists should be updated monthly. A complete physical inventory should be taken at the end of each quarter so that damaged items can be repaired and missing ones replaced quickly. If there is a good deal of catering business, there might be an above-average loss due to damage and/or theft. If so, a physical inventory should be taken more frequently.

9

Production and Service Planning

Creative catering makes each event special. Dare to be different!

Laura Silverman, CCE
Senior Catering Manager
Pier Sixty Six Resort & Marina
Fort Lauderdale, Florida
President National Association of
Catering Executives, 1991–92

Production and service planning must be correlated with client needs to ensure smooth-running functions, satisfied guests, and fair profits for the hotel. All factors must be evaluated so that the appropriate plans can be developed. Coordination is vital. Attention to detail is critical. You cannot take anything for granted.

PRODUCTION PLANNING

A production plan lists the types and amounts of finished foods and beverages needed, when they must be ready, and when they should be produced. The chef and banquet manager must have copies of the banquet event orders (BEO) so that they can incorporate them into the daily production and work schedules.

Quantity of Food Needed

The chef needs to requisition foods from the hotel storeroom. If the kitchen staff needs something unusual that the hotel does not normally carry in stock, he or she will need to prepare a purchase requisition a few days before the meal function and give it to the

236

purchasing department. The purchasing agent will then have enough time to shop around for the product and get the best possible value.

The amount of food that must be requisitioned and produced depends primarily on the:

1. Number of guests expected
2. Style of service
3. Expected edible yields.

You should plan to prepare enough foods to handle the guaranteed guest count, plus a set percentage above that amount. Generally speaking, if the guarantee is 100 guests, you should plan for 10 percent more; if the guarantee ranges from 100 to 1,000 guests, you should plan for 5 percent more; and if the guarantee exceeds 1,000 guests, you should plan for 3 percent more.

If the guests are having a sit-down, preplated meal, it is relatively easy to compute the food-requisition amounts because you have a great deal of control over the portion sizes. For instance, if the main course is roast bottom round of beef, the serving size is 6 ounces, and the edible yield percentage for the raw roast beef is 75 percent, you will need to requisition about 55 pounds of raw beef for a party of 100 guests. Fifty-five pounds will be needed to serve 100 guests, plus 10 extra guests. The calculations are:

1. Divide serving size by edible yield percentage. This will tell you how much raw product you need per serving.

$$\frac{6 \text{ oz.}}{.75} = 8 \text{ oz.}$$

2. Divide 16 oz. by the amount of raw product needed per serving. This will tell you the number of edible servings you can get from one raw pound.

$$\frac{16 \text{ oz.}}{8 \text{ oz.}} = 2$$

3. Divide number of guests by the number of edible servings per raw pound. This will give you the amount of raw beef you must requisition.

$$\frac{110 \text{ servings}}{2} = 55 \text{ pounds}$$

If you plan to use reception service and/or buffet service for a meal function, it is not as easy to determine the amount of foods to requisition and to produce. There are some rules of thumb though, that can help you make a reasonable estimate. For instance, in a reception where foods are displayed on buffet tables, guests will generally consume about seven hors d'oeuvres during the first hour of the reception. Guests generally will eat more during the first hour of a reception.

Another rule of thumb suggests that blue-collar persons will eat and drink more than white-collar and pink-collar employees.

Still another rule of thumb notes that if you crowd people into a room, they tend to eat and drink less than if they have more space to roam around and visit. A crowded room makes it more difficult for guests to revisit the buffet tables.

Recall that the way in which you display your foods on a buffet table will encourage or discourage overconsumption. For instance, putting the less expensive items up front, the more expensive items further back, and having a chef serve meat can give you an extra margin of control.

In some cases, you may not be too concerned if you overproduce foods for a buffet. For instance, if you can get the client to agree to eat the same types of menu items that are used in the hotel's restaurant outlets, overproduction is no problem because you can recycle any leftovers. If the menu items cannot be recycled, either you must have a sharp pencil when making your estimates, or you will need to increase your competitive bid price for the catered meal function to take into account the additional food costs.

Unfortunately, it is very difficult to make an accurate determination of the amount of food to requisition and produce when you are dealing with self-service buffets and receptions unless you sell foods by the piece and clients agree to purchase a set amount. For that matter, even per-person pricing can be based on a specific amount and types of food items offered.

If there are no restrictions placed on the self-service function though, you cannot compute reasonably accurate estimates unless there is a good deal of relevant historical data upon which to base them. But even if you do take a lot of time to estimate your needs, you have limited control over the serving sizes. As a result, you should always add a margin of safety to avoid stockouts.

Quantity of Beverage Needed

It is much easier to determine how much alcoholic beverage you will need than it is to forecast your food requirements. Unlike food, beverage is a standardized, manufactured product. You do not have to worry about spoilage and quality and yield variations.

Furthermore, as long as your liquor storeroom is well stocked, you will never run out of product. You cannot quickly prepare and serve an extra roast beef dinner if you are out of cooked roast beef, but as long as there is beverage in house, you can make drinks.

Usually the banquet and reception bars are set up with a par stock of beverages, ice, glassware, garnishes, and other necessary supplies about a half-hour to an hour before the catered event is scheduled to begin.

The normal par stock used is influenced by the:

1. Number of guests expected
2. Hotel's experience with similar catered events
3. Amount of storage space available at the bar.

Joseph E. Seagram & Sons Inc. has developed rules that can be used to estimate the approximate amount of liquor needed for an average reception of 100 guests. For instance, if you have 100 guests, you would expect about half of them to consume 3 glasses of wine apiece during the reception. Since each 750 milliliter (ml) bottle of wine contains about 5 drinks, you will need about thirty 750 ml bottles. Consumption trends indicate that you will need about 25 bottles of white or sparkling wine and 5 bottles of red. (Generally speaking, for every 2 bottles of red served, you expect to serve 10 bottles of white or sparkling.)

Joseph E. Seagram & Sons Inc. also suggests that during the typical reception for 100 guests, 50 percent of them will consume 3 spirit drinks apiece. To accommodate the group adequately, consumption trends indicate that the basic portable bar should be stocked with:

Type of Spirit	No. of Liters
Blend	1
Canadian	1
Scotch	2
Bourbon	1
Gin	1
Vodka	3
Rum	2
Brandy/Cognac	1

Generally, you should expect liquor consumption to average at least $2^{1}/_{2}$ drinks per guest during a one-hour reception, particularly if the event attracts a mixed-company crowd. Average consumption tends to drop at very large receptions and it usually increases at male-only events. However, if you schedule enough help and stock enough inventory to handle 2½ drinks per hour, you should be able to accommodate any type of beverage function adequately.

If the beverage function's drink menu varies significantly from the type you normally serve, bartenders will need to change the types and amounts of beverages usually stocked at the portable bars. For instance, if a drink menu will offer only red and white table wine, gin, bourbon, vodka, scotch, and an assortment of soft drinks, the bartender will need to adjust the typical opening par stock requisitioned from the liquor storeroom.

Usually you do not need to worry about stocking an exact amount of beverage at the banquet or reception bars because you can always depend on the bar back to replenish the supply quickly. Also, experience shows that if you run out of something temporarily, most guests will wait until the bar back replenishes the supply or they will select another beverage. For instance, if you cannot serve a glass of burgundy because you are waiting a few minutes for more to be retrieved from the liquor storeroom or another hotel bar, the typical guest will not mind the wait. Or, if you have a substitute red wine, many guests will gladly accept it.

You should though, make an effort to forecast your needs as accurately as possible because this will help ensure a smooth-running event. In addition, if beverages need to be iced down, it behooves you to make sure that you have plenty of ice available; you cannot take a room-temperature item and chill it quickly unless you have the specialized equipment needed to do this.

In most instances, it makes no difference if you overstock a banquet or reception bar because the merchandise can be used at other hotel bars. However, if the hotel needs to purchase specific beverages for the catered function that are not used in other hotel bars, you will need to compute as accurately as possible the amount you should order.

For example, a meal function might require a unique dinner wine that must be special ordered by the purchasing agent. If the expected guest count is 100, you will need to order enough wine to serve 110 persons.

Usually you will estimate two and one-half servings of wine per guest for the typical dinner banquet. In our example then, you will need to order enough wine to serve 275 glasses (110 × 2.5). Since the standard wine glass holds a 5-ounce portion (approx. 148 ml), you will need to special order about fifty-five 750 ml bottles of wine. The calculations are:

1. Divide the amount of liquor per 750 ml bottle by the serving size. This will tell you how many potential drinks you can obtain per container.

$$\frac{750 \text{ ml}}{148 \text{ ml}} = 5.07 \text{ potential drinks per bottle}$$

2. Divide the number of servings needed by the number of potential drinks per container. This will tell you how many containers you will need to special order.

$$\frac{275 \text{ servings}}{5.07} = 54.24 \text{ 750 ml bottles, rounded to 55 750 ml bottles needed.}$$

If you take into account overpouring, waste, and the fact that usually you cannot get all of the liquid out of a bottle (some of it will stick to the sides), you will need to increase your special-order size. For instance, if you assume that you will lose 1 ounce (approximately 30 ml) per 750 ml bottle, your special-order size will be about fifty-seven 750 ml bottles of wine. The calculations are:

$$\frac{720 \text{ ml}}{148 \text{ ml}} = 4.86 \text{ potential drinks per bottle}$$

$$\frac{275 \text{ servings}}{4.86} = 56.58 \text{ 750 ml bottles, rounded to 57 750-ml bottles needed.}$$

Some suppliers may not allow you to special order anything in less than case-size lots. In our example then, you may need to special order sixty 750 ml bottles (5 cases, 12 bottles per case) because the liquor distributor may not want to bust a case for you. If you are faced with this situation, you may need to add a liquor surcharge to the client's final billing.

Alternatively, you could charge the client only for the amount of wine consumed, keep the leftover product, and run it as a special in one of the hotel's restaurant outlets.

Some unopened leftovers could also find their way into complimentary fruit baskets left for special guests in their hotel suites.

Opened and unopened wine could be sent to the client's hospitality suite or used for another function. For instance, if the client has booked three meal functions, perhaps the leftover wine can be used for the next event.

The supplier may be willing to exchange unopened leftovers for something you normally use. While the typical supplier may not want to take back in trade one or two bottles, he or she is usually quite willing to take back unopened cases in trade. If the client agrees, you could charge the client by the case, order extra from the supplier, keep the few leftover loose bottles, return the unopened cases to the supplier, and credit the client for the returns.

Finally, you could charge the client by the bottle or by the case and let him or her take home any leftover wine. Before you do this though, check the local liquor code to see if it is legal. For instance, the hotel may need to hold a package-goods liquor license before you can let the client take home unopened liquor. And opened stock may have to be served solely for consumption on premises.

To avoid the leftover problem, you could special order, say, four cases of wine (forty-eight 750 ml bottles), put it all out on the dining tables, and when it runs out, back it up with another wine. However, make sure that you advise the client before doing this.

Quality of Food Needed

The quality of foods used by the hotel is dictated by the product specifications and standardized recipes prepared by hotel executives. For instance, a hotel that is part of a chain organization will have a vice president of purchasing and a vice president of food and beverage operations on the corporate level who usually have the final responsibility for making these quality determinations.

Before you requisition foods, you must examine the standardized recipes very carefully so that you know exactly what you need. For example, if the recipe calls for Kraft cheese, you must requisition this brand name. You cannot requisition Borden cheese because the recipe is specifically geared for Kraft. Since Borden will be a bit different, the finished product will not be the same if you use Borden instead of Kraft.

Likewise with other product identification factors. You must requisition the correct product quality, size, color, package size, degree of preservation, type of processing, and so forth, if you expect to maintain quality control. Actual quality that differs from the standard, expected quality, no matter how slight, is unacceptable.

In addition to quality control, product specifications and standardized recipes help ensure cost control. When you cost out your standardized recipes, you will use purchase prices based on the types of ingredients noted in them. If you use a substitute, and do not account for any difference in cost, your final accounting will show an actual food cost that is more or less than what you budgeted. If the actual cost exceeds the budgeted standard cost, the hotel will suffer a loss. If the actual is less than the standard, clients will be cheated because they will have received foods that were not consistent with the menu prices quoted.

Quality of Beverage Needed

As with food, the quality of beverage served will depend on the product specifications and standardized recipes used to prepare finished drinks. Unlike food though, there usually is one more thing to consider: the client's desires to have certain brand names of liquor served at the catered event.

Some clients will not specify brand names. Since well brands usually cost less than call brands, some clients will be satisfied with them. Consumer preferences though, indicate that while people are drinking less, they are drinking higher quality products. Premium brands are in vogue and more clients today are asking the hotel to provide a choice of high-quality wines, spirits, and beers.

Brand names are the primary selection factors used when developing liquor product specifications, standardized recipes, drink menus, and stock requisitions. However, when requisitioning liquor from the liquor storeroom, there are a few additional factors that must be noted.

For instance, you will need to note the container sizes for each product needed. Generally speaking, for spirits, you will use 750 ml or 1 liter bottles if you free pour the drinks, and 1.5 liter or 1.75 liter bottles if you use a mechanical dispensing unit to prepare drinks.

When requisitioning beers, more than likely you will want 12-ounce bottles or cans. If you have a portable draft-beer dispensing unit, you would requisition the appropriate container size (probably a pony keg) that fits it.

Wines come in various container sizes. Generally this flexibility allows the client more cost-saving opportunities. For instance, you can purchase wines in 750 ml and 1.5 liter bottles. Less expensive products, such as well wines (that is, "house" wines), can be purchased in larger bottles and in bag-in-the-box containers (that is, a large plastic cryovac bag of wine inside a cardboard box that is usually designed to be used as a self-dispensing package).

As with food, your drink product specifications and standardized recipes help ensure cost and quality control. Without these guidelines, it will be very difficult to forecast accurately the alcoholic-beverage costs. In this case, price quotations offered to potential clients may not be as competitive as they should be.

Food Prepreparation

Food prepreparation (that is, preprep) activities generally are performed a day or more before the meal function. They include all the food production steps that can be performed ahead of time that will not compromise the quality of finished menu items. For instance, if the menu calls for vegetables and dip, a pantry person can prepare these items the day before and refrigerate them. Or if the menu calls for an egg action station, a cook can preprep some egg mixes, dice the vegetables, and lay out the bacon on sheet pans the night before.

Generally speaking, the larger the function, the more preprep that must be done in advance. For instance, a banquet of 5,000 prime rib dinners would require you to start preplating the meals at least three hours in advance and putting them in a hot cart. You would start out plating the rare portions, and end up plating the well-done portions. Alternatively, you could plate the cooked meat cold the day before, hold under refrigeration, and heat, sauce, and garnish prior to serving.

Some hotels have adopted the "sous vide" form of prepreparation. This involves the production of finished or semifinished menu items about a week or more before they are needed. After they are produced, the foods are then vacuum packed and stored in the refrigerator until needed.

Sous-vide production has expanded the number and type of menu items that can be preprepared. For instance, if you have a party next week and grilled salmon steaks will be on the menu, today you can sear, season, vacuum package, and then cook them in their plastic pouches. When done, the individually packaged steaks must be cooled rapidly and stored in the refrigerator. A few minutes before service, you reheat and plate them.

The sous-vide technology requires you to invest in some additional kitchen equipment. However, the method offers several culinary advantages. For instance, grilled salmon steaks can be cooked in their own juices and seasonings and several of them can be served at one time. Under normal cooking procedures, you would be unable to serve grilled salmon steaks to a large group of people while simultaneously maintaining quality control.

Unfortunately, sous-vide procedures can contribute to foodborne illness if they are not monitored closely. Sanitation is extremely important when sealing food products in plastic. If harmful bacteria are left in the package, they may grow to the point where some guests consuming the food may become ill.

The menu planner should try to include as many preprep items as possible. This makes it much easier to plan food production. It gives you more control over the labor work schedules. You can utilize production labor more efficiently. And it ensures that the correct amount of foods will be available when it is time to prepare the finished products.

Bar Prepreparation

Bar preprep is much easier than food preprep. Generally, it includes stocking the portable bars with all nonliquor nonperishables whenever it is convenient to do so. Then, just prior to service, you preprep your nonliquor garnishes, requisition the liquor, load the ice bins, and ice down wine bottles and bottles or cans of beer.

If the banquet bars are permanent or semipermanent fixtures, bar backs and/or bartenders can restock them after a catered event according to the specifications noted on the banquet event order (BEO) for the next function. For instance, when a party is over, the manager can take an ending inventory and determine the liquor usage for that function. The bar back and/or bartender can then replenish the bar with nonperishables so that the bar production workers the next day need only spend a few minutes prepreping the perishables.

Food Preparation

Food preparation (that is, prep) activities are performed just prior to the point of service. For example, your preparation schedule for hot foods should dovetail with your guest-service schedule. You would not want to produce these products too far in advance, or else they will lose culinary quality. Nor would you want to produce them to customer order, as this will slow down service.

A good food production schedule combines the preprep and prep activities. For instance, if you have a baked-chicken item on the menu, you can do some preprep work the night before, such as washing the products, seasoning them, and laying them out on sheet pans. About an hour or so before service, you will prep them, that is, put them in the oven to cook.

Finish Cooking

Finish cooking involves cooking to guest order. For instance, the chef must wait for the guest to order a rare steak; he or she does not prep it in advance.

Finish cooking is the most difficult part of the food production plan. It is also the most labor intensive. You need to schedule a lot of worker hours. And the worker hours must be provided by highly skilled food handlers who can work under the demanding conditions that accompany most finish-cooking activities.

For instance, a chef working at an egg action station must be quick, efficient, and accurate. He or she normally will be producing two or three guest orders at a time and will need to remember them as well as those that are coming in from other guests waiting in line.

Some finish cooking is easier than others. For instance, with a roast beef item, you can preprep the roast the night before, prep it two or three hours before service, and finish cook it, that is, carve and serve it, to customer order. In this case, the finish cooking involves a relatively easy task.

Bar Preparation

In most instances, bar prep is synonymous with bar service, that is, the same person who prepares the drink also serves it and, if applicable, collects cash or a drink ticket.

In those instances where a service bar is used, that is, a bar used only by cocktail servers to obtain drinks for their guests, the prep and service activities are separated. The bartender preps drinks only when the servers order them. For cost-control purposes, usually a server must give a precheck ticket, or some other record, such as a duplicate guest check, to the bartender before a drink can be prepared. If applicable, the servers are responsible for cash or drink-ticket collection.

Food Work-Station Setup

Action stations, serving lines, and buffet tables must be set up prior to service. In some hotels, the kitchen staff has this responsibility, while other properties split the work between the kitchen and convention-service staffs. For instance, cooks may be responsible for setting up the serving lines in the kitchen or in the service corridor, and setting up the action stations, while the kitchen and banquet-setup crews together set up the buffet tables. Generally speaking, the kitchen handles the foods and convention service handles the table setups.

Replenishing the Food Work Stations

The kitchen is normally responsible for replenishing the food supplies on buffet tables, action stations, and serving lines. Usually a food runner is employed to handle this task. In some cases though, the service staff might take on this duty. For instance, the kitchen crew may be responsible for stocking back-up foods in hot carts and delivering them to a service corridor. A food server can then be assigned to replenish depleted food work stations with foods taken from these hot carts.

Employees assigned this responsibility typically must do more than merely refill serving containers. They must be able to anticipate customer needs, combine half-empty pans and make the combination appear as attractive as any other container, and react to the chef's last-minute instructions. They also may need to pitch in and help keep buffet tables and landing space clear of soiled tableware and trash.

Replenishing the Bars

Bar backs are responsible for replenishing liquor, ice, garnishes, glassware, and direct operating supplies, such as coasters, swizzle sticks, and cocktail napkins. Most bartenders will also jump in and help restock merchandise in an emergency, such as when the bar back is helping out at another beverage function that is short-handed.

Cocktail servers may also help out in a pinch. For instance, if there are one or two special drink requests that cannot be pre-pared by the bartender because he or she does not have the stock available, a cocktail server may just go to another hotel bar to fill them.

Number of Food Production People Needed

Food production differs somewhat from food service in that the food handlers usually have responsibility for food production throughout the hotel. Handling the catered meal function may not be their only duty. While the banquet-service staff concentrates solely on the scheduled meal function to which it is assigned, the typical food handler must juggle many tasks.

It is therefore, a bit more difficult to determine exactly how much food production labor is needed for a particular meal function. On the one hand, the cooks on duty in a restaurant outlet may be able to handle the entire catered event along with their other responsibilities. At the other end of the spectrum is the catered function that requires a completely separate kitchen crew. For some meal functions, you may not have any additional variable labor costs, whereas for others, the food production payroll will be a significant portion of total expenses.

In general, the number of food production work hours needed for a catered event will depend on the:

1. *Number of guests.*

2. *Amount of time scheduled for the catered event.*

3. *Applicable union and company personnel policies.*

4. *Type of service style used.*   For instance, action stations require more production labor, whereas the typical buffet that offers only standardized menu items will need less.

5. *Amount of convenience foods used.*   Processed foods are less expensive to prep and serve. You need fewer labor hours to reconstitute them. You also avoid expensive labor expertise because the products require less skill to handle. However, their purchase prices usually are very high because of the built-in labor and energy costs that the manufacturer must recapture.

6. *Amount of scratch production.*   This is the opposite of convenience-foods usage. The closer a food ingredient is to its natural state, the lower its purchase price will be. A significant amount of scratch production results in a low food cost. However, you will end up with a high labor cost since you take on all of the preprep and prep burdens. If the local labor market is tight, the resulting labor cost incurred may be prohibitive.

7. *Amount of finish cooking needed.*   Too much finish cooking wreaks havoc with a food-production labor budget. If the client wants a great deal of this, chances are he or she must be willing to pay a handsome labor surcharge.

8. *Type of menu items offered.*   Some products take more time to preprep and prep. For instance, it takes more time to produce meat loaf than roast beef, vegetable soup than onion soup, and gallantine of capon than roast duckling.

9. *Number of last-minute requests.*   Flexibility is one of the hallmarks of a successful hotel catering department. You must be flexible enough to accommodate some unscheduled requests. For instance, you should be ready to produce one or two individual fruit plates or vegetable platters on a moment's notice.

10. *Number of special diets.*   It can take almost as long to produce two or three special diets as it does to take care of 50 standard guest meals. If you know about these needs in advance you can be ready for them. However, once you start producing a different menu item for each guest, you immediately lose the advantages that catering enjoys over regular restaurant food production and service.

11. *Accuracy of meal-time estimates.*   It is not unusual for a meal function to start late and end late. This, unfortunately, may result in overtime premium pay for some production staff. It also can cause overtime premium pay in other departments, such as housekeeping and convention service, because their work schedules may be thrown out of line.

When catered functions run behind schedule, you must expect to incur a higher labor cost. It is also likely that the foods may have lost a good deal of their culinary quality. Ironically, when this scenario occurs, the guests cause you to pay more for the privilege of hearing them complain about the foods' marginal quality.

Some catering managers prepare staffing charts to help them determine the number of food-production work hours needed, how many persons to call in to work the function, and how these people should be scheduled. These charts usually relate the number of work hours needed to the number of expected guests. For instance, if you expect 100 guests, you go down the column headed by 100 and in each cell there will be a number of suggested work hours needed for each job position.

Assume you are allowed 16 food production hours for 100 guests. If the meal function will last four hours, you can divide the 16 work hours into four, 4-hour shifts and bring in four persons. You also can schedule one 8-hour person, and two 4-hour employees. Or you can plan any other acceptable combination.

How you apportion the allowable number of work hours will depend on many of the factors discussed above. For instance, considerable preprep indicates that maybe you should have an 8-hour person come in the day before. A lot of finish cooking implies an opposite strategy.

Distributing work hours over a work schedule also depends on how many food production persons you want on board before, during, and after the meal function. Usually you will need to stagger the work schedule in such a way that most of your production work hours are used when the bulk of the production must be completed, with the remaining hours left over to cover the start-up and tear-down periods.

Staffing charts work much better in the typical restaurant operation where the menu, production, and service are standardized and there is a consistent pattern of customer arrivals and departures, popularity of menu items, and amount of time it takes to turn the tables. They also work well in service planning because, once you know the timing of the function, menu, number of guests, and style of service needed, you can usually lock into a standardized work schedule.

Kitchen staffing charts must be continually revised unless your catering business settles into some sort of predictable pattern. The director of catering will usually keep a close eye on the staffing chart and change it as needed. He or she also will be forever looking for that elusive pattern that can make it much easier to forecast food production payroll expenses and develop accurate food production work schedules.

Number of Bar Backs and Bartenders Needed

The number of bar backs needed for a catered function will depend primarily on the:

1. Number of bars scheduled
2. Capacity of each bar to hold in-process inventories
3. Distance between the bars and the kitchen and storerooms
4. Degree of ease or difficulty associated with retrieving back-up stock
5. Number of guests
6. Hours of operation
7. Variety of liquor stock, glassware, garnishes, and direct operating supplies needed at the bars
8. Applicable union and company personnel policies.

Unless the catered event is very small, you will need at least one bar back. The typical banquet bar, especially the portable one, does not have a lot of storage capacity. It usually will need periodic replenishment.

If a small beverage function is scheduled, perhaps the bartender can do double duty and take on the bar back's responsibility. However, this could reduce service efficiency and cause guest dissatisfaction if the bartender is in the liquor storeroom and is temporarily unavailable to mix drinks.

The number of bartenders needed for a catered event will depend primarily on the:

1. Number of bars scheduled
2. Types of drinks that must be prepared
3. Number of drinks that must be prepared
4. Number of guests

5. Hours of operation
6. Amount of bar-back work that must be performed
7. Applicable union and company personnel policies.

You will need at least one bartender for each bar location. For all but the very small beverage functions, usually you schedule two bartenders for each bar plus any wine-service personnel needed for the meal. Even for small beverage functions of, say, 50 to 60 guests, you may need two bartenders, or more, if the event is scheduled for only forty-five minutes to one hour. In this case, speed is a high priority. With such a short time frame, guests will normally swamp the bar to make sure they get their desired number of drinks before it closes. One bartender may be unable to handle this onslaught.

For large beverage functions, such as a convention's opening night cocktail reception, hotels generally will try to get by with one bartender for every 100 guests, whereas the typical professional meeting and convention planner prefers a ratio of one bartender for every 75 guests.

The 1/75 ratio is usually the minimum necessary if you expect all guests to arrive at the same time. If you do not have enough bartenders when a crowd hits the door, some guests may have to wait up to an hour to get a drink.

If you have over 1,000 guests, the ratio of one bartender to each 100 guests is appropriate. With a large crowd, guests cannot move around as much. With 8 to 10 bartenders, the preparation and service tends to be quicker and more efficient because the bartenders can help each other and keep the lines moving.

The timing of a beverage function can also influence the number of bartenders needed. For instance, if 200 persons are leaving a business meeting and going directly to a cocktail reception, you many want to set a ratio of one bartender for each 50 guests so that they will be served quickly. If there is a break period between the end of the business meeting and the beginning of the cocktail reception, where guests can go back to their sleeping rooms to freshen up, they will not arrive all at once. They will come in a few at a time. Consequently, you could use fewer bartenders to handle the group.

To alleviate pressure on the bartenders, you could schedule a few cocktail servers to pass glasses of champagne, still wines, bottled waters, and juices. This also adds an extra touch of elegance to the event.

If the catered function calls for cocktail servers and/or a sommelier, perhaps you can reduce the number of bar backs and bartenders you would normally schedule. For instance, one cocktail server could be cross-trained (that is, a combination bartender and cocktail server) and scheduled as a floater (that is, fill in as a bartender or server as needed). This flexibility could easily save a few labor hours over the long term.

By the same token, a food server, busperson, captain, or other member of the catering and kitchen staffs could be used to help out the bartenders and bar backs. For instance, it might be more economical to schedule one 6-hour busperson to handle bussing and bar back duties than to schedule one 4-hour bar back and one 4-hour busperson.

If you decide to mix and match job positions and adopt these types of creative scheduling techniques, you will need to check the union joint bargaining agreement, if applicable, and/or the company's personnel policies and procedures manual to see if it is permissible. Furthermore, you must ensure that the relevant staff members have received the proper type and amount of cross-training.

Number of Cashiers Needed

If a cashier is needed to sell drink tickets, you will need at least one on duty. Normally you will need only one cashier if the catered function is small and/or if it is a leisurely event where guests are not pressed for time. Larger functions, as well as those where speed is required, require more cashiers. Under these conditions, generally you will need to schedule one cashier for every two bartenders.

If you are using cashiers, you may want to schedule a plain-clothes security guard to supervise and protect the cash-handling operations. A plain-clothes guard sometimes is preferable to a uniformed guard because some guests may become a bit anxious if they see uniformed security.

If you have a security guard scheduled to supervise the liquor service, and if the group being serviced is not too large, he or she could also oversee the cash-handling operations. With a large group of guests though, you should consider scheduling at least one security guard to supervise liquor preparation and service and one to oversee the cash-handling procedures.

Number of Ticket Takers Needed

If guests must use tickets to enter a function room, or if they need to use them to get into a meal function, you may or may not need to schedule a ticket taker to collect them. In most cases, clients will handle this chore personally; however, on some occasions you will be asked to provide this service.

Ideally, the client would handle the collection of all entry tickets. You should avoid coming between the client and his or her guests in what sometimes could be a confrontational occurrence. You do not want to be put in a position where the hotel must impose client sanctions on guests. Furthermore, some guests may not appreciate the hotel assuming this control position.

Drink tickets and meat tickets do not usually cause confrontational problems. Consequently, if guests are required to use them, there generally is no need to schedule separate ticket takers. In these cases, bartenders and chefs can collect them.

Number of Banquet-Setup Crew Members Needed

The number of persons needed to set up, tear down, and/or clean the function room will depend primarily on the:

1. Amount of lead time available
2. Size of the catered event
3. Size of the room
4. Location of the room in the hotel
5. Amount of time available between functions. For example, how much time do you have to tear down and clean up after a breakfast function and set up for an afternoon reception?
6. Applicable union and company personnel policies.

If you have a lot of time available, and/or if the function planned is for 50 guests or less, usually convention service can get by with only one crew member. For larger functions, or if time is precious, usually no less than two persons must be scheduled.

Two or more crew members may also be needed if some tasks require the strength and agility of at least two persons to accomplish. For example, setting up a platform, rolling out and setting up a portable dance floor, or hanging signage or decorations may require two persons working in tandem.

Usually the hotel wants function rooms set up as soon as possible. All nonperishable items should be set out in advance so that staff members can concentrate on the last-minute details and not have to worry about doing things during "prime" times (that is, times when guest service is a priority) that could have been done quite comfortably during "slack" times (that is, down times when guests are not being served).

SERVICE PLANNING

Unlike production planning, service planning is a much easier task. Once you know the timing of the function, menu, number of guests, and style of service, you usually can forecast an accurate estimate of the number of service work hours needed, the number and types of servers required, and the most efficient work schedule that should be followed.

Types of Servers Needed

Depending on the type of catered event, the banquet manager will need to schedule one or more of the following types of service personnel:

1. Maitre d' hotel
2. Captain
3. Food server
4. Cocktail server
5. Sommelier
6. Busperson.

Service Duties

Service personnel are responsible for a wide array of duties. Unlike production staff members, servers are often called upon to jump in at a moment's notice and handle unscheduled requests and/or activities. For instance, while the typical client would not consider asking the chef to change the menu at the last minute, he or she may not be shy about asking the maitre d' hotel to set up an extra dining table, slow down service because the speaker is running a bit late, or push two tables together so that a subgroup of guests can create its own party atmosphere.

Service personnel must be very flexible. All of them should be trained to perform the following functions:

1. Napkin folds
2. Table settings
3. Placing table pads and tablecloths
4. Presetting foods on dining tables
5. Greeting/seating guests

6. Taking food/beverage orders from guests (if applicable). This would be done only if guests have a choice of entrees and/or beverages.

7. Serving food and beverage

8. Submitting food/beverage guest orders to chefs and bartenders (if applicable). As with number 6, this would be done only if guests have a choice of entrees and/or beverages.

9. Opening wine bottles

10. Pouring wine

11. Hot beverage service

12. Cold beverage service

13. Crumbing tables

14. Bussing tables

15. Carrying loaded cocktail, oval, and crescent-shaped trays

16. Stacking trays

17. Emptying trays

18. Tableside preparation

19. Using different service styles

20. Handling last-minute requests for food, beverage, and/or service

21. Handling complaints

22. Directing guests to other facilities in the hotel

23. Handling disruptions

24. Dealing with intoxicated guests

25. Refusing liquor service to minors

26. Requisitioning tableware from the executive steward.

Service Ratios

Service ratios, that is, the number of service personnel needed to handle a given number of guests, are usually established by the catering executive and the hotel's top management team. These ratios are the heart of the service staffing guide.

The number of service personnel needed depends on many factors. The primary ones are:

1. *Number of guests.*
2. *Length of the catered function.*

3. *Style of service used.*

4. *Menu, especially its length and complexity.*

5. *Timing of the event.* For instance, you may need more servers if there will be a considerable amount of time between courses and other activities, such as guests' listening to speakers, dancing, or watching stage shows. Similarly, if the group needs to be fed very quickly, you will need more service personnel, though, since you will not need them very long, you might be able to handle the catered event adequately without exceeding your labor budget.

6. *Room setup.* Is the layout and design conducive to quick, efficient service, or should bottlenecks be expected?

7. *Location of function room.* How much distance is there between the kitchen and the function room? How easily can you go from the kitchen to the function room? Is there enough aisle space? Is the service corridor large enough? Are there enough service elevators?

8. *The probability that overtime must be scheduled.* For instance, experience may suggest that a particular type of catered event, and/or a particular type of group, will tend to run late. This could result in overtime premium pay for a few service personnel. However, if you can anticipate this problem, you should be able to schedule enough employees to handle the event properly without resorting to overtime.

9. *Number of head-table guests.* These guests require much more service attention than do the others.

10. *The amount and type of extraordinary requests.* For instance, a client may want extra labor to seat guests after they go through a buffet line. Some guests may request extra condiments, which will add to the service work load. And some clients, at the last minute, may want the room rearranged somewhat; usually the service personnel have to handle this type of last-minute request because the setup crew may be unavailable on short notice.

11. *Applicable union and company personnel policies.* Unionized hotels may schedule only the minimum number of service personnel called for in the union contract. Nonunion hotels whose competitors are unionized may also follow these standard ratios.

Experience shows that the minimum number of servers as well as the minimum number of each service-job classification that must be scheduled according to union regulations usually are insufficient to provide the level of service required by most catered events. You generally will need more servers if, for example, you need to serve a large luncheon very quickly, or if you must provide French service for a dinner function.

The joint bargaining agreement's requirements typically provide enough servers to accommodate only the small and/or easy-to-handle groups. These service minimums though, at least give you something to work with when forecasting the number of servers needed.

Many hotels develop strict service ratios and do not vary from them even though a particular situation may call for it. For instance, some properties will budget one server for every 32 guests regardless of the style of service, the type of menu, or whether the servers are responsible for wine service.

If you adhere strictly to this 1:32 ratio, you may risk customer dissatisfaction. Some catered events can be handled adequately under this payroll-cost constraint. However, most functions will need more help or else they cannot be serviced efficiently.

Irrespective of the quality of a catered function's food and beverage, room setup, and overall ambience, poor service reduces significantly the guests' appreciation and enjoyment of the event. Customer surveys consistently show that patrons rank the quality of service very high on their lists of desired restaurant attributes. They usually place it no lower than second on their lists, ranking it just slightly behind the culinary quality of the food and beverage.

Poor service will overshadow any other favorable aspect of the event. Guests will never be pleased if the service is lacking. They will usually remember a bad experience much longer than a good one. The catering executive who tries to shave service costs to the bone will undoubtedly make a lot of clients and guests unhappy. He or she will also jeopardize repeat patronage.

If the hotel puts you on a very tight labor budget, at times you will be between a rock and a hard place. You will be asked to maintain the budget, yet provide a level of service that will satisfy guests and encourage clients to return. You cannot risk coming in overbudget. If the catered event's projected revenue will not cover the extra labor costs, the least you should do is ask the client to alter his or her menu or service requirements, or agree to pay a modest labor surcharge so that you can schedule adequate staff.

Experience shows that the number of service personnel needed can vary from a low of about one staff member for every 8 guests to a high of approximately one staff member for every 40 guests.

According to meeting planners, the minimum service ratio for the conventional sit-down meal function with American-style service with some foods preset, is one server for every 20 guests. If you are using rounds of 10, you should schedule one server for every 2 dining tables. If you are using rounds of 8, two servers should be scheduled to handle 5 dining tables.

The minimum busperson ratio for this sit-down meal is one busperson for every 3 servers. If you are using rounds of 10, you should schedule one busperson for every 6 dining tables. If you are using rounds of 8, one busperson should be scheduled for every 8 dining tables.

Some hotels will schedule one busperson for every two servers. This is usually done for functions that include several VIPs or where extraordinary service is requested by the client. Generally speaking though, you can make do with one busperson for every three servers because servers normally are expected to perform some bussing duties during the catered event.

If the conventional sit-down meal function requires poured-wine service, you normally will need one server for every 16 guests. You should schedule one server for every two rounds of 8, or two servers for every three rounds of 10. One busperson for every six rounds of 10, or every eight rounds of 8, will usually suffice.

If the meal function is served buffet-style, usually servers and buspersons can handle significantly more guests. For instance, the minimum service ratio of one server for every 20 guests and one busperson for every 3 servers could very easily be increased to one server for every 40 guests, and one busperson for every 4 servers.

In some cases you may want to maintain the ratio of one server for every 20 guests for a buffet-style meal function. For instance, if the kitchen schedules a small crew, or if it has to handle several parties, it may be unable to refresh the buffet tables and help serve guests. You could use the balance of your wait staff to focus on these tasks.

If the buffet requires considerable replenishment during the meal, you may need to schedule servers to handle the food-running chores. In this situation, normally one food runner (or other service employee) is needed for every 100 to 125 guests. You will need more runners if they are expected to accommodate several buffet stations spread throughout the function room. Conversely, if there are only a few buffet stations, other food servers who could share the work load, and/or a limited menu, you should be able to schedule fewer runners. Moreover, if the chef employs food runners, you may be able to avoid this responsibility.

If the meal function requires Russian or French service, you can usually serve the guests adequately if you follow the service ratios noted above for the conventional sit-down meal with poured-wine service.

If the meal function includes Russian or French service, along with poured-wine service, generally you will need at least one server for each dining table and one busperson for every three dining tables. This ratio is appropriate whether you are using rounds of 8 or rounds of 10.

Head tables usually receive the best service. If the catered function has head tables, you should plan to schedule at least one server for each head table. If the head table includes more than eight guests, you should use two servers.

Ideally, the head table would have its own busperson. If you cannot afford this, or do not need a separate busperson, you should assign the head table and one or two other nearby dining tables to one busperson. If possible, you should not have head-table servers handling both the serving and bussing chores. They should devote their efforts to guest service.

Regardless of the style of service, you usually will need to schedule at least one floor supervisor. This supervisor could be a banquet captain or a maitre d' hotel.

Generally speaking, you should plan to schedule at least one banquet captain for each catered event. For very large meal functions, you should plan to schedule one banquet captain for every block of 250 guests (that is, for every block of 25 rounds of 10). Alternatively, you could schedule one banquet captain for every ten to twelve servers.

The banquet captain for a small catered event can supervise both the meal service and the reception service. For example, if there are only 100 guests, one floor supervisor is sufficient to handle both segments.

If you need to schedule more than one banquet captain, you should assign one maitre d' hotel to coordinate their duties. For instance, if you have a meal function for 1,000 guests, you typically would assign one maitre d' hotel and four banquet captains to supervise service. If there is a premeal reception, the maitre d' hotel should supervise both the meal service and the reception.

You should not try to serve a function without a sufficient number of floor supervisors. These men and women play an extremely important role in coordinating service and seeing to it that all guests are served efficiently. For instance, with a sit-down meal function, it is important to have all courses served at approximately the same time. This will not happen by itself. It is a difficult feat to achieve, and is almost impossible to accomplish without adequate supervision.

If you need to staff a reception, you must schedule enough servers to supervise the food stations. Generally speaking, you should have one server responsible for every three food stations. If the stations are spread throughout the function room, and there is considerable distance between each one, you will need more servers.

The servers responsible for overseeing the food stations can also perform some bussing duties. For instance, they can help replenish the tableware, bus the landing space, and remove waste. Depending on the size and complexity of the reception, you may be able to get by with few, or no, buspersons.

You will need more servers if you intend to pass food trays during a reception. For a small catered event, one or two servers would suffice. As the function size increases, you normally need to schedule one server to handle one-fourth of the function room, one-eighth of the function room, and so forth. Generally, you should plan to schedule at least two servers for every 75 guests.

You also will need more buspersons if you have servers pass trays during the reception. The servers usually will be unable to pitch in and help with the bussing duties because they will be too busy with guests. You should expect to schedule at least one busperson for every three to four servers.

Even if there is no food served during a reception, you still should schedule at least one or two buspersons to keep the landing space clear. Perhaps a dining-room busperson or two could be brought in earlier than the others to cover the reception's bussing needs; then after the reception, they can help out during the meal function's rush period.

If you are using cocktail servers during a reception to pass trays of premade drinks, you will need at least one cocktail server for every two to three food servers. Usually you need considerably less cocktail servers than food servers in this situation because guests tend to approach the food servers more frequently than they do the cocktail servers. For instance, a guest might take a glass of wine from a tray and nurse it all night, whereas he or she will usually take more than one piece of food.

Very few catered events use cocktail servers to take guest drink orders, return to a service bar to fill them, and then go back on the floor to serve them. This type of service is infeasible for large group functions. Generally it is done only for small functions, especially those that cater to VIPs. The typical type of cocktail service used for standard catered events requires the guests to approach the portable bars, get their drinks, disappear into the crowd, and return when they want more drinks.

If you do use this type of cocktail service to take guest orders though, your labor costs will increase significantly. In this situation, at best a server can usually make only three or four passes per hour through his or her assigned floor area. During each pass, he or she will usually be able to carry, at the most, only 12 to 16 drinks. In the best-case scenario then, you would need one cocktail server to handle 48 to 64 drinks per hour. Furthermore, since this type of service is less efficient and requires more coordination and effort, you will need more bartenders to handle the work load.

Many receptions last only about one hour. Some will last up to two hours. If it is a one-hour period, you normally expect each guest to consume at least $2^1/_2$ drinks. For a two-hour period, you expect each guest to consume at least 3 drinks. If you have a one-hour cocktail reception for 100 persons, and the client wants cocktail servers to take drink orders from guests, you will need about three bartenders and five to six cocktail servers to handle the drink orders efficiently. If you have a two-hour reception though, guests will not drink so quickly, and some of them will tend to leave before the reception ends; consequently, you may be able to get by with fewer bartenders and cocktail servers. Unfortunately in this instance, most guests will do the bulk of their drinking during the first hour, so you may be unable to reduce your service requirements significantly.

When clients are faced with the exorbitant labor cost associated with having cocktail servers take guest orders, they generally decide against it. But even if a client is willing to pay the extra labor charges, you still might want to discourage such a labor-intensive style of service because there are too many opportunities for the catered event to bog down. For instance, at a predinner reception, if guests need to wait too long for their drinks, the reception, and ultimately the dinner, will probably run much longer than scheduled.

On the other hand, sometimes slower cocktail service can be a virtue. For instance, if there is a host bar at a cocktail reception, guests may be tempted to overindulge, whereas if they give their orders to a server, their consumption will probably be much less.

Work Scheduling

The banquet manager usually sets aside one day each week to prepare the service work schedules for the following week. Each week, he or she must prepare a fixed work schedule and a variable work schedule.

The fixed schedule represents the minimum number of persons and number of work hours needed to keep the hotel catering department open and active, regardless of the volume of business expected. For instance, if there is at least one catered function each day, you will need a handful of permanent full-time and/or permanent part-time persons scheduled to provide the level of service expected by guests.

If a hotel does a great deal of catering business, these fixed employees can be scheduled solely for catered functions. If the catering business varies, with several peaks and valleys, you can still have permanent staff members assigned to catering, though you might have to share them with another hotel department. For instance, you might have a 40-hour-per-week employee assigned to catering, with the understanding that, if catering business is slow, he or she will work in the room-service department.

The more fixed employees you have, the easier it is to prepare your weekly work schedules. It is also more conducive to employee satisfaction. Fixed employees usually have steady, predictable work schedules. They will appreciate the ability to plan their personal lives more accurately.

Variable labor is incremental labor. It will fluctuate with the volume of catering business. The catering department usually must schedule a large number of variable employees each week.

Unlike some of the hotel's restaurant-outlet managers, the banquet manager will need to prepare a variable work schedule each week. Catering business can be predictable, but the uniqueness of each catered function forces you to call A-list and B-list employees every week in order to prepare a proper work schedule.

The work schedules will be based primarily on the:

1. Types of functions booked that week
2. Expected lengths of each function
3. Number of guests anticipated
4. Styles of service required
5. Allowable labor costs
6. Employee availabililty
7. Guest satisfaction needs.

Typically you would use this information, any applicable union regulations, and the staffing guidelines set forth in the hotel's staffing charts to prepare the appropriate work schedules.

When preparing work schedules, you will need to allocate a sufficient number of work hours to cover the preopening and teardown periods. You should stagger your servers so that some arrive and leave earlier than others. You should aim to have the maximum number of workers available when the catered functions are in high gear, and fewer scheduled at function beginnings and endings.

Scheduling the appropriate number of work hours, while simultaneously adhering to your labor budget, is hard to accomplish in some situations. For instance, if you are working in a union property, the union contract may require you to guarantee each employee you call in a minimum 4-hour work schedule that day. If you need a few persons one day to cover 3-hour shifts, you are free to schedule them for three hours apiece. However, you must pay them for four hours.

It was noted earlier in this chapter that the minimum number of servers required in the typical joint bargaining agreement usually does not cause problems for you because this minimum normally is insufficient to handle most types of catered events. However, the minimum number of guaranteed work hours can cause problems if you have several bookings that lend themselves to scheduling several service personnel for less than the minimum.

Even a nonunion hotel may have a policy of paying a minimum number of work hours. For instance, it may wish to follow these standards in order to compete with unionized hotels for workers. To say the least, this will make it more difficult to schedule economically some catered functions.

Timing of Service

The client and the catering sales representative normally discuss the timing of the service and relay their desires to the service staff. The banquet manager must take these desires and develop a plan that will provide maximum efficiency and a minimum number of bottlenecks.

Service will make or break the catered function. If half the guests are waiting for their entrees while the other half are eating dessert, there is a problem. Also, if the head table, which usually receives the best service, is finished before other guests, the head-table guests will have to wait for the others to finish, or will have to begin the program while some guests are still being served or are still eating.

Timing problems can be minimized or avoided by scheduling extra servers. However, this may be cost prohibitive.

An inexpensive way to minimize timing problems is to preset as much food and beverage on the dining tables as the client will allow and/or which can be done safely. This is especially important if the client is in a hurry. For instance, if the group has only one hour for lunch, many food items, such as appetizers, salads, rolls, butter, relishes, and desserts, can be preset on the dining tables.

Some hotels offer luncheons that are entirely preset. For instance, salad and/or sandwich luncheons can be preset in such a way that guests can sit down and eat quickly. Servers would need to handle only beverage service and special requests.

To ensure proper timing, as well as smooth-running service, the banquet captain will normally call the roll of all service personnel about one hour before the catered function is scheduled to begin. All employees are called by name to confirm attendance. Work stations are assigned. Servers are informed of any special diets, special service requests, and so forth. Also during the roll-call, the captain will describe all menu items so that guest inquiries can be answered without the need for servers to run back to the kitchen and check with the chef.

For most receptions, normally there is a scheduled starting and ending time. At the beginning, usually a few guests will arrive. By the time the reception is half over, all guests will usually be present. Toward the end of the reception, you should begin to see guests leaving a few at a time.

Some receptions will have all guests there when they open. For instance, a cocktail reception that begins immediately after the convention group's last business meeting of the day will usually have maximum attendance when the doors open.

About 15 minutes before you want the meal service to start, you should begin calling guests. You can dim the lights in the prefunction area, ring chimes, start music, or make announcements to signal guests that it is time to enter the dining room for dinner. Servers should be standing ready at their stations when guests walk into the room, not against the wall talking with each other.

For most conventional meal functions, the salad course will usually take about 20 to 30 minutes, and the entree about 30 to 50 minutes, from serving to removing of plates. Dessert can usually be handled in approximately 20 to 30 minutes. Normally, the entire banquet service will be about $1^1/_4$ hours for the typical luncheon and two hours for the typical dinner event.

More elaborate meal functions may take a bit more time to serve. While the added diversions can enhance the dining experience, long meal functions tend to make guests a little anxious. Even if you are using elaborate service styles or other similar attractions, guests will begin to think something is wrong with the hotel catering department if the meal lasts much longer than two hours. In addition, recall that some potential guests will be very reluctant to attend the catered event if they suspect it will run on too long.

Tear-Down Procedures

As the function winds down, servers can begin performing a bit of tear-down work. For instance, prior to serving dessert, they can crumb tables and remove nonessentials (such as salt and pepper shakers and extra flatware). While the guests are enjoying their dessert, the servers can refill the condiment containers and put them away.

As guests begin to trickle out, servers can see to it that all utensils and tableware requisitioned from the executive steward are cleaned and returned properly. They can inventory all service equipment. And they can see to it that any necessary paperwork, such as meal-ticket accounting, is completed correctly.

Soon after all guests have left, all dining and buffet tables must be stripped. Soiled and leftover clean napery must be returned to housekeeping. Unless the tables must be set up for the next function, they will need to be broken down and put away by the banquet-setup crew.

Housekeeping or convention-service staff members will need to come in and clean the floors, walls, hallways, mirrors, windows, and fixtures. In some hotels, servers help out this crew; for instance, at the end of the function, a server may run a vacuum cleaner over the heavy-traffic areas.

While housekeeping or convention service may be handling the cleaning chores, an employee or two might be able to help set up for the next scheduled function. For instance, if you are tearing down after a luncheon, and there is a dinner scheduled later, the banquet-setup crew might want to get a head start by simultaneously tearing down and resetting the room. The crew would most likely appreciate any help service personnel can contribute.

Some servers may need to package a few leftovers for the client and/or guests to take home. For instance, half-empty beverage containers, centerpieces, and other decorations may be fair game for any guest who wants to take a souvenir of the catered event.

The kitchen staff will also need to recycle a few leftover foods. Sometimes these foods can be used for the next catered function, by the hotel's restaurant outlets, or in the employee dining room.

If the leftover foods have lost some of their culinary quality, it probably is best to discard them. For instance, foods that have been on a buffet table for an hour or more may be perfectly edible. However, they probably have deteriorated to the point where their appearance, taste, and texture are below your quality standards. You should not risk offending a guest by recycling and serving them again.

If the leftover foods are protein-rich, moist foods, they may have been contaminated during service. These potentially hazardous foods present excellent growing conditions for harmful bacteria. For instance, roast beef, cream-based soups, custards, and protein-rich salads made with mayonnaise or other similar dressings should not be reserved unless you are certain they are safe to eat. If there are any doubts, they should be discarded immediately before they have a chance to come into contact with wholesome foods and contaminate them.

Some clients may ask you to donate leftover foods they have paid for to a homeless shelter or some other similar charitable organization. This is certainly a socially redeeming activity we can all support. However, if someone contacts a food-borne illness from these foods, the hotel may be liable for damages.

Some states (such as California) have good samaritan laws that absolve you of liability as long as you used reasonable care when preparing, collecting, and delivering the leftover foods to charitable organizations. If you were not negligent in handling these products, and if you sincerely believe they are safe to eat, you can donate them and not worry about being sued. However, if there is any question about the wholesomeness of the foods, you should discard them. Not only do you risk a lawsuit, you do no one a favor by distributing foods that could make people sick.

CATERING SAFETY AND SANITATION

Food and beverage production and service must be carried out in a safe and wholesome manner. Anyone handling foods and beverages must be trained to practice basic safety and sanitation procedures to ensure that employees and guests do not fall victims to accidents or food-borne illnesses.

All commercial food-service operations must adhere to the sanitation standards set forth by their local health districts. These agencies inspect periodically food and beverage production and service personnel, equipment, and facilities to ensure that they comply with local rules and regulations.

Catering executives should consider following the sanitation guidelines developed by the Educational Foundation of the National Restaurant Association (NRA) when training employees. In fact, any employee who completes successfully the Educational Foundation's sanitation course will earn a certification that is viewed favorably by all local health districts.

Production and service equipment and facilities must meet

pertinent standards of safety and sanitation. All commercial construction must meet building-code guidelines. For instance, in most cities and counties in the United States, all food-contact equipment must display the familiar blue seal of the National Sanitation Foundation (NSF). Equipment that does not carry this seal usually cannot be used in commercial food and beverage operations.

Underwriter's Laboratory (UL) and the American Gas Association (AGA) inspect and certify equipment compliance with generally accepted safety standards. For instance, a gas oven displaying the AGA seal is safe to use in commercial production. Most local building codes usually require all equipment and permanent installations to meet or exceed safety standards promulgated by these types of independent inspectors.

The safe and sanitary food and beverage operation also meets standards set by other local government inspector-powered agencies. For instance, the fire marshall will inspect periodically for fire hazards, such as blocked exits, overcrowding, and discharged fire-extinguisher systems.

The Department of Labor is also concerned with safety matters. For example, if you hire a few teenagers to work as buspersons or food runners, they will not be able to perform all types of work. Usually youngsters under 18 years of age cannot operate machinery, such as slicers, food processors, and dough-cutting machines. They also typically cannot fill, refill, or light fuel containers, such as Sterno pots.

The local workers compensation agency normally is responsible for enforcing the federal Occupational Safety and Health Act (OSHA). The agency may also insure employees for job-related injuries. Hotels can call upon the agency to help them develop effective employee safety-training guidelines. Furthermore, the agency can visit your property, point out areas of concern, and note what you can do to eliminate these hazards.

There are several safety and sanitation problems that must be controlled by the catering executive. Experience shows that the major ones are:

1. *Tableside and action-station cooking.* Exhibition cooking poses many risks, even if it is performed by trained professional chefs who have a great deal of experience with this type of work.

Some parts of the country may prohibit exhibition cooking. You should check the local fire code to see if it is allowed in your area. And, if it is allowed, check further to see if any restrictions exist.

Action-station cooking does not seem to be nearly as dangerous as tableside cooking. Usually there is sufficient aisle space allocated to minimize the threat of accidents.

Tableside cooking, especially the type involving flaming dishes, poses the most serious risk. For example, to enhance guest and employee safety, the Sheraton Corporation has a company policy prohibiting this practice.

Rarely does tableside cooking result in a major hotel fire. The accident would have to be very serious for any fire to combat the modern hotel's sprinkler system. However, guest injury is another matter.

Flaming dishes are an attractive addition to the catered event. They provide an exciting and entertaining change of pace. Clients and guests are always pleased with these types of presentations. Unfortunately, the curious guest who gets a little too close to the action is liable to inhale hazardous gas and/or come into contact with a spark or flame.

Inhaling gasses tends to be more of a risk than the fire itself. Usually whenever you flame a dish, an extra server is stationed nearby to watch the spectacle and react to any emergency. This minimizes the fire hazard. However, you may not be able to control gasses because usually you cannot see them leaking until some harm occurs.

You must be very careful when using Sterno, butane, propane, or other types of cooking fuels. Propane is especially troublesome and risky. When using propane, it does not matter how much training the chef has had. A leaking tank is not obvious. Furthermore, lighting the burners can provide some anxious moments if too much gas is allowed to enter the burners before you light them.

Propane is a dangerous fuel. It is recommended that it be used only outdoors. It is so combustible that, depending upon temperature, humidity, and the amount of air space between the tanks and the grills, there is as much as a 60 percent chance that the equipment will malfunction and cause a serious accident.

Most tableside cooking units use butane fuel. This is usually the best fuel to use. It is much safer than propane. It also is preferable to Sterno because you can control the temperature and size of the flame much better with butane than you can with Sterno.

Tableside cooking should be limited to a single saute or wok station that is no closer to guests than the diameter of a 60-inch round dining table. The work area must be well ventilated. You should not allow exhibition cooking in a low-ceilinged room or in a room that does not have proper ventilation.

If a client prefers the excitement and attraction of tableside cooking, you can indulge this request safely by providing a flaming display on an elevated platform situated away from the dining areas on one side of the function room. The display can be used to prepare a handful of portions, with the bulk of production performed in the kitchen.

Another compromise is to have a flaming parade around the perimeter of the function room with the lights dimmed. For instance, food servers can carry a few flaming baked Alaska desserts or a few flaming kabobs from the kitchen to a dining-room service area. Once there, servers can douse the fires, plate up the foods, and serve a few guests. As with the flaming display, the remaining production and preplating can be done in the kitchen.

2. *Burns.* Even if you do not provide flaming tableside cooking, guests are still subject to accidental burns. For instance, if you have unprotected candle flames on each dining table, napery can be set afire if the candles tip over. Or guests may accidentally burn themselves or their clothing if they reach over the flame without realizing how hot it is. If you want to put candles on each table, you should use votive-type containers, such as chimneys, because these setups can prevent accidental burns or fires.

Buffet service also presents several potential hazards that can cause burns. For instance, hot chafing dishes can be very dangerous to the unsuspecting guest. Handles and utensils can get very hot. And the steam created by the typical chafing-dish setup can build up and escape, thereby seriously burning someone who happens to be nearby.

If Sterno or some other similar fuel is used to keep the contents of chafing dishes hot, the fuel can "go wild," that is, if the lid on the Sterno container is left open too wide, vapor can build up under the steam table pan, ignite, and suddenly you have a flame surrounding the bottom of the pan and possibly even enveloping the whole chafing dish.

Many chafing dishes and coffee urns have little Sterno pots under them. You must make sure that these pots are covered correctly to prevent the fuel from going wild.

If you use Sterno, do not allow anyone to refuel the containers while they are in use. Sometimes you cannot see the slight flame emitted by the fuel. If you try to refuel while the pot is still burning, you may burn yourself very badly. In fact, a young chef in a Las Vegas hotel lost his life when his chef's jacket caught fire while he was trying to refuel Sterno pots on the buffet table.

All Sterno refueling should be done in a production or service-corridor area, not on the buffet table. Better yet, if a pot has burned out, you should cover it, set it aside, and use another full pot in its place. Later on you can refuel all the pots, long after the flames have been extinguished.

Even though we in the industry tend to refer to Sterno as a generic product, it is in fact, a brand name. There are other less expensive fuels you can use. However, according to Anthony Marshall, Dean of the School of Hospitality Management at Florida International University, and a well-known attorney, we should use only the Sterno brand. He warns that, unlike the Sterno brand, other brands are poisonous. (If in doubt, always look for the tell-tale skull-and-crossbones decal.) If they are left unlighted on a buffet table, guests may think they are some type of dip, consume some, and possibly die. In fact, Dean Marshall notes a specific incident where a woman died after consuming an off-brand fuel left sitting on the table and the property was held responsible for her death.

Hot carts positioned throughout the function room pose another burn hazard. Portable steam tables can be a problem. Similarly, hot-beverage setups can also be dangerous.

To prevent these types of accidental burns, you must see to it that any exposed hot surface is clearly marked. For safety purposes, most manufacturers will mark hot surfaces at the factory when the equipment is being manufactured. In fact, some local government agencies may require this type of marking before the equipment can be used in local commercial food-service operations.

3. *Falls.*   Guests are subject to falls. Most of them are unfamiliar with the function room. Some of them are not careful when roaming around the room, thereby bumping into other guests and servers. And many of them may not immediately recognize portable electrical and/or sound drop cords laced throughout the area.

To minimize the possibility of guests falling, you should never allow any loose item to be placed on the floor. For instance, if a drop cord must be used, it should be secured and marked conspicuously.

Similarly, if there is a slope in the floor, it should be marked clearly. Furthermore, all tables, carts, tray stands, and other equipment must be placed in the correct locations and secured properly.

4. *Broken glass.*   Broken and chipped tableware is another hazard that seems to be more prevalent in catered events than in regular restaurant service. The time pressures associated with most catered functions increase the risk that guests will inadvertently find damaged items.

Usually chipped plateware can be found and removed from service before it ends up in front of guests. However, the same cannot always be said about broken glassware. Indeed, the possibility of guests finding a piece of broken glass is always present whenever employees are rushing to serve a group of people.

The trend today is to have shorter cocktail receptions. A one-hour reception, or less, is more common since the shorter time period might reduce guest consumption of alcohol. However, for those groups that still like to drink, the shorter reception means that bartenders will be working very quickly to serve the same number of drinks. The pressure to prepare and serve a lot of drinks quickly tends to increase the risk of broken glassware.

Hurried buspersons and other employees who clear tables and landing space may also increase the number of broken glasses and the possibility of a guest getting a piece of glass in his or her food or beverage.

Buspersons should be taught to dump ice out of glasses before placing them in bus trays. Ice in bus trays causes glasses to slip around and bang into each other. The potential for chipped and broken glassware increases, along with the increased possibility that glass chips will get into the food and beverage supply.

Likewise, glasses should not be stacked in bus trays. Flatware should never be placed into glasses. And plates should not be mixed with glasses. All of these actions increase the possibility of broken glass getting into a guest's drink or meal.

Ice or cold water should never be put into hot glasses. The glasses may crack and split. This would not be troublesome if the glass broke completely before it was served to a guest. There is a serious problem though, if the glass merely sprouts a hairline crack; when the guest sees this, he or she will be leery of all other food and beverage offerings. Worse yet, if a guest actually drinks from this glass, he or she might receive a cut lip.

Glasses should never be used to dip ice out of an ice bin. If the glass breaks, you will need to empty the bin and clean it thoroughly. You should use plastic scoops to dip ice and put it into glasses; metal scoops should not be used because they can chip the glasses. The last thing you want is a guest receiving a piece of glass in his or her drink.

5. *Food-borne illness.*   One of the hotel catering department's worst nightmares is to cause an outbreak of food-borne illness. Imagine the agony suffered by the Hyatt Corporation when many catering guests became ill after consuming foods that were prepared with contaminated fresh shell eggs.

Food-borne illness can be traced to many origins. The products may be contaminated when purchased. They may become contaminated during production and service. Or they can become contaminated if stored under improper conditions.

Improper storage conditions, for an excessive period of time, generally is the biggest problem faced by the typical hotel catering department. The "time/temperature" dilemma rears its ugly head whenever potentially hazardous foods must be held for long periods of time on a buffet table.

Potentially hazardous foods must be stored at 45 degrees F or below, or 140 degrees F or above. The 45 to 140 degrees F range is the danger zone. If potentially hazardous foods must go through the danger zone (such as when they are cooked), they must go through it as quickly as possible because at these temperatures, harmful bacteria will thrive.

Foods on a buffet table are especially vulnerable to the time/temperature problem. For instance, if you offer a meat loaf entree, a chafing dish may be unable to maintain the required temperature. If a guest or employee contaminates this cooked food, and the food is not served for a while, harmful bacteria can multiply and eventually someone may become ill.

If you are serving cold potentially hazardous foods on a buffet table, they must be kept at or below 45 degrees F. For instance, a cold potato salad made with protein-rich ingredients should never be allowed to sit out unrefrigerated for more than a few minutes. It must be displayed on a cold table.

To prevent these time/temperature problems, you must ensure that the service equipment can hold foods at the proper temperatures, see to it that foods are not kept on the buffet table any longer than necessary, and eliminate guest-contamination possibilities by installing sneeze guards in front of the foods.

You could also minimize these types of problems if you are willing to forego the use of some of the more troublesome foods. For instance, if eggs are to be used in a menu item that will not be cooked, such as hollandaise sauce, you could use pasteurized, frozen eggs instead of fresh shell eggs. You also could refuse to serve raw meat or seafood.

10

Other Client Services

Catering is everchanging; always be prepared to change, always be prepared to learn. You are only as good as your last party.

Patrick Grady
Director of Catering
Marriott at The American University
Washington, DC

Some catered events require much more than food and beverage service. In addition to food and drink, some clients will need unique audio, visual, and/or lighting services. Some will require specialized dining-table and buffet-table presentations. And others may need something extra special to ensure that guests come away from the functions with many happy memories.

Clients who are planning several meal and beverage functions, such as the meetings and conventions clients, also may ask for something more than food and beverage service if only to relieve the monotony. They may also want something unusual to recharge guests' batteries so that they have an extra storehouse of energy to draw on when tackling the remaining business sessions.

Unique attractions are also used by clients to highlight celebratory catered events. Awards dinners, weddings, new-product introductions, and the like, are made more exclusive and memorable if clients provide a smorgasbord of food, beverage, and other services specifically designed to maximize their impact on guests.

Hotels can sometimes be in a difficult position when dealing with clients who want other services. After all, if clients spend a lot of money for these things, how much will they have left over for food and beverage? You certainly do not want to speak ill of clients' ideas, but it is your responsibility to point out that they should strike a proper balance between decor and food and beverage.

273

Guests are most impressed with the quality and value of food and beverage received; other services cannot overcome mediocre products. You need to be cautious though, when discussing these points; at no time should you attempt to feather your nest at the expense of the client's needs and desires.

The catering executive must be prepared to entertain a variety of special requests for other client services. Usually only the small, refueling type of catered meal functions are built solely around food and beverage service.

Most events require some sort of additional service. It can range from the mundane (such as the need for a videotape player, television monitor, overhead projector, and screen) to the spectacular (such as the client who requests a skydiving stunt or one who needs to transport an elephant in a service elevator).

The catering executive will need to coordinate many special requests. He or she will need to help plan, organize, and implement a plethora of unusual and unique requirements. He or she may also need to advise clients of the most effective and economical combination of special services needed to ensure success. Like the band leader, the catering executive must see to it that all food, beverage, and special services are playing from the same sheet of music.

PROVIDING OTHER CLIENT SERVICES

Hotel caterers specialize in providing food and beverage service. While some are capable of providing additional services, others prefer to leave these to outside experts.

A hotel cannot be all things to all people. It realistically must draw the line somewhere. Cost considerations render it virtually impossible for it to house all of the specialties that clients might potentially need.

When dealing with services other than food and beverage, usually the hotel is faced with five options. It can: (1) provide as many of them as possible itself; (2) steer the client to outside service contractors; (3) expect clients to find their own outside service contractors; (4) authorize concessions, that is, provide in-house space for outside service contractors to set up shop; or (5) use some combination of these four possibilities.

Hotel Providing Other Client Services

A hotel usually will provide its own special services only if it is economically feasible to do so, or if there are no other outside alternatives that can be trusted to do the work correctly and efficiently.

Some special services can be very profitable, particularly if they are not labor intensive. For instance, providing a few pieces of audiovisual (AV) equipment and one technician to a convention usually does not involve a lot of variable costs. Consequently, its contribution margin can add considerably to overall hotel profits.

Unfortunately though, some special services are very capital intensive. For instance, most lighting equipment is very expensive. To make matters worse, it tends to become obsolete very quickly, thereby requiring you to replace it periodically with even more expensive items. It is cost prohibitive to let this equipment sit idle. Unless the hotel uses it often, you may not earn an adequate return on your investment.

Providing a full range of AV services can be another expensive undertaking. AV technology is changing so rapidly that it is difficult to keep pace. A complete in-house AV system is a major investment, but one that is required in conference centers and resorts located in rural areas where outside service contractors are not readily available.

In some instances, a hotel may be happy to break even with such services as lighting and sound if it means that clients will spend freely on food and beverage services. In this case, it may be good business to offer the client a loss leader if it helps secure other profitable business for the hotel.

Outside Service Contractors

Some hotels have a list of approved outside service contractors that they recommend to potential clients whenever special client services are needed. These contractors usually are the ones hotels feel are capable of doing the job properly.

Before adding a contractor to the approved list, he or she normally must have adequate references. A hotel does not want to risk recommending someone whose ineptness will cause client and guest dissatisfaction and ruin the chances of repeat patronage.

Some hotels may not want to recommend any outside service contractor because it represents a possible conflict of interest. They fear someone may accuse them of taking kickbacks. They also run the risk of clients complaining that they were steered to inadequate, costly outsiders whose inabilities should have been well-known to the catering executives.

Most of the time the hotel expects clients to find their own outside service contractors whenever something extra special is needed. Some hotels do not have the resources to handle these services. Nor are some properties eager to assume liability for them.

The catering staff normally is capable of working with any contractor. In fact, the hotel usually has a written "handbook" of pertinent information that these outside service providers must have in order to plan and implement their work correctly.

Sometimes friction may arise if a client wants to use an outside service contractor that the hotel would like to avoid. A service contractor may have a good working relationship with the client, but you may not enjoy the same good fortune. Generally though, you must be able to work with any outside service contractors selected by clients.

Many potential clients, especially large conventions that hold events throughout the country, have long-term contracts with several outside service providers. This is an effective cost-saving procedure since a service contractor will normally offer clients a generous volume discount if they purchase a large amount of services. The hotel will need to work with these outsiders if it wants to book the catering business.

In-House Concessionaires

Large hotels that do not want to provide their own special services, yet do not want to inconvenience potential clients, may grant a few outside service contractors concession status. These contractors then, will automatically receive a client's business unless he or she wants to make other arrangements with another service contractor. (See Figure 10.1.)

The hotel usually allocates the concessionaire some warehouse space within the hotel so that necessary equipment and materials can be stored. The concessionaire will also need a bit of space to house employee work areas. Usually the concessionaire has its own back-up warehouse facilities off site. By having on-site space though, clients can be serviced quickly and efficiently. Furthermore, emergencies or last-minute requests can be handled immediately when employees and equipment are readily available at a moment's notice.

Combination of In-House and Outside Services

Occasionally the hotel may provide some services itself while the client is expected to secure others. For instance, if a convention needs specialized sound and lighting services, you may be able to provide microphones and speakers, but the client may have to use an outside service contractor to provide the necessary lighting.

Figure 10.1. Example of typical AV services offered by hotel in-house concessionaires. (Courtesy John Steinmetz, The Westin Bonaventure, Los Angeles, CA.)

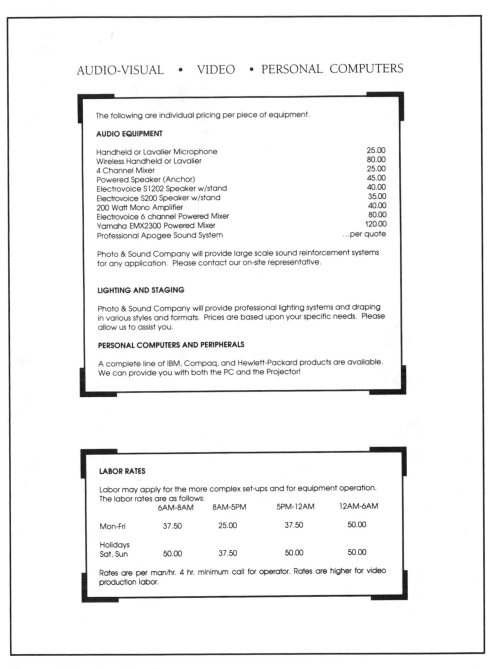

AUDIO-VISUAL • VIDEO • PERSONAL COMPUTERS

The following are individual pricing per piece of equipment.

AUDIO EQUIPMENT

Handheld or Lavalier Microphone	25.00
Wireless Handheld or Lavalier	80.00
4 Channel Mixer	25.00
Powered Speaker (Anchor)	45.00
Electrovoice S1202 Speaker w/stand	40.00
Electrovoice S200 Speaker w/stand	35.00
200 Watt Mono Amplifier	40.00
Electrovoice 6 channel Powered Mixer	80.00
Yamaha EMX2300 Powered Mixer	120.00
Professional Apogee Sound System	...per quote

Photo & Sound Company will provide large scale sound reinforcement systems for any application. Please contact our on-site representative.

LIGHTING AND STAGING

Photo & Sound Company will provide professional lighting systems and draping in various styles and formats. Prices are based upon your specific needs. Please allow us to assist you.

PERSONAL COMPUTERS AND PERIPHERALS

A complete line of IBM, Compaq, and Hewlett-Packard products are available. We can provide you with both the PC and the Projector!

LABOR RATES

Labor may apply for the more complex set-ups and for equipment operation. The labor rates are as follows:

	6AM-8AM	8AM-5PM	5PM-12AM	12AM-6AM
Mon-Fri	37.50	25.00	37.50	50.00
Holidays Sat, Sun	50.00	37.50	50.00	50.00

Rates are per man/hr. 4 hr. minimum call for operator. Rates are higher for video production labor.

Figure 10.1. (continued)

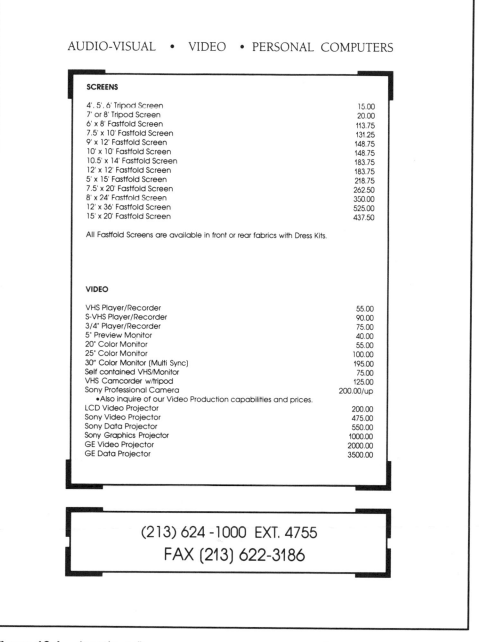

AUDIO-VISUAL • VIDEO • PERSONAL COMPUTERS

SCREENS

4', 5', 6' Tripod Screen	15.00
7' or 8' Tripod Screen	20.00
6' x 8' Fastfold Screen	113.75
7.5' x 10' Fastfold Screen	131.25
9' x 12' Fastfold Screen	148.75
10' x 10' Fastfold Screen	148.75
10.5' x 14' Fastfold Screen	183.75
12' x 12' Fastfold Screen	183.75
5' x 15' Fastfold Screen	218.75
7.5' x 20' Fastfold Screen	262.50
8' x 24' Fastfold Screen	350.00
12' x 36' Fastfold Screen	525.00
15' x 20' Fastfold Screen	437.50

All Fastfold Screens are available in front or rear fabrics with Dress Kits.

VIDEO

VHS Player/Recorder	55.00
S-VHS Player/Recorder	90.00
3/4" Player/Recorder	75.00
5" Preview Monitor	40.00
20" Color Monitor	55.00
25" Color Monitor	100.00
30" Color Monitor (Multi Sync)	195.00
Self contained VHS/Monitor	75.00
VHS Camcorder w/tripod	125.00
Sony Professional Camera	200.00/up
•Also inquire of our Video Production capabilities and prices.	
LCD Video Projector	200.00
Sony Video Projector	475.00
Sony Data Projector	550.00
Sony Graphics Projector	1000.00
GE Video Projector	2000.00
GE Data Projector	3500.00

(213) 624 -1000 EXT. 4755
FAX (213) 622-3186

Figure 10.1. (continued)

AUDIO-VISUAL   •   VIDEO   •   PERSONAL COMPUTERS

PRESENTATION SUPPORT

Flipchart Easel	15.00
Flipchart Pad*	10.00
Watercolor Marker*	1.50
Electric Arrow Pointer	15.00
Laser Dot Pointer	40.00
Overhead Acetate Roll*	11.00
Overhead Acetate Sheet*	.50
Transparency Pen*	2.00
80 Capacity Slide Tray	5.00
140 Capacity Slide Tray	5.00
T-30 VHS tape*	10.00
T-60 VHS tape*	10.50
T-120 VHS Tape*	12.50
LCD Computer Panel	95.00
Caramate/Audioviewer	35.00
SAFE-LOK Projection Stand	12.50
34" Cart	15.00
54" Cart	17.50

*Note: These items are purchased by end user, and are not "rented". You retain possession at the end of the meeting.

MISCELLANEOUS

Wireless Slide Proj. Remote	20.00
2 Projector Dissolve Unit	40.00
3-Tier Projector Stacker	27.50
2-Tier Sony Video Proj. Stacker	50.00
1000W Followspot	75.00
Xenon Followspot	125.00
3 Light Video Kit	45.00
Lecternette w/Base	50.00
Audio Cassette Recorder	25.00
Audio Cassette with 2 Proj. Dissolve	45.00
Stereo Cassette Deck (Tascam)	40.00
3 Channel Stereo Cassette	60.00
4 Channel Reel-to-reel Deck	70.00
Navitar 6"-9" Lens with EIII bracket	20.00
Keystone Correcting Lens (PC lens)	15.00
Hayes 1200 Baud Modem	35.00
Hayes 2400 Baud Modem	50.00
Walkie-Talkie, 2 channel	25.00

This is a partial listing of our extensive inventory. Please allow us to help you if you cannot easily find the item you require. We look forward to assisting you with a most successful meeting at the Westin Bonaventure! Thank you.

Figure 10.1.   (continued)

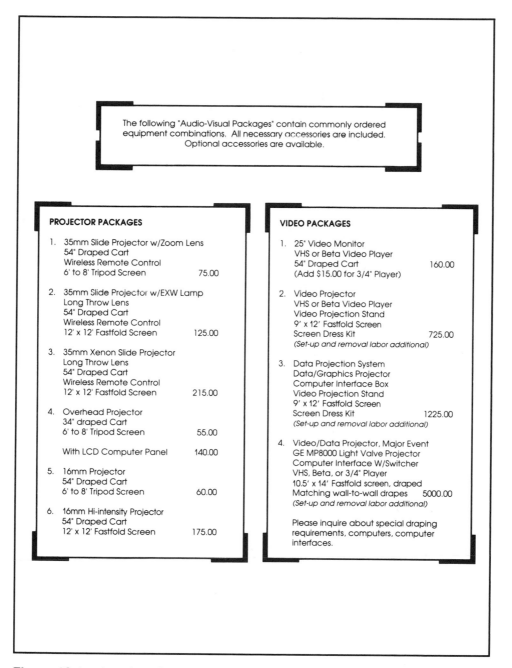

The following "Audio-Visual Packages" contain commonly ordered equipment combinations. All necessary accessories are included. Optional accessories are available.

PROJECTOR PACKAGES

1. 35mm Slide Projector w/Zoom Lens
    54" Draped Cart
    Wireless Remote Control
    6' to 8' Tripod Screen   75.00

2. 35mm Slide Projector w/EXW Lamp
    Long Throw Lens
    54" Draped Cart
    Wireless Remote Control
    12' x 12' Fastfold Screen   125.00

3. 35mm Xenon Slide Projector
    Long Throw Lens
    54" Draped Cart
    Wireless Remote Control
    12' x 12' Fastfold Screen   215.00

4. Overhead Projector
    34" draped Cart
    6' to 8' Tripod Screen   55.00

    With LCD Computer Panel   140.00

5. 16mm Projector
    54" Draped Cart
    6' to 8' Tripod Screen   60.00

6. 16mm Hi-intensity Projector
    54" Draped Cart
    12' x 12' Fastfold Screen   175.00

VIDEO PACKAGES

1. 25" Video Monitor
    VHS or Beta Video Player
    54" Draped Cart   160.00
    (Add $15.00 for 3/4" Player)

2. Video Projector
    VHS or Beta Video Player
    Video Projection Stand
    9' x 12' Fastfold Screen
    Screen Dress Kit   725.00
    (Set-up and removal labor additional)

3. Data Projection System
    Data/Graphics Projector
    Computer Interface Box
    Video Projection Stand
    9' x 12' Fastfold Screen
    Screen Dress Kit   1225.00
    (Set-up and removal labor additional)

4. Video/Data Projector, Major Event
    GE MP8000 Light Valve Projector
    Computer Interface W/Switcher
    VHS, Beta, or 3/4" Player
    10.5' x 14' Fastfold screen, draped
    Matching wall-to-wall drapes   5000.00
    (Set-up and removal labor additional)

    Please inquire about special draping
    requirements, computers, computer
    interfaces.

Figure 10.1.   (continued)

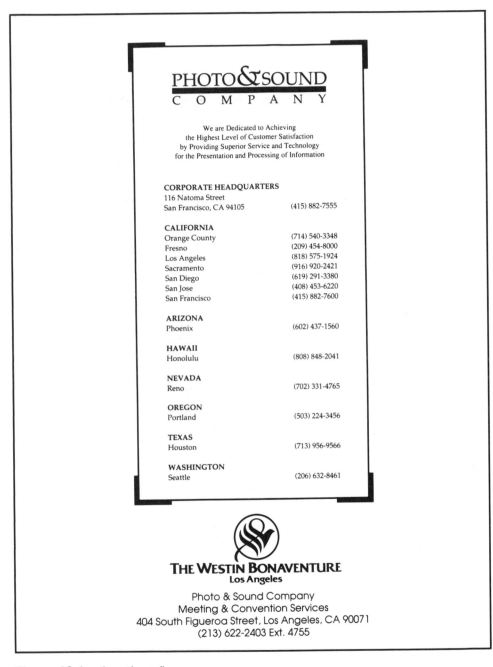

Figure 10.1. (continued)

Usually the hotel can provide a handful of the most commonly needed client services. For instance, it is the rare property that cannot provide the basic AV equipment, such as overhead projectors, screens, microphones, speakers, slide projectors, television monitors, videotape players, and film projectors. If nothing else, it can rent a few of these items and relieve the client of this chore.

Occasionally a hotel may want to offer a few complimentary client services in order to secure a large catering contract. For example, if a client needs a microphone for the luncheon speaker, a hotel may provide it free of charge. This type of service is relatively inexpensive to provide because you can usually tap into the hotel's house sound system (that is, the hotel's public address system) very easily. But the client will not see it this way. He or she will appreciate the additional consideration and remember it when it is time to plan the next catered function.

AUDIOVISUAL

Audiovisual (AV) services are probably the most common type of extra services needed by catering clients. You or another professional must be able to counsel your clients regarding the best options for them to use. You should be able to help them match their particular needs with the most effective and efficient AV systems.

The catering manager must be careful not to represent the department as being AV experts if in fact it is not true. The manager is asking for trouble if he or she gives this impression. To be on the safe side, if the hotel decides to provide extensive AV services, it should have an AV professional on staff.

The purpose of AV is to communicate. Presentations are made to sell, train, and inform. The most effective and memorable presentations use AV to "show and tell." Without AV, presentations are apt to lack the "punch and power" needed to make a lasting impression on guests.

If the message is to be presented only once in an information session, such as a sales meeting, a flip chart or overhead projector with transparencies may be sufficient. However, if the objective of the meeting is to teach a group of people, or lead them in a brainstorming session, an electronic board would be a better choice.

If complex financial data are being presented to groups, a carousel slide projector and slides may be the best choice, along with back-up written copy provided after the meeting. By controlling the timing of each slide, the moderator will ensure that everyone is looking at the same information at the same time. By passing out hard copy after the meeting, he or she also ensures that no one is reading ahead and not paying attention to the data at hand.

If visual presentations need to be altered while they are being displayed, you can use an overhead projector, transparencies, and transparency marking pens. For the more adventurous group, and the one with a little extra money in its budget, you could hook up a personal computer to the appropriate overhead projection machinery. The computer can be stand-alone, or it can be on-line, connected to a satellite location in another part of the hotel, or even in another part of the country.

Types of AV Services

Clients usually can find the AV services they need very easily because there are several types and varieties available. The general types of AV services clients can order are:

1. *Microphone.*   There are at least seven types of microphones: (a) lectern; (b) table; (c) floor; (d) lavalier (also called a necklace or lapel microphone); (e) halo (also called a suspended or boom microphone); (f) hand-held; and (g) omnidirectional.

2. *Projection screen.*   There are two basic types of projection screens: front-screen projection and rear-screen projection. With front-screen projection, the media projector is located within or behind the audience. Images are projected onto one of the following screen surfaces: (a) Matte white—the most common screen surface. It diffuses the available light evenly over a wide area. It is especially useful in large, wide rooms. (b) Glass-beaded—the surface contains chemically-coated glass beads. This produces superior image brightness (about three times the matte white). However, the optimal viewing angle is much narrower. (c) Lenticular—this type of surface is similar to a lens, in that it controls light and sends it to a predetermined area. It is most often used in stereo projection where viewers must wear 3-D glasses. These screens are normally not very large. The biggest one available measures approximately 6 feet by 6 feet.

With rear-screen projection, the media projector is placed behind the screen and images are projected through the screen surface. The screen surfaces used are made of glass, acrylic, or vinyl.

When compared to front-screen projection, the primary advantages are:

a. No interference with projection beam of light.

b. No tripping over drop cords or other equipment.

c. No need to dim all function-room lights, which permits attendees to take notes easily.

Its major disadvantages though, are:

a. It takes up a lot of space. Depending on the screen size and type of lens used, you will usually need about 15 to 30 feet behind the screen.

b. The area behind the screen must be completely dark.

c. Since the area in front of the screen must be light, the room must have separate lighting controls.

The size and type of screen required are related to the audience needs, room size, and room dimensions. To determine the maximum screen size, subtract four feet from the minimum ceiling height. If you use the maximum height, guests seated in the back row will be able to see the screen unobstructed by heads in the front rows.

If you plan to use slides, the screen should be square in order to accommodate both vertical and horizontal slides. In this case though, neither type of slide will completely fill the screen. Usually a professionally-prepared slide presentation will include only horizontal slides so that each image will fill completely a horizontally formatted screen.

The appropriate screen size must be used to ensure comfortable viewing for all audience members. While function-room size and layout are important factors, generally speaking the recommended screen size depends primarily on the audience size. Function planners should use the following screen sizes:

Audience Size	Recommended Screen Size (in Feet)
25 to 50	4 × 4
50 to 75	5 × 5
250 to 500	10 × 10
500 to 1,000	12 × 12
Over 1,000	14 × 14

3. *Overhead projector.* This equipment bounces an image off of a 45-degree mirror onto a lens placed above the object. The object is either a transparency or it could be an acetate sheet which can be written on with a special marking pen by a speaker during his or her presentation. Overhead projectors can be used in a lighted room, though subdued lighting is best.

Overhead projectors come in various sizes. The standard projector accommodates transparencies measuring 8 1/2 inches by 11 inches. Smaller sizes are more convenient if clients are using smaller transparencies. For instance, one of the smallest overhead projectors available is the Oxberry PPS-70, which is specifically designed to accommodate minitransparencies measuring approximately 4 inches by 5 inches.

4. *Sound.*   A good presentation depends on the quality of the equipment used to convey it. Without a good sound system, the most carefully planned display will flop.

There are two general types of sound systems: distributed and clustered. The distributed system is preferred when human voices need to be projected. Loudspeakers are placed strategically along the ceiling so that all of the audience is equidistant from the signal (that is, sound) source. The clustered system is used primarily for music. In this case, loudspeakers are usually placed about 15 to 30 feet above and around the stage.

The sound system includes four major components:

(a) Signal sources—the most common ones are microphones, audiotape, videotape, and filmstrip with audio track.

(b) Audio mixer—this equipment combines several signal sources and sends mono or stereo signals to the amplifier and ultimately to the speakers. The mixing system is usually an audio "box" that accepts multiple microphone, sound projector, or tape player hookups and allows these inputs to be "mixed" through a sound system with the help of an amplifier. Modern mixers automatically adjust for volume, sound level between speakers, feedback, and equalization, thereby minimizing labor costs.

(c) Amplifier—this equipment takes the signal from the audio mixer and boosts it to the level required by the speakers.

(d) Speaker—there are various types and sizes. They must be arranged in the room in such a way that they can fill it completely with sound.

The sound system can be adapted to include auxiliary equipment. For instance, if a client wants to broadcast a meeting to a satellite location, the appropriate telephone hookups can usually be added very easily to accommodate this need.

Many hotels have a built-in house sound system. These systems usually are adequate for public addresses and background music.

However, they usually are not designed to project musical instruments or singing.

5. *AV technician.*   For elaborate AV presentations, usually the client will need to hire at least one technician. For instance, if you are using four or more sound sources in a function room, it is recommended that you schedule one AV technician for that room who will coordinate and supervise the production.

In addition to AV technicians, a catered function may need a show coordinator. A coordinator would be necessary for an elaborate, complex event where it is essential to coordinate several productions during a short period of time.

6. *Audio recorder.*   The two basic types are: reel-to-reel and cassette tape recorders. Several sizes are available.

7. *Video recorder.*   Videotape cameras are commonly used to record entire events or parts of events. In fact, it is not unusual for some guests to use their own cameras to tape the proceedings for their own libraries.

8. *Carousel slide projector.*   This equipment is used to project images from horizontal and vertical slides onto a screen. The slides are placed in front of a single-light source one at a time. There are similar slide projectors that do not use a carousel to hold the slides. However, the most commonly used slide projector is still the Kodak Carousel.

Some slide projectors have automatic focus, automatic timers for continuous operation, and cordless remote control units. You can also synchronize your presentation with an audiotape player by inserting inaudible pulse tones on the tape that advance the slides automatically.

9. *Messager slide projector.*   This equipment is much smaller than the typical carousel projector. Instead of using a carousel to hold the slides, a magazine is used to stack the slides, which are then gravity fed in front of two light sources. Two light sources allow the images to blend (that is, "fade") into each other, thereby eliminating dark spots and ensuring smooth transitions.

This projector is more convenient to use than the carousel slide projector. For instance, the user does not have to insert slides into a carousel; he or she merely needs to stack them in the magazine. Moreover, the user knows exactly which slide is projected on the screen because each slide's number can be displayed on a digital readout attachment.

10. *Xenon slide projector.*   This equipment is typically used in large function rooms for large groups. In a large room, the projected images must be big enough for everyone to see. The images projected by the typical carousel slide projector begin to lose clarity and focus if they are enlarged too much. However, the Xenon slide projector uses a very bright bulb and thus, projects a much sharper, crisper large picture that can be seen easily from afar.

This projector is a more complicated device in that it usually must be adjusted to accommodate each slide's unique features. Consequently, it cannot be operated by an amateur. An AV technician usually must be employed to run it.

11. *TV monitor.*   A TV monitor is similar to a regular TV; the major difference is that the monitor produces a much-higher picture quality.

If a client needs to show a video, he or she can usually select one of three types of video systems. They are:

    a.   Use a regular TV set wired to accept video.

    b.   Use a TV monitor wired to accept video.

    c.   Use a video projection system (usually referred to as a big-screen TV) wired to accept video. This system uses a video projector, a special projection screen (that can be up to 30 feet wide), a video playback unit, and a patch into the hotel's in-house sound system.

As a general rule of thumb, when viewing videotapes, you should:

    a.   Use a 19 inch TV monitor for 10 people or less.

    b.   Use a 25 inch TV monitor for 11 to 25 people.

    c.   Use a 35 inch to 46 inch TV monitor for 26 to 50 people.

    d.   Use a big-screen TV for groups over 50 people.

You also could use a combination of these four options. For instance, in a room with 20 to 40 people, you can use two TV monitors with a common, portable sound speaker.

12. *Videotape player.*   Sometimes referred to as a VCP (video cassette player). It is designed specifically to play prerecorded video tapes to be shown on a TV monitor. A VCR (video cassette recorder) can also be used to show prerecorded video tapes.

13. *Audiotape player.*   This equipment is designed to play prerecorded audiotapes. Some types of equipment used to record audio presentations can also be used to play prerecorded tapes.

14. *Camera.* There are two basic types: film cameras and video cameras. Generally speaking, if a camera is needed, the client will use a videotape camera.

15. *Film projector.* This equipment is used to project prerecorded motion picture film images onto a projection screen. There are usually four types available: 35 mm; 16 mm; Super-8; and 8 mm. Most projectors have built-in sound speakers which are adequate for small groups. To accommodate large audiences, most projectors can be patched into the hotel's in-house sound system.

16. *Opaque projector.* This equipment is similar to an overhead projector, the major difference being that its light is reflected from above instead of from underneath. It can be used on solid materials, such as book pages, photographs, or small three-dimensional objects. Unlike the overhead projector though, when using this equipment, the room must be dark in order to see the images projected onto the screen.

17. *Slide/sound synchronizer.* This is a combination slide and audiotape presentation. For instance, a carousel slide projector can be advanced automatically by inaudible pulses on one stereo channel, while the other channel can present audio messages, such as music or voice-over narration.

18. *Dissolve unit.* This equipment allows two or three carousel slide projectors focused on the same screen to create a smooth transition from one slide to another. As the slides advance, they will fade into each other.

19. *Simultaneous translation.* With this service translators sit in a booth and listen to a speaker. As the speaker talks, they immediately translate his or her remarks and deliver the translation into a microphone that feeds into headsets worn by audience members.

There are two basic types of simultaneous-translation systems: cabled and wireless. The wireless is more expensive, but is more convenient to use. It allows maximum mobility.

Some systems allow audience members maximum control over the headset volume. Although these are more expensive than those without this option, again, they are more convenient to use. They also are preferred by audience members who wish to listen selectively to a speaker's remarks.

Most systems allow audience members to interact with the speaker and each other. For instance, an attendee might want to ask the speaker a question. The question can be easily translated back to the speaker and his or her translated responses communicated to the audience just as quickly. You can use several translators to accommodate a number of languages.

If you receive requests for this type of service, and you wish to provide it yourself, you should check with local embassies, consulates, colleges, or universities for bilingual persons. Be certain though, that anyone hired to do this type of work has had formal simultaneous-translation training and/or work experience.

20. *Closed circuit TV (CCTV).* Usually only the major conference centers have this type of capability. The video camera and TV monitors are usually used by groups to set up interactive training sessions. However, the systems can also be used for other purposes, such as providing security for exhibition areas, VIPs, and cash bars.

21. *LCD (liquid crystal display) panel.* This is an electronic device that sits on top of an overhead projector in lieu of a standard transparency. It is sometimes referred to as an electronic transparency. It is designed to project computer-generated data on the screen. Some models have built-in electronic storage and random-access retrieval capability, which enable the presenter to use some data while storing the rest of it for a later discussion.

22. *Projection table.* Standard projection tables vary in height, weight, and size. They are designed to hold projection equipment. They usually have detachable, adjustable legs that can be manipulated for height and storage. And they usually have locking casters, heavy-duty cords, and several plug outlets.

Some projection tables are more elaborate. They are designed to interact with other projection equipment. For instance, some have electronic pointers that can be used to enhance a slide presentation.

23. *Slide.* Most slides used today are 35 mm, color film, and measure 2 inches square (including the mounting). To ensure consistent focus, you should use only glass-mounted slides.

24. *Motion picture film.* Most educational and industrial films today are either 16 mm or Super-8. Occasionally you will find an 8 mm film. The soundtrack is usually dubbed onto the film during the printing or processing stage. For best results, the soundtrack should be patched into the hotel's in-house sound system.

25. *Videotape.* The most common videotape formats used today are:

   a. VHS (a $1/2$ inch format)
   b. U-matic (a $3/4$ inch format)

    c.   Betacam (a broadcast-quality, $1/2$ inch format)

    d.   1-inch (a broadcast-quality format).

If a client will be using two different formats, he or she will need two separate videotape players. None of these videotape formats are compatible with the others' equipment.

    26. *Multi-media system.*   This is a complete sight/sound environment. It combines audio, visual, and special-effects equipment (such as lasers, computers, and smoke-making machines).

    Off-the-shelf multi-media shows can be purchased or rented. For instance, you can rent a standard slide show and insert a few of your own slides to personalize the production. This is much cheaper than commissioning a major production that may be used only once.

    27. *Transparency.*   The typical transparency is a multi-or single-colored display printed on a thin sheet of transparent plastic or acetate. It is placed on an overhead projector and projected onto a screen.

    28. *Electronic board.*   This equipment resembles the traditional whiteboard, but anything written on it can be reduced and printed on paper by an attached printer for immediate distribution to attendees.

    29. *Easel.*   A three-legged stand designed to hold signs, chalk boards, posters, flip charts, and other types of illustrative material.

    30. *Flip chart.*   This is a large pad of paper (usually measuring 20 inches by 24 inches) designed to be used by a speaker to illustrate topics. It is placed on its own stand or on a separate easel. Usually it is set up to include several different colored marking pens and some masking tape that can be used to tape completed pages on the wall for later reference by the group.

    31. *Chalkboard.*

    32. *Pad and pencil.*

Recording

Sometimes a client may wish to record a catered event. For instance, it is common to audio record business meetings to have a record of the meeting, distribute tapes to persons unable to attend, and/or have a record for written transcription later on.

    When audio recording an event, generally the best results are obtained by patching into the hotel's in-house sound system. This results in a much better quality sound than if you use tape recorders placed strategically at the podium or throughout the function room.

If a client wishes to audio record an event for presentation later on to people who cannot attend the meeting, you should suggest using a reel-to-reel format. This produces the highest quality tape which can be edited easily. Unfortunately, this format is bulky, expensive, time consuming, and does not allow you to duplicate tapes easily.

Cassette recording is much less expensive. It is easy to use and the tapes can be duplicated very quickly. Unfortunately, it produces a poor sound quality and the tapes are very difficult to edit. This format though, is usually adequate if, for example, the objective is to have a verbal record that will be transcribed by a stenographer after the meeting ends.

If the client wants to use the cassette format, you should suggest that he or she use the Marantz PMD system, or a comparable system. The Marantz PMD is commonly used when a master recording device is needed. It is compact, easy to use, and you can monitor what is being recorded.

Some clients will want a video recording of the events. If so, they are best advised to use videotape instead of motion picture film. It is less costly, more versatile, and more durable than film.

When video recording, the technician will usually want to place one or more monitors around the room to check for accuracy as well as to broadcast the event to guests who are not close enough to see the action first hand. This way, the technician can show action as it happens, including the speaker's face, the audience reactions, and audience members asking questions. If an instant replay is desired, it can easily be presented.

When designing the function-room layout with video recording in mind, make sure the cameras are located so that they can "see" everything you want to record. They also should be located outside the traffic lanes. Another important factor is lighting. To ensure a clear, sharp picture, all subjects must be well lit.

Another important part of any recording is the recording microphone. Microphones and microphone placements are very critical. If the audience asks questions, you will need microphones placed strategically throughout the room. Otherwise there will be blank spots on the tape. Furthermore, the speaker may need to repeat the questions.

A speaker using an overhead projector or other similar equipment may want to use a lavalier microphone so that his or her hands are free to manipulate the equipment. This type of microphone will also ensure that the sound will not fade while the presenter is moving about the stage.

Omnidirectional microphones should be used when it is critical to record all sounds. Usually the best one you can use is the PZM type, or its equivalent. This is a condenser microphone that resembles a flat metal plate with a bubble on top of it. It has a very wide sound-pickup range, which makes it very useful for recording any events or meetings that take place around a large conference table. In addition, it is an unobtrusive piece of equipment that is virtually unnoticeable by guests.

When taping any event, make sure that all master tapes are prelabeled. The client should give the AV technician preprinted labels he or she can use to mark the tapes after they are used. You do not want a mislabeled, or unlabeled, tape to ruin an otherwise sterling event.

Someone should test the recording system before the client and guests enter the room. Start by going to each microphone and naming its type and location. The AV technician should then play back the tape to ensure that a proper recording is being made.

If a recording is critical, you might suggest that the client use two separate systems. This way you are ensured of a back-up system in case the first one fails to record. If both systems are recording, you then have an overlap that can be used to ensure that nothing is lost during tape changes.

Selecting an AV Service Contractor

When a client needs to use an outside AV service, you may be asked to recommend one. If so, you should investigate those available in your local area and develop a list of approved suppliers.

Before adding a firm to your approved supplier list, it must be able to perform adequately. Nevada Audio Visual Services, Inc., suggests you evaluate the following characteristics before deciding if a service contractor can handle clients' needs.

1. You should seek AV professionals with a proven reputation. Ask for references. Call the references and ask:

 a. How capable technically were the AV representatives?

 b. Did the firm have all necessary equipment?

 c. How responsive was the firm to last-minute requests?

 d. Was the final bill equal to the original competitive bid?

2. Look for an AV service contractor with communication technology specialists certified by the International Communication Industries Association. An AV firm with these specialists on staff is committed to continuing education within this highly technical and ever-changing industry.

3. The proximity of the AV firm to the hotel.

4. The availability of deliveries and installations after normal business hours.

5. The number of field representatives.

6. The number of delivery vehicles.

7. Do all field representatives and drivers carry beepers or cellular phones so that they can be contacted quickly?

8. Rental charges for equipment. Ensure that you are quoted the total charge for delivery, setup, and post-production.

9. Charge (if any) for back-up, emergency equipment.

10. Deposits required.

11. Refund policies. For instance, if an equipment order is canceled at the last minute, will some of the deposit be returned? Inquire also about the procedures used to reconcile disputed charges.

12. Setup time needed.

13. Rehearsal time needed.

14. Staging area(s) required.

15. Client assistance provided. Many clients will need assistance in planning their AV needs. The approved AV service contractor is able to provide sufficient input and assistance in developing these plans. A client may also need some help in computing his or her budget for AV production, equipment, labor, delivery, installation, and post-production costs.

16. Labor charges. This can be the biggest part of a client's AV budget. However, armed with the correct information about the catered event, the AV firm will be able to develop a detailed labor schedule that complies with union contracts and gives the client a realistic expectation of total labor costs.

Unfortunately, actual labor charges tend to exceed the budgeted ones because the client and the AV service contractor cannot anticipate everything about the scheduled function. For instance, there may be a problem getting into the facility to set up sound equipment because another catered function is running late. Delayed access to function rooms, as well as tight turnarounds, last-minute, on-site changes, and incomplete agendas are the most common reasons for labor cost variances.

These cost variances may increase if union labor must be scheduled. Many hotels and AV companies have contractual agreements requiring union labor for AV services. With complex, elaborate setups, more than one union may be involved. Since most labor contracts include hourly minimums, meal penalties, overtime rates, and show calls, the actual labor charge can be significantly greater than the budgeted one.

The more your AV service contractor knows about the catered function, the easier it will be to predict accurately the final, actual labor cost. Furthermore, the event's show coordinator will then be able to select and schedule a crew capable of handling the event properly.

17. The firm's ability to coordinate with other service contractors. For instance, if a separate lighting service contractor is required, both firms will need to work together smoothly to avoid glitches that can add to final costs and cause guest dissatisfaction.

18. Other services that can be provided by the AV firm. Some clients appreciate a one-stop shopping opportunity. It is good practice to be able to recommend to them AV firms that can perform other related services. For instance, some AV service contractors offer a wide variety of services, such as theme parties, laser and pyrotechnics shows, video conferencing, personalized slide presentations, and simultaneous translation.

Accommodating a Client's AV Needs

If a client is using AV services, the function must be held in a room where sound is transmitted effectively. The walls should have absorbent panels and be at least one inch thick. If air walls (i.e., moving partitions) are used, they should be metal or fiberglass and about two to four inches thick. Be sure that seals and gaskets are intact and tightly secured to prevent sound leaks.

Wool or thick-pile rugs are excellent floor coverings. These will absorb unwanted sounds, such as those created by foot steps and moving equipment.

The function room's ceiling should not be too high or else sound can reverberate. If the local building codes require very high ceilings, you will need to have some sort of acoustical material installed to reduce this effect or, if the client allows, position the speakers appropriately so that this problem is minimized. Usually if there is any potential for sound reverberation, you can quickly overcome it by installing temporarily fabrics, tiles, or other acoustical material.

If you have anything to say about room decor, avoid using permanent acoustical tiles. While they represent an effective and efficient way to minimize sound reverberation, unfortunately they are not very attractive. Permanently installed acoustical tiles may detract considerably from the function room's attractiveness.

If a client is using an outside AV service contractor, be certain that the firm is apprised of the hotel's logistics. For instance, the firm must be aware of accessibility, freight elevators, height and width of the doorways, and so forth in order to plan and implement the project correctly. The firm should also be informed of other events in the hotel that could interfere with installation and teardown procedures. These are very important factors that must be known ahead of time or else a satisfactory AV budget cannot be prepared.

Since AV service requires additional electrical power, and if your hotel's policy is to charge extra for it, be absolutely sure that the client realizes this. Do not point this out at the last minute. Experience shows that most clients are unaware of these subtle, hidden charges. It is up to you to disclose them up front so that clients can plan accordingly.

Finally, make certain the client realizes that all outside services will be billed at the actual cost, which may or may not be the same as the competitive bids submitted. You do not wish to dwell on the negative, but experience shows that the least little thing can throw off an AV schedule and drive up its labor costs.

ENTERTAINMENT

Many catered events offer some type of entertainment. The offerings run the gamut from the mundane to the spectacular. At one end of the spectrum is the one-man keyboard player, while at the opposite end are internationally famous singers headlining major show productions.

As with any outside service contractor, the hotel could develop an approved supplier list for potential clients to use. This would be relatively easy for those hotels that offer entertainment in their restaurant and bar outlets or have a corporate entertainment director.

If a client requires entertainment though, usually the responsibility for booking, scheduling, and coordinating it falls on his or her shoulders. Generally speaking, clients get in touch with booking agents and work closely with them and the catering executive to plan and implement the desired production.

The hotel's major involvement in the entertainment decision is to take it into account when planning the catered event. For instance, if a dance band is scheduled, everything from banquet setup to work scheduling will be influenced. Considering the major impact that entertainment will have, the catering executive cannot work effectively unless he or she is privy to this information.

The hotel must also know if there are any additional services that must be provided. The entertainment contract will indicate what they are and who is responsible for securing them. Generally speaking, the key variables the hotel must consider are:

1. *Lighting requirements.*   Will the entertainment provide its own? Will there be a separate outside lighting service contractor? Will the hotel's permanent system suffice?

2. *Number of dressing rooms needed.*   Also note where they must be located.

3. *Sound systems.*   Many entertainers have their own systems and technicians. Your responsibility is to provide sufficient space and electrical power. Hotel policy may require you to charge the client for this extra space and electrical power.

4. *Rehearsal time and facilities needed.*   If you need to hold the function room space for a day or two before the event so that rehearsals can be held, you will probably need to charge the client extra for this accommodation.

5. *Setup time.*   In lieu of rehearsal time, or in addition to it, you may need to hold a function room for an extra day or two so that the entertainment production can be set up properly.

6. *Security.*   Some entertainers have their own security guards. Others may depend on the hotel for all security or for additional security to supplement their own.

7. *Staging requirements.*   In addition to setting up a stage and runway, you must know if you need to dovetail with the lighting and AV service contractors.

8. *Dance floor.*   You also want to know if one or more dance floors are needed.

9. *Buffer area.*   This is the space between the entertainers and the audience. Some big-name acts want quite a distance between them and their fans, primarily for security purposes.

10. *Liability.*   A glance at the contract will tell you if there is any potential liability concern. For instance, some magicians use unusual and potentially dangerous props which could expose the hotel to a lawsuit if guests are injured.

You also need to know if the hotel will be responsible for the entertainer's personal property. If so, you must control the handling of these items.

11. *Complimentary food, beverage, and/or sleeping rooms.* You may want to offer entertainers the hospitality of the house as a goodwill gesture. Alternatively, you may let them run a tab and then charge it back to the client. Or you can arrange for the booking agents to pay for these services and bill it back to the clients. Before making a decision though, you will need to get the client's permission up front before doing anything.

12. *Operational restrictions.* Some entertainers have demands that may impact the rest of the hotel's operations. For instance, a singer may require a smoke-free ballroom, sleeping room, and dressing room. Or an entertainer may request special foods and beverages.

LIGHTING

Lighting is most commonly used to provide safety and security. It is primarily used to illuminate public and work areas properly so that they meet local building-code requirements as well as create a relaxed atmosphere.

Lighting can be much more than this. Lighting is magic. In can be used to overcome a plain, pedestrian environment, highlight persons, products, and specific function-room decors, illuminate speakers and other entertainers, focus attention on a particular spot, create a more exciting and dramatic dance floor, frame an area, and provide other decorative touches.

Lighting can also be used to tell a story. For instance, you can use laser equipment to project company logos, pictures of awards recipients, names of VIPs, and so forth on a wall so that guests can view them when they enter the facility.

Depending on the client's needs, he or she can obtain lighting service in at least three ways: (1) use the hotel's permanent lighting system; (2) rent lighting equipment and personally install, operate, and tear it down; or (3) employ an outside lighting service contractor.

Hotel Lighting System

The typical hotel does not own specialized lighting equipment that can be used to create light shows or any other type of unusual production. Normally it can provide a few spotlights and other similar equipment. However, usually its in-house system is not set up to accommodate unusual requests.

The typical hotel though, usually is capable of accommodating the outside service contractor. Sufficient electrical power, space, overhead beams, and so forth are normally included in the original building design in anticipation of these needs.

Conference centers, resorts, and hotels in rural areas may have sufficient lighting equipment and resources to handle most special requests. These properties usually feel obliged to provide such services because clients expect this type of convenience. Furthermore, if you are located in an out-of-the-way area, you cannot rely on nearby service contractors.

If a client requires only enough lighting to illuminate the function room, then no additional lighting service is required. But if lighting will be used as a form of decoration, few hotels can provide a complete service package.

Rent Lighting Equipment

If a client has unusual lighting demands, he or she can save a considerable amount of money by renting the equipment in lieu of employing a lighting service contractor. Rental rates are usually very competitive, whereas this is not usually the case with lighting service contractor fees. Additional savings can be earned if a client can coordinate and share expenses with a preceding or succeeding group who have similar lighting needs.

Your clients should not choose this option unless they are familiar with the use of this equipment. They also should avoid it if local unions prohibit this type of work. Furthermore, you should warn them that the potential savings could prove illusory if, for example, they need to hire additional labor to handle the work. In some cases, it may be more economical and convenient to select an outside lighting service contractor.

If a client prefers this option, be certain that he or she signs an insurance waiver and/or liability waiver indemnifying the hotel. Furthermore, make sure the hotel's insurance carriers and local building codes permit you to allow unlicensed and inexperienced clients to do this type of work on your premises. If there are any liability concerns, you should not let clients do their own work.

Employ a Lighting Service Contractor

An outside lighting service is an extremely labor-intensive, capital-intensive service. Consequently, clients will pay a pretty penny for it. The results of professionally developed light shows are very attractive and will certainly guarantee a memorable affair. However, these memories will not come cheap.

Lighting shows can be very expensive for several reasons. The major ones are:

1. Most designs are unique and therefore, will take some time to perfect.

2. Highly skilled, expensive union labor is typically used.

3. The hotel design may inhibit efficient installation.

4. The lighting service contractor must house an inventory of very expensive equipment that is subject to rapid obsolescence.

5. Liability insurance that service contractors must carry is very expensive.

6. Rehearsal time must be paid for.

7. The installation may be subject to inspection by the local government's building-codes agency.

8. Portable electrical power generators may be needed if the hotel does not have sufficient electrical power, or if it cannot be drawn from the main power panel and redistributed to the proper locations.

9. When the system is being installed and tested, other hotel departments, such as banquet setup, may have to postpone their work.

10. Coordination with other hotel departments and outside service contractors can be expensive and time-consuming.

11. If the lighting show requires a lot of electrical power, the hotel may charge extra for it. There may also be a surcharge if a function room must be shut down for a day or two so that installation and testing can be completed.

Selecting a Lighting Service Contractor

If the hotel decides to develop an approved supplier list, it should use selection criteria similar to those noted for AV and entertainment services. As with all outside services, you are primarily interested in the firm's ability to provide timely, adequate service.

OTHER SERVICES

Clients occasionally will require other services the hotel is unable to provide. If outside service contractors must be used, once again, the hotel may have an approved supplier list for the client's convenience. If not, it is up to the client to secure the necessary services and coordinate them with the hotel catering executive.

The most common types of other service contractors used by clients are:

1. Decorator
2. Designer
3. Florist
4. Photographer
5. Transportation
6. Media coverage
7. Specialized security
8. Religious
9. Printer
10. Host/hostess
11. Amenity/Souvenir manufacturer.

INTERMEDIARIES

At times, the catering executive will not work directly with a client. Instead, he or she will be dealing with an intermediary hired by the client to arrange a catered function.

Intermediaries are sometimes referred to as "10 percenters." This name is based on how they charge for their services. Generally, they charge 10 percent of the client's total bill for catered events. If the client schedules a large affair, the percentage fee may be reduced.

Clients typically use intermediaries when the catered event represents a major undertaking. For instance, if there will be several meal and beverage functions, two or more hotels involved, and many outside service contractors, a potential client may feel more comfortable employing a seasoned professional experienced in producing these types of detailed affairs.

Intermediaries are often used for civic and political fundraising events where it is necessary to solicit financial support and to sell tickets. Fundraising fashion shows, theme parties, charity auctions, and art shows are typically planned and implemented by professional intermediaries.

Intermediaries may also be used by clients planning the following types of events:

1. Theatrical production
2. Pyrotechnics show
3. Laser show
4. Video conference
5. Festival
6. Fair
7. Testimonial roast
8. Reunion
9. Awards program
10. New-product introduction
11. Company party
12. Convention
13. Training program
14. Exhibition.

The catering executive typically has mixed feelings about intermediaries. Their professionalism is certainly welcome. They know what they are doing. Unlike some clients, they do not need to be educated about every little detail. Furthermore, the client is paying for their work.

Intermediaries generally are more astute shoppers than the typical catering clients. They tend to drive harder bargains. They sometimes want more control over events than the typical catering executive is willing to surrender. It is sometimes inefficient to funnel your proposals and comments through a third party. And there may be some uneasy moments if, in addition to getting a fee from the client, an intermediary solicits a commission from the hotel for including the property in the event. Because some properties will not pay this type of commission, a client may not be exposed to all potential hotel catering departments capable of handling his or her needs.

Some catering executives feel that it is too difficult to work with intermediaries. For instance, some of them will never let you talk directly to the client, which presents problems when you are trying to produce an event "as seen through the eyes" of another. Without direct client contact, there is no way of knowing if your proposals are consistent with client wishes. If the client is disappointed, he or she will more readily blame the caterer, not the intermediary.

Another potential problem with intermediaries occurs when clients contact you directly instead of going through their intermediaries. If the contact involves a discussion of prices, you have a particularly significant dilemma if the intermediaries are marking up your prices and rebilling clients. Before talking to any client who is represented by an intermediary, you should meet with both of them so that these potentially troublesome occurrences do not arise.

Independent Meeting Planner

Professional meeting planners, sometimes referred to as "contract planners" or "multiple management companies," are probably the most common type of intermediary used by clients. A client can hire them to plan and implement the entire function. Or they can be used to perform specific services, such as site selection, negotiations, or registration of convention attendees.

Independent meeting planners specialize in producing convention programs, business meetings, training programs, and other similar events. They are capable of coordinating all necessary business functions, meal functions, beverage functions, and outside service contractors. They usually meet the needs of small and medium-sized companies that require professional assistance, yet do not have the resources to hire in-house planners. Most government clients also engage these types of intermediaries.

Special-Event Planner

These intermediaries are sometimes engaged by corporations to plan and implement company parties and other similar affairs. They usually have a select clientele list that are served on a periodic, predictable basis. For instance, a special-event producer may plan a particular company's annual picnic every year. Clients tend to prefer this type of long-term arrangement because it ensures continuity and variety.

Professional sports teams typically use special-events planners to coordinate after-game parties, half-time events, parades, and so forth.

Major events, such as the Olympics, corporate centennial celebrations, building openings, presidential inaugurations, and so forth, usually use several planners. For instance, the Coca Cola Company's 100th birthday celebration in Atlanta required the services of several special-events specialists, with each one responsible for one specific part of the event.

If several special-events planners are used, one of them may be responsible for overseeing and coordinating everyone's efforts. He or she may also need to develop a master plan for the event and decide how each planner will be used.

Independent Party Planner

This intermediary is similar to the special-event planner. The primary difference is that he or she tends to work more often with noncorporate clients. For instance, a small group of persons wishing to organize a 20-year high school reunion will tend to use this type of intermediary to help publicize, plan, and implement the function.

Professional reunion planners are the most rapidly growing segment of the independent party planning community. According to the National Association of Reunion Planners (NARP), by 1995, one of three high school reunions will be planned, organized, implemented, and supervised by a professional planner.

High school reunions are the most common type of reunion function. However, other reunions, such as family, military, company alumni, and so forth, are quickly becoming commonplace as clients realize how easy it is to develop what was once thought to be an impossible task.

Independent party planners usually take over all aspects of the function. They usually book the site, handle mailings, book entertainment, prepare a memory book, and so forth. Many of them also "lend" clients the deposits required by hotel caterers, thereby allowing clients to avoid coming out of pocket for up-front expenses; they can wait until their guests pay before they have to pay the planners.

Many independent party planners are brokers who subcontract most or all portions of the function. For instance, if a group wants to hold a prom function, it may contact this type of intermediary who will then select the hotel caterer, help plan the menu, hire a decorator, and engage the appropriate entertainment.

Ground Transportation

The typical ground-transportation firm handles primarily guest baggage. A firm can be hired by the convention client to pick up guest baggage at the airport and bring it to the hotel. When the convention is over, the baggage is brought back to the airport.

Some ground-transportation firms specialize in transporting clients' personal property. A local transport operator may pick up air-freighted or rail-freighted convention materials, such as equipment and product samples, and deliver them to the exposition hall. The same firm can also retrieve leftover merchandise and return it to the airport or railway yard.

Some ground-transportation firms specialize in providing limousine service for guests. They can pick up and drop off guests as well as be on call for personal needs during the conventions. Usually this type of service is employed because in many cases it is a low-cost alternative to using taxicabs.

There are also ground-transportation firms that move clients and guests to off-site locations. Convention attendees who need to tour a local manufacturing plant can use a local bus company to handle their transportation needs.

A few ground-transportation companies specialize primarily in entertainment. Some trips, such as charter boat rides and trail rides, are planned strictly for their entertainment value.

Travel Agency

The travel agent's typical responsibilities are to sell individual or package tours, rental cars, sleeping rooms, and transportation tickets. Some of them though, have expanded their role to include meeting-planning services. For instance, if a client uses a travel agent to secure airline and sleeping-room reservations, it is a small leap to using them to book a meeting room and catered luncheon. For small meetings, the travel agent may be a viable option for clients.

Combined Travel Agency and Independent Meeting Planner

A recent trend in the industry is the merger of these two specialized intermediaries. The travel agency has the transportation expertise, and the planner has convention- and meeting-management abilities. Together they make a formidable option for clients. In many instances, this combination gives even the smallest client a one-stop shopping opportunity.

Destination Management Company

Destination management companies range from those who provide very specialized services to full-service firms capable of handling all group logistics. For instance, some companies provide only ground transportation (such as busses, limos, and vans), while others can handle personally, or can subcontract, everything a client needs. For instance, full-service firms can book entertainment, plan theme parties, coordinate tours and spouse programs, and handle off-site events (including catering) at museums and other local attractions.

Full-service firms can also provide personnel; for instance, exhibitors may want to hire local models to work exhibit booths.

Trained registration personnel can also be hired. And "moving decor," such as costumed models, caricature artists, and celebrity look-a-likes, can be used to help carry out an event's theme. Generally speaking, it is much cheaper for the out-of-town corporate and association clients to hire these persons locally than to pay transportation and per-diem maintenance for company employees.

Destination management companies are oftentimes used to secure props for theme parties. For instance, a destination management company can see to it that a 1960s party has a vintage Mustang or Corvette display. Appropriate balloon art and pyrotechnics displays can also be coordinated by this intermediary.

Many out-of-town clients are willing to pay a local destination management company to provide guidance in an unfamiliar area. It is very difficult for a client to judge the quality of services available if he or she has never visited the area. This intermediary can relieve the client of this burden because most destination management companies are intimately familiar with the local entertainers, lighting companies, and AV contractors. Furthermore, these firms can handle negotiations and oversee every detail, thereby ensuring a successful event.

Clients whose events are held in a different area every year prefer working with destination management companies. These intermediaries have made it easy for clients to indulge this preference by locating themselves in major convention cities. Some national firms, such as USA Hosts, have local offices in several major convention cities that provide large corporate clients one-stop service as well as favorable quantity-discount prices.

There are independent destination management companies that work only one part of the country. Because of their specialized approach, clients may find them to be the best option. For instance, Tour Gals, an independent firm located in Atlanta, may be the best choice for planning spouse programs in that area.

Some independent destination management companies belong to referral groups, which allows them to compete with the national firms. For instance, the independent firm Activity Planners in Las Vegas belongs to CONTACT, which is a loose federation of destination management companies whose major purpose is to provide referral opportunities to members.

Convention and Visitors Bureau (CVB)

The local CVB can provide free of charge some of the same services provided by other intermediaries. It is an especially attractive option for the out-of-town client who wants to book an event in a local area, but is unfamiliar with it. The CVB can provide useful information about the area, such as family attractions, transportation, hotels, and amount of available exhibit hall space, that can be used by a client to evaluate its suitability for an event.

The CVB can be an extremely valuable one-stop-shopping source for clients. For instance, if a client wants to plan a convention, he or she can send the CVB a list of requirements for meeting and sleeping accommodations and meal and beverage services. The CVB will assemble a list of suitable properties and outside service contractors, thereby relieving the client of the tedious task of shopping around. In most cases, the CVB can save clients at least two or three days time.

The CVB's most tangible benefit for clients is the time saved. In addition to providing suitable alternative selections for clients, it can also provide considerable logistical support at the local level. Not only will it provide a list of outside service contractors, it can also help clients schedule and coordinate their work.

Since the typical CVB is funded by local member hotel properties, a client usually can use its planning services free of charge. It also can offer promotional material to clients free of charge. Clients can get free name-tag holders, brochure shells, small mementos, registration personnel, and other similar fare. Most bureaus will use their advertising budgets to absorb these types of costs.

11

Staffing

I know I cannot do the job by myself! You must always remember
the people who work with you. It is the people who make the
system work.

Daniel H. Dodson
Banquet Manager
Scottsdale Princess Hotel
Scottsdale, AZ

One cannot overestimate the importance of staffing in the service
industry. The catering department's reputation rests on its ability
to prepare and serve a consistent quality of food and beverage.
Without the proper amount and type of personnel, the hotel cannot
hope to develop or maintain a sterling reputation.

What motivates a client to book business at a particular hotel?
What is the difference between one large hotel's catering department and another's? Certainly each hotel lays claim to some sort of
unique benefit that it alone can provide to clients. However, if you
scratch the surface of any hotel's reputation, chances are you will
find that its perceived level of service is its most salient feature.

There is an old saying in the food-service business that supermarkets sell food, restaurants sell service. The same thing can be
said about the typical hotel catering department. Conceivably a
client could rent a hall and perform all the shopping, cooking,
serving, and cleaning chores. And he or she could probably do it at
less than half the cost of hiring a caterer. Why then, would he or she
agree to book a catering function knowing full well that it will not
be cheap?

The obvious answer is that clients, like all customers, are willing to pay for someone else to do the work. But, more than that,
they are willing to pay a premium for someone to do the work in a
timely and efficient manner, and certainly better than they can do
it themselves.

One of the best things that can happen to you is for clients to say yes, they did spend a great deal, but they got their money's worth. In other words, they received value for their dollars.

Conversely, one of the worst things that can occur is for clients to perceive that they did not get a good value. No matter how low the price is, if a client does not perceive value, it is too high.

Staffing is critical. It is an organization's life blood. Experience shows that customer satisfaction and repeat patronage are influenced primarily by food and beverage quality, service, and sanitation and cleanliness. An inadequate, undermanned, undertrained staff is incompatible with the successful hotel catering operation.

EMPLOYEE RECRUITMENT

The wise catering executive does not rely solely on the hotel's human-resources department to secure adequate staffing. You cannot merely pick up the phone and call the employment manager whenever you have a job opening. Rather, it is very important to adopt a proactive stance in order to satisfy your staffing needs.

Staffing is an ongoing activity primarily because the typical hotel catering department's staffing requirements fluctuate widely. This is especially true for the group of employees who work part time and/or work very unpredictable schedules.

There is a critical core of permanent, fixed-cost, full-time and part-time managerial and hourly staff members. Many of these people are career oriented and/or satisfied with their current positions. Consequently, they are apt to remain with you. This does not mean though, that this core will never change. As with anything else, it is subject to change at a moment's notice. For instance, a permanent part-time head bartender may suddenly leave you to take a full-time bartending job at a competing hotel.

The majority of your staff are variable-cost employees who tend to work for more than one hotel. While many of them prefer part-time status, some of them are looking for full-time employment. If they secure something permanent, chances are they may leave you on short notice.

Many variable-cost employees may be busy when you need them. For instance, some of them may be working their regular jobs and cannot break away to help you, while others may be working at another hotel's catered function that day.

Your variable-cost employees also tend to move into and out of the industry. It is not unusual for food and cocktail servers and buspersons to qualify for employment in other segments of the service industry. For instance, the people skills and customer-contact skills that food servers develop are the major prerequisites for many job positions in department stores, supermarkets, and boutiques.

An unfortunate fact of life in the service industry is the labor shortage that frustrates your efforts to build and maintain an adequate staff. Not only must you compete with other hotels for a diminishing labor pool, you also need to fight other retailers. For instance, a recent trend in food service is for qualified, experienced chefs to leave the restaurant industry and join the supermarket industry.

It seems that many supermarket companies are making a major investment in deli operations and are willing to employ expensive chefs to develop prepared foods for customer take out. Complicating your efforts to compete with the supermarket industry is the fact that it generally will offer more attractive work schedules and pay more than the typical food-service operator. For instance, several food-service publications report that entry-level wages and discretionary employee benefits in supermarket delicatessens exceed those paid in the hotel and restaurant industries.

To say the least, maintaining an adequate number of qualified employees is no easy task. No one likes to encounter severe employee turnover. However, the fluctuating demands for staff members in the catering industry have resulted in a certain amount of "structural" (that is, unavoidable) turnover.

Experience shows that if a food-service operation has normal employee turnover, the manager may spend as much as one-third of his or her working hours recruiting, interviewing, and training new staff members. This time investment can be reduced slightly if the hotel has a full-service, centralized human-resources department. However, you must resist the temptation to lean too heavily on the human-resources department because it is risky to delegate completely this responsibility. Unless you are intimately involved with staffing procedures, chances are you will be unable to handle your clients' needs effectively.

The catering executive must be willing to cultivate constantly potential employees. This is especially important for your hourly staff. Your A-lists and B-lists can never be too long. You do not want to get to the end of them and find that you still do not have enough people to staff the upcoming catering events.

You also need to cultivate and develop your fixed-cost employees. Since the typical way of doing this is to promote people from the variable-cost employee group, it is even more important to spend as much time as possible recruiting entry-level employees.

Job Specification

For management positions, a job candidate must have technical work experience along with the requisite human skills. For many hourly positions, you also prefer job candidates with a reasonable amount of catering work experience. However, conceivably you could hire persons for many positions who have minimal or no work experience in our industry.

If a person has the willingness to do the work, and possesses customer-contact skills and a positive attitude toward the catering industry, you can train them to perform capably. With patience and understanding, you can turn energetic people into excellent food and cocktail servers.

The lack of technical skills can place an additional burden on you and the rest of your staff because of the extra training that must be done. Managers in the food-service industry are accustomed to hiring and training neophytes. In fact, many of them prefer to do this because they do not have to retrain new hires and break old habits. They feel that it may be much easier to start with a blank slate.

It is one thing to hire someone without catering work experience, but quite another to hire a person who has no work experience in customer-contact positions. There is no way to predict how someone will react when put into a high pressure situation where guests are blowing off steam. Experience shows that the various personality tests available do not adequately predict a newcomer's initial reactions.

Likewise if you contemplate hiring someone who has never worked a paid job outside the home. If you hire such a person, you encounter all the problems associated with hiring someone with no catering work experience plus those that crop up whenever someone is introduced to the realities of the work place. Not only must you teach these novices how to perform their jobs, you also must teach them the protocols of working for an employer.

When recruiting job candidates, you also must see to it that they possess the appropriate credentials. For instance, some positions may need to be staffed solely with union members. A few may require college degrees or similar training. Secretaries should be certified in word processing, computerized recordkeeping, and other related tasks. Other positions may require persons who have current alcohol server awareness training certificates. And some employees may need current health cards issued by the local health district.

Minimum age is another job specification for job candidates who prepare, sell, and/or serve alcoholic beverages. In most parts of the United States, these persons must be at least 21 years old. As a general rule, hotels will hire minors for kitchen preprep, food runner, and other similar jobs. However, the catering department usually will not hire minors because it is almost impossible to keep them away from alcoholic-beverage service.

Job Description

It is imperative to maintain up-to-date, current job descriptions so that job candidates know exactly what to expect if they come to work for you. You do not want to be put into the position of relating inaccurate information. This will cause unnecessary grief, job dissatisfaction, and unnecessary employee turnover.

The job descriptions should paint accurate pictures of all job duties that must be performed. Experience shows that often job candidates misinterpret job parameters because the job descriptions are too vague. The recruiter may exacerbate this problem further by failing to address the specific job needs during the interview process.

It is thought that a job misinterpretation is one of the key variables responsible for excessive employee turnover. Generally speaking, if you can keep an hourly person for 30 days, and a management person for one year, chances are that he or she is satisfied with the job and the company and is likely to remain for a while. If you paint a realistic picture up front, and then see to it that reality does not vary significantly from this description, your employee turnover will probably be much less than the industry average.

Labor Pool

The catering executive should work closely with the hotel's human-resources department to develop an adequate labor pool. He or she should inform human resources of potentially fruitful areas to seek job candidates so that its efforts are not wasted. For instance, if you feel that the local college will generate adequate job candidates, you should encourage the human-resources department to recruit on campus.

The catering department also should not be afraid to adopt a proactive stance. It should have a long-term staffing plan which notes expected terminations and resignations, and anticipated total staffing needs. It should also take the lead whenever possible and seek out job candidates and send them to human resources for interviewing and possible hiring.

The following labor-pool sources can yield capable job candidates:

1. *Promote from within the catering department.*   Employees like promotion-from-within policies since this gives them an opportunity to move up in the company. Experience shows that career ladders and career scaffolds attract potential employees who would otherwise not perceive your hotel as a good place to work.

2. *Use the hotel's job bidding process.*   Usually a hotel will post job openings on the employee bulletin board. Interested employees can then bid, that is, apply, for them. For instance, a person currently employed in the hotel's coffee shop may want to apply for a full-time catering position.

3. *Job referral.*   Current catering employees may have friends or relatives who might wish to apply for job openings. This could be a win-win situation, in that the current employee may receive some type of bonus while the catering department gets another good employee who knows what to expect. Unfortunately, some conflict-of-interest and nepotism problems could arise whenever this sort of inbreeding occurs. Because of these problems, some hotels severely restrict this hiring practice.

4. *Use employees from other hotel departments.*   A part-time employee in another department may be a good addition to your A-list or B-list. This can be another win-win situation, assuming it does not violate hotel policy. You must be careful when doing this though, because some jealousy and hard feelings can develop. For instance, it could be rather ticklish if a part-time coffee-shop employee finds your department more inviting and requests a transfer.

Using other hotel department employees also could cause overtime problems. For instance, if in one week an hourly employee works five full days in the coffee shop and one full day for you, he or she would have to be paid overtime premium pay for the sixth day. Federal regulations mandate that an hourly employee must be compensated $1\frac{1}{2}$ times his or her regular rate of pay for all hours worked in excess of 40 per week. Furthermore, in some states an hourly employee may be entitled to overtime premium pay for all hours worked in excess of 8 per day (if the normal work week is 5 days, 8 hours per day) or 10 per day (if the normal work week is 4 days, 10 hours per day).

5. *Union hiring hall.*   A unionized hotel may need to use the union hiring hall for permanent and temporary hires if the job positions are unionized. In some cases, the union may sponsor

internships and apprenticeships that can provide you with a steady, albeit ever-changing, supply of young, enthusiastic, workers.

6. *Culinary schools.*   This is a good source of permanent, full-time employees. It also represents a good pool of part-time workers who need to earn work-experience hours to complete their degree requirements. The instructors themselves may be interested in working part time. Or they may be willing to work for you during their summer vacations.

7. *Colleges and universities.*   You should concentrate your recruiting efforts on the many universities and 2-year colleges offering hospitality management training. You may be able to attract graduates for full-time positions. And since most college programs require students to earn a minimum number of work hours in the hospitality field, you should try to set up a system whereby your part-time staff is continually replenished with underclassmen.

Many other college majors might be willing to work part time. Our industry is flexible enough to work around most young persons' school schedules. Students are usually favorably disposed to part-time hotel work because of your ability to satisfy almost anyone's personal schedules. You should call the schools' placement offices and ask them to post job openings on their job bulletin boards.

8. *High schools.*   This labor source is similar to colleges and universities. The major difference though, is that most students are too young to work around alcoholic beverages. They also may be too young to work past curfew. Usually catering departments will not hire anyone under 21. However, you might consider working with vocational schools to develop catering internships and other similar job opportunities. When the interns reach majority age, they may look favorably on your current job offerings.

9. *Other retail establishments.*   Some other retailers, such as department stores and supermarkets, employ part-time persons who may be interested in adding more work hours to their current personal work schedules. You may be able to help them do this by giving them one or two days of work per week. At the very least, you can put them on your A-list or B-list.

10. *Manufacturing plants.*   Some persons working in these industries may be interested in moonlighting activities. They may want to extend their current part-time earnings, or they may want to work a sixth day. You can accommodate them with a regular day each week, or you can put them on your A-list or B-list.

11. *Homemakers.*   These are one of the best sources for A-list or B-list people. Experience shows though, that you will need to be

extra flexible with them because they will not work if your needs conflict with their personal family responsibilities.

12. *Seniors.*   Many retired persons want to keep active in the work-a-day world. They are becoming more and more of a fixture in many retailers' part-time labor pools. Several types of food-service operations are anxious to hire them on a part-time basis. They usually bring a favorable combination of work experience, enthusiasm, patience, personableness, and dedication that makes them extremely valuable employees.

Experience shows that we are guilty of trying to convert part-time employees, especially seniors, into full-time employees. Since this is usually an unattractive option, you should avoid this temptation lest you lose valuable part-time personnel.

13. *Private industry councils.*   Many businesspersons support institutes and other similar organizations that can be good sources of full-time and part-time labor. For instance, groups such as the Urban League, are very active in sponsoring employment job fairs, apprenticeship programs, and job training opportunities that can dovetail very nicely with your employment efforts.

14. *Employment agencies.*   Public and private employment agencies may yield full-time job candidates. Public agencies operated by the state unemployment security departments can be good sources of hourly wage earners. They may be preferable to private employment agencies because they do not charge fees for their services. Usually because of the fees involved, employers tend to use outside private "head hunters" only when it is necessary to hire middle and top management personnel.

15. *Government job-training agencies.*   There may be one or more local government agencies sponsoring job-training programs on their own or with the cooperation of the federal government. For instance, the local workers compensation insurance program may sponsor several rehabilitative training programs for injured employees who cannot go back to their old jobs. You could be part of these training efforts by providing jobs for the trainees. In some cases, your cooperation can result in payroll savings since some programs grant tax credits and/or pay part or all of the wages during the training periods. Moreover, a successful trainee could end up taking a full-time, permanent position with your hotel.

16. *Day-labor operations.*   These organizations are similar to public and private employment agencies. The major difference is that they usually "lease" people to you on a daily basis. For instance, if you need a few extra hands to set up an outdoor tent, a call to the local "manpower" agency could yield specifically the exact amount of labor required. You get only the amount of help needed. And it is more convenient to pay one price for it rather than putting everyone through the normal, expensive hiring procedure.

Day-labor operations may hire street people. This tends to turn off the typical employer. However, experience shows that, if you use these organizations properly, and assign workers only those jobs they are capable of doing, you can obtain very favorable results.

17. *Other hotels.* While it is not neighborly to steal employees from your competitors, you should not let this stop you from spreading the word about job opportunities at your property. Furthermore, since all hotels use many part-time persons, there is ample opportunity to offer someone one or two work days at your property while allowing him or her to keep the other job.

Usually some of your employees are working for several hotels anyway. For example, a few of them may be on the B-list of every major property in town. You might as well take the initiative and maximize the potential of this labor source by using good taste in publicizing your job opportunities.

18. *Professional associations.* This is one of the most prolific sources of sales and management personnel. Many hospitality managers belong to one or more professional associations. For instance, many catering professionals belong to the National Association of Catering Executives (NACE).

One of the benefits association members enjoy is being kept apprised of current career opportunities available in their field of expertise and interest. You should use these built-in grapevines to advertise current job vacancies.

19. *Reduce your employee turnover.* The seeds of employee turnover or employee retention are planted when a job candidate is interviewed and take root when the new hire gets a chance to experience reality and compare it to your promises.

Turnover and retention are also directly related to the type and amount of job training and development provided to employees. Studies show that the lack of training and development is one of the main reasons people leave their jobs.

It has been said that, depending on the type of job position, it costs at least several hundred to several thousand dollars to replace a hospitality-industry worker. The costs of hiring, orienting, training, putting up with lower productivity for a while, and so forth, can add up very quickly. If you can reduce turnover, the potential payroll savings are very handsome. Moreover, a reduction in employee turnover relieves the pressure for you to cultivate other labor sources.

Job Application

The job application is the most common method used to screen initially potential employees. Usually applications are filled out in the human-resources department by walk-ins, that is, persons who respond to classified ads, or who merely stop by to see if you need help.

The job application can be an excellent prescreening device. The employment manager can use it to weed out quickly unqualified job candidates who do not possess the requisite experience, education, and other pertinent background characteristics.

If you find someone to fill a job position, you would still need to send him or her to the human-resources department to complete a job application and go through the rest of the job-processing procedure. Chances are that since you found the person, the total procedure will be expedited.

Job Interview

If a walk-in seeks a job, usually he or she is given a prescreening interview if the job application reveals some promising information. Typically the prescreening interview involves a discussion of things such as: when can the person report for work? what is the depth of his or her work experience? will the person feel comfortable working under your property's particular rules and regulations? and so forth.

A prescreening interview is also an excellent opportunity to determine if a job candidate is likely to succeed at your hotel property. For instance, Holiday Inns uses a prescreening process to determine if a job candidate has the proper attitudes, skills, and work habits needed to perform effectively. Managers ask job candidates approximately 25 questions, the responses to which are compared to those of current successful Holiday Inns employees. A statistically significant positive correlation of responses suggests that the job candidate will excel with the company.

If a job candidate survives the prescreening interview, the interviewer should take the time to check references before moving him or her along in the job-processing procedure. Telephone calls should be made to verify information indicated on the job application and during the prescreening job interview.

A reference check may also include some testing procedures. For instance, your hotel may have a policy of giving all job applicants integrity tests, drug tests, physical exams, job-skills tests, and so forth, before they can qualify for the next step in the employment process.

If the reference check yields favorable information, the job candidate usually is then interviewed by you or someone on your staff. In some cases, he or she may be interviewed by you and other management personnel in the catering department. This is especially true if the person is applying for an entry-level sales or management position.

After this interview, it is usually up to you to determine if the hotel should offer the position to the job applicant. If you want to hire the person, human resources will then extend the job offer formally, complete the employment process, and schedule the new hire's first work day.

ORIENTATION

The human-resources department is responsible for orienting all new hires. This procedure normally takes the better part of one work day.

Orientation usually involves providing new hires with nonjob related information. For instance, new hires are usually:

1. Introduced to the company's philosophy
2. Fitted for uniforms
3. Given an employee handbook and explanation of the information it contains
4. Given a welcoming by the hotel's general manager and other major department heads
5. Exposed to general lectures dealing with property security procedures, company history, career opportunities, and so forth
6. Given a property tour
7. Assigned locker-room space, parking place, name tag, and so forth
8. Introduced to supervisor and coworkers.

TRAINING

Usually the human-resources department and the catering department share the training efforts. For instance, human resources may provide general training in life safety, customer courtesy, complaint handling, telephone procedures, drug and alcohol awareness, and so forth, with catering taking responsibility for the initial and on-going specific job-related training.

The Food & Beverage Committee of the Hotel Sales & Marketing Association International (HSMAI) developed training guidelines that can be used to familiarize a catering department's new hire with all pertinent hotel operating and nonoperating activities. Depending on the position, a new hire should be exposed to one or more of the following systems:

1. *Banquet sales manual.* All catering sales representatives should be familiar with your catering policies and procedures. New entry-level salespersons who are unfamiliar with the general sales systems used in the hotel industry should pay particular attention to the following:

    a. Catering files and filing procedures

    b. Tracing procedures

    c. Solicitation procedures

    d. Catering sales analysis

    e. Booking procedures

    f. Procedures used to prepare banquet event orders (BEO), prefunction sheets, and convention resumes

    g. Dates and space reservation procedures

    h. Confirmation procedures

    i. Cancellation procedures

    j. Specific job responsibilities

    k. Sales techniques

    l. Credit procedures

    m. Guarantee procedures.

2. *Food and beverage department.* If relevant, the new hire should be exposed to some or all of the following food and beverage operating procedures:

    a. Food and beverage controller's office

        (1) General banquet food and beverage cost requirements

        (2) Exposure to banquet food and beverage cost calculations

        (3) General food and beverage accounting procedures

        (4) Food controls

(5)   Beverage controls

(6)   Guarantee and attendance calculations

(7)   Variance analysis

(8)   Profit and loss statement analysis

(9)   Computing total banquet costs

(10)   Percentage analysis

(11)   Payroll cost analysis

(12)   Profit ratios

b. Kitchen

(1)   Executive chef's responsibilities

(2)   Banquet chef's responsibilities

(3)   Banquet menus

(4)   Banquet change orders

(5)   Staffing

(6)   Stock requisitions

(7)   Food preprep

(8)   Food prep

(9)   Banquet dish-up

(10)   Evaluating potential menu items

(11)   Month-end inventories

(12)   Portion control

c. Steward

(1)   Payroll forecasts

(2)   Review of banquet menus

(3)   Staffing

(4)   Stock requisitions

(5)   Equipment preparation

(6)   Equipment inspection

(7)   Equipment storage

(8)   Coordination with kitchen and service

(9)   Salvage procedures

(10)   Sanitation procedures

(11)   Refrigeration

(12)   Equipment par stocks

(13)   Equipment inventories

(14) Supplies storage

(15) Equipment and supplies purchasing

d. Banquet manager

    (1) General service procedures

    (2) Coordination with kitchen and steward

    (3) General supervisory procedures

    (4) Banquet rooms

    (5) Function-room setups

    (6) Premeal service meetings

    (7) Seating charts

    (8) Function-room maintenance

    (9) Menu meetings

    (10) Preconvention meetings

    (11) Coordination of tableware and napery

    (12) Payroll forecasts

    (13) Rehab. meeting (forecasted repair and maintenance needs)

    (14) Work scheduling

    (15) Housekeeping work sheets

    (16) Styles of service

e. Beverage

    (1) Banquet menus

    (2) Coordination with steward and banquet manager

    (3) Stock requisitions

    (4) Change orders

    (5) Guarantees

    (6) Sales and cost data

    (7) Prefunction meetings—roll-call and briefing

    (8) Stocking banquet bars

    (9) Bar tear down

    (10) Beginning and ending bar inventories

    (11) Cash reconciliation

    (12) Drink-ticket reconciliation

    (13) Month-end inventories

    (14) Work scheduling

      f. Room service
- (1) Hospitality suites
- (2) Liquor control
- (3) Room service checks
- (4) Coordination with room setup
- (5) Amenity service packages available

      g. Food and beverage manager
- (1) Daily revenue and payroll report
- (2) Filing system
- (3) Restaurant outlets
- (4) Bar outlets
- (5) Forecasting
- (6) Payroll analysis
- (7) Menu analysis
- (8) Coordination with the district or regional director of food and beverage (if applicable)
- (9) Coordination with the corporate vice president of food and beverage (if applicable).

3. *Purchasing.*
   a. Product availability
   b. Seasonal variations
   c. Special items not commonly used
   d. Banquet menu reviews
   e. Banquet order sheets
   f. Order sizes
   g. Purchase price trends
   h. Plant visits.

4. *Convention service.*
   a. Review of function-room setup check lists
   b. Banquet room assignments
   c. Banquet room capabilities and limitations
   d. Hospitality suites
   e. Clearing space for catering functions
   f. Preconvention meetings.

5. *Tour and travel.*
   a. Travel agents

    b. Tour wholesalers

    c. General sales procedures

    d. Meal coupons

    e. Other coupons

    f. Product and service prices.

6. *Front office.*

    a. Reservations

    b. Front-desk procedures

        (1) Check in

        (2) Check out

        (3) Baggage handling

    c. Coordination with sales department

    d. Room and suite tours

    e. Bell desk

    f. Concierge.

7. *Credit/accounting.*

    a. Credit procedures

    b. Deposit requirements

    c. Collections

        (1) Procedures

        (2) Problems

        (3) Outside collection agencies

        (4) Types of accounts.

8. *Human resources.*

    a. General personnel procedures

    b. Coordination with hotel departments

    c. Compensation packages.

9. *Engineering.*

    a. Sound

    b. Lighting

    c. Utilities available in function rooms

    d. Charges for utilities, labor, and equipment.

10. *Public relations and advertising.*

    a. Food and beverage promotions

    b. Newspaper clippings

      c. Outside calls

      d. Attend functions at other hotels

      e. Contact individuals responsible for buying catered functions

      f. Familiarization with competing hotel catering departments' offerings.

11. *Safety.*

      a. Recognizing safety hazards

      b. Slippery floor procedures

      c. Customer safety

      d. Proper utilities hookups

      e. Setting up crosswalk areas

      f. Fire codes

      g. Health codes

      h. Evacuation routes.

12. *Laundry and valet.*

      a. Napery controls

      b. Stock requisitions

      c. Soiled napery storing procedures

      d. Usage charges

      e. Uniforms and costumes.

The department head should use these suggested training guidelines to develop an appropriate training program for each new hire. The new hire's progress should then be monitored, with the department head submitting a training report to the director of catering at the conclusion of the training period.

The training report should be reviewed with the trainee before preparing the final draft. For instance, each time an entry is made in the report, the trainer and trainee should visit together for a few moments to discuss the entry and determine if any changes need to be made in the program. This is also a good time to discuss the trainee's progress and clear up any problems.

For some new hires, it would be useful to have them prepare a personal report at the end of their training period. For instance, if you are training a new catering sales representative, you may want to ask him or her to submit a written report detailing what was learned after visiting and working in all other pertinent hotel departments. This report can give you a valuable insight into the trainee's communications skills. It can reveal if additional training is needed. It can also tell you if the training programs need to be modified.

COMPENSATION

The typical compensation package includes a combination of some of the following: salaries, wages, gratuities, commissions, bonuses, tips, required employee benefits, and discretionary employee benefits. All compensation packages are developed and coordinated by the human-resources department. You should know specifically the types and amounts of compensation allowed for each job position so that potential job candidates will not be misled when you are cultivating them.

Management positions normally receive predetermined salaries unrelated to the amount of time worked. Some managers though, may receive performance bonuses and/or commissions. For instance, a catering sales representative may receive a modest fixed salary plus a percentage of all business booked.

Nonmanagement, wage-earner positions are usually compensated on an hourly basis. Some of them may also receive a preset split of the gratuities collected for each catered event. If a client leaves a tip, the wage earners typically will share it as well.

Required employee benefits are usually referred to as payroll taxes. They include primarily the hotel's contribution to the federal government social security, medicare, and unemployment-tax programs. Some states also require employers to contribute monies to their unemployment-tax programs and the state-operated workers compensation programs.

As a general rule, the minimum cost of required employee benefits is equal to about 15 to 18 percent of your total payroll expense. For instance, if you pay a server $10.00 per hour, the hotel's hourly out-of-pocket expense for this employee is about $11.50 to $11.80 per hour after factoring in these payroll taxes.

In some parts of the country, the hotel's total payroll-tax expense is much higher because the tax percentages will be applied to the payroll expense plus the amount of gratuities and declared tips. For instance, if a $10.00 per hour server averages an additional $5.00 per hour gratuity and tip income, the hourly payroll-tax expense for this employee will be about $2.25 to $2.70 (15 to 18 percent of $15.00). The hourly out-of-pocket expense for this employee then, is about $12.25 to $12.70.

Typical discretionary benefits are health, dental, optical, and life insurance paid for by the company or offered to employees at a reduced rate. Some hotel companies also provide stock-option plans, profit-sharing plans, pension plans, free meals, matching contributions to selected charities, paid vacations, paid sick days, insurance coverage for dependents, formal training, career opportunities (such as promotion from within), reimbursement of educational expenses, flexible work scheduling, uniform allowances, and reduced-cost meals, beverages, and sleeping rooms at other company-owned or -operated hotel properties.

Only full-time employees qualify for the full range of discretionary benefits. Hotels may offer a limited number of discretionary benefits to part-time employees who work at least 20 hours per week. Employees working 19 hours or less per week usually do not qualify for discretionary benefits.

Some hotels, especially unionized properties, have generous overtime-pay policies that exceed those mandated by federal and state labor regulations. They may also have very generous holiday-pay policies. For instance, union and/or company policy may require you to pay double time instead of time-and-one-half for all overtime worked, straight time for all state and federal holidays not worked, and double time for all state and federal holidays worked.

Discretionary benefits are not cheap. The National Restaurant Association (NRA) estimates that the least-expensive, bare-bones health insurance package costs a minimum of about $120 per month for each covered employee.

The NRA also estimates that the cost of required benefits, discretionary benefits, and administrative expenses needed to operate the human-resources function is approximately 40 percent of your total payroll cost. According to its estimates, an employee earning $10.00 per hour then, actually costs you approximately $14.00 per hour after factoring in all payroll-related expenses.

12

Financial Controls and Reports

In order for your company to be successful and profitable, you must give the party for two the attention to detail that the party for two thousand requires!

Gayle Skelton and Donald Hillis
A Catered Affaire
Dallas, Texas

Control procedures must be used to ensure that actual performance is in line with planned performance. The control cycle begins when a potential client considers booking business at your hotel and it does not end until the catered function is completed to everyone's satisfaction.

Before a control system can be implemented, you must set standards of performance. If you book a beverage function and you expect each bottle of liquor to yield approximately 15 drinks, the actual number of drinks served per container must be consistent with this standard. If your bartenders pour more or less than 15 drinks per container, you may have a control problem. If they pour too many drinks per container, usually the customers are receiving a reduced portion size. If they pour too few drinks per container, chances are there is excessive waste or customers are receiving excessive portion sizes.

It is management's duty to set the required standards and policies by which all catered events will be run. All operational procedures—from booking the business, to purchasing, receiving, storing, issuing, producing, and serving the finished products, to function-room selection and setup, to final bill tabulation and collection—must be standardized. If all employees follow the standard operating procedures, chances are you will reach your cost-control and quality-control goals with minimal difficulty.

One of management's primary responsibilities is to see to it that actual results are in line with the standards. To do this, management must develop data-gathering and data-analysis procedures that can be used to compute actual results and compare them to the standards. If there are variances between the standards and the actual results, management must move to identify and solve the underlying problem(s). Experience shows that this correction phase of control is the most difficult one because it is not always easy to diagnose what went wrong. If you cannot get at the root of the problem, it is impossible to solve it.

For example, if your bartenders are consistently pouring more drinks per container than you expect, there are many potential causes for this variance. Unintentionally underpouring each drink is the most logical cause, though mechanical problems with the liquor-dispensing machinery, inadequate recordkeeping, and failure to account properly for those guests who ask for short pours, are also possible reasons.

Another difficult aspect of the control process is the potential to overcontrol everything. You should not cost-control yourself out of business. You cannot spend a dollar to control a dime. There comes a point where some controls are not cost effective. For instance, computerized automatic liquor-dispensing units will increase your ability to control drink service. Unfortunately, the expensive investment in these systems may never be recovered in a reasonable period of time.

Overcontrol can also put a manager in the position of concentrating solely on inanimate objects and ignoring clients and guests. You cannot dwell so much on cost-related matters that you begin to lose sight of the customer. You must satisfy your clients and guests. However, if you are spending too much time gathering and processing cost data, you may be neglecting them.

It is very difficult to strike just the right balance between effective control and customer service. Experience shows that if you take good care of the guest, your expenses and profits will fall into line. But if you concentrate solely on every penny, eventually you will not have to worry about control because you will have no business left to control.

Michael Hurst, past president of the National Restaurant Association (NRA), summed it up best when he remarked that you can achieve maximum control by closing your business; this is the only way to avoid control problems. If you want to stay in business and build it into a profitable enterprise, Mr. Hurst suggests that you manage from the front door, not the back door. Taking care of the clients and guests and providing consistent value is the best recipe for success in the food and beverage industry.

The purpose of this chapter is to discuss the generally accepted control procedures used in the hotel catering industry. By adopting them, the director of catering takes a giant step toward minimizing variances and maximizing client and guest satisfaction.

BANQUET EVENT ORDER (BEO)

The banquet event order (BEO), sometimes referred to as the function sheet, is the basis of the hotel's internal communication system between departments. It is also the basic building block upon which the hotel catering department's accounting and recordkeeping systems are constructed. (See Figure 12.1.)

A BEO is prepared for each meal and beverage function, and copies are sent to the departments noted in chapter 5 that will be directly or indirectly involved with the events.

Usually all hotel departments receive a copy of each BEO about three weeks before the catered function is held. This ensures that all department heads have enough time to schedule and complete their necessary activities that support the events.

BEOs are usually numbered sequentially for easy reference. It is important to assign an identifying number to each BEO so that department heads can resolve any discrepancy easily and quickly. For instance, if banquet setup is unclear about a particular event's requirements, it can call the catering office for additional information regarding BEO 175. This is certainly easier and more accurate than using clients' names or other forms of identification, all of which can be garbled and misinterpreted after two or three phone calls.

The typical BEO contains the following information:

1. BEO number
2. Function date
3. Type of function
4. Client name
5. Client address
6. Client contact person, or person in charge
7. Person who booked the event and authorized signature
8. Name of function room
9. Beginning time of function

BANQUET EVENT ORDER

Distribution
General Manager
Accounts Receivable
Front Office Cashier
Valet Parking
Inventory Control
Sales
Food & Beverage Director
Chef
Executive Steward
Bar Manager
Catering Director
Banquet Manager
Audiovisual
Banquet Housemen
File

Date: _____

Name: _____

Address: _____

In Charge: _____

Booked by: _____

Food

Beverage

Special Attention:

Food and Beverage Prices:

Master Account Number:

Approved by: _____

Date: _____

Figure 12.1.   Example banquet event order (BEO).

10. Expected ending time of function
11. Number of guests expected
12. Number of guests to prepare for
13. Menus
14. Style of service
15. Function-room setup
16. Special instructions (such as sleeping room blocks, center-pieces, table sets, bar arrangements, unique underliners, VIPs, and other special amenity orders)
17. Prices charged
18. Master billing account number
19. Billing instructions
20. Reference to other BEOs or other relevant records
21. Date BEO was completed
22. Signature of person preparing (or approving) the BEO
23. List of departments receiving a copy of the BEO.

PREFUNCTION SHEET

Some hotels want to warn all departments well in advance of future catering activity. For instance, management may want everyone to have a good idea of the amount and types of catering business booked for next month. This can be done by preparing a monthly prefunction sheet which briefly notes the types of groups and number of guests expected the following month.

The prefunction sheet serves many purposes. Its major advantage is that it allows each department head to preplan his or her staffing needs for the long term. Other advantages are: kitchen and purchasing can use this information to plan tentative ordering, prepreparation, and preparation schedules; the storeroom can plan its inventory-management procedures more effectively; convention service and the steward departments will have plenty of time to secure additional furniture, equipment, and tableware if needed; and housekeeping can plan its heavy-cleaning routines much easier if it knows what to expect.

CHANGE ORDER

Usually clients have opportunities to make alterations in their booked functions. For instance, they may be able to order changes in the menu one week before the event is scheduled, switch from table service to buffet service three days before, and decide to add extra bars 24 hours in advance.

At times several changes must be made at the last minute. For example, if a function that initially expects 400 guests suddenly expands to 600 guests, the catering department may need to move the buffet line into the prefunction space in order to accommodate additional seating.

Sometimes a change may be suggested by the catering executive. For instance, if the purchasing agent has a problem getting a particular wine, the catering sales representative will need to meet with the client and discuss alternate brands that can be served for the same price.

These types of alterations must be communicated to all hotel departments who are involved with the catered event. The most efficient way to do this is to prepare an addendum to the original BEO.

The BEO addendum is usually referred to as a banquet change order or banquet change sheet. It contains the original BEO's identification number as well as other pertinent identifying factors. It also notes very specifically the changes that must be made. The department head must note unequivocally what must be eliminated and what must be added to the scheduled catered event.

To avoid confusion, the hotel should use a simple color-coded system to ensure changes are recorded accurately. For instance, one property uses a three-color system: white—original BEO; green—revisions; pink—guarantees. In this case, if a change must be communicated, all relevant departments will receive them on green or pink paper, update their original BEOs, and reduce the paper flow so that only one document is retained.

CONVENTION RESUME

A convention resume is a summary of function room uses for a particular convention or meeting. It is normally used whenever a client books two or more catered events to be held consecutively. (See Figure 12.2.)

The convention resume may more appropriately be referred to as the function room resume because this report emphasizes function room use for a particular client. It usually includes the major highlights, while deferring to the pertinent BEOs for specific details. For instance, if you book a one-week convention, and there are 15 meal, beverage, and business-meeting functions, the convention

CONVENTION RESUME

Distribution   Date: _____
General Manager
Accounts Receivable   Name: _____
Front Office Cashier
Valet Parking   Address: _____
Inventory Control
Sales   In Charge: _____
Food & Beverage Director
Chef   Booked by: _____
Executive Steward
Bar Manager
Catering Director
Banquet Manager
Audiovisual
Banquet Housemen
File

Date   Hours   Function   Room   Guest Count

Room, Equipment, Labor Charges:

Room Setups:

Equipment Setups:

Special Attention:

Billing Instructions:

Master Account Number:

                                      Approved by: _____

                                      Date: _____

Figure 12.2. Example convention resume.

resume will highlight each function, when the function rooms will be booked, and when they will be down. This document usually includes:

1. Function dates
2. Types of functions
3. Client name
4. Client address
5. Client contact person, or person in charge
6. Person who booked the events and authorized signature
7. Beginning times of functions
8. Expected ending times of functions
9. Number of guests expected
10. Furniture and equipment needs
11. Function room names
12. Room setups
13. Special instructions
14. Room charges
15. Labor charges
16. Equipment charges
17. Master billing account number
18. Billing instructions
19. Reference to other relevant records
20. Date convention resume was completed
21. Signature of person preparing (or approving) the function resume
22. List of departments receiving a copy of the function resume.

CATERING CONTRACT

The hotel typically requires clients to sign formal catering contracts before the events are scheduled to take place. This is especially true when dealing with large functions.

Sometimes a hotel will forego the use of formal contracts and instead rely on signed BEOs or signed letters of agreement. These documents may be every bit as legally enforceable as formal contracts. Usually though, they do not include the typical boiler-plate language (that is, standardized legalese) found in most formal contracts.

You should never book and confirm a catered event without a signed agreement. Usually an unwritten contract cannot be legally enforced in a court of law unless you are dealing with an agreement worth $500 or less. But even with small parties, it is good business practice to detail in writing both your and the client's responsibilities and obligations.

If you have standardized contract forms, you can give a copy to a potential client to read and study before progressing any further. This gives the client enough time to examine the terms and conditions and to ask questions about anything unclear.

Experience shows that many clients are unfamiliar with the language of the food and beverage industry. For instance, several years ago there was a dispute about the meaning of the term "chicken." Since it was not defined in the purchase-order contract, the supplier shipped hens. But the buyer wanted to purchase broiler (or fryer) chickens. The dispute ended up in litigation where, unfortunately for the buyer, the court found for the seller since the term "chicken" encompasses several types and varieties and the seller was able to interpret its meaning loosely.

You are not in business to intentionally fool clients. But you must realize that, for example, some of them may see the notation "buffet service with meat tickets" and jump to the conclusion that guests can take and eat all they want. If they are not familiar with the term "meat ticket" it is up to you to explain it thoroughly and head off any potential trouble. The last thing you want is an unhappy group of guests.

Many hotels develop standardized contracts that contain a considerable amount of boiler-plate clauses with enough blank space available to write in specific details as needed. For typical functions, the standard boiler-plate contract will usually suffice. But if there is anything unusual that must be addressed, the hotel's legal counsel, or other representative, must add it.

If a convention client requires atypical services, the hotel's and the client's legal representatives may work together to develop a mutually agreeable contract. They would need to negotiate and ultimately reduce their agreement to writing. This agreement can then be added to the standard boiler-plate contract or it can stand alone.

Some hotel catering departments do not have to get involved with contract preparations. If you are part of the hotel sales department, the director of sales may handle all contract negotiations. He or she may take care of adding clauses, explaining hotel policies, detailing the hotel's responsibilities and obligations, and so forth. Only occasionally would you need to participate in these developments.

The basic catering contract usually includes the following details:

1. Contract date
2. Function date(s)
3. Function time(s)
4. Appropriate client and hotel signatures
5. Function room(s) tentatively assigned
6. Menus
7. Style(s) of service
8. Function-room setup(s)
9. Other client services, such as:
   a. Audiovisual
   b. Lighting
   c. Sleeping rooms
   d. Transportation
   e. Security
10. Head-count guarantees (and/or dollar amount guarantees)
11. Estimated cost summary
    a. Food and beverage charges
    b. Consumption taxes
    c. Gratuities
    d. Labor charges
    e. Room charges
    f. Cancellation penalty
    g. Deposits
    h. Other charges
12. Billing procedures
13. Procedures that must be used if changes are necessary
14. All hotel catering policies (see Chapter 1)
15. Client's responsibilities and obligations
16. Other standard contract language, such as:
    a. Person signing contract represents he or she has full authority to bind legally the client
    b. The contract shall be binding upon the parties, as well as their heirs, administrators, executors, successors, and assigns

c. Client has read the contract and completely understands its contents

d. Client stipulates that he or she is not signing the contract under duress.

CREDIT MANAGEMENT

If a client is eligible for credit, the hotel's credit manager will evaluate the client's credit rating and, if credit is approved, set up a master account number. He or she will then detail the hotel's deposit requirements and billing procedures.

Usually very few clients are eligible for credit. As a general rule, clients are expected to pay in advance. This is especially true for those clients who may not generate repeat business, such as one-time political fundraising events. It is also typical in the catering industry to require advance payments from the SMERF market.

Probably the major reason hotels are reluctant to advance credit is the fact that the services provided are completely consumed. You can repossess a car or other tangible asset if a customer reneges, but this option does not exist when selling catering services.

Credit terms though, can be a major selling tool. For instance, all other things being equal, a client may select your property because it offers generous credit terms. The more generous the credit terms, in effect, the lower the price will be for the catered event because the client can hang on to his or her money for a while longer and leave it in the bank to draw interest income.

Offering credit also tends to increase sales revenue. While some of the added sales may result in bad debts, a judicious use of credit will more than offset them. The theory of offering credit is to increase sales, suffer a bit of bad debt expense, but generate incremental net profits to more than offset the bad debts. In the long run, you may be able to earn significantly more profit than if you operated on a cash-only basis.

There is a slight trend in the hotel catering industry to allow clients to use their personal or company credit cards to pay for catering services. This procedure virtually eliminates credit risk for the hotel. It also makes the hotel's job a lot easier since the credit-card company handles all the credit verification chores and billing procedures. Unfortunately, this service is very costly; depending on the type of card used, the hotel will pay anywhere from about 2 to 5 percent of credit-card charges to the credit-card company.

Most hotels offering catering services operate their own credit department (which is sometimes referred to as the hotel's "city ledger"). Since many catered functions exceed several thousand dollars, bank and travel and entertainment credit cards cannot be used to pay for them because their credit limits may be too low. The typical hotel will usually take a credit-card payment only for small functions. For example, if you are serving a business luncheon for twenty-five guests in a private dining room, you may be willing to treat this affair as if it were a normal restaurant transaction.

Deposit

Repeat clients eligible for credit may not need to put up a deposit. However, generally they are expected to put up about 25 percent to 80 percent of the estimated final bill, depending on the size of the catered function and the client's credit rating.

Usually the deposit must be made at least 30 days prior to service. If a contract is signed several months in advance, you may extract a minimal earnest-money deposit at that time of, say, 5 percent. You then might require the client to increase this deposit to, say, 25 percent 30 days before the booking date.

When taking a deposit, the credit manager will issue a receipt to the client. The deposit will be recorded in the client's file, a copy of a check-received memorandum will be issued to the client, and a copy of this receipt will also be placed in the client's file.

Billing Procedures

When dealing with clients eligible for credit, the credit manager will bill them according to the terms and conditions noted in the catering contract. The final accountings will be prepared immediately after the catered events. Some clients will be billed for the total amount due, while others will be given a credit period during which they are required to follow a specific payment schedule.

In a few cases, credit-worthy clients will not have to pay immediately after the event. Usually the hotel will set up a billing cycle that is mutually agreeable to both parties. Moreover, tradition and competition may enter the picture, whereby specific credit periods are granted to certain clients as a matter of standard operating procedure. Some corporate clients are accustomed to 7-day to 2-month billing cycles for all their purchases. Government clients are also accustomed to these billing cycles. You may need to offer these credit terms in order to be competitive with other hotels soliciting these clients.

Collection Procedures

If a client fails to make a scheduled payment, the credit manager usually sets into motion preplanned collection procedures.

If a client is late, normally the credit manager will call the client immediately and discuss the problem and possible solutions. If this effort fails to produce results, sterner measures are instituted. A registered letter may be sent, or the bill may be faxed. These procedures take away the opportunity for the client to say that the bill was lost in the mail.

If all these efforts yield nothing, then the hotel may turn the problem over to its corporate credit department. This office usually has more sophisticated collection procedures. It also will take the drastic step of turning over the account to an independent bill-collection agency.

Other Credit Procedures

The credit department may need to be involved with other credit-related issues. The credit manager, either alone or in conjunction with the catering executive, could be faced with the following:

1. Tax-free clients must demonstrate this status by providing evidence of tax-free numbers and any other related documentation.

2. If clients are promised complimentary products and/or services, the final billings must be adjusted accordingly.

3. Some hotels pay referral fees or other types of commissions. If so, the credit manager may need to provide data necessary to compute them correctly.

4. A hotel may want to offer clients cash discounts if they pay their bills before the due dates. If so, the credit manager will need to adjust the final billings or, alternatively, see to it that cash rebates are mailed to clients.

5. If a client cancels the catered event after the cancellation grace period expires, the credit manager will need to determine if he or she forfeits the entire deposit, or if part of it can be refunded. In some cases, particularly when clients cancel at the last minute, perhaps the deposit is insufficient consideration. If so, the credit manager will need to compute the appropriate charges and institute collection procedures.

6. Some clients may have refunds due. For instance, you may want a client to put up a refundable deposit for AV equipment. When the equipment is returned on time and in an acceptable condition, the credit manager may credit the deposit to the final billing, or he or she may process a separate refund check.

Another form of refund is buying back drink tickets from guests who did not use all of them. Usually the hotel will not buy back those that were purchased by the client and given to the guests. However, if a guest purchases extra drink tickets and does not use them all, the hotel may have a policy of repurchasing them.

7. Returns and allowances may need to be factored into the final billing. If you had to make a last-minute menu substitution that is less expensive than the original selection, the credit manager may need to adjust the final billing. Conversely if the hotel had to use a more-expensive substitute. In this case, the hotel may not wish to pursue the matter because it is not the client's fault that the original item could not be procured. However, the client and catering executive may meet and perhaps split the difference. If so, the credit manager may need to take this into account when processing the final billing.

FOOD AND BEVERAGE COST CONTROL

Effective product-cost control is based on standardized operating procedures. To ensure consistent, predictable business results, top management must establish budgetary standards, quality standards, labor standards, layout and design standards—the list is endless.

If there is one major, overriding problem afflicting many businesses in the food and beverage industry, it is the lack of standards. This is understandable due to the fact that they are difficult to establish, implement, monitor, and revise. The poorly trained manager only has so much time. When rushed, he or she may neglect company standards and permit unacceptable practices.

Even those establishments that have complete sets of standards can fall prey to the inability or unwillingness of managers to apply them consistently. The best control procedures are worthless if they are not used correctly.

Management must develop and implement a consistent cycle of control. Moreover, it must monitor the control system continually so that needed changes can be made quickly and efficiently.

The food and beverage operation's cycle of control begins with the purchasing function. It continues through receiving, storing, issuing, production, and service. Checks and balances are inserted throughout the cycle in order to pinpoint responsibility and reveal any problems.

The main purpose of product-cost control, or any other expense control, is to ensure that actual costs parallel standard (that is, budgeted) costs. Unlike the typical restaurant business, catering is in a better position to minimize variances between standard and actual costs. After all, you know what to expect and when to expect it. Consequently, it is easier to forecast your needs and prepare for them accordingly.

Experience shows though, that catering's advantage over the typical restaurant operation is not as large as it may initially appear. For instance, even though you know what to expect, guests are notorious for arriving late, leaving late, and/or requesting special attention at the last minute.

The potential to minimize variances between actual and standard costs is generally a bit easier for the typical catering department. But while this may be true, the system is not error-free. It can be as close as possible to being error-free though, if you pay close attention to every major operating activity.

Purchasing

The food and beverage cycle of control begins in the purchasing agent's office. This person is responsible for selecting and procuring the needed products at the most economical prices. Values obtained by the purchasing department establish initially the ultimate costs of doing business.

Probably the most critical cost-control tool used by the purchasing agent is the product specification. (See Figure 12.3.) Food and beverage costs, as well as the quality of finished menu items, cannot be predicted accurately unless you are using standardized,

Intended Use	Packaging Procedure
Exact Name	Degree of Ripeness
Brand Name	Product Form
U.S. Grade	Color
Product Size	Trade Association Standards
Expected Yield	Chemical Standards
Package Size	Inspection Procedures
Type of Packaging	Instructions to Suppliers
Preservation Method	Quantity Limits
Point of Origin	Cost Limits

Figure 12.3. Typical information included on food, beverage, and nonfood supplies specifications.

consistent product specifications. You must use the same ingredients time after time or else the finished products' costs and culinary qualities will vary unpredictably.

Another major cost-control technique is to identify appropriate suppliers who can handle your needs adequately and include them on an approved supplier list. When ordering, only these approved suppliers should be used. Exceptions must be authorized by top management.

The purchasing agent also contributes to cost and quality control by preparing and entering the optimal order sizes for each ingredient purchased. If you underorder, you risk stockouts and unhappy guests. If you overorder, you risk spoilage and excessive inventory carrying charges.

Catering lends itself nicely to computing optimal order sizes because, unlike typical restaurant service, most catered events are very predictable. If, for instance, you expect 100 dinner guests, and you normally prepare for 105, you then order enough merchandise to prepare and serve 105 meals. In most cases, you do not have to anticipate customer demands because you know about them well in advance. Furthermore, if the ingredients used for catered events are also used in the hotel's restaurant outlets, you can even order a little additional safety stock and not worry about it going bad in storage.

Receiving

Unlike the typical restaurant operation, hotels usually do a very good job receiving their shipments. They usually assign at least one full-time receiving agent to ensure that deliveries are consistent with purchase orders and the hotel's product specifications.

Hotels usually follow the invoice receiving technique. This system requires the receiving agent to:

1. Compare the delivery slip (that is, invoice) to the purchase order. You must be certain that the shipment is the correct one and that it contains all the items originally ordered.

2. Compare the products delivered with the invoice and the purchase order. All three must match.

3. Inspect the quality of each item. The shipment must meet the product specifications. If not, it should not be accepted unless a superior authorizes receipt.

4. Inspect the quantity of each item. Weights, volume, counts, and so forth must be accurate.

5. Arrange for credit from the supplier, if applicable. If there is any problem with product quality or quantity, the receiving agent must get a credit slip from the driver. If the driver is an independent trucker, you will need to send a request for credit memorandum to the supplier's credit department. Before your accounting department's accounts payable division pays the bill, it must account properly for any and all credits.

6. Sign invoice, retain a copy to send to accounting, and arrange to store the shipment.

Storage and Issuing

The major purpose of storage is to protect the merchandise from theft and spoilage. Theft is minimized by keeping everything under lock and key, restricting access to the storeroom facilities, and using a standardized issuing system whereby anyone wanting merchandise from the storeroom must complete and sign an authorized stock requisition and take responsibility for the products. (See Figure 12.4.)

Spoilage is minimized by maintaining appropriate sanitation standards and rotating the stock correctly. Products must also be stored in the appropriate temperature and humidity environment.

Canned goods and other dry storage groceries should be stored at about 70 degrees F (50 degrees F is ideal), with approximately 50 percent relative humidity.

Frozen foods should be stored at 0 degrees F or less. Ideally, the freezer thermostat would be set at −10 degrees F so that when the door is opened to get something, the interior temperature will not rise above 0 degrees F.

Refrigerated meats, seafood, and poultry should be stored at the coldest temperature possible without freezing; dairy products at about 34 to 38 degrees F; and fresh produce at about 36 to 40 degrees F. Each of these product categories requires approximately 85 percent relative humidity. Ideally, you will have at least three separate walk-in refrigerators so that these recommended temperatures and humidities can be maintained.

Products in the typical hotel storage facilities normally do not spoil to the point where they are inedible. Usually they lose just enough culinary quality to render them unfit for service. For instance, flaccid lettuce could be eaten without risking food-borne illness; however, you cannot expect customers to pay for it. The challenge of maintaining culinary quality is a little more daunting in the food and beverage industry than it is, say, in a homemaker's kitchen.

				Unit	
Quantity	Unit	Description	Issued	Price	Amount

FOOD REQUISITION No. XXXXX

Dept.: _____ Date: _____ 19 ___

Ordered by: _____

Issued by: _____

Received by: _____

Distribution

White Copy: Controller

Yellow Copy: Storeroom

Pink Copy: Chef

Figure 12.4. Example food requisition form.

Production

Preprep and prep procedures offer several opportunities for cost overruns. To combat this tendency, the catering executive should work with the chef and/or food and beverage director to develop adequate production controls. The major production controls that should be emphasized are:

1. Always use standardized recipes. Standardized recipes are just as important as product specifications. It is useless to purchase the same quality merchandise every time if you do not use consistent preprep and prep procedures. (See Figure 12.5.)

STANDARD RECIPE FORM		
Product Name:		
Equipment Needed:		
Yield:		
Serving Size:		
Preparation Time:		
Temperature(s):		
Ingredients	Quantities	Method

Figure 12.5. Example standard recipe form.

2. Develop a standardized production plan. The timing of preprep and prep activities is another crucial factor impacting product costs. This is particularly true for foods, since if you produce foods too far in advance, chances are you will have a lot of finished items past their peak of culinary quality that cannot be served.

Since you have a good idea of how much to produce and when the finished items will be served, you normally can develop a very accurate production plan. It is this knowledge that gives you a cost-control advantage over the typical restaurant operation; predictability minimizes cost variances.

3. Supervise portioning procedures. Experience shows that we tend to overportion foods. Guests who help themselves tend to take more than they can eat. And employees have the tendency to put a little more on the guest's plate, especially if the guest is witnessing the dish-up process.

It is also true that we have a tendency to create excess scrap, that is, waste, during the production process. This is especially the case if we are rushed. Since you usually have sufficient lead time and know what to expect, chances are correct production planning can virtually eliminate this problem.

Many food-service experts believe that if you use standardized product specifications and recipes, if you make a conscious effort to reduce avoidable waste, and if you maintain portion control, the odds are excellent that your actual costs will be in line with your standard costs. Minimizing or eliminating cost variances should be one of the food-production manager's major goals.

Service

Usually if you have enough servers, you will not encounter any significant service problems that could cause cost and quality variances. However, good service does not just happen. Someone must supervise and monitor the service function to ensure cost and quality standards are met and all guests are satisfied.

The most critical aspects of service control are:

1. Dish-up should be done as close as possible to service time. Culinary quality suffers if finished items have to sit any longer than necessary. Products past their peak of quality cannot be served; usually they end up in the garbage, with your product costs increasing accordingly. Service costs may also increase if you need to plate and serve quite a bit of food to replace products that cannot be served.

2. An expeditor should be used to coordinate production and service. This person usually sees to it that servers' needs are communicated properly to production people and that guest orders are delivered from the kitchen and served to the guests in a timely manner. Usually a supervisor or manager fills this critical role as part of his or her overall responsibilities.

3. A food checker should be used to inspect the quality of finished menu items. He or she should also be responsible for ensuring that only the correct amount of meals and beverages are served. As meals are carried from the kitchen to the banquet room, the food checker will keep a running tally of them and compare the total served to the expected number of guests noted on the banquet event order (BEO). As with the expeditor position, this role may be filled by an existing supervisor or manager.

In some cases, the expeditor could also perform the food checker's duties. For small catered events, he or she could keep the tally as well as maintain coordination between production and service.

Food and Beverage Cost Control Recordkeeping System

Your cost-control efforts are incomplete if you do not have some way of gathering and analyzing cost data.

You will need an effective data-gathering and analysis procedure for at least two reasons: one, you must have some way of calculating standard and actual product usage; and two, these data might be needed to calculate a client's final billing.

If you are primarily interested in calculating standard and actual costs, you should use the *standard-cost* recordkeeping system.

The standard-cost system is a rather long, arduous procedure that is not usually performed in the typical food-service operation unless it is fully computerized. It is usually too difficult and time-consuming to operate this system by hand.

The system requires you to calculate the standard cost for each menu item. You must precost each menu item, that is, you must determine the exact standard cost for each one. This requires you to cost out each recipe and calculate the expected (or potential) product cost per serving. (See Figure 12.6.)

Once you have the potential product cost for each serving, you need to multiply it by the number of servings used. This gives you the total standard cost.

To determine the total actual cost, you must take a physical inventory of all foods and beverages left at the end of the catered

PRODUCT COST ANALYSIS			
Product: _____			
Ingredients	Unit Price	Amount Used	Ingredient Cost

Total Product Cost: _____

Number of Servings: _____

Cost per Serving: _____

Target Cost Percentage: _____

Menu Price: _____

Figure 12.6.   Example product cost worksheet.

function and cost it out. This ending inventory is then inserted into the following formula in order to compute the total actual cost:

	Beginning inventory (the previous ending inventory)
plus:	Issues from the storeroom
plus:	Direct purchases (that is, deliveries that bypass the storeroom and go directly to production)
minus:	Ending inventory
equals:	Total actual cost

The total standard cost is compared to the total actual cost. If there is a significant variance, you need to go back through the cycle of control and see if you can spot the problem(s). That is, you must examine your purchasing, receiving, storing, issuing, preprep, prep, and service procedures to see what needs to be corrected. You then make the necessary correction(s) so that future catered events do not suffer the same fate.

Usually a food-service manager will cost out recipes only once in a while. It is not an ongoing effort because it is very difficult to revise costs that are apt to change frequently. Of course, when submitting a competitive bid to a client, the catering executive may want to calculate current recipe costs. Likewise you may need the current standard costs if you book an event that will be priced according to the amount of food and beverage consumed.

Another way of gathering and analyzing cost-related data is to use the *product-analysis* recordkeeping system. This system (sometimes referred to as the critical-item inventory system) concentrates on food and beverage usage, not on their costs.

This system is not as accurate as the standard-cost system, but it is much easier to use. However, while it exchanges a bit of accuracy for time savings, the information it yields is sufficient to control product costs. Experience shows that it is the most common type of product-cost recordkeeping system used in the food-service industry.

In summary, this system involves a comparison of banquet-room counts to production counts. For instance, if the kitchen plates up 125 steak dinners, the banquet records should reveal that 125 guests were served. The kitchen usage should compare favorably with head counts, plate counts, meal tickets, meat tickets, or any other service records used. Any variance must be investigated and the underlying problem(s) corrected.

The products counted are usually only the critical, that is, expensive, items. If you book a party for 100 T-bone steaks, you tend to concentrate your food-cost control efforts solely on the meat. You should take the time to compare kitchen counts with banquet-room counts. And in addition, you should match these data with the stock requisition records and check for consistency. If everything works out right, there will be 100 T-bone steaks noted on the stock requisition, 100 prepared, and 100 served.

Some food-service experts are critical of this system primarily because you neglect other product costs. However, the product costs you neglect are not nearly as expensive as the ones you monitor. While not infallible, the system does provide a reasonable measure of product cost control. Furthermore, this system provides enough information to calculate the final billings of those catered functions that are priced according to the amount of guest consumption.

Some food-service experts also criticize this system because if you rely on it exclusively, you will ignore raw-product purchase prices and edible-portion costs. If this happens, you may not have sufficient data upon which to base menu prices. You also do not know if your month-end actual cost calculations reflect reality because you have no standard cost with which to compare it.

It would appear that the product-analysis system will be with us for some time since the standard-cost system cannot effectively be used unless the food and beverage property is fully computerized or a large central accounting staff is maintained. The cost of an integrated property computer system is expensive and may not be cost effective for the typical food and beverage operation. However, without a computer system, it is difficult and time-consuming to maintain accurate, current recipe costs.

A form of product analysis that is used exclusively for beverages is sometimes referred to as the *ounce system* of control. Under this procedure, the manager establishes a standard number of drinks that should be poured from each container, and the actual number of drinks served should be consistent with the standard.

For instance, if you use 1 liter containers of vodka, and the average drink size is 1.5 ounces, the potential number of drinks per bottle is 22.5 (33.8 ounces/1.5 ounces = 22.5 drinks). At the end of the beverage function, if you note that 2.7 bottles of vodka were used, the sales records for vodka should reflect approximately 60 drinks served (2.7 bottles × 22.5 drinks = 60.75 drinks). In this example, after taking an ending inventory and calculating the expected number of drinks served, you should have approximately 60 drink tickets in the ticket lock box. You expect 60 drinks to be served (standard usage), so you should collect about 60 drink tickets (actual usage).

Usually at the end of the beverage function, the manager will calculate the usage of each brand of liquor and determine the total number of potential drinks served. This total serves as your basis of comparison, the standard to which is compared the actual number of drink tickets collected.

You expect the actual number of drinks served to be a bit less than the standard. If the bartenders do not use a liquor-dispensing machine, and have to free pour, chances are there will be some overpouring. Furthermore, with free pouring, you cannot get all the liquor out of the bottle; some of it will remain on the sides of the bottle since you usually do not have time to wait for every drop to drip out.

Faced with this situation, you may need to adjust your standards. You may plan to lose, say, one-half ounce of liquor per container and revise your standards downward. For instance, in the vodka example noted above, you might expect 22 drinks per container instead of 22.5.

For complete control, you will need to relay the beverage-usage data to the head cashier so that he or she can audit the performance of the cashier assigned to the beverage function. The basic comparison here is between the number of drink tickets sold, the number collected by bartenders, and the amount of cash collected. The cash collected and the number of drink tickets sold should match exactly. However, you expect the number of drink tickets collected to be a little less than the number sold and the cash collected because a few guests may not use each drink ticket purchased.

If the bartenders collect cash from guests, you might want to use the *standard-sales* recordkeeping system for beverage functions. This system (sometimes referred to as the potential-sales system) is very similar to the ounce system, in that it concentrates on usage and not on product costs. The major difference is that it allows you to control cash as well as product usage.

To use this system, you need to calculate a bottle value for each container of liquor stocked in inventory. The bottle value represents the amount of sales revenue a container of liquor should generate. For instance, if the 1.5 ounce serving of vodka noted in the example above sells for $3.75 per drink, the bottle value of a liter of vodka is approximately $84.38 (33.8 ounces/1.5 ounces = 22.5 drinks; 22.5 drinks × $3.75 = $84.38). If you note at the end of the function that 1.7 liters of vodka were used, the cash collected should be approximately $143.45 (1.7 bottles × $84.38 = $143.45).

At the end of every beverage function, you must calculate usage rates for each brand of liquor. Each brand's usage rate must then be converted to its standard sales revenue. After calculating each brand's standard sales revenue, a grand total of standard sales revenue must be determined. This grand total serves as your overall standard sales figure, which is then compared to actual sales revenue, that is, total cash collected. The comparison should show very little variance.

A variation of the standard-sales recordkeeping system is to keep track of disposable glassware usage. For instance, if you use 9-ounce cups for mixed drinks at $3.00 apiece, and there are 100 cups missing at the end of the event, the cash collected should equal $300, and the beverage inventory usage should be consistent with the preparation and service of 100 mixed drinks.

Although most hotels will not use disposable ware instead of glassware for beverage functions, there may be some occasions when it is appropriate. For instance, plastic cups may be preferred in exhibit halls, parties on the hotel grounds, and other off-premises sites.

Controlling Product Costs for Buffets, Receptions, and Open Bars

If guests are able to serve themselves, or can order drinks without using drink tickets or other forms of documentation, your cost-control procedures need to be adjusted to take into account average usage figures. Since you do not control portions or guest-usage rates, your purchasing, production, and service strategies must be based on historical averages. This requires you to analyze previous catered events periodically in order to keep up to date on average customer usage in your property.

Another key area that will need revision is the recordkeeping system used. If you use the product-analysis system, you must be sure to use relevant averages or else you will have no control over the critical items. For instance, if you are serving veal cutlets on an all-you-can-eat buffet line for 100 guests, and in the past you note that each guest takes, on the average, $1\frac{1}{2}$ servings, at the end of the event, the kitchen and banquet-room counts should balance at around 150 servings.

Unfortunately, when working with averages, there is a greater opportunity for "inventory shrinkage." For instance, in the veal-cutlet example above, you have no way of knowing if five of the 150 servings were pilfered by employees unless you use additional subtle cost-control procedures designed specifically to thwart this activity. This is particularly troublesome if the client's final billing is based on guest consumption.

Unfortunately in our industry, there are many opportunities for undetected pilferage and shoplifting if you must work with average cost data. Mystery shoppers, extra supervision in the function room and kitchen, and other similar techniques usually must be used to minimize them.

Product-Cost Reduction Techniques

While cost reduction technically is not the same as cost control, many persons see no difference between them. The typical food and beverage operation spends about one-third of its sales revenue on product costs. Any little decrease therefore, will have a major favorable impact on net profits.

Some of the more common product-cost reduction techniques used in the food-service industry are:

1. *Seek long-term competitive bids from suppliers.*   This allows you to maximize your purchasing power. Suppliers may be willing to offer price concessions if they can count on your business.

2. *Qualify for purchase-price discounts.*   Many suppliers will grant quantity discounts if you purchase a huge amount of one type of item. Before agreeing to a huge purchase though, make sure that the hotel has enough storage space and cash or trade credit available to handle it.

If you submit large purchase orders, you may qualify for a volume discount. This type of discount is offered if you purchase a large dollar amount of several types of items.

Some suppliers offer promotional discounts, whereby they may reduce the purchase price if you agree to promote their products in your operation. If you allow them to put table-tent advertisements on your dining-room tables, you might receive a 1 or 2 percent price reduction.

Cash discounts may also be lucrative alternatives. These are granted by some suppliers if you pay your bills before the due dates. Purchasing agents will routinely ask suppliers if they offer any type of discount for prompt payment.

3. *Other purchasing opportunities.*   Suppliers occasionally offer other cost-reduction opportunities the hotel may find attractive. You may be willing to take advantage of:

a. New products. These usually carry some sort of temporary introductory price that is much lower than normal. You could stock up on some of these things and use them to accommodate a few catering functions. For instance, a new frozen chicken entree may come on the market. You may be able to get two free cases for every one you purchase at the regular price. If you have the storage room and the budget, you could stock up on this product and offer it as a low-cost alternative to some of your clients who are on tight budgets.

b. Stock-discontinuation sales. Similar to the new-product introductory prices, these money-saving items can increase your net profits or allow you to be more competitive when soliciting cost-conscious clients.

c. Consider trading for products instead of paying cash. Some hotels have trade-out arrangements with certain suppliers. For instance, instead of paying cash for your canned groceries, you might find a supplier who is willing to accept payment in kind. While trading is not commonly done for food commodities (it is more common with services, such as outdoor advertising), it is worth pursuing because bartering can save a good deal of money. It is cheaper to pay a $100 invoice with $100 worth of sleeping rooms and menu items because your out-of-pocket costs are much less than $100. And if you allow these trade credits to be used only during your slow periods, there will be no extra pressure on your production and service staffs.

4. *Use more raw food ingredients.* These are much cheaper than preprepared convenience items. Unfortunately, you will usually spend more for labor and energy since you will need to do most, if not all, of the preprep and prep work. Generally though, unlike the typical restaurant, the typical hotel has sufficient production space and labor on hand to make raw-ingredient use an economical option.

PAYROLL COST CONTROL

Food-service experts agree that the manager's first line of defense against payroll-cost variances is the work schedule. Your work-scheduling skills will have the major impact on your ability to minimize variances between the standard and actual payroll costs.

The work schedule represents the standard payroll cost. It is based on the hotel property's staffing guide. And the staffing guide is based primarily on the number of guests expected. As the guest count increases, the number of payroll hours and staff members needed also increases.

Unfortunately, the relationship between number of guests and number of work hours and staff members needed is not easily predictable. For instance, there is no neat formula that tells you how many work hours you need for each guest, nor is there a calculus that reveals the additional number of work hours that should be scheduled if five more guests show up. Furthermore, you cannot always predict if you need more staff members to handle a few more guests; for example, usually if one server can handle 14 guests, he or she may be able to handle 16 with no additional trouble.

The optimal payroll cost is a very illusive figure in the food-service business. Unlike food and beverage costs, payroll costs are not completely variable. They have been tagged with several descriptions, such as semivariable costs, semifixed costs, and step-wise variable costs. The fact remains though, that if you plot payroll costs against sales revenue on a graph, you will not get a straight line.

Factors Affecting Payroll Cost

The optimal payroll cost is a bit unpredictable because there are so many factors affecting it. While some factors are controllable, many of them are not. The degree of control that can be exercised can vary considerably among hotel properties. Indeed, if you manage a particular property and have mastered its payroll-cost control vagaries, you may find that a transfer to another property will cause you to regress temporarily to the bottom of the learning curve in that some things you did at the old property cannot be effectively used at the new one.

The key factors that affect the amount and cost of payroll needed are:

1. Menu
2. Style of service
3. Guest count
4. Guest-arrival patterns
5. Facility layout and design
6. Type of equipment
7. Employee tenure
8. Employee turnover
9. Local labor-market conditions
10. Hours of operation
11. Union regulations
12. Federal and state labor department regulations
    a. Minimum wage
    b. Tip credit
    c. Meal credit
    d. Child-labor restrictions
    e. Overtime premium pay.

Payroll Cost Control Recordkeeping System

As with any type of cost control recordkeeping system, the primary objectives are to compute standard and actual costs, compare them, and evaluate and correct any unacceptable variances.

The standard payroll cost is computed by costing out the work schedule. If you are lucky, a healthy part of the work schedule will be fixed. But if the bulk of your work schedule is variable, you might have to calculate standard costs daily.

The hotel caterer must expect the typical work schedule to lean heavily in the direction of variable-cost employees since many catered functions booked in your property may need completely different crews. Furthermore, if the client is paying separately for labor, you will need to cost out the work schedule.

You *cannot* avoid calculating standard payroll costs. Competitive bids rely on accurate cost estimates. Since payroll is a considerable chunk of the total cost needed to prepare for and serve a catered event, chances are the catering sales representatives will continually ask you for current payroll-cost estimates.

Actual payroll costs are computed by costing out the time records. Some time records are fixed; for example, secretaries', supervisors', and managers' salaries may not vary. However, variable-cost employees normally use a time clock and/or sign a time sheet.

The fixed costs and variable work hours are converted to a total, actual payroll cost. This actual is then compared to the standard. As always, if there is a significant variance, the problem(s) must be uncovered and corrective action taken.

Payroll Cost-Reduction Techniques

The typical food and beverage operation spends at the very least approximately 25 percent of each sales revenue dollar for payroll, with about another 5 percent or more going for employee benefits. Payroll, employee benefits, and payroll-related administrative costs can easily exceed one-third of a food-service operation's sales revenue. As a result, no payroll cost control procedure is considered complete unless it includes one or more cost-reduction techniques.

Some payroll cost-reduction techniques used in the hospitality industry are:

1. *Employee leasing.*   Instead of hiring employees, you lease the entire staff from a leasing company. This can save money because the leasing company consolidates and handles all the human-resources administrative details, thereby relieving the hotel of this costly burden. The leasing company also can consolidate several small employers' employee benefits needs, qualify for large-employer discounts, and pass on some of the savings to its clients. According to the employee-leasing industry, clients typically save between 2 to 4 percent of their current labor costs by using employee leasing.

2. *Hiring "rehab" employees.*   In some instances, if you agree to participate in rehabilitative efforts by hiring the handicapped, allowing the local workers compensation agency to place trainees in your property, or hiring individuals in certain targeted social or income groups, you may receive a monetary reward. For instance, the workers compensation agency may pay part of a trainee's wages for a few weeks. Or you might qualify for an income tax credit if you hire the handicapped.

3. *Use independent contractors in lieu of employees.*   For some tasks, you may be able to employ independent contractors instead of hiring employees to do the work. For instance, instead of hiring cloak-room attendants, you might want to hire an independent service. This can be more convenient in the long run since you do not have to maintain extensive personnel files, process payroll checks, and handle all other relevant administrative details. You merely send a check once a month to the service and use the time saved to pursue other more profitable activities.

4. *Use part-time employees in lieu of full-time employees.*   Usually part-time employees working 19 hours or less per week do not receive discretionary benefits. They also grant you a great deal of flexibility. The down side though, is the fact that you need to have more persons on the payroll, which can increase significantly your uniform, employee-meal, and other personnel-related costs.

5. *Use more preprepared convenience foods.*   When using convenience foods, you do not need as many employees, nor do you need very many highly skilled (hence costly) employees. The drawback though, is the increased food costs.

Food purchase prices are much higher for convenience products because they include the cost of food, production labor, and energy needed to produce them. Generally, frozen-food entrees can be used to maximize the productivity of current production labor as it allows food handlers to increase significantly the numbers of guests that can be served.

6. *Institute more self-service options.*   This reduces payroll at the expense of food and beverage costs. The hope is that the extra foods and beverages guests will take when left on their own will not wipe out entirely the payroll-cost savings.

7. *Eliminate overtime premium pay.*   The labor laws, as well as union regulations, require you to pay overtime premium pay under certain circumstances. For instance, an employee may need to be compensated one and one-half times the regular rate of pay for any hours worked in excess of eight per day.

At times you may fall victim to this problem because some catered events are bound to run over and you will need to keep some persons on board to take care of the stragglers. If these overruns are common, you would be much better off scheduling one or two persons to come in later during the event. They can stick around and take care of closing down. And instead of being stuck with overtime premium pay, you would be able to pay the more economical straight-time wage.

Another way to prevent overtime premium pay is to negotiate with clients and ask them to agree in advance that if the events run over, they will be responsible for paying the additional labor charges.

Alternatively, you could schedule a supervisor or manager to handle any unpredictable last-minute overruns. Usually management employees do not have to be compensated at overtime premium rates. They normally receive straight salaries that do not vary with the amount of hours worked.

8. *Reduce costly employee turnover.*   Proper employee selection, orientation, and training should help reduce employee turnover and the subsequent costs of hiring replacement personnel.

9. *Use labor-saving equipment.*   Under some circumstances, you may be able to reduce your payroll costs by investing in labor-saving devices. For instance, a computerized automatic bar may increase worker productivity enough for you to reduce the number of bartenders needed.

The expensive investments that usually must be made in this type of equipment though, may not be recovered easily. Chances are you will not see enough of a payroll-cost reduction to justify any major investments. However, if an investment can pay for itself in about three years or less, generally it is considered a good choice.

Be careful though, when estimating the cost savings that supposedly accompany labor-saving equipment. Our industry has been unable to take full advantage of many labor-saving technological advances since after all, we are in the personal service business. It can be easy to overestimate cost savings, particularly if we rely on enthusiastic equipment salespersons for these estimates.

10. *Institute a profit-sharing plan.*   This and other similar forms of employee-motivation techniques can reduce employee turnover as well as increase employee productivity. Over the long haul, the extra pay and benefits given to long-term employees usually pale in comparison to the increased sales revenue and profits generated by experienced staff members.

CONTROL OF OTHER EXPENSES

Usually the catering executive concentrates on controlling product and payroll costs primarily because they represent a very large chunk of the sales-revenue dollar. This "prime cost" (that is, product cost plus payroll cost) is about 55 to 60 percent of the typical food-service operation's sales revenue. Consequently, it is understandable that a manager's cost-control efforts will be aimed in this direction.

But there are a handful of other controllable expenses that deserve some of your attention. Generally speaking, these are: direct operating expenses (such as napery, tableware, soaps, chemicals, and paper products), utilities, repairs and maintenance, and administrative and general expenses (such as telephone, postage, and office supplies).

The key to controlling these expenses is to be on the lookout for waste, pilferage, and incorrect equipment use.

Waste is a typical problem when using paper products, production equipment, soaps, chemicals, and other similar items. For instance, it is not uncommon for employees to use too much chemical in the rinse water, be overly generous with the use of paper napkins and doilies, turn on the oven long before it is needed, and neglect sorting soiled napery correctly. While these actions do not necessarily cause significant decreases in net profit, they will add up quickly if you do not monitor them closely.

Office supplies and telephone use are subject to employee pilferage as well as to waste. Subtle controls, such as taking frequent inventories of office supplies and restricting long-distance telephone use, should be applied in order to minimize these problems.

Employees must be trained adequately in equipment use before allowing them to operate it. If they do not know how to use equipment correctly, they may injure themselves and the equipment. In addition to increased workers-compensation costs, experience shows that incorrect equipment use is the major cause of exorbitant repairs and maintenance expenses. Moreover, incorrect equipment use will reduce drastically the equipment's useful life. One of the paradoxes of the food and beverage business is that we would never allow someone to drive a car without a driver's license, yet we are willing to let someone operate a $40,000 dish machine without proper training.

COMPUTERIZED CONTROL PROCEDURES

The hotel catering department can gain many benefits by computerizing its operations. However, since computerization is an expensive undertaking, to justify its investment, a computer system must offer substantial benefits to the hotel property and to its guests.

Hotel catering departments may be able to reap the following potential benefits:

1. Improved guest service
2. Streamlined handling of paperwork and data
3. Improved control over day-to-day operations
4. Generation of complete, timely reports
5. Reduced cost of paper supplies
6. Increased sales revenue
7. Increased employee productivity
8. Reduction of clerical staff
9. Job enrichment, due to the reduction of repetitive tasks
10. Ability to keep current sales and expense data on file.

Selecting a Computer System

You should take your time and consider carefully all available options before making a computer-investment decision. Some catering executives suggest that you let the following rules guide your decision:

1. Never be the first user of a computer system. The first user usually is placed in a high-risk position.

2. Avoid purchasing or leasing a computer system from a firm that has many large clients, unless you are one of them. The largest users will receive priority service from the computer firm.

3. Before buying a system, always observe someone else using a similar system at a similar hotel property. Interview the users and seek their opinions.

4. Decide specifically what you want the system to do for you. This tells you the type of software you will need to purchase or rent.

5. Once the software is selected, look for the appropriate hardware. Be certain that the hardware is compatible with other computer systems used at your property. If possible, never select hardware that requires you to take data from one machine, reformulate

it, and enter it into another machine. Data reentry tends to reduce significantly the benefits of computerization.

6. Select an adequate computer-service firm. The firm should provide sufficient training and technical backup. The company should have a "help hotline." Furthermore, the firm must be able to adapt the standard software to coincide with your property's overall system.

A good back-up service is important even if the hotel property has computer people on staff. Many on-site computer people are front-office oriented and may find your department perplexing.

Computer Uses

Software available to the food and beverage industry can be purchased to perform the following tasks:

1. Desk-top publishing for menus, brochures, and other similar promotional materials
2. Sales analysis
3. Bookings analysis
4. Cancellation report
5. Group-booking log
6. Daily tracer-list printout of current and previous clients
7. Sales-call report
8. Group-profile sheet
9. Banquet event order (BEO)
10. Function resume
11. Lost-business report
12. Prefunction sheet
13. Catering contract
14. Daily event schedule
15. Forecast
16. Daily function-room schedule
17. Work schedule
18. Room layout
19. Space management
20. Link to outside suppliers and service contractors
21. Payroll processing
22. Recipe costing

23. Menu pricing
24. Inventory management
25. Recipe-nutrition analysis
26. Invoice control
27. Product-cost analysis
28. Payroll-cost analysis
29. Equipment scheduling
30. Word processing
31. Time clock
32. Production schedule
33. Break-even analysis
34. Menu planning
35. Tip reporting
36. Tip allocation
37. Server analysis
38. Stock requisition
39. Department-by-department comparison
40. Open-guest-check report
41. Cashier analysis
42. Communication with other hotel departments
43. Link with corporate headquarters
44. Billing
45. Inventory reorder
46. Yield management.

Glossary

ABC Alcohol Beverage Commission.

ACF American Culinary Federation.

ACOM Association for Convention Operations Management.

ACTION STATION Found at receptions and buffet meals. Chefs prepare foods to order and serve them to guests. Sometimes referred to as Exhibition Cooking.

AGA American Gas Association.

AH & MA American Hotel & Motel Association.

AIR WALL Portable divider used to partition large function room into smaller rooms.

AIWF American Institute of Wine and Food.

A LA BROCHE Cooked on a skewer.

A LA CARTE Ordering individual items from a menu, as opposed to TABLE D' HOTE. All items prepared and served to order and priced separately.

A LA KING Cooked in white cream sauce with vegetables.

A LA MAITRE D' HOTEL Specialty of the house.

A LA MODE (1) In the style of; (2) ice cream on pie; (3) mashed potatoes on beef.

A LA NEWBERG Sauce of butter, cream, egg yolk and (sometimes) sherry.

A L' ANGLAISE English style.

A LA PROVENCALE With garlic and olive oil.

A LA VAPEUR Steamed.

A L' ETUVEE Stewed.

A L' HUILE D'OLIVE   In olive oil.

A-LIST   Includes the catering department's steady-extra employees. They are the first ones called to work when temporary help is needed.

AMERICAN SERVICE   Another name for PLATED SERVICE.

ANGELS ON HORSEBACK   Baked bacon-wrapped oysters.

ANTIPASTO   Italian appetizers; usually includes olives, peppers, salami, marinated vegetable salads, sliced cold meats, and other similar foods.

APPETIZER   First course of a meal, such as a soup or fruit cup.

ARCHITECTURAL CUISINE   Menu items where foods are stacked, such as endive boats filled with other salad greens. Also called Vertical Cuisine.

ASPIC   Calves' foot jelly. It comes in powder form or in sheet-gelatin form. It is melted in a sauce pan and used to coat and protect buffet foods or foods that will be shown in competition.

AU GRATIN   Foods sprinkled with crumbs and/or cheese and baked until browned.

AU JUS   Served with natural juices.

AU LAIT   With milk.

AU NATUREL   Plainly cooked.

AU CHAMPIGNONS   Cooked with mushrooms.

AV   Audiovisual.

BAKED ALASKA   Cake base with ice cream, covered with meringue, and then browned just before service.

BALL   Formal social gathering for dancing. Dinner is usually served. Dancing is often done between courses and after dinner.

BANQUET   Formal, often ceremonial, dinner for a select group of people.

BASE PLATE   Large empty plate set in the center of each place setting and used as a base for several courses. Usually removed prior to entree course.

BANQUET EVENT ORDER (BEO)   Lists menu and details for a catered event.

BEARNAISE SAUCE   A derivative of the hollandaise mother sauce. It is prepared by adding a tarragon reduction to hollandaise. Bearnaise must be kept on or near heat or it will separate and break down.

BECHAMEL   Sauce of flour, butter, milk, diced onions and carrots, and veal or chicken stock.

BEEF STROGONOFF   Sauteed tenderloin tips served in a sour-cream sauce over noodles.

BEIGNET   (1) French doughnut, square-shaped, minus the hole, lavishly sprinkled with powdered sugar; (2) foods dipped in batter and deep fried.

BEURRE   Butter.

BIEN CUIT   Well done, as in "steak cooked well done."

BISQUE   Soup thickened with vegetable puree; usually a shell-fish soup.

BLANCHI   Blanched.

BLANQUETTE   White meat in cream sauce.

BLINTZ   Thin pancakes stuffed with a cream cheese mixture, fruit, or meat.

B-LIST   Includes the catering department's casual laborers. They are called to work if sufficient temporary employees are not available on the A-list.

BLOCK   A number of sleeping rooms reserved for a large group.

BLUE CHEESE   White cheese, marbled with blue-green mold. Spicy flavor.

BOEUF A LA BOURGUIGNONNE   Traditional beef stew with vegetables in burgundy wine sauce.

BOMBE   Molded dessert of ice cream, whipped cream, and fruit.

BONBON   Any sweet candy.

BOOTH   Area occupied by an exhibitor at a trade show or exhibition.

BOOTH AREA   Amount of square footage included in a booth.

BORDELAISE   With Bordeaux wine.

BORSCHT   Russian beet soup; served chilled.

BOTTLED WATER   Defined by the U.S. Food & Drug Administration as "water that is sealed in bottles or other containers and intended for human consumption." Common types sold are:
　　Carbonated (sparkling) water   "Naturally carbonated" refers to water whose carbon dioxide content is from the same source as the water; "carbonated water" refers to water to which carbon dioxide has been added.
　　Drinking water   Water from a government-approved source. It must undergo some type of processing, such as filtration or disinfection.
　　Natural water   Water from protected underground sources, such as springs or wells. It cannot be processed, but it may be filtered or purified.
　　Seltzer   Filtered tap water that has been artificially carbonated and flavored with mineral salts.
　　Spring water   Water from a deep underground source that flows naturally to the surface. If it is unprocessed, it may be labeled "natural."

BOULA BOULA   Blend of green turtle and green pea soups with unsweetened, browned, whipped cream on top.

BOUILLABAISE   Wine-flavored mixed seafood stew.

BOURGEOISE   Plain, family-style.

BOUQUETIERE   Mix of vegetables in season.

BOX LUNCH   Light lunch in a box.

BOXED   Draped with linen that is folded, creased at corners, and pinned.

BRAISE   Moist heat cooking method used to tenderize and flavor meats.

BREAKFAST   Early-morning meal.

BREAK-OUT SESSION Small groups formed from large-group meeting. The small groups normally discuss specific details introduced during the general, large-group meeting. Also called Concurrent Session.

BRICK CHEESE Light-yellow- to orange-colored cheese. Brick shaped. Mild flavor.

BRIE CHEESE Cheese with edible white crust and creamy, yellow-white interior. Mellow flavor.

BRIOCHE A buttery, egg-rich, yeast dough bread, usually ball-shaped with a smaller ball pressed on top.

BRUNCH Midmorning meal. Usually includes breakfast and luncheon food selections.

BUFFET SERVICE Presentation of food, offered on a table from trays, chafing dishes, and other similar equipment. Often self-served with some assistance.

BUSINESS MARKET Companies that purchase catering services. There are three levels: shallow (low-budget); mid-level (usually involves a sit-down meal); and deep (fancy meal function).

BUTLER SERVICE Food is presented on trays by servers. Utensils are included for guests to serve themselves.

BY THE BOTTLE Liquor served and charged for by the full bottle. Usually all bottles that have been opened must be paid for by clients.

BY THE DRINK Liquor served and charged for by the number of drinks prepared and served.

BY THE PIECE Food served and charged for by the piece. Typical pricing method used for a reception.

CAFETERIA SERVICE Similar to buffet service, except guests do not serve themselves; they are served by counter attendants and may utilize trays to carry all selections.

CALL BRAND Client specifies particular liquor label (i.e., brand). Opposite of HOUSE BRAND or WELL BRAND.

CAMEMBERT CHEESE Cheese with edible white crust and creamy yellow interior. Mild to pungent flavor.

CANAPE Cold appetizer with bread or cracker base.

CANDELABRA Ornamental branched holder for more than one candle.

CANOPY Drapery, awning, or other roof-like covering.

CAPER Pickled green bud of a Mediterranean bush.

CAPON Castrated young chicken; tender, plump, and juicy.

CAPTAIN Oversees servers at meal functions.

CART SERVICE Foods are prepared at tableside. Servers then compose individual plates for each guest.

CARVER In-room attendant who carves and serves meats during a reception or buffet.

CASH BAR   Private room bar setup where guests pay for drinks. Opposite of OPEN BAR.

CATERER   Person or company providing food, beverage, equipment, and other services. May be on-premises or off-premises.

CATERING MANAGER   Maintains client contacts. Responsible for servicing accounts.

CATERING SALES MANAGER   Oversees sales efforts. Responsible for administering the sales office.

CAVIAR   Sturgeon roe (eggs); lightly salted.

CENTERPIECE   Decorations such as flowers placed at the center of a banquet, conference, or buffet table.

CEPE   Wild, strong-flavored mushroom.

CHANTERELLE   Yellow, trumpet-shaped, delicately flavored wild mushroom.

CHARGER   Another name for BASE PLATE.

CHASER   Mild drink taken after consuming hard liquor.

CHATEAUBRIAND   Thick tenderloin steak cut from the center, or "barrel," of the tenderloin.

CHAUD   Hot.

CHAUD-FROID   Hot/cold jellied sauce used to decorate show pieces.

CHEDDAR CHEESE   White- to orange-colored cheese. Varied shapes and styles, with or without rind. Flavor ranges from mild to sharp, depending on the amount of aging.

CHEF'S CHOICE   Selection of food items (such as types of vegetables) determined by the chef to accompany an entree.

CHEMISE   With skins, as in "boiled potatoes with skins on."

CHIFFONADE   Foods served with shredded vegetables.

CHOCOLAT   Chocolates.

CHOP SUEY   Chinese stew.

CHRIE   Council on Hotel, Restaurant & Institutional Education.

CLC   Convention Liaison Council.

CMAA   Club Managers Association of America.

COEUR   Heart, as in "hearts of lettuce."

COFFEE BREAK   See REFRESHMENT BREAK.

COLBY CHEESE   Light-yellow- to orange-colored cheese. Cylindrical shape. Mild flavor.

COMPOTE   Stewed fruit; usually served in a glass.

CON CARNE   With meat.

CONCESSION   The privilege of maintaining a subsidiary business within the hotel.

CONCESSIONAIRE   The operator or owner of a concession.

CONFERENCE   Traditional annual meeting. Attendees come together for meetings, general sessions, and so forth to further a common purpose.

CONFITURE   Jam.

CONSERVES   Preserves with nuts.

CONSOMME   Clear soup, served hot or chilled.

CONTINENTAL BREAKFAST   Light morning meal usually consisting of rolls, pastries, butter, jam or marmalade, chilled juices, and hot beverages.

CONVENTION   A conference that includes exhibits.

CONVENTION AND VISITORS BUREAU (CVB)   Local agency usually supported by hotel sleeping-room taxes. Responsible for attracting out-of-town guests and conventions to the area.

CONVENTION RESUME   A summary of function-room use for a convention or meeting.

CONVENTION SERVICE MANAGER   Handles all catering services except food and beverage services.

COQUILLES ST. JACQUES   Scallops prepared with butter; served in a scallop shell.

CORDIAL   A liqueur usually served after dinner.

CORKAGE   The charge placed on liquor purchased by the client outside the hotel and brought into the property. The charge usually includes the cost of labor, ice, glassware, and mixers.

CORPORATE SPECIAL-EVENT PLANNER   Firm that helps corporate clients plan and implement company parties.

COUPE   Ice-cream dessert.

COURT BOUILLON   (1) Fish stock; (2) a rich, spicy soup or stew, made with fish fillets, tomatoes, onions, and sometimes mixed vegetables.

COVER   Place setting for one person. Another name for PLACE SETTING.

COVERS   Actual number of meals served at a catered meal function or in a food-service facility.

CREAM CHEESE   White cheese, usually foil wrapped in rectangular portions. Mild, slightly acidic flavor.

CREPE   Thin pancake.

CROISSANT   Crescent-shaped puff pastry roll.

CRU   Raw, uncooked.

CUT-OFF DATE   Time when client must release tentatively reserved function-room space or commit to its purchase.

DAIS   Raised platform. Head tables and some action stations are usually situated on a dais.

DAMASK   Woven silk or linen fabric used for napery.

DEMI   Half.

DEMI TASSE   Small cup of coffee.

DIABLE   Deviled.

DINNER   Evening meal for a group.

DIRECTOR OF CATERING   Assigns and oversees all catering functions. Responsible for marketing, production, and service.

DIRTY RICE   A cajun dish of pan-fried cooked rice sauteed with green peppers, onions, celery, stock, and giblets.

DOMESTIC LIQUOR   Beer, wine, and spirits produced in the country where it is served. Opposite of IMPORTED LIQUOR.

DOUBLE CLOTH   Use of two tablecloths on a banquet table for decorative purposes. Usually two different colors are used.

DRAPERY   Decoratively arranged tablecloths or skirting on the front of head tables and around reception and buffet tables.

DRY SNACK   Finger foods, such as peanuts, pretzels, potato chips, and corn chips, usually served at receptions.

DUCHESSE POTATOES   Mashed potatoes mixed with eggs; forced through a pastry tube.

DU JOUR   Of the day.

EAU   Water.

ECLAIR   Pastry filled with custard or whipped cream.

EDAM CHEESE   Creamy-yellow cheese with red-wax coating. Cannonball shape. Mild, nut-like flavor.

EGGS BENEDICT   Poached eggs on English muffin with Canadian bacon (or ham) and hollandaise sauce.

EI   Educational Institute of the AH & MA.

ELECTRONIC-POUR SYSTEM   Mechanical liquor-dispensing system. Dispenses exact portions and keeps track of number of portions used. Some can also automatically ring up sales to guests. A major product- and cash-control device used in the bar business.

EN BROCHETTE   Broiled and served on a skewer.

EN CASSEROLE   Food served in the same dish in which it was baked.

EN COQUILLE   In shell or shell-shaped ramekin.

ENERGY BREAK   Refreshment break where nutritious foods and beverages are served. May also include stretching or other forms of exercise.

ENGLISH SERVICE   Another name for FAMILY-STYLE SERVICE.

ENTREE   Main meal course. (In Europe, it is the term used to describe the appetizer.)

EPICE   Highly spiced.

EPINARDS EN FEUILLES   Leaf spinach.

EXHIBITION   An event (usually a trade show) where products and services are displayed by exhibitors. Also called Exposition.

EXHIBITOR   A company occupying an exhibit booth.

ESCA   Exposition Service Contractors Association.

ESCARGOTS   Snails cooked in broth.

FAMILY-STYLE SERVICE   Platters and bowls of foods are set on the dining tables, from which guests serve themselves. Usually involves guests passing the containers to each other.

FETA CHEESE   Soft, flaky white cheese. Salty, pickled flavor.

FILET MIGNON   Most expensive cut of the beef tenderloin.

FINAN HADDIE   Smoked haddock.

FINES HERBES   Herb mixture.

FINGER BOWL   Hot water, sometimes scented, and fresh napery served to a guest after the meal so that the hands and face can be cleansed.

FLAMBE   Meat dish or dessert item flamed with spirits.

FLOOR-LENGTH LINEN   Covers table across top and down to floor.

FLORENTINE   Served with spinach.

FOIE   Liver.

FOIE GRAS   Seasoned goose liver.

FOND   Bottom.

FOURNEE   Baked.

FRAISES   Strawberries.

FRAMBOISES   Raspberries.

FREE POUR   Alcoholic beverages poured by hand without the use of shot glasses or other measuring devices.

FRENCH SERVICE   Platters of food are composed in the kitchen. Each food item is then served by server from platters to individual plates. Alternatively, foods are prepared tableside, plates are composed, and then served to guests.

FRIT   Fried.

FROID   Cold.

FROMAGE   Cheese.

FUME   Smoked.

FUNCTION   A catered meal or beverage event.

FUNCTION SHEET   Another name for BANQUET EVENT ORDER (BEO).

FUSION CUISINE   Menus that include a blend of foods from several cultures. Also called Crossroads Cuisine.

GALLANTINE Boned meat pressed into symmetrical shape. Usually includes truffles. When the loaf is sliced, a decorative pattern is revealed. Served cold.

GARNI Garnished.

GARNISH Food decoration, usually edible, that adds color and form to food presentation.

GATEAU Cake.

GLACE (1) Ice; (2) ice cream; (3) iced.

GOBLET Glass with stem and foot.

GORGONZOLA CHEESE White cheese, marbled with blue-green mold. Spicy flavor.

GOUDA CHEESE Creamy-yellow cheese, with or without red-wax coating. Mild, nutlike flavor.

GOULASH Hungarian meat dish seasoned with paprika.

GRANITEE A coarse-textured sorbet.

GRAS Fat.

GRATUITY Mandatory charge added to food and beverage prices. Usually equal to 15 to 19 percent of food and beverage prices.

GRILLE Grilled or broiled.

GROUND TRANSPORTATION FIRM Outside service contractor that transports people, baggage, and/or equipment from airport, railway station, or bus terminal to hotel and back.

GRUYERE CHEESE Pale-yellow, firm-textured cheese, with or without holes. Used to make fondue.

GUARANTEE The minimum number of servings to be paid for by the client, even if some are not consumed. Usually a hotel requires the guarantee to be solidified 48 hours in advance.

GUMBO Cajun soup. Usually includes shrimp or chicken.

HAND SERVICE One server is assigned for each two guests. Servers wear white gloves. When serving, they stand behind their guests holding two composed plates. When the signal is given, all guests are served at the same time.

HARICOTS VERTS Thin (French-cut) green beans.

HEAD COUNT Actual number of people attending a catered function.

HEAD TABLE Table used to seat VIPs, speakers, and other dignitaries.

HIGHBALL GLASS Traditional glass used to serve an alcoholic mixed drink.

HOLLANDAISE SAUCE Sauce of egg yolks, clarified butter, lemon juice, and spices.

HOMARD Lobster.

HORS D'OEUVRES Small appetizers.

HOSPITALITY SUITE Room or suite of rooms used to entertain guests.

HOST BAR   Another name for OPEN BAR.

HOUSE BRAND   Brand poured when client does not specify particular liquor label (i.e., brand). Another name for WELL BRAND. Opposite of CALL BRAND.

HOUSEMAN   Service-staff member who handles function-room setup and tear down.

HOUSE WINE   Wine recommended by the catering sales representative. Usually offered to clients at a reasonable price. It is the property's wine WELL BRAND.

HSMAI   Hotel Sales & Marketing Association International.

HUILE   Oil.

HVAC   Heating, ventilation, and air conditioning.

ICE CARVING   Decorative carving from large block(s) of ice used to enhance a buffet or reception table.

IFSEA   International Food Service Executives Association.

IMPORTED LIQUOR   Beer, wine, and spirits not produced in the country where it is served. Opposite of DOMESTIC LIQUOR.

INCENTIVE EVENT   Celebratory event intended to showcase persons who meet or exceed sales or production goals.

INCENTIVE TRAVEL   A reward given by companies to employees who meet or exceed sales or production goals.

INCLUSIVE   Price charged clients that includes all applicable gratuities and consumption taxes.

IN-HOUSE SERVICE   Service provided directly and entirely within the property.

INTERMEZZO   The break in dinner just prior to the entree. A sorbet is usually served. A short period of dancing may also be included.

IRISH STEW   Lamb stew with dumplings.

ISES   International Special Events Society.

JARDINIERE   Diced, mixed vegetables.

JIGGER SPOUT   Adapter on a liquor bottle used to eject a premeasured amount.

JOB DESCRIPTION   List of duties that make up a particular job position.

JOB SPECIFICATION   List of qualities (such as work experience and education) a job applicant must have in order to be considered for a particular job.

KEG   Container holding bulk quantities of beer, wine, soda pop, or soda pop syrup.

LA BAGUETTE   Long French bread; crunchy crust.

LETTER OF AGREEMENT   Document used in lieu of a formal contract. It lists services, foods, beverages, and so forth. It becomes binding when signed by hotel and client.

LIEDERKRANZ CHEESE   Creamy-white, aromatic cheese. Soft, with edible white crust. Delicate piquant flavor.

LIMBURGER CHEESE   Creamy-white, very aromatic cheese. Robust flavor.

LINEN   Tablecloths and Napkins. Another name for NAPERY.

LIQUEUR CART   Rolling cart that includes a selection of cordials. Usually passed after dinner.

LITER   Metric unit of measurement used to package spirits and wines. Equal to approximately 33.8 ounces.

LOCAL BEER/WINE   Beer or wine produced or distributed locally.

LOSS LEADER   Item offered by a retailer at cost or less than cost to attract customers. Also referred to as a Price Leader.

LUNCHEON   A light noon-day meal.

LYONNAISE   Cooked with onions.

MACEDOINE   Mixture of vegetables or fruits.

MAITRE D' HOTEL   Floor manager. Responsible for all aspects of meal service.

MANHATTAN CLAM CHOWDER   Clam soup made with tomatoes.

MANPOWER AGENCY   Firm specializing in providing day-labor workers.

MARKET SUBGROUP   Term used to describe a market that piggybacks on another market.

MEDALLION   Small, round piece of meat.

MEETING PLANNER   Person hired by large companies, professional associations, and trade associations to plan, organize, implement, and control meetings, conventions, and other similar activities.

MINESTRONE   Italian vegetable soup.

MINIMUM   Smallest number of covers and/or beverages served at a catered event. A surcharge may be added to the client's bill if the minimum is not reached.

MOCK BEARNAISE SAUCE   Made by adding a tarragon reduction to mayonnaise, which is more stable than hollandaise and therefore, will not break. In off-premises catering, if sauce cannot be prepared on-site, mock bearnaise must be used because the real product will not travel without breaking.

MONTERY JACK CHEESE   Creamy-white cheese. Mild flavor.

MORILLE   Wild morel mushroom; honeycombed appearance; delicate flavor.

MORNAY SAUCE   Cream sauce thickened with eggs and grated cheese.

MOUSSE   (1) Light, airy dessert dish made with beaten egg whites and whipped cream; (2) finely ground meat, seafood, or poultry served in a mold.

MOUSSELINE   Hollandaise sauce (or mayonnaise) with whipped cream.

MOUTARDE   French mustard.

MPI   Meeting Planners International.

MUENSTER CHEESE   Creamy-white cheese with yellow, tan, or white surface. Mellow to mild flavor.

NACE   National Association of Catering Executives.

NAEM   National Association of Exposition Managers.

NAME BRAND   Another name for CALL BRAND or PREMIUM BRAND.

NAPERY   Tablecloths, napkins, and other fabric table coverings.

NAPKIN FOLD   Napkins folded decoratively.

NAPOLEAN   Flaky, iced French pastry with cream or custard filling.

NEUFCHATEL   White cheese, usually foil wrapped in rectangular portions. Mild flavor.

NEW ENGLAND CLAM CHOWDER   Clam soup made with milk and potatoes.

NOIR   Black.

NOIX   Walnuts.

NOUILLE   Noodle.

NRA   National Restaurant Association.

NSF   National Sanitation Foundation.

O'BRIEN   Sauteed with onions and green peppers.

OEUF   Egg.

OFF-PREMISES CATERING   Foods usually prepared in a central kitchen and transported for service to an off-site location.

OIGNON   Onion.

OPEN BAR   Private room bar setup where drinks are paid for by the client or a sponsor. Opposite of CASH BAR.

OSHA   Occupational Safety and Health Act.

OUTLET   Food and beverage area in the hotel, such as a restaurant, bar, snack bar, or cafeteria.

OVER-SET   Number of covers set over the guarantee. Paid for by the client only if actually consumed.

PA SYSTEM   Hotel's in-house public-address system.

PAIN   Bread.

PAIN GRILLE   Toast.

PANACHE   Mixed vegetables (usually two vegetables).

PARMENTIER   Served with potatoes.

PARTY PLANNER   Similar to corporate special-event planner. Works with noncorporate clients to design and implement private parties.

PASTRY CART   Selection of desserts on a rolling serving cart.

PATE   A combination of finely ground meats and spices forming a loaf. Some pates are spreadable, some are sliced. Classical meats used include goose liver, duck liver, chicken liver, and veal. Usually served as an appetizer.

PCMA   Professional Convention Management Association.

PEACH MELBA   Ice cream served on peach half, topped with raspberry syrup and whipped cream.

PECHE   Peach.

PEEK-A-BOO CUISINE   Menu items where some foods are hidden, such as beans hiding under meat. Also called Surprise Cuisine.

PELE   Peeled.

PER PERSON   Food and/or beverage priced according to the number of guests expected to attend the catered event.

PETITE MARMITE   French soup with small pieces of beef and vegetables, served in small covered pots with toast float.

PICCALILLI   Pickled relish of chopped cucumber, green tomato, and onion.

PIECE DE RESISTANCE   Main dish (entree).

PIGS IN BLANKETS   Method of preparation. For example: (1) franks baked in pie crust or mashed potatoes; (2) baked oysters wrapped in bacon; (3) sausage wrapped in a pancake.

PIPE AND DRAPE   Light-weight tubing and drapery used to separate exhibit booths, staging areas, and other similar locations.

PIQUANT   Spicy; highly seasoned.

PLACE SETTING   Another name for COVER.

PLATED BUFFET   Selection of preplated foods and entrees set on a buffet table. Can also be set on a roll-in cart.

PLATED SERVICE   Foods arranged on individual plates in the kitchen and then served to guests.

PLUS, PLUS   Addition of gratuities and consumption taxes to the standard prices charged for food and beverage. Designated on the catering contract and BEO by the notation "+ +."

PODIUM   Raised platform where a speaker stands when delivering his or her remarks. The table model is called a Lectern.

POIRE   Pear.

POIS   Peas.

POMME   Apple.

POMME DE TERRE   Potatoes.

POMMES AU FOUR   Potatoes baked in their skins.

POMMES NOUVELLE   New potatoes.

POMMES PONT NEUF   Long pieces of fried potatoes, also called Pommes Frit (french fries).

POMMES PUREES   Mashed potatoes.

PONY GLASS   A small stemmed glass used for cordial service.

PORC   Pork.

PORT DU SALUT CHEESE   Creamy-yellow cheese. Firm, resistant rind with soft interior. Full flavored.

POTAGE   Soup.

POULE   Hen.

POULET   Young chicken.

PRE-EVENT (FUNCTION) MEETING   Meeting between client and hotel to review upcoming function and make last-minute adjustments.

PREFUNCTION SPACE   Entry area to a ballroom. Usually used to house receptions, refreshment breaks, and displays.

PREMIUM BEER   High-priced beer. Has a higher alcoholic content than light beer and regular beer.

PREMIUM BRAND   Most expensive liquor brands offered by the hotel. Sometimes referred to as a CALL BRAND.

PREP AREA   Space used for food production not visible to guests.

PRESET SERVICE   Placing plated foods on dining tables prior to seating guests.

PROFESSIONAL ASSOCIATION   Group of persons who practice a particular professional activity.

PROPOSAL   Communication sent by hotel to potential client detailing the hotel's offerings and the asking prices.

PROVOLONE CHEESE   Light-golden-yellow to light-golden-brown cheese. Shiny surface. Yellowish-white interior. Usually smoked. Mild, sharp, and piquant flavors.

PUREE   Mashed.

QUART   Unit of volume measurement equal to $1/4$ gallon, or 32 ounces.

QUENELLE   Dumpling.

QUICHE LORRAINE   A custard pie of onion, bacon, and mushroom.

RAGOUT   Stew with rich gravy.

RAMEKIN   Dish used for both baking and serving.

RECEPTION   Stand-up social function where beverages and light foods are served. Foods may be presented on small buffet tables or passed by servers. May precede a meal function.

RECHAUFFE   Reheated; warmed over.

RECOGNITION EVENT   Less-elaborate incentive event.

REDUCTION   The base from which the flavor of a sauce is derived. The volume of liquid in the saucepan diminishes as the liquid evaporates, thereby concentrating the flavor.

REFRESH   To clean function room after meetings, or during meeting break periods. Usually refill water pitchers, remove soiled articles, change glassware, and perform other light housekeeping chores.

REFRESHMENT BREAK   Time between meeting sessions. May include coffee, soft drinks, and/or food items. Some are planned around a theme.

REFROIDI   Chilled.

RISER   Platform used to build a stage or stairs.

ROLL-IN   Foods and/or beverages preset on rolling tables and then moved into function room at designated time.

ROOM TURNOVER   Amount of time needed to tear down and reset a function room.

ROTI   Roast.

ROULADE   Rolled.

ROULEAU   Roll of.

ROUX   Mixture of butter or other fat and flour used to thicken sauces and soups.

RUSSIAN SERVICE   Foods are cooked at tableside. Servers put them on platters and present platters to guests seated at dining tables. Guests serve themselves.

SANS ARETE   Boneless.

SANS PEAU   Skinless.

SAUCE AU BEURRE   Butter sauce.

SAUCE ROBERT   Brown gravy with lemon juice, minced onions, dry mustard, and white wine.

SAUERBRATEN   Beef seasoned with onions, vinegar, and brown sauce.

SAUTE   Fried lightly in a little fat.

SEMINAR   A group receiving instruction and direction from an expert in the subject matter.

SERVICE BAR   Bar located outside of function room or outlet in a service area not visible to guests.

SERVICE CHARGE   Charges added to standard food and beverage prices. Usually used to defray the cost of labor, such as housemen, servers, technicians, and other personnel. May be in addition to or in lieu of a gratuity.

SERVICE CONTRACTOR Outside company used by clients to provide specific products or services.

SET PLATE Another name for BASE PLATE.

SHERBET GLASS Short glass container with foot and stem.

SHISH KABOB Lamb pieces and vegetables cooked on a skewer.

SHOT Single-serving measurement of spirits.

SHOULDER Period of slow business. Time between a hotel's peak and low seasons.

SHOW PLATE Decorative plate preset at each place setting and removed before service begins.

SHUCKER Person who opens fresh clams and oysters at a food station in view of guests.

SIGNATURE ITEM Product or service for which the hotel is well known. The hotel specializes in providing this item.

SILVER SERVICE Another name for RUSSIAN SERVICE.

SKIRTING Pleated or ruffled table draping used on buffet, reception, and head tables.

SMERF MARKET Acronym for social, military, education, religious, fraternal market.

SNIFTER A large, short-stemmed goblet used for cordials.

SOMMELIER A wine steward.

SORBET A frozen product having a mushy consistency. Designed to be a palate cleanser. Served just prior to the entree. It has a tart flavor, never sweet. It usually has a wine or champagne base.

SOUFFLE Baked, fluffy dessert or main dish of milk, egg yolks, stiffly beaten egg whites, and seasonings.

SOUPCON Very tiny amount; hint of.

SPECIAL EVENTS MARKET Functions that are planned in advance, arouse expectations, and have celebration as the motivating force.

SPONSORED BAR Another name for OPEN BAR.

STATION A server's assigned area. Also refers to the individual buffet tables located throughout a reception area, with each table offering one food item or representing one theme.

STEADY A server employed full time by the hotel property.

STEAK TARTARE Raw, ground filet mignon; highly seasoned.

STILTON CHEESE Rich, waxy cheese marbled with blue-green mold and wrinkled rind.

STOCK REQUISITION Document used to obtain merchandise from the hotel storeroom. Used to control product usage.

SUPPER Light evening meal. Usually served after 9:00 PM.

SUPREME (1) Sauce cooked with a browned roux, thinned with chicken stock, and seasoned with lemon juice and parsley; (2) silver bowl used for iced items.

SWISS CHEESE White or pale-yellow cheese with many large holes. Sweet, nutlike flavor.

T & T Tax and tip.

TABLE D'HOTE Full-course, fixed-price meal.

TABLE WINE Class of wine naturally fermented to about 12 percent alcohol. Typically used as a house wine.

TALLOW CARVING Display piece carved from a combination of hardened lamb's fat and wax. Usually all white, but can be tinted.

TAP Device used for starting or stopping the flow of beverage from a container.

TENT Portable shelter. Usually used to house outdoor functions.

TERRINE Similar to a pate. It is baked in an earthenware dish from which it is served.

THEME PARTY Party at which all foods, beverages, decorations, and entertainment relate to a single theme.

TICKET EXCHANGE Banquet-control procedure whereby guests exchange an event coupon from their registration packet for an actual event ticket and seat assignment. Increases control. Also tends to reduce the number of no shows.

TIP Voluntary gift clients give to hotel employees for extra-special service.

TRADE ASSOCIATION Group of persons employed in a particular trade.

UL Underwriter's Laboratory.

UNDERLINER Plate used under bowl, glass, condiments, and so forth.

UNION CALL Additional servers obtained from a labor source shared by several hotels. Hotel hires servers as needed from this common labor source to work individual catered functions.

URBAN/RUSTIC CUISINE Menu item that includes primarily pastas, olive oil, vegetables, vinegar, olives, oven-dried plum tomatoes, shaved cheese, and breads. Served hot or cold.

VEAU Veal.

VELOUTE White sauce. Used as a base for other sauces.

VERT Green.

VICHYSSOISE Potato/chicken-broth soup. Served chilled.

VOL AU VENT A puff-pastry shell, or cup, usually filled with a creamed meat entree or fruit/custard dessert.

WALDORF SALAD   Dish of diced apples, celery, chopped walnuts, mayonnaise, and whipped cream.

WATER STATION   Table or side stand with pitchers of water and glassware. Intended to be a self-service station.

WELL BRAND   Another name for HOUSE BRAND.

WORKSHOP   Persons meeting together to learn new techniques, skills, and knowledge. Usually involves participants training each other.

YIELD   Number of usable servings per raw unit.

NOTE: A number of items in this Glossary are excerpted from *The Convention Liaison Council Glossary,* 1986. Reprinted with permission of the Convention Liaison Council, September 18, 1991.

Selected References

BOOKS

Milton T. Astroff and James R. Abbey. *Convention Sales and Service, 3rd Ed.* (Dubuque, IA: Wm. C. Brown, 1991)

Don Bell. *Food and Beverage Cost Control* (Berkeley, CA: McCutchan, 1984)

Don Bell. *Wine and Beverage Standards* (New York: VNR, 1989)

Michael M. Coltman. *Cost Control For the Hospitality Industry, 2nd Ed.* (New York: VNR, 1989)

The Convention Liaison Council Glossary (Washington, DC: Convention Liaison Council, 1986)

Convention Liaison Council Manual, 4th Ed. (Washington, DC: Convention Liaison Council, 1985)

Paul R. Dittmer and Gerald G. Griffin. *Principles of Food, Beverage, and Labor Cost Control for Hotels and Restaurants, 4th Ed.* (New York: VNR, 1989)

Joe Jeff Goldblatt. *Special Events: The Art and Science of Celebration* (New York: VNR, 1990)

Leonard H. Hoyle, David C. Dorf, and Thomas J.A. Jones. *Managing Conventions and Group Business* (East Lansing, MI: The Educational Institute of the American Hotel & Motel Association, 1989)

Costas Katsigris and Mary Porter. *The Bar and Beverage Book, 2nd Ed.* (New York: John Wiley, 1991)

Douglas C. Keister. *Food and Beverage Control, 2nd Ed.* (Englewood Cliffs, NJ: Prentice-Hall, 1990)

Manfred Ketterer. *How to Manage a Successful Catering Business, 2nd Ed.* (New York: VNR, 1991)

Pamela Goyan Kittler. *Food and Culture in America* (New York: VNR, 1989)

John B. Knight and Lendal H. Kotschevar. *Quantity Food Production, Planning, and Management* (New York: VNR, 1988)

Lendal H. Kotschevar and Charles Levinson. *Quantity Food Purchasing, 3rd Ed.* (New York: Macmillan, 1988)

Robert A. Lipinski. *Professional Guide to Alcoholic Beverages* (New York: VNR, 1989)

Charles Levinson. *Food and Beverage Operation: Cost Control and Systems Management* (New York: Prentice-Hall, 1990)

Judy Serra Lieberman. *The Complete Off-Premise Caterer* (New York: VNR, 1991)

Francis Talyn Lynch. *Garnishing* (Los Angeles: HPBooks, 1987)

Irving J. Mills. *Tabletop Presentations* (New York: VNR, 1989)

Leonard Nadler and Zeace Nadler. *The Comprehensive Guide to Successful Conferences & Meetings* (San Francisco: Jossey-Bass, 1987)

Barbara Nichols (Ed). *Professional Meeting Management* (Birmingham, AL: Professional Convention Management Association, 1985)

Jack D. Ninemeier. *Planning and Control for Food and Beverage Operations, 3rd Ed.* (East Lansing, MI: The Educational Institute of the American Hotel & Motel Association, 1991)

Jack D. Ninemeier. *Principles of Food and Beverage Operations, 2nd Ed.* (East Lansing, MI: The Educational Institute of the American Hotel & Motel Association, 1990)

Thomas F. Powers and Jo Marie Powers. *Food Service Operations: Planning and Control* (New York: John Wiley, 1984)

Restaurant Industry Operations Report (Washington, DC: National Restaurant Association, annual publication)

Anthony Rey and Ferdinand Weiland. *Managing Service in Food and Beverage Operations* (East Lansing, MI: The Educational Institute of the American Hotel & Motel Association, 1985)

Joyce Rubash. *Master Dictionary of Food and Wine* (New York: VNR, 1990)

Denny Rutherford. *Introduction to the Conventions, Expositions and Meetings Industry* (New York: VNR, 1990)

Raymond S. Schmidgall. *Hospitality Industry Managerial Accounting, 2nd Ed.* (East Lansing, MI: The Educational Institute of the American Hotel & Motel Association, 1990)

Arno Schmidt. *The Banquet Business, 2nd Ed.* (New York: VNR, 1990)

Bernard Splaver. *Successful Catering, 3rd Ed.* (New York: VNR, 1991)

John Stefanelli. *Purchasing: Selection and Procurement for the Hospitality Industry, 3rd Ed.* (New York: John Wiley, 1992)

Derek Taylor. *How to Sell Banquets* (New York: VNR, 1981)

M.C. Warfel and Marion L. Cremer. *Purchasing for Food Service Managers, 2nd Ed.* (Berkeley, CA: McCutchan, 1989)

Mickey Warner. *Recreational Foodservice Management* (New York: VNR, 1989)

G. Eugene Wigger. *Catering to Every Whim: A Complete Guide to Catering Sales, Administration and Operations* (Englewood Cliffs, NJ: Prentice-Hall, 1991)

Ronald A. Yudd. *Successful Buffet Management* (New York: VNR, 1990)

Brother Herman E. Zaccarelli. *Foodservice Management by Checklist: A Handbook of Control Techniques* (New York: John Wiley, 1990)

JOURNALS

Association Meetings
The Laux Company, Inc.
63 Great Road
Maynard, MA 01754
(508) 897-5552

Catering Business
633 Third Avenue
New York, NY 10017
(212) 984-2293

Catering Impact
4265 San Felipe
Suite 500
Houston, TX 77027
(713) 869-7650

Catering Today
P.O. Box 222
Santa Claus, IN 47579
(812) 937-4464

Conventions and Expositions
1575 I Street NW
Washington, DC 20005
(202) 626-2769

Corporate Meetings and Incentives
747 Third Ave.
New York, NY 10017
(212) 418-4220

Fancy Food Magazine
1414 Merchandise Mart
Chicago, IL 60654
(312) 670-0800

Food Arts
387 Park Avenue South
New York, NY 10016
(212) 684-4224

Gastronome
980 Madison Ave.
Suite 202
New York, NY 10021
(212) 570-1302

Hotels & Restaurants International
1350 East Touhy Ave.
Des Plaines, IL 60018
(708) 635-8800

Inside ISES
7070 Hollywood Blvd.
Suite 410
Los Angeles, CA 90028
(800) 344-ISES

The Meeting Manager
1950 Stemmons Freeway
Dallas, TX 75207-3109
(214) 746-5222

Meeting News
1515 Broadway
New York, NY 10036
(212) 869-1300

Meetings & Conventions
500 Plaza Drive
Secaucus, NJ 07096
(201) 902-1700

Nation's Restaurant News
425 Park Ave.
New York, NY 10022
(212) 371-9400

Restaurants & Institutions
1350 East Touhy Ave.
Des Plaines, IL 60018
(708) 635-8800

Restaurant Business
633 Third Ave.
New York, NY 10017
(212) 986-4800

Restaurant Hospitality
1100 Superior Ave.
Cleveland, OH 44114
(216) 696-7000

Restaurants USA
1200 17th Street NW
Washington, DC 20036
(202) 331-5900

Sales and Marketing Management
633 Third Ave.
New York, NY 10017
(212) 986-4800

Special Events
6133 Briston Pkwy
P.O. Box 3640
Culver City, CA 90231-3640
(213) 337-9717

Successful Meetings
633 Third Ave.
New York, NY 10017
(212) 986-4800

KEY INDUSTRY ASSOCIATIONS AND RESOURCES

American Culinary Federation (ACF)
P.O. Box 3466
Suite 300
St. Augustine, FL 32085
(904) 824-4468

American Hotel & Motel Association (AH & MA)
1201 New York Ave. NW
Washington, DC 20005-3917
(202) 289-3100
(202) 289-3199 (FAX)

American Institute of Wine & Food (AIWF)
1550 Bryant Street
Suite 700
San Francisco, CA 94103
(415) 255-3000

Association for Convention Operations Management (ACOM)
1819 Peachtree Street
Suite 560
Atlanta, GA 30309
(404) 351-3220
(404) 351-3348 (FAX)

CaterSource
P.O. Box 14776
Chicago, IL 60614
(312) 975-8446

Club Managers Association of America (CMAA)
P.O. Box 26308
Alexandria, VA 22313
(703) 739-9500

Convention Liaison Council (CLC)
1575 I Street NW
Washington, DC 20005
(202) 676-2723

Council on Hotel, Restaurant & Institutional Education (CHRIE)
1200 17th Street NW
7th Floor
Washington, DC 20036
(202) 331-5990
(202) 331-2429 (FAX)

Exposition Service Contractors Association (ESCA)
1516 South Pontius Ave.
Los Angeles, CA 90025
(213) 478-0215

Hotel Sales & Marketing Association International (HSMAI)
1300 L Street NW
Suite 800
Washington, DC 20005
(202) 789-0089

International Caterers Association (ICA)
220 South State Street
Suite 1416
Chicago, IL 60604
(312) 922-0966

International Food Service Executives Association (IFSEA)
1100 S. State Road 7
Suite 103
Margate, FL 33068
(305) 977-0767
(305) 977-0874 (FAX)

International Special Events Society (ISES)
7080 Hollywood Blvd.
Suite 410
Los Angeles, CA 90028
(800) 334-4737
(213) 461-5770

Meeting Planners International (MPI)
1950 Stemmons Freeway
Dallas, TX 75207
(214) 746-5222

National Association of Catering Executives (NACE)
304 West Liberty
Suite 201
Louisville, KY 40202
(502) 583-3783
(502) 589-3602 (FAX)

The National Off-Premise Caterers Roundtable Association
P.O. Box 2881
Bakersfield, CA 93302
(805) 325-1715
(805) 861-1365 (FAX)

National Association of Exposition Managers (NAEM)
719 Indiana Ave.
Indianapolis, IN 46202
(317) 638-NAEM
(317) 687-0017 (FAX)

National Restaurant Association (NRA)
1200 17th Street NW
Washington, DC 20036-3097
(202) 331-5900
(202) 331-2429 (FAX)

Professional Convention Management Association (PCMA)
100 Vestavia Office Park
Suite 220
Birmingham, AL 35216
(205) 823-7262
(205) 822-3891 (FAX)

Society of Company Meeting Planners (SCMP)
2600 Garden Road
Suite 208
Monterey, CA 93940
(408) 649-6544

Index